SCRIPTURAL TRACES: CRITICAL PERSPECTIVES ON
THE RECEPTION AND INFLUENCE OF THE BIBLE

20

Editors
Claudia V. Camp, Texas Christian University
Matthew A. Collins, University of Chester
Andrew Mein, Durham University

Editorial Board
Michael J. Gilmour, David Gunn, James Harding, Jorunn Økland

Published under

LIBRARY OF HEBREW BIBLE/
OLD TESTAMENT STUDIES

692

Formerly Journal for the Study of the Old Testament Supplement Series

Editors
Claudia V. Camp, Texas Christian University
Andrew Mein, Durham University

Founding Editors
David J. A. Clines, Philip R. Davies and David M. Gunn

Editorial Board
Alan Cooper, Susan Gillingham, John Goldingay,
Norman K. Gottwald, James E. Harding, John Jarick, Carol Meyers,
Daniel L. Smith-Christopher, Francesca Stavrakopoulou, James W. Watts

READING OTHER PEOPLES' TEXTS

Social Identity and the Reception of Authoritative Traditions

Edited by

Ken Brown, Alison L. Joseph,
and Brennan Breed

LONDON • NEW YORK • OXFORD • NEW DELHI • SYDNEY

T&T CLARK
Bloomsbury Publishing Plc
50 Bedford Square, London, WC1B 3DP, UK
1385 Broadway, New York, NY 10018, USA
29 Earlsfort Terrace, Dublin 2, Ireland

BLOOMSBURY, T&T CLARK and the T&T Clark logo
are trademarks of Bloomsbury Publishing Plc

First published in Great Britain 2020
This paperback edition published in 2022

Copyright © Ken Brown, Alison L. Joseph, Brennan Breed and contributors, 2020

Ken Brown, Alison L. Joseph, Brennan Breed have asserted their right under the Copyright, Designs and Patents Act, 1988, to be identified as Editors of this work.

All rights reserved. No part of this publication may be reproduced or transmitted in any form or by any means, electronic or mechanical, including photocopying, recording, or any information storage or retrieval system, without prior permission in writing from the publishers.

Bloomsbury Publishing Plc does not have any control over, or responsibility for, any third-party websites referred to or in this book. All internet addresses given in this book were correct at the time of going to press. The author and publisher regret any inconvenience caused if addresses have changed or sites have ceased to exist, but can accept no responsibility for any such changes.

A catalogue record for this book is available from the British Library.

Library of Congress Cataloging-in-Publication Data
Names: Brown, Ken, 1982- editor. | Joseph, Alison L., editor. | Breed, Brennan W., editor.
Title: Reading other peoples' texts : social identity and the reception of authoritative traditions / edited by Ken Brown, Alison L. Joseph and Brennan Breed.
Description: New York : T&T Clark, 2020. | Series: Library of Hebrew Bible/Old Testament Studies 2513-8758 ; 692 | Includes bibliographical references and index. | Summary: "This volume draws together ten essays by scholars of the Hebrew Bible, New Testament, Greco-Roman religion and early Judaism, to address the varying ways that conceptions of identity and otherness shape the interpretation of biblical and other religiously authoritative texts"-- Provided by publisher.
Identifiers: LCCN 2019058123 (print) | LCCN 2019058124 (ebook) |
ISBN 9780567687333 (hardback) | ISBN 9780567687340 (pdf)
Subjects: LCSH: Bible--Influence. | Bible--Social aspects. | Bible--Criticism, interpretation, etc. | Judaism. | Greece--Religion. | Rome--Religion.
Classification: LCC BS538.7 .R43 2020 (print) | LCC BS538.7 (ebook) | DDC 220.6--dc23
LC record available at https://lccn.loc.gov/2019058123
LC ebook record available at https://lccn.loc.gov/2019058124

ISBN:	HB:	978-0-5676-8733-3
	PB:	978-0-5677-0520-4
	ePDF:	978-0-5676-8734-0

Series: Library of Hebrew Bible/Old Testament Studies, ISSN 2513-8758, volume 692
Scriptural Traces, volume 20

Typeset by Forthcoming Publications Ltd

To find out more about our authors and books visit www.bloomsbury.com and sign up for our newsletters.

Contents

List of Contributors	vii
Preface	ix
Abbreviations	xi

SOCIAL IDENTITY AND SCRIPTURAL INTERPRETATION:
AN INTRODUCTION
    Ken Brown and Brennan Breed   1

BOUNDARIES AND BRIDGES:
JOURNEYS OF A POSTCOLONIAL FEMINIST IN BIBLICAL STUDIES
    Musa W. Dube   33

READING WITHOUT HISTORY
    Michael L. Satlow   50

WHAT HAPPENS TO PRECURSOR TEXTS IN THEIR SUCCESSORS?
    Robert L. Brawley   68

REDACTION AS RECEPTION: GENESIS 34 AS CASE STUDY
    Alison L. Joseph   83

BETWEEN OUR ANCESTORS AND THE OTHER:
NEGOTIATING IDENTITY IN THE EARLY RECEPTION OF THE WATER
FROM THE ROCK
    Ken Brown   102

ABRAHAMIC IDENTITY IN PAUL AND *LIBER ANTIQUITATUM BIBLICARUM*
    Kyle B. Wells   124

HERACLES BETWEEN SLAVERY AND FREEDOM: SUBVERSIVE TEXTUAL
APPROPRIATION IN PHILO OF ALEXANDRIA
    Courtney J. P. Friesen   151

PERSPECTIVES ON A PLURIFORM CLASSIC
    C. L. Seow   169

ICONOCLASTIC READINGS:
OTHERING IN ISAIAH 44 AND IN ITS RECEPTION
IN BIBLICAL SCHOLARSHIP
    Sonja Ammann   196

BIBLICAL SCHOLARS' ETHOS OF RESPECT:
ORIGINAL MEANINGS, ORIGINAL TEXTS,
AND RECEPTION HISTORY OF ECCLESIASTES
    Brennan Breed   212

Bibliography   237
Index of References   266
Index of Authors   278
Index of Subjects   284

List of Contributors

Sonja Ammann, Assistant Professor of Old Testament, University of Basel

Robert L. Brawley, Albert G. McGaw Professor of New Testament (Emeritus), McCormick Theological Seminary

Brennan Breed, Associate Assistant Professor of Old Testament, Columbia Theological Seminary

Ken Brown, Lecturer, Whitworth University

Musa W. Dube, Professor of New Testament, University of Botswana

Courtney Friesen, Assistant Professor of Classics, University of Arizona, Tucson

Alison L. Joseph, Senior Editor of The Posen Library of Jewish Culture and Civilization; Adjunct Assistant Professor, Jewish Theological Seminary

Michael Satlow, Professor of Judaic Studies and Religious Studies, Brown University

Choon-Leong Seow, Vanderbilt, Buffington, Cupples Chair in Divinity and Distinguished Professor of Hebrew Bible, Vanderbilt Divinity School

Kyle Wells, Senior Minister of Christ Presbyterian Church, Santa Barbara; Adjunct Professor, Westmont College

Preface

If all reading is an encounter with the Other, the same is true of all effective writing. This volume is a product of extended dialogue between the participants, beginning with several engaging conversations during the Lautenschlaeger Award colloquium in Heidelberg in May 2016, continuing in a second colloquium in Chicago in March 2017, and refined through subsequent discussion via digital media. To describe any subject with depth and nuance depends on engagement with a diverse set of conversation partners, who can broaden one's horizons and sharpen one's observations, and this book embodies how fruitful engagement with the Other can be.

Apart from the first two chapters, all of the essays collected in this volume were presented at a colloquium focused on "Reading Other Peoples' Texts," held March 12–14, 2017 at the Martin Marty Center for the Advanced Study of Religion, at the University of Chicago Divinity School. They have subsequently been revised or rewritten in light of the discussions in Chicago and afterward. One result of these discussions was to make clear that our focus on interpretation and identity could be fruitfully enriched through a more concerted engagement with postcolonial theory and its insights into the portrayal of the Other. To that end, we have added a detailed introductory chapter addressing these issues, and a further essay by Musa W. Dube focused on the implications of postcolonialism and identity for biblical scholarship.

The colloquium on which this volume is based was generously funded by the Manfred Lautenschlaeger Foundation, in partnership with the Research Center for International and Interdisciplinary Theology (Forschungszentrum für Internationale und Interdisziplinäre Theologie; FIIT) at the University of Heidelberg. It brought together several winners of the 2016 Manfred Lautenschlaeger Award for Theological Promise with senior scholars working on the Hebrew Bible, the New Testament, and early Judaism. The Manfred Lautenschlaeger Award (formerly the John Templeton Award for Theological Promise) recognizes ten international scholars annually for their dissertations or first monographs in all areas of theology and religion. The aims of the award are to bring together junior scholars in conversation about their current research, and to facilitate future collaboration, through financial and logistical support, including through funding colloquia such as this.

We would especially like to thank Michael Welker (Director of the FIIT), and his Administrative Assistant, Bettina Höhnen, for organizing the Lautenschlaeger Award and for all their support, as well as Ryan Coyne (Director of the Martin Marty Center) for his generous hospitality and great effort to host the colloquium, Julia L. Woods (Administrative Assistant at the University of Chicago Divinity School) for her invaluable aid and endless patience, Mat Collins (co-editor of Scriptural Traces) for his enthusiasm about the book and efforts to push it through to publication, Sarah Blake (Editorial Assistant at T&T Clark) for her assistance, and our copy-editor, Duncan Burns, for his excellent attentian to detail in finalizing the manuscript for publication.

Abbreviations

AB	Anchor Bible
AfOB	Archiv für Orientforschung: Beiheft
AGJU	Arbeiten zur Geschichte des antiken Judentums und des Urchristentums
AIL	Ancient Israel and Its Literature
AJP	*American Journal of Philology*
AJSR	*Association for Jewish Studies Review*
ArBib	The Aramaic Bible
ATD	Das Alte Testament Deutsch
AThANT	Abhandlungen zur Theologie des Alten und Neuen Testaments
BAR	*Biblical Archaeology Review*
BASOR	*Bulletin of the American Schools of Oriental Research*
BBB	Bonner biblische Beiträge
BBC	Blackwell Biblical Commentaries
BBR	*Bulletin for Biblical Research*
BETL	Bibliotheca Ephemeridum Theologicarum Lovaniensium
Bib	*Biblica*
BibInt	*Biblical Interpretation*
BibInt	Biblical Interpretation Series
BibRec	*Biblical Reception*
BJS	Brown Judaic Studies
BJSUCSD	*Biblical and Judaic Studies from the University of California, San Diego*
BK	Biblischer Kommentar
BRLJ	Brill Reference Library of Judaism
BZABR	Beihefte zur Zeitschrift für altorientalische und biblische Rechtsgeschichte
BZAW	Beihefte zur Zeitschrift für die alttestamentliche Wissenschaft
CAD	*The Assyrian Dictionary of the Oriental Institute of the University of Chicago*. Chicago: The Oriental Institute of the University of Chicago, 1956–2006
CBET	Contributions to Biblical Exegesis and Theology
CBQ	*Catholic Biblical Quarterly*
CBQMS	Catholic Biblical Quarterly Monograph Series
CC	Continental Commentaries
CCSG	Corpus Christianorum: Series Graeca
CCSL	Corpus Christianorum: Series Latina

CM	Cuneiform Monographs
CPG	*Clavis Patrum Graecorum*
CSEL	*Corpus Scriptorum Ecclesiasticorum Latinorum*
CTJ	*Calvin Theological Journal*
DCLS	Deuterocanonical and Cognate Literature Studies
ET	English Translation (where verse numbering differs from the Hebrew)
DSD	*Dead Sea Discoveries*
FAT	Forschungen zum Alten Testament
FOTL	Forms of the Old Testament Literature
FRLANT	Forschungen zur Religion und Literatur des Alten und Neuen Testaments
GPBS	Global Perspectives on Biblical Scholarship
GRBS	*Greek, Roman, and Byzantine Studies*
HALOT:SE	The Hebrew and Aramaic Lexicon of the Old Testament: Study Edition. Edited by Ludwig Koehler, Walter Baumgartner et al. 2 vols. Leiden: Brill, 2001
HAR	*Hebrew Annual Review*
HBAI	*Hebrew Bible and Ancient Israel*
HBM	Hebrew Bible Monographs
HSCP	*Harvard Studies in Classical Philology*
HSM	Harvard Semitic Monographs
HThANT	Historisch-Theologische Auslegung des Neuen Testaments
HThKAT	Herders Theologischer Kommentar zum Alten Testament
HTR	*Harvard Theological Review*
HUCA	*Hebrew Union College Annual*
ICC	International Critical Commentary
IJA	*The Bezalel Narkiss Index of Jewish Art* at http://cja.huji.ac.il
JAJSup	Journal of Ancient Judaism Supplements
JBL	*Journal of Biblical Literature*
JBLMS	Journal of Biblical Literature Monograph Series
JCS	*Journal of Cuneiform Studies*
JNES	*Journal of Near Eastern Studies*
JQR	*Jewish Quarterly Review*
JR	*Journal of Religion*
JSJ	*Journal for the Study of Judaism*
JSJSup	Supplements to the Journal for the Study of Judaism
JSNT	*Journal for the Study of the New Testament*
JSOT	*Journal for the Study of the Old Testament*
JSOTSup	Journal for the Study of the Old Testament Supplement Series
JSP	*Journal for the Study of the Pseudepigrapha*
JTS	*Journal of Theological Studies*
KAT	Kommentar zum Alten Testament
KJV	King James Authorized Version
LBH	Late Biblical Hebrew
LHBOTS	The Library of Hebrew Bible/Old Testament Studies
LNTS	The Library of New Testament Studies

LSTS	The Library of Second Temple Studies
LUÅ	Lunds universitets årsskrift
LW	*Luther's Works: The American Edition*. 55 vols. Philadelphia: Concordia and Fortress, 1955–86
LXX	The Septuagint
MT	The Masoretic Text
NAB	New American Bible
NICNT	New International Commentary on the New Testament
NICOT	New International Commentary on the Old Testament
NJB	New Jerusalem Bible
NJPS	*The JPS TANAKH: The Holy Scriptures, The New JPS Translation according to the Traditional Hebrew Text*. Philadelphia: The Jewish Publication Society, 1985
NovT	*Novum Testamentum*
NovTSup	Supplements to Novum Testamentum
NPNF	Nicene and Post-Nicene Fathers
NRSV	The New Revised Standard Version
NTOA	Novum Testamentum et Orbis Antiquus
NTS	*New Testament Studies*
OBO	Orbis Biblicus et Orientalis
OBT	Overtures to Biblical Theology
OG	The Old Greek translations
OLA	Orientalia Lovaniensia Analecta
OTP	*Old Testament Pseudepigrapha*. Edited by James H. Charlesworth. 2 vols. New York: Doubleday, 1983, 1985
OTR	Old Testament Readings
OtSt	Oudtestamentische Studiën, Old Testament Studies
PG	Patrologia Graeca
PIASH	Proceedings of the Israel Academy of Sciences and Humanities
PMLA	*Proceedings of the Modern Language Association*
PTS	Patristische Texte und Studien
RBS	Resources for Biblical Study
RevQ	*Revue de Qumrân*
SAACT	State Archives of Assyria Cuneiform Texts
SC	Sources Chrétiennes
SCS	Septuagint and Cognate Studies
SemeiaSt	Semeia Studies
SHANE	Studies in the History [and Culture] of the Ancient Near East
SJ	Studia Judaica
SJLA	Studies in Judaism in Late Antiquity
SO	Symbolae Osloenses
SPhiloA	Studia Philonica Annual
SSN	Studia Semitica Neerlandica
STDJ	Studies on the Texts of the Desert of Judah
StSam	Studia Samaritana
SubBi	Subsidia Biblica
SUNT	Studien zur Umwelt des Neuen Testaments

SymS	Society of Biblical Literature Symposium Series
TCSt	Text-Critical Studies
TDOT	*Theological Dictionary of the Old Testament*. Edited by G. Johannes Botterweck and Helmer Ringgren. Translated by John T. Willis et al. 8 vols. Grand Rapids: Eerdmans, 1974–2006
TrGF	*Tragicorum graecorum fragmenta*. Edited by Bruno Snell et al. 5 vols. Göttingen: Vandenhoeck & Ruprecht, 1971–2004
TSAJ	Texte und Studien zum antiken Judentum / Texts and Studies in Ancient Judaism
TynBul	*Tyndale Bulletin*
VT	*Vetus Testamentum*
VTSup	Supplements to Vetus Testamentum
WA	Weimar Ausgabe: Martin Luther. *Werke: Kritische Gesam[m]tausgabe*. 121 vols. Weimar: Hermann Böhlaus, 1883–
WBC	Word Biblical Commentary
WUNT	Wissenschaftliche Untersuchungen zum Neuen Testament
ZABR	Zeitschrift für altorientalische und biblische Rechtsgeschichte / Journal for Ancient Near Eastern and Biblical Law
ZAW	*Zeitschrift für die alttestamentliche Wissenschaft*

SOCIAL IDENTITY AND SCRIPTURAL INTERPRETATION: AN INTRODUCTION

Ken Brown and Brennan Breed

"Memory is an aggressive act." David Roskies[1]

In early 1609, the English colony at Jamestown was not yet two years old. Ill-equipped, on the brink of starvation, and already in conflict with the surrounding Powhatan tribes, most of the first colonists had died, and Jamestown's survival was in grave doubt. Back home in England, public support was wavering, and disputes arose over the future of the colony. Although Jamestown had been founded primarily as a financial investment of the Virginia Company, its royal charter also presented the colony as an agent of Christian mission.[2] So when the settlement needed support, a series of sermons and religious tracts were published to promote it, which

---

1. David G. Roskies, *Against the Apocalypse: Responses to Catastrophe in Modern Jewish Culture* (Cambridge: Harvard University Press, 1984), 10; the context is an anecdote regarding an old custom among Polish Jews of breaking in a new pen by writing "Amalek," and crossing it out, in practical obedience to Deut. 25:19, "You shall blot out the memory of Amalek from under heaven. Do not forget!" Cited and discussed by Elliott Horowitz, *Reckless Rites: Purim and the Legacy of Jewish Violence*, Jews, Christians, and Muslims from the Ancient to the Modern World (Princeton: Princeton University Press, 2006), 107–10. For further discussion, see below, n. 39.

2. The first royal charter, dated April 10, 1606, is reprinted in William Waller Hening, *The Statutes at Large: Being a Collection of All the Laws of Virginia from the First Session of the Legislature, in the Year 1619* (Richmond: S. Pleasants, 1809), 1:57–66; §3 describes the colony's role "in propagating of Christian religion to such people, as yet live in darkness and miserable ignorance of the true knowledge and worship of God" (58).

appealed not just to hopes for exotic adventure and financial bounty, but also to Christian duty.³

Particularly notable is a sermon by Robert Gray, published in London on April 28, 1609, which defends the colony through a creative application of Josh. 17:14-18. In the biblical passage, Joshua commands the Israelite tribe of Joseph to "drive out the Canaanites" and take possession of their land. Gray insists that the passage offers "a precept" that applies also to their own situation:

> [I]t is everie man's dutie to travell both by sea and land, and to venture, either with his person or with his purse, to bring the barbarous and savage people to a civill and Christian kinde of government, under which they may learne how to live holily, justly, and soberly in this world, and to apprehend the meanes to save their soules in the world to come, rather than to destroy them, or utterly to roote them out.... Yet forasmuch as everie example in the scripture, as I saide, is a precept, we are warranted by this direction of Joshua to destroy wilfull and convicted Idolaters, rather than to let them live, if by no other meanes they can be reclaimed.⁴

Here Gray affirms that, ideally, Christians should avoid war and violence, even among the non-Christian natives of Virginia, but if the latter refuse to accept Christian faith and rule, they can and must be destroyed, just as Joshua commanded the destruction of the Canaanites. This possibility was not merely hypothetical. Less than a month after this sermon

---

3. On religious self-legitimation in James I's empire, cf., e.g., John Parker, "Religion and the Virginia Colony, 1609–1610," in *The Westward Enterprise: English Activities in Ireland, the Atlantic, and America 1480–1650*, ed. K. R. Andrews, N. P. Canny, and P. E. H. Hair (Liverpool: Liverpool University Press, 1978), 245–70; Alfred A. Cave, "Canaanites in a Promised Land: The American Indian and the Providential Theory of Empire," *American Indian Quarterly* 12 (1988): 277–97; Edward L. Bond, "England's Soteriology of Empire and the Roots of Colonial Identity in Early Virginia," *Anglican and Episcopal History* 66 (1997): 471–99; Robert Appelbaum and John Wood Sweet, eds., *Envisioning an English Empire: Jamestown and the Making of the North Atlantic World* (Philadelphia: University of Pennsylvania Press, 2005), esp. James Horn, "The Conquest of Eden: Possession and Dominion in Early Virginia," 25–48; Karen Ordahl Kupperman, *The Jamestown Project* (Cambridge: Belknap, 2007), esp. 241–77.

4. Robert Gray, *A Good Speed to Virginia* (London: W. Welbie, 1609), 19. This sermon is discussed by Cave, "Canaanites in a Promised Land," 283; and Karen B. Manahan, "Robert Gray's *A Good Speed to Virginia*," in *The Literature of Justification*, ed. Edward J. Gallagher (Lehigh University Digital Library, 2006), http://digital.lib.lehigh.edu/trial/justification/jamestown/essay/4/.

was published, on May 23, 1609, the Virginia Company received a new royal charter, which granted the authority to "expulse, repel, and resist by Force and Arms, as well by Sea as by Land, and all Ways and Means whatsoever" any who attempted to live within the bounds of Virginia without the Company's leave, including the native population.[5] By August, the First Anglo–Powhatan War would erupt, lasting until 1614 and bringing heavy casualties on both sides.[6]

Gray's appeal to Joshua to justify violent conquest was not new. Already in 1513, the geographer Martín Fernández de Enciso had argued at a conclave of Spanish theologians that the Indies were to the Spanish what Canaan was to the Jews,[7] and several sixteenth-century English writers made similar arguments as well.[8] Yet consider the assumptions upon which such interpretations are built: First, by reading a text originally addressed to the ancient tribe of Joseph (Josh. 17:14), as though it also applied to his seventeenth-century English compatriots, Gray assumes a unified, "Christian" identity for English society (embodied, in this case, in the Virginia Company), and presents it as a legitimate successor of the Israelites.[9] This ignores the varied identities, cultures, religious beliefs, and ethnic backgrounds combined within King James's

---

5. Reprinted in Hening, *The Statutes at Large*, 1:80–98, esp. 94–5, cf. Horn, "The Conquest of Eden," 44.

6. See J. Frederick Fausz, "An 'Abundance of Blood Shed on Both Sides': England's First Indian War, 1609–1614," *Virginia Magazine of History and Biography* 98, no. 1 (1990): 3–56; Ethan A. Schmidt, *The Divided Dominion: Social Conflict and Indian Hatred in Early Virginia* (Boulder: University of Colorado Press, 2015), 45–61.

7. From this meeting came the *Requerimento*, based on Deut. 20:10-18, which asserted Spain's divine right to take possession of the New World. See Lewis Hanke, *The Spanish Struggle for Justice in the Conquest of America* (Philadelphia: University of Pennsylvania Press, 1949), 31–6; Yvonne Sherwood, "Francisco de Vitoria's More Excellent Way: How the Bible of Empire Discovered the Tricks of [the Argument from] Trade," *BibInt* 21 (2013): 215–75.

8. E.g., George Peckham, "A True Report of the Late Discoveries, and Possession Taken in the Right of the Crowne of England of the Newfound Lands," in *The Principal Navigations Voyages Traffiques & Discoveries of the English Nation*, ed. Richard Hakluyt (1589; repr., Glasgow: James MacLehose & Sons, 1904), 8:89–131, esp. 101–2; cf. Cave, "Canaanites in a Promised Land," 281–3.

9. Much of the sermon is devoted to arguing that God has blessed "us" with prosperity and multitudes just as he did Israelites in Joshua 17, so that "we may justly say, as the children of Israel say here to Joshua, we are a great people, and the land is too narrow for us"; Gray, *A Good Speed to Virginia*, 9, cf. 7–16.

newly forged empire,[10] as well as the even more substantive differences between the "English" and the ancient Israelite tribes.

At the same time, Gray collapses all distinctions between the non-Christian peoples of Virginia—they are all alike "the barbarous and savage people"[11]—without regard for the natives' own perceptions of identity, culture, religion, or ethnicity, as well as their own claims upon the land and its governance. No effort is expended seeking to understand how the Powhatan identified themselves or what differentiations *they* made: Insofar as they rejected English rule and Christian faith, they are portrayed as "wilfull and convicted Idolaters," deserving the same fate as the Canaanites. These identifications then serve as the basis for Gray's interpretation of the biblical text itself as a "precept," applicable not only to late Bronze Age Canaan, but also to seventeenth-century Virginia.

Not everyone accepted the legitimacy of conquest, however, even among supporters of Jamestown. For example, in sharp contrast to Gray, William Crashaw delivered a sermon in London on February 21, 1609, addressed to the "Lord Gouvernour and Captaine Generall of Virginia," in which he explicitly denied that the commands in Joshua apply to the English:

> The Israelites had a *commandment* from God to dwell in *Canaan*; we have *leave* to dwell in Virginia; they were *commanded to kill* the heathen; we are *forbidden to kill* them but are commanded to *convert* them.[12]

Yet despite his more positive standpoint towards the natives, Crashaw no less than Gray assumes an identification between his present audience and those described in the Bible; he simply points to different biblical models. In particular, he highlights Genesis 23, in which Abraham bought a field "in the land of Canaan" (Gen. 23:2), on which to bury his wife Sarah. Crashaw argues that:

---

10. Gray even alludes to the recent joining of England and Scotland under one king (James VI of Scotland was simultaneously James I of England), describing it as the joining of "the wood of Israel and Judah in one tree" (cf. Ezek. 37:16-22); Gray, *A Good Speed to Virginia*, 9.

11. Gray, *A Good Speed to Virginia*, 19.

12. William Crashaw, *A Sermon Preached in London before the Right Honourable the Lord Lawarre, Lord Governour and Captaine Generall of Virginea, and Others of His Maiesties Counsell for that Kingdom, and the Rest of the Adventurers in that Plantation* (London: W. Welby, 1610), F3 r.–v., emphasis original; cf. D3 v.

A Christian may take nothing from a Heathen against his will, but in faire and lawfull bargaine: *Abraham* wanted a place to burie in, and liked a peece of land: and being a great man, and therefore *feared*, a iust and meeke man, and therefore *loved* of the heathen, they bad him *chuse where hee would, and take it*: No, saith *Abraham,* but *I will buie it,* and so he paide the price of it: so must all the children of *Abraham* doe.[13]

While Crashaw admits a distinction between "us" and "the Israelites," he still identifies Christians as "children of Abraham," who are obligated to do as he did. No less than Gray, Crashaw assumes a direct connection between how the ancient inhabitants of Canaan were treated, and how the contemporary natives of Virginia should be handled. Just as Abraham purchased land from the Hittites in Canaan, so the English must not take Virginia by force.[14]

Therefore, whether to justify violence or condemn it, both Gray and Crashaw apply biblical identifications directly to their contemporaries, in order to support an explicit contrast between Us and Others, whose fate they debated, but whose opinion they never asked. Yet there is no necessary reason why the English had to approach the Powhatan in this way. Though the Spanish and Portuguese had already used biblical texts to justify their own conquests, the French had instead relied on native alliances and trading outposts to advance their interests.[15] So the precise contours of the relationship between the English settlers and the indigenous peoples remained an open question. Nevertheless, once the

---

13. Crashaw, *A Sermon Preached in London*, D3 r., emphasis original.

14. "[F]irst we will take nothing from the *Savages* by power nor pillage, by craft nor violence, neither goods, lands nor libertie, much lesse life (as some of other Christian nations have done, to the dishonour of religion). We will offer them no wrong, but rather defend them from it"; Crashaw, *A Sermon Preached in London*, D3 v., emphasis original. This was also not a novel idea, and was emphasized already by the Spaniard Bartolomé de Las Casas, *A Short Account of the Destruction of the Indies*, ed. and trans. Nigel Griffen (1552; repr., London: Penguin, 1992), which condemned the Spanish slaughter of the natives, and denied that Christians may lawfully invade the New World. The work was first translated into English in 1583; de Las Casas, *The Spanish Colonie*, trans. M. M. S. (London: T. Dawson, 1583).

15. On the differences of structure and identity between these empires, including their use of the Bible, see Nicholas Canny and Anthony Pagden, eds., *Colonial Identity in the Atlantic World, 1500–1800* (Princeton: Princeton University Press, 1989); Willie James Jennings, *The Christian Imagination: Theology and the Origins of Race* (New Haven: Yale University Press, 2010), esp. 15–203; Yvonne Sherwood, "Comparing the 'Telegraph Bible' of the Late British Empire to the Chaotic Bible of the Sixteenth Century Spanish Empire: Beyond the Canaan Mandate into Anxious

particular constructions of group identity and otherness found in the biblical narratives of Canaan were invoked, they shaped the expectations and moral frameworks of the English settlers, and provided a seemingly natural validation for their own ambitions.

Such links between interpretation and identity, frequently tied to a contrast between Us and the Other, are not just relevant to the analysis of colonial England's self-justifications. They exemplify the ways in which all communities identify themselves through both association and differentiation. Appeals to religiously authoritative texts frequently justify and clarify these identifications, which are in turn applied back onto the texts themselves.

This is not straightforward, particularly regarding texts that have been composed initially by peoples very different from those reading them, living in other geographic, social, cultural, and religious contexts. Though many later readers claim to stand in a direct lineage with the group(s) that composed their authoritative texts, such lineages are rarely uncontested. Further, even the scriptural texts themselves draw linguistically, culturally, and theologically from still earlier communities and traditions, and they have often continued to be transformed through their histories of transmission and reception. Yet these differences are regularly—though only selectively—bridged over, as the text becomes "ours," and is read in light of "our" own situations and beliefs. This happens again and again, as various particular groups adopt and adapt the same texts for themselves, often in mutually exclusive ways. The otherness of the text is not erased, just redirected, ever and anew.

In these new contexts, not only the meaning of the language, but also the texts' claims of authority, identity, and social relation must be negotiated anew. With regard to biblical texts specifically, various communities of Jews, Christians, Muslims, and others have not only come to differing conclusions regarding which texts to grant scriptural authority, in which forms, they have also read *themselves* into the texts in mutually exclusive ways. By identifying their own communities—and their enemies—with the characters and groups described within the Bible, they have applied its affirmations, commands, prohibitions, promises, and condemnations directly to their own or Other communities.

The study of reception history is an attempt to organize and trace the endlessly variable streams of tradition, interpretation, influence, and reuse that are fostered by this dialectic between text and reader.

Parables of the Land," in *In the Name of God: The Bible in the Colonial Discourse of Empire*, ed. C. L. Crouch and Jonathan Stökl, with Cat Quine, BibInt 126 (Leiden: Brill, 2014), 4–62.

Particularly in biblical studies, the history of the text's reception has become a major focus of research,[16] but the manner in which reception is shaped by perceptions of identity and otherness has so far received less direct attention.[17] In order to address that lack, this chapter introduces the foundational concepts of identity and otherness, and explores their relation to interpretation. The following chapters will then reflect on various additional methodological issues and case studies stretching from antiquity to the present.

Identity and Otherness

Ask "Who are you?" and one typically expects to hear a personal name, or perhaps a reference to some group or community. Yet no matter the answer, it will only reflect a small part of the person's self-conception and identity, which inevitably presuppose a range of social contexts and relations. Neither personal names nor group identifications are inherent;

---

16. See, e.g., Hans-Josef Klauck et al., eds., *Encyclopedia of the Bible and Its Reception* (Berlin: de Gruyter, 2009–); Michael Lieb, Emma Mason, and Jonathan Roberts, eds., *The Oxford Handbook of the Reception History of the Bible* (Oxford: Oxford University Press, 2011); Emma England and William John Lyons, eds., *Reception History and Biblical Studies: Theory and Practice*, LHBOTS 615/ Scriptural Traces 6 (London: Bloomsbury T&T Clark, 2015); Dan Batovici and Kristin De Troyer, eds., *Authoritative Texts and Reception History: Aspects and Approaches*, BibInt 151 (Leiden: Brill, 2017); Brennan W. Breed, *Nomadic Text: A Theory of Biblical Reception History* (Bloomington: Indiana University Press, 2014).

17. Identity Theory has been fruitfully applied to biblical and other Jewish and Christian literature; see, e.g., E. P. Sanders et al., eds., *Jewish and Christian Self-Definition*, 3 vols. (Philadelphia: Fortress, 1980–1982); Mark G. Brett, ed., *Ethnicity and the Bible*, BibInt 19 (Leiden: Brill, 1996); Ehud Ben Zvi and Diana V. Edelman, eds., *Imagining the Other and Constructing Israelite Identity in the Early Second Temple Period*, LHBOTS 456 (London: Bloomsbury, 2014); J. Brian Tucker and Coleman A. Baker, eds., *T&T Clark Handbook to Social Identity in the New Testament* (London: Bloomsbury T&T Clark, 2014); Samuel Byrskog, Raimo Hakola, and Jutta Maria Jokiranta, eds., *Social Memory and Social Identity in the Study of Early Judaism and Early Christianity*, NTOA/SUNT 116 (Göttingen: Vandenhoeck & Ruprecht, 2016); Michal Bar-Asher Siegal, Wolfgang Grünstäudl, and Matthew Thiessen, eds., *Perceiving the Other in Ancient Judaism and Early Christianity*, WUNT 394 (Tübingen: Mohr Siebeck, 2017). But such approaches have not yet had much impact on studies of reception history specifically. For one example, see Yvonne Sherwood, *A Biblical Text and its Afterlives: The Survival of Jonah in Western Culture* (Cambridge: Cambridge University Press, 2000), 21–31, regarding anti-Jewish interpretations of the book of Jonah.

they are given, imposed, offered, shared, negotiated, accepted, or rejected, by individuals and by those with whom they interact. Identity is not "just there," it must be actively established, as individuals and groups seek to associate and dissociate themselves and others.[18] As Stuart Hall notes, "cultural identity is not a fixed essence at all, lying unchanged outside of history and culture.... It is not a fixed origin to which we can make some final and absolute Return."[19] Instead, identity varies and changes over time, and a person can share multiple, overlapping, or conflicting identities, some embraced and others imposed, some recognized and others unrecognized.[20] In this sense, identity is a "polythetic classification," defined not by a narrow set of conditions, but by a broad class of related, overlapping, and partial similarities.[21]

18. Richard Jenkins, *Social Identity*, 4th ed. (London: Routledge, 2014), 18. On the relation between (social) identity and language; see, e.g., Fredrik Barth, ed., *Ethnic Groups and Boundaries: The Social Organization of Culture Difference* (Oslo: Scandinavian University Press, 1969; repr., Long Grove: Waveland, 1998); John J. Gumperz, ed., *Language and Social Identity*, Studies in Interactional Sociolinguistics 2 (Cambridge: Cambridge University Press, 1982); Anthony P. Cohen, *The Symbolic Construction of Community* (London: Routledge, 1985); Richard K. Blot, ed., *Language and Social Identity* (Westport: Praeger, 2003); Asif Agha, *Language and Social Relations*, Studies in the Social and Cultural Foundations of Language 24 (Cambridge: Cambridge University Press, 2007).

19. Stuart Hall, "Cultural Identity and Diaspora," in *Identity: Community, Culture, Difference*, ed. Jonathan Rutherford (London: Lawrence & Wishart, 1990), 222–37, here 226. Similarly, Kobena Mercer emphasizes the ways identity can shift "through strategic inflections, reaccentuations and other performative moves in semantic, syntactic and lexical codes"; Kobena Mercer, "Diaspora Culture and the Dialogic Imagination: The Aesthetics of Black Independent Film in Britain," in *Welcome to the Jungle: New Positions in Black Cultural Studies* (New York: Routledge, 1994), 53–66, here 63.

20. See Jenkins, *Social Identity*, 17–25. "One's identity—one's identities, indeed, for who we are is always multi-dimensional, singular *and* plural—is never a final or settled matter. Not even death freezes the picture: identity or reputation may be reassessed after death, some identities—sainthood or martyrdom, for example—can only be achieved beyond the grave" (18–19).

21. Cf. R. Needham, "Polythetic Classification: Convergence and Consequences," *Man* NS 10 (1975): 349–69; following Ludwig Wittgenstein, such "polythetic" categories are characterized by "family resemblances" rather than strict criteria of inclusion or exclusion. For an application of this concept to biblical studies (though not in relation to identity theory), cf. Carol A. Newsom, "Spying Out the Land: A Report from Genology," in *Bakhtin and Genre Theory in Biblical Studies*, ed. Roland Boer, SemeiaSt 63 (Atlanta: Society of Biblical Literature, 2007), 19–30.

To speak of a person's or group's identity, therefore, does not specify an innate reality that naturally precedes any attempt to define it. There is no identity in isolation, only in connection and contrast with others: Individuality and commonality, identity and difference, are held in tension in all perceptions of who We are. As such, the ways in which a community identifies itself as a unified group, an Us, cannot be separated from how it distinguishes itself from others, seen as Them. Yet such distinctions are regularly hierarchical and discriminatory, not only excluding but rejecting Them as fundamentally different, or Other.[22]

Postcolonial and feminist thinkers such as Johannes Fabien and Gayatri Spivak have highlighted this recurring phenomenon in human history, building on the notion of woman as the Other in Simone de Beauvoir's *The Second Sex*, as well as Edward Said's account of the Orient as a carefully constructed Other, whose exotic depictions served to bolster colonial Europe's sense of self-worth. They emphasize that the Other is not merely that which is different from Us; it is a subjectively imposed image to which its object is subsumed or domesticated as a counterpoint to Our own identity.[23] Often, it serves to justify Our own superiority and power over the Other, by describing Them as morally and intellectually inferior, or even pathological. As Frantz Fanon puts it, the "natural" state of the colonized Other is portrayed as "barbarism, degradation and bestiality," not as an objective account of history, but instead *in order that* the colonists can present themselves as helping the conquered: "[C]olonialism is not simply content to impose its rule upon the present and the future of a dominated country.... By a kind of perverted logic,

---

22. Throughout this volume "Us" and "Them" or "the Other" will be used as standard terms (without quotation marks) to designate the implied community of the speaker, and those excluded from it, respectively.

23. See Simone de Beauvoir, *The Second Sex*, trans. Constance Borde and Sheila Malovany-Chevallier (1949; repr., New York: Random House, 2009); Edward W. Said, *Orientalism* (New York: Random House, 1978; repr., 2014); Said, *Culture and Imperialism* (New York: Vintage, 1994); Johannes Fabian, *Time and the Other: How Anthropology Makes Its Object* (New York: Columbia University Press, 1983; repr. 2014); Gayatri C. Spivak, "Three Women's Texts and a Critique of Imperialism," *Critical Inquiry* 12 (1985): 243–61; Spivak, "The Rani of Sirmur: An Essay in Reading the Archives," *History and Theory* 24 (1985): 247–72; Spivak, *In Other Worlds: Essays in Cultural Politics* (New York: Routledge, 1988); cf. also Homi K. Bhabha, *The Location of Culture*, 2nd ed. (London: Routledge, 2004); Neil Lazarus, ed., *The Cambridge Companion to Postcolonial Literary Studies* (Cambridge: Cambridge University Press, 2004); Jana Gohrisch and Ellen Grünkemeier, eds., *Postcolonial Studies Across the Disciplines*, Cross/Cultures 170 (Amsterdam: Rodopi, 2013).

it turns to the past of the oppressed people, and distorts, disfigures and destroys it."[24] In these ways, colonized subjects are created that the so-called Other is forced to occupy.[25]

Since such acts of identification impose conceptual distinctions on the world, there will always be an arbitrary quality to the results. In fact, as migration has become increasingly common—both within and between nations—more and more individuals find themselves torn between established social or cultural identities.[26] Many perceive themselves neither as fully a part of their parents' cultures, nor fully integrated into their new ones, but are often able to move between them in ways that others cannot.[27] These gaps, contradictions, and excesses are unavoidable, despite frequent but futile attempts to deny them, precisely because identity is a constructive act, and therefore forever open to re-articulation.

All of these aspects of the dynamic construction of identity and otherness can be seen in the sermons supporting Jamestown.[28] For example,

---

24. Frantz Fanon, *The Wretched of the Earth*, trans. Constance Farrington (London: Paladin, 1963), 209; discussed by Rasiah S. Sugirtharajah, *Postcolonial Criticism and Biblical Interpretation* (Oxford: Oxford University Press, 2009), 17.

25. Cf., e.g., V. Y. Mudimbe, *The Invention of Africa: Gnosis, Philosophy, and the Order of Knowledge* (Bloomington: Indiana University Press, 1988), esp. 1–23; Neil Lazarus, "Introducing Postcolonial Studies," in *The Cambridge Companion to Postcolonial Literary Studies*, 1–18, esp. 7–15. Willie Jennings also describes the process of developing a hierarchy of cultural difference that was implicit (and explicit) in the construction of "whiteness"; see Jennings, *Christian Imagination*, esp. 15–64.

26. For example, Spanish-speaking people of African descent who emigrate from the Dominican Republic to New York City do not fit without remainder into the categories of "Hispanic/Latinx" or "Black/African-American," even though these identifications are well-established in the cultural discourse of the United States.

27. This experience of being caught between cultures is often referred to as "hybridity," "third space," or "third culture"; see Bhabha, *The Location of Culture*; and Amar Acheraïou, *Questioning Hybridity, Postcolonialism and Globalization* (London: Palgrave Macmillan, 2011), who emphasizes that the phenomenon is not only a product of modern colonialism, but "has been a feature of all societies, from the Sumerians…to modern times" (1); Jan Nederveen Pieterse, *Globalization and Culture: Global Mélange*, 3rd ed. (Lanham: Rowman & Littlefield, 2015), 67–126.

28. For the application of postcolonial approaches to the Bible more generally, see, e.g., Musa W. Dube, *Postcolonial Feminist Interpretation of the Bible* (St. Louis: Chalice, 2000); Kwok Pui-lan, *Postcolonial Imagination and Feminist Theology* (London: SCM, 2004); Sugirtharajah, *Postcolonial Criticism and Biblical Interpretation*; Rasiah S. Sugirtharajah, *Exploring Postcolonial Biblical Criticism: History, Method, Practice* (Chichester: Wiley-Blackwell, 2011); Musa W. Dube,

in the very first paragraph of his sermon, Gray asserts that "this earth... is the greater part of it possessed and wrongfully usurped by wild beasts, and unreasonable creatures, or by brutish savages, which by reason of their godles ignorance and blasphemous idolatrie are worse then those beasts which are of most wilde and savage nature."[29] This affirms a clear hierarchy, in which the English are set above and in stark contrast to the natives in Virginia, who are not just Other, but sub-human, "worse" than the wildest and most savage animals. Later in the sermon, Gray similarly asserts that:

> The report goeth, that in Virginia the people are savage and incredibly rude: they worship the divell, offer their young children in sacrifice unto him, wander up and downe like beasts, and in manners and conditions differ very little from beasts.[30]

This characterization of the Powhatan (whom he does not name) as idolaters who sacrifice their own children to the devil is not based on any firsthand reports by those who actually met them. It merely repeats stereotypes concerning "Indians" already popular among sixteenth-century defenders of colonization.[31] Whatever legitimate basis these charges may or may not have in the practices of some tribes, they are ultimately derived from the identification with the Canaanites, who are similarly accused of idolatry and child sacrifice in Deut. 12:31 and elsewhere.[32] In fact, what Gray is doing here is in an important sense merely a continuation of what the authors of Deuteronomy and Joshua were themselves doing: reinforcing the corporate identities of their own communities (almost certainly in periods much later than those they describe) by depicting the Other as a degenerate people whose destruction is justified.[33]

Andrew M. Mbuvi, and Dora R. Mbuwayesango, eds., *Postcolonial Perspectives in African Biblical Interpretations*, GPBS 13 (Atlanta: Society of Biblical Literature, 2012).

29. Gray, *A Good Speed to Virginia*, 6.

30. Gray, *A Good Speed to Virginia*, 19. By contrast, describing his *own* people, Gray asserts: "This hath always beene reported...that the English were always accounted more warlike, valorous and couragious than the French, but the French were always beyond them in prudence and pollicie" (7).

31. See Cave, "Canaanites in a Promised Land," 279.

32. E.g., Lev. 18:24; Deut. 18:10-12.

33. Deuteronomy 12 and its reception will be discussed in a later section of this chapter.

Yet one must be careful not to generalize too quickly. Even among supporters of colonization, the Other was not always portrayed as irredeemable, or even as fundamentally different. For instance, though Crashaw similarly refers to the natives as "savages," who are in desperate need of Christian instruction and rule, he also seeks to break down the barrier, at least to a certain extent:

> [T]ime was when wee were savage and uncivill, and worshipped the divell, as now they do, then God sent some to make us civill, others to make us christians. If such had not been sent us we had yet continued wild and uncivill, and worshippers of the divell: for our *civilitie* wee were beholden to the Romanes, for our *religion* to the Apostles and their disciples. Did we receive this blessing by others, and shall we not be sensible of those that are still as we were then?[34]

For Crashaw, the differences between "us" and the natives are by no means proof of their subhuman nature, much less a justification for their destruction, for "we" too were once "savages" like them, and only became something else due to receiving the blessings of civility and religion from "others."[35] An ironic admission of this is found in one of Captain John Smith's reflections on his time in Virginia: "Much they blamed us for not converting the Savages, when those [English colonists] they sent us were little better if not worse."[36] In reality, the colonists were a diverse group,

---

34. Crashaw, *A Sermon Preached in London*, C4 v., emphasis original.

35. Similarly, Robert Johnson also associates the natives with Canaanites, who "sacrifice their children to serve the divel," but emphasizes their *commonality* with the English: "as we our selves and our forefathers...were strangers from the Commonwealth of Israel, and lived long time without God in the world were yet at length reduced home to that familie of saints and sonnes of God, so now appeareth the same grace, which God out of his secret counsell begins to extend and give to the remnants of those scattered Gentiles, our kinsmen and younger brethren (as I may say) the sundrie nations of America"; Robert Johnson, *The New Life of Virginia* (London: F. Kyngston, 1612), reprinted in *Collections of the Massachusetts Historical Society*, 2nd ed. (Boston: N. Hale, 1826), 8:199–227, esp. 202. Another proponent of this view was Alexander Whitaker, who actually went to Virginia, and personally converted Pocahontas to Christianity after her capture/kidnapping in 1613; cf. Kupperman, *The Jamestown Project*, 245.

36. John Smith, *Advertisements for the Unexperienced Planters of New-England, or Any-Where* (London: J. Haviland, 1631), 5; repr. in *The Complete Works of John Smith (1580–1631) in Three Volumes*, ed. Philip L. Barbour, The Institute of Early American History and Culture (Williamsburg: University of North Carolina Press, 1986), 3:272; cf. Kupperman, *The Jamestown Project*, 228, 357 n. 26.

with varying motivations, backgrounds, and self-perceptions, forced to build new identities in a dramatically different social context half a world away from their homes, with varying results.

This raises an important caution: Though claims of identity presuppose a distinction between Us and Them, this is sometimes over-emphasized, as though *all* identifications were inevitably contrastive. They often are, but they can also serve to overcome difference, to assert that We are part of a larger (and, in reality, more diverse) group. For Crashaw, English identity is partly built on what unites them with "others": the Romans, the Apostles, Israel, *and* the Gentiles. The hierarchical distinctions between Us and Them are not thereby eliminated, but they are porous. It is possible to change from one group to another, to stop being a "savage" and become one of Us. Conversion, rather than destruction, is the goal.[37] In fact, even Gray encouraged conversion, though he was willing to contemplate more extreme measures if it failed. Identity may presuppose contrast, but it can also emphasize commonality.[38]

Of course, even the more positive examples among the English colonizers still define both themselves and the natives according to their *own* conceptions of identity, religion, and civility, with little if any regard for how such matters were perceived by the colonized. But affirmations of identity are not just a tool of the self-styled elite; they can also serve to unite and give direction to minoritized, oppressed, and othered communities. The construction of self—whether by adopting alternative identifications, by re-appropriating imagery and language intended to other that very community, or by opting out of such language altogether—can be an act of oppositional agency that gives voice, power, and hope that resistance is possible.

---

37. In line with this, several of the Virginia Company's own tracts and broadsides, such as *A True and Sincere Declaration of the Purposes and Ends of the Plantation Begun in Virginia* (London, 1610), affirmed that its foremost goal was to "preach, & baptize into *Christian Religion*, and by propagation of that *Gospell*, to recover out of the armes of the Divell, a number of poore and miserable soules…from out of all corners of the earth," secondly, to honor the king, and thirdly, to secure marketable commodities (2–3; emphasis original). Catherine Armstrong, *Writing North America in the Seventeenth Century: English Representations in Print and Manuscript* (Hampshire: Ashgate, 2007), 131–2, notes that in practice the third goal, not the first, provided the chief motivation for most of the colonists (133–8; cf. also Kupperman, *The Jamestown Project*, 210–17).

38. Jenkins particularly challenges the overemphasis on difference within many conceptions of identity theory; *Social Identity*, 21–7.

Unfortunately, no records of biblical interpretation among the Powhatan have been preserved, but one can see examples of textually mediated identity-formation among the marginalized in many other contexts. For instance, medieval Jews living under Christian and Islamic rule sometimes also appealed to the biblical conquest accounts for models to describe their own hopes for deliverance, by identifying their oppressors with biblical enemies such as the Amalekites.[39]

In all these cases, whether to impose power over the Other, or to challenge it, conceptions of identity inevitably project complex social structures, often largely unconscious, which link certain groups and individuals together, while excluding others. In that process, the interpretation of religiously authoritative texts can be both a product of and a justification for social identifications. Yet how this works in practice requires further attention.

Identity and Interpretation

All reading is an encounter with someone else, an engagement with an Other who does not share one's own perspectives, experiences, or identity.[40] But paradoxically, this is only possible due to the *communal* nature of language: Our words produce meaning only in relation to a system of language, which depends (at least minimally) on a shared social and cultural environment, which precedes any given use of it. As Mikhail Bakhtin explains, "Prior to [the] moment of appropriation, the word does not exist in a neutral and impersonal language…but rather it exists in other people's mouths, in other people's contexts, serving other people's intentions: it is from there that one must take the word."[41] Language is

---

39. See, e.g., Naḥmanides' commentary on Exod. 17:9; for additional examples, cf. Gerson D. Cohen, "Esau as Symbol in Early Medieval Thought," in *Studies in the Variety of Rabbinic Cultures* (Philadelphia: The Jewish Publication Society, 1991), 243–69; Horowitz, *Reckless Rites*, 107–46; Katell Berthelot, "The Paradoxical Similarities between the Jews and the Roman Other," in *Perceiving the Other in Ancient Judaism and Early Christianity*, ed. Michal Bar-Asher Siegal, Wolfgang Grünstäudl, and Matthew Thiessen, WUNT 394 (Tübingen: Mohr Siebeck, 2017), 95–109.

40. This encounter is further mediated through some*thing* else, a text that itself does not fully reflect the identity of its author; cf. Jacques Derrida, *Limited Inc.*, trans. Samuel Weber and Jeffrey Mehlman, ed. Gerald Graff (Evanston: Northwestern University Press, 1988), 47–51; Breed, *Nomadic Text*, 102–4.

41. Mikhail M. Bakhtin, *The Dialogic Imagination: Four Essays*, ed. Michael Holquist, trans. Caryl Emerson and Michael Holquist (Austin: University of Texas Press, 1981), 293–4.

unavoidably "other people's," crafted and sustained by others, by which we constitute our own thoughts and statements, and hence our sense of self.

As such, reading "other people's" texts does not just depend on abstract assumptions and beliefs, but also on deeply personal perceptions of who We are, as individuals and as groups. The perceived meaning of a statement is always contingent upon who is saying it, who is hearing it, and what kinds of social relations exist between them. Since these perceptions are at least partially subjective and variable, this inevitably results in a tension between how a speaker or author perceives their (implied or intended) audience, and how any particular, actual audience perceives itself. Such tensions are not merely situational; they also reflect deep-seated and often unconscious ideological commitments.

One realm in which this is seen is the manner in which individuals address one another, or accept being addressed. Louis Althusser has referred to this phenomenon as "interpellation": the recognition by a hearer or reader that they are the "subject" (or addressee) of a statement or "hail."[42] To recognize oneself as subject, one implicitly accepts the authority of a speaker to address one, which in turn presupposes certain ideological commitments and social constructions of identity. For example, the hail of a police officer yelling "Stop right there!" assumes a different range of social relations than a good friend shouting "Wait right there!"[43]

Similarly, when a text hails its reader as "you" or "us," it also presupposes certain identities for the author and reader, and certain relations of authority and obligation between them, which can be accepted or challenged by any particular audience. For example, consider the wildly differing relations between author and reader implied by such genres as a love sonnet and a legal subpoena. It is not just that one assumes affection and the other conflict; each presupposes a broad range of social systems involving love and courtship on the one side, or justice and legality on the other. Both seek to compel a response from the addressee, but the means by which they do so are irreconcilable: Love cannot be compelled by legal force, while a subpoena depends on the authority of the state. Neither text

---

42. See Louis Althusser, "Ideology and Ideological State Apparatuses (Notes towards an Investigation)," in *Lenin and Philosophy and Other Essays*, trans. Ben Brewster (New York: Monthly Review Press 1971), 127–86; cf. also Roland Boer, "Louis Althusser: The Difficult Birth of Israel in Genesis," in *Marxist Criticism of the Hebrew Bible* (London: Bloomsbury T&T Clark, 2015), 23–46.

43. Cf. Althusser, "Ideology and Ideological State Apparatuses," 170–7, esp. 172, 174.

is understandable without an understanding of these social and ideological contexts, though the implications of rejecting their hail are by no means the same. Thus, while the interpellation differs, in each case accepting the text's address implies accepting its ideological assumptions—at least in part—which are often left unsaid.[44]

Likewise, as Carol Newsom and Roland Boer have emphasized, the ways in which scriptural texts address their audiences are also built on certain ideological (including religious) assumptions, with attendant implications of authority and identity.[45] Such interpellations may be intended by the text's author(s) or editor(s), but they need not always be: Sometimes later readers perceive interpellations in a text that may never have been intended by its author(s). For instance, if the Song of Songs was initially composed as erotic poetry, it would have interpellated its intended audience in a very different way than perceived by later Jewish and Christian readers, who have interpreted the book as an allegory for divine love.[46] In other cases, the differences between intended and perceived interpellation may not be as obvious, but they can be assumed to be common, particularly when literature is read by new communities in later periods or other cultures. Further, if these insights are combined with the recognition that conceptions of identity are built on both association

---

44. Of course, the hail can also be rejected. One can see such critical questioning of interpellation, for instance, in the work of many black feminist and womanist writers, who keenly question the framing assumptions of white feminist scholarship; see, e.g., bell hooks, "The Oppositional Gaze: Black Female Spectators," in *Black Looks: Race and Representation* (Boston: South End Press, 1992), 115–31.

45. E.g., Carol A. Newsom, "Woman and the Discourse of Patriarchal Wisdom: A Study of Proverbs 1–9," in *Gender and Difference in Ancient Israel*, ed. Peggy L. Day (Minneapolis: Fortress, 1989), 142–60; Boer, *Marxist Criticism of the Hebrew Bible*; Roland Boer and Jorunn Økland, eds., *Marxist Feminist Criticism of the Bible*, The Bible in the Modern World 14 (Sheffield: Sheffield Phoenix, 2008); cf. also Larry L. Welborn, "Towards Structural Marxism as a Hermeneutic of Early Christian Literature, Illustrated with Reference to Paul's Spectacle Metaphor in 1 Corinthians 15:30-32," *The Bible & Critical Theory* 8 (2012): 27–35; Deane Galbraith, "Interpellation, Not Interpolation: Reconsidering Textual Disunity in Numbers 13–14 as Variant Articulations of a Single Ideology," *The Bible & Critical Theory* 10 (2014): 29–48.

46. On such allegorical readings of the Song of Songs, cf., e.g., H. H. Rowley, "The Interpretation of the Song of Songs," *JTS* 38 (1937): 337–63; E. Ann Matter, *The Voice of My Beloved: The Song of Songs in Western Medieval Christianity* (Philadelphia: University of Pennsylvania Press, 1990); Arthur Green, "Shekhinah, the Virgin Mary, and the Song of Songs: Reflections on a Kabbalistic Symbol in Its Historical Context," *AJSR* 26 (2002): 1–52.

and contrast, it is evident that the perceived address of the text—and its interpretation—is inevitably grounded in deeply personal, socially conditioned perceptions of who We are, *and* who We are not.

Cases of this can again be seen among the defenders of Jamestown, as in Gray's sermon on Joshua 17. The text he is citing is a narrative, recounting something that is purported to have happened in a particular time and place, but by identifying his readers with the original addressees in Joshua, Gray reads this text as a "precept" that is more broadly applicable. In other words, through this social identification, Gray also dramatically alters the hail of the text, transforming a story into a statute. Yet we have already noted that this phenomenon is not limited to colonialist rhetoric, nor is it exclusively a "post-biblical" phenomenon. So in the next section, we will illustrate the broader significance of these links between interpretation and identity through a different example, only tangentially associated with colonialism.

Corporate Identity and Otherness in Deuteronomy 12 and Its Reception

Deuteronomy 12:13-14 commands that all sacrifice be confined to a single sanctuary:

> Take care lest you offer your burnt offerings *in every place* [בכל־מקום] you see. But [only] at the place that YHWH will choose / has chosen[47] in one of your tribes—there you shall offer your burnt offerings and there you shall do all that I [= YHWH] command you.

This command is attributed directly to the deity, as the ultimate source of authority in Israelite society. Yet it explicitly rejects the legitimacy of sacrificing at various local altars, which was widely practiced in ancient Israel, as reflected in many biblical texts and confirmed by the archaeological record.[48] Further, as Bernard Levinson has shown, Deuteronomy's

---

47. On the textual variant regarding whether God *will* choose, or already *has* chosen, see below.

48. E.g., Gen. 12:7-8; 35:1-7; 1 Sam. 1:3; 7:17; 1 Kgs 18:20-46; on the multiple cult-sites in Israel and Judah, cf. Eleonore Reuter, *Kultzentralisation: Entstehung und Theologie von Dtn 12*, BBB 87 (Frankfurt: Hain, 1993), esp. 192–212; Wolfgang Zwickel, *Der Tempelkult in Kanaan und Israel: Studien zur Kulturgeschichte Palästinas von der Mittelbronzezeit bis zum Untergang Judas*, FAT 10 (Tübingen: Mohr Siebeck, 1994); Karel van der Toorn, *Family Religion in Babylonia, Syria and Israel: Continuity and Change in the Forms of Religion*, SHANE 7 (Leiden: Brill,

demand for cult centralization directly *rewrites* the altar law in Exod. 20:22-26, which states that (v. 24):

> You shall make for me [= YHWH] an altar of earth and sacrifice on it your burnt offerings and your well-being offerings, your sheep and your cattle; *in every place* [בכל־המקום] where I cause my name to be remembered I will come to you and bless you.

Where Exodus presumes that altars would be constructed in every place (בכל־המקום), and prescribes how they should be built, Deuteronomy denies that they should be built in every place (בכל־מקום) except the one, central sanctuary, using Exodus' own language to deny its presuppositions.[49]

The religious and ideological assumptions implied by this cultic revision are manifold, but for the present discussion consider just one: In what appears to be a secondary introduction, in Deut. 12:1-7, the command is sharpened, not just as a reform of existing cultic practice, but as a rejection of foreign contamination.[50] According to this frame (cf. 12:29-31), it was not the audience's own ancestors who worshipped differently; it was *foreigners* who served "*their* gods" on "*their* altars"—not "your altars" or "our altars"—and it is "*their*" practices that must not be followed (Deut. 12:2-4):

> **You** must completely destroy *all the places* [כל־המקמות] where the nations whom you dispossess served *their* gods, on the mountain heights, on the hills, and under every leafy tree. Tear down *their* altars, smash *their* pillars, burn *their* sacred poles with fire, and cut down the idols of *their* gods, and thus eliminate *their* name from this *place*. **You** shall not worship YHWH **your** God in such ways.

1996), esp. 236–65; John Day, ed., *Temple and Worship in Biblical Israel*, LHBOTS 422 (London: T&T Clark, 2005); Reinhard G. Kratz and Hermann Spieckermann, eds., *One God—One Cult—One Nation: Archaeological and Biblical Perspectives*, BZAW 405 (Berlin: de Gruyter, 2010).

49. On the subversive rewriting of Exod. 20:22-26 in Deuteronomy 12, see esp. Bernard M. Levinson, *Deuteronomy and the Hermeneutics of Legal Innovation* (New York: Oxford University Press, 1997), esp. 23–52; cf. also Reuter, *Kultzentralisation*, 123–7.

50. This introduction in Deut. 12:1-7, along with 12:8-12 (all of which addresses the reader primarily, though not exclusively, in the plural) is generally thought to be later than the commands in 12:13-23 (which address the reader consistently in the singular), meaning that this framing is *already* part of the reception of the altar law; cf. Levinson, *Hermeneutics*, 24–5; Reuter, *Kultzentralisation*, 97–112.

Through this dichotomy, the proscribed practice of sacrificing "in every place" is redefined as foreign, even though the text Deuteronomy 12 rewrites is none other than the Covenant Code (Exodus 20–23), attributed (at least in the final form of the Pentateuch) to Yhwh himself. Thus, already in Deuteronomy, an explicit contrast between "you" and "the foreigner," is used to attribute traditional Israelite and Judahite practice—accepted in Exodus—to "them," while demanding from "you" a wholehearted allegiance to the innovative cultic practice.[51] In this way, the earlier "biblical" text is substantively rewritten in order to impose a conception of social identity on its audience, which implicitly rejects and repudiates the identity assumptions of the earlier "biblical" text.[52] Moreover, the Other is not just rejected in Deuteronomy 12; their cultic sites must be completely destroyed to prevent contamination. Other passages in Deuteronomy go further, commanding the destruction of the peoples of the Land themselves (esp. Deut. 7:1-6; 20:16-18), and even the execution of one's own kin who worship "their" gods (esp. Deuteronomy 13).[53]

Yet if worship of "one" God in only "one" place is thus established as foundational to the implied audience's identity—it is literally what distinguishes Us from Them—which "one" place does the text have in view? Surprisingly, the traditional Masoretic Text of Deuteronomy does not make it explicit, referring only to "the place Yhwh your God will choose" (e.g., Deut. 12:5, 11, 14, 18, 21, 26), and various communities who have embraced Deuteronomy as scripture have come to radically different conclusions on this point, each in line with their own conceptions of themselves as the "true" addressees of the text.[54] Most Jews

---

51. On this "tendentious" redefinition of traditional Israelite practice as "Canaanite"; see also Levinson, *Hermeneutics*, 148–9.

52. The term "biblical" is here placed in quotation marks to indicate that Exodus 20, in whatever form it existed, would not yet have been considered "biblical" at the time that Deuteronomy 12 was written and edited.

53. Cf., e.g., Philip D. Stern, *The Biblical Ḥerem: A Window on Israel's Religious Experience*, BJS 211 (Atlanta: Scholars Press, 1991); Joel N. Lohr, *Chosen and Unchosen: Conceptions of Election in the Pentateuch and Jewish-Christian Interpretation*, Siphrut 2 (Winona Lake: Eisenbrauns, 2009), 208–25; Nathan MacDonald, *Deuteronomy and the Meaning of "Monotheism,"* 2nd ed., FAT II/1 (Tübingen: Mohr Siebeck, 2012), 108–23; Christian Hofreiter, *Making Sense of Old Testament Genocide: Christian Interpretations of* Herem *Passages* (Oxford: Oxford University Press, 2018).

54. Cf., e.g., Reinhard G. Kratz, "'The Place which He Has Chosen': The Identification of the Cult Place of Deut. 12 and Lev. 17 in 4QMMT," in *Meghillot* 5–6 (2007): *57–*80; Gary N. Knoppers, *Jews and Samaritans: The Origins and History of Their Early Relations* (Oxford: Oxford University Press, 2013), 169–216.

have identified the "place" with Jerusalem or its temple, an interpretation already explicit in other texts of the Hebrew Bible, and continued in later Jewish literature.[55] By contrast, the Samaritan community, who trace their lineage to the old Northern Kingdom of Israel (an identification rejected by rabbinic Judaism), once had a temple at Mt. Gerizim in Samaria, and they continue to read this and several parallel expressions not in the future tense, referring to a place YHWH *will* choose, but in the past tense, referring to "the place YHWH *has chosen*," which they identify as Mt. Gerizim.[56]

It is debated which version of the altar command is earlier, but the two communities have continued to disagree about the correct form and interpretation of the text since antiquity.[57] This dispute once again reflects deeply held social and ideological commitments, and it has had real consequences: After the Assyrian Empire destroyed Northern Israel

---

55. See, e.g., 1 Kgs 8:16 (especially in the LXX); 2 Kgs 23:27; Ps. 78:68; Neh. 1:8-9; 2 Chron. 6:5-6; 7:12; as well as 4QMMT B 51–66; for the latter, see Florentino García Martínez and Eibert J. C. Tigchelaar, eds., *The Dead Sea Scrolls Study Edition* (Leiden: Brill, 1999), 2:796–7; cf. Kratz, "'The Place which He Has Chosen'," *58–*67; Stefan Schorch, "The Samaritan Version of Deuteronomy and the Origin of Deuteronomy," in *Samaria, Samarians, Samaritans: Studies on Bible, History and Linguistics*, ed. József Zsengellér, SJ 66 / StSam 6 (Berlin: de Gruyter, 2011), 23–37.

56. See Deut. 27:4 in the Samaritan Pentateuch, and the added command to build an altar on Mt. Gerizim at the end of their versions of the Ten Commandments, Exod. 20:14 [ET 20:17] and Deut. 5:18. On the Samaritans and their scriptures more broadly, see also Menachem Mor and Friedrich V. Reiterer, with Waltraud Winkler, eds., *Samaritans: Past and Present, Current Studies*, SJ 53 / StSam 5 (Berlin: de Gruyter, 2010); Zsengellér, *Samaria, Samarians, Samaritans*; Robert T. Anderson and Terry Giles, *The Samaritan Pentateuch: An Introduction to Its Origin, History, and Significance for Biblical Studies*, RBS 72 (Atlanta: Society of Biblical Literature, 2012); Jörg Frey, Ursula Schattner-Rieser, and Konrad Schmid, eds., *Die Samaritaner und die Bibel: Historische und literarische Wechselwirkungen zwischen biblischen und samaritanischen Traditionen / The Samaritans and the Bible: Historical and Literary Interactions between Biblical and Samaritan Traditions*, SJ 70 / StSam 7 (Berlin: de Gruyter, 2012); Benyamim Tsedaka, with Sharon Sullivan, eds., *The Israelite Samaritan Version of the Torah* (Grand Rapids: Eerdmans, 2013); Benedikt Hensel, *Juda und Samaria: Zum Verhältnis zweier nach-exilischer Jahwismen*, FAT 110 (Tübingen: Mohr Siebeck, 2016).

57. Though most have concluded that the indefinite future form in the MT is older, and has been modified in a sectarian direction by the Samaritans, a few have argued that the Samaritan version is older, and has been deliberately obscured in the MT; e.g., Schorch, "The Samaritan Version of Deuteronomy," 23–37; cf. Kratz, "'The Place which He Has Chosen,'" *67–*73; Knoppers, *Jews and Samaritans*, 184–8; Hensel, *Juda und Samaria*, 178–83.

and Samaria in 722 or 720 BCE, and the Babylonian Empire destroyed Jerusalem and its temple in 587 or 586 BCE, many of the former inhabitants of the land were exiled. But then Babylon itself was conquered by the Persian Achaemenid Empire in 539 BCE, which allowed the exiled Judeans to return and rebuild over the following centuries. Meanwhile, others had remained behind, or resettled, in Samaria, and archaeological investigations of Mt. Gerizim have confirmed that a YHWHistic sanctuary was also in use there since at least the early fifth century BCE.[58]

As a result, communities in both Judah (by then known as Yehud) and Samaria came to maintain separate YHWHistic temples, and both claimed to be true "Israelites."[59] At least some in each group also denied the legitimacy of the other's sanctuary and claims to Israelite identity. For instance, according to the book of Ezra–Nehemiah, when the returnees laid the foundation for the restored temple in Jerusalem, some people already living in the land came to them, claiming that they also worshipped "your God," and wished to help restore his temple (Ezra 4:1-2).[60] The returnees refused, saying, "It is not for *you* but for *us* to build a house for *our* God, for *we alone*[61] will build [a house] for YHWH, the God of Israel, as King Cyrus of Persia has commanded *us*" (Ezra 4:3). In other words, the returnees in Ezra–Nehemiah claim sole legitimacy as members of the people of "Israel," in contrast to those already living in the land, including the residents of Samaria (e.g., Ezra 4:2, 10). From that point on,

---

58. See Yitzhak Magen, "The Dating of the First Phase of the Samaritan Temple on Mount Gerizim in Light of the Archaeological Evidence," in *Judah and the Judeans in the Fourth Century B.C.E.*, ed. Oded Lipschitz, Gary N. Knoppers and Rainer Albertz (Winona Lake: Eisenbrauns, 2007), 157–212; Hensel, *Juda und Samaria*, 35–50.

59. On Jewish and Samaritan claims to "Israelite" identity in this period, see, e.g., Knoppers, *Jews and Samaritans*, esp. 135–68; Hensel, *Juda und Samaria*, esp. 35–282.

60. Lisbeth Fried emphasizes that the people are referred to as "enemies" (Ezra 4:1), and are quoted as appealing to "'Your God' [4:2], and not 'our God'.... By having the 'enemies' put it this way, the biblical author makes a separation between the two communities of worshippers—the Judeans and their 'enemies'"; Lisbeth S. Fried, *Ezra: A Commentary*, A Critical Commentary (Sheffield: Sheffield Phoenix, 2015), 191. Cf. also Donna Laird, *Negotiating Power in Ezra–Nehemiah*, AIL 26 (Atlanta: Society of Biblical Literature, 2016).

61. אנחנו יחד could instead be translated "we together," but the sense is contrastive; "we alone" is accepted by, e.g., the NRSV; *HALOT SE* 1:405; Jacob M. Myers, *Ezra, Nehemiah: Introduction, Translation, and Notes*, AB 14 (Garden City: Doubleday, 1965), 30; Hugh G. M. Williamson, *Ezra, Nehemiah*, WBC 16 (Waco, TX: Word, 1985), 41–2, with further bibliography; Fried, *Ezra: A Commentary*, 189.

Ezra–Nehemiah claims that the latter actively opposed the restoration of Jerusalem and its temple (Ezra 4:6-16; Nehemiah 4–6).

Though it is disputed to what extent these portrayals accurately describe the situation in the sixth or fifth centuries BCE, opposition between competing groups who self-identified as "Israel" certainly grew over the following centuries, eventually resulting in a decisive break between "Jews" and "Samaritans."[62] Matters came to a head in the late second century BCE, when the Hasmonean (Jewish) king John Hyrcanus marched against Samaria and destroyed the temple on Gerizim.[63] Less than two centuries later, the same fate befell Jerusalem as well, when the Romans destroyed its temple in 70 CE.[64] Since then, each community has continued to view Jerusalem or Gerizim respectively as the only legitimate cultic site, and anticipates the eventual restoration of the temple there.[65]

The Gospel of John even highlights the dispute over these two sanctuaries, when Jesus is challenged by a Samaritan woman: "*Our* ancestors worshipped on this mountain [= Gerizim], but *you* [= the Jews] say that Jerusalem is *the place* where one must worship" (Jn 4:20). Jesus responds, "Believe me, woman, an hour is coming when you will worship the Father neither on this mountain nor in Jerusalem…. An hour is coming and is now here, when the true worshippers will worship the Father in spirit and truth" (4:21, 23). Whether intended by John or not, many later

---

62. On Ezra–Nehemiah and their relation to history, see, e.g., Lester L. Grabbe, *Ezra–Nehemiah*, OTR (London: Routledge, 1998); Mark J. Boda and Paul L. Redditt, eds., *Unity and Disunity in Ezra–Nehemiah: Redaction, Rhetoric, and Reader*, HBM 17 (Sheffield: Sheffield Phoenix, 2008); Isaac Kalimi, ed., *New Perspectives on Ezra–Nehemiah: History and Historiography, Text, Literature, and Interpretation* (Winona Lake: Eisenbrauns, 2012); Knoppers, *Jews and Samaritans*, esp. 135–240; Hensel, *Juda und Samaria*, 283–344; cf. also Michael L. Satlow, *How the Bible Became Holy* (New Haven: Yale University Press, 2014), 69–100.

63. This is described by the first-century CE Jewish historian Josephus, *B.J.* 1.62-65; *A.J.* 13.254-56; see Knoppers, *Jews and Samaritans*, 172–3; Jonathan Bourgel, "The Destruction of the Samaritan Temple by John Hyrcanus: A Reconsideration," *JBL* 135 (2016): 505–23; Hensel, *Juda und Samaria*, 50.

64. On the whole history of this period, see, e.g., Lester L. Grabbe, *An Introduction to Second Temple Judaism: History and Religion of the Jews in the Time of Nehemiah, the Maccabees, Hillel and Jesus* (London: T&T Clark, 2010); Grabbe, *A History of the Jews and Judaism in the Second Temple Period*, 2 vols., LSTS 47, 68 (London: T&T Clark, 2004, 2008).

65. Cf., e.g., Isaac Kalimi, "The Hiding of the Temple Vessels in Jewish and Samaritan Literature," in *Fighting over the Bible: Jewish Interpretation, Sectarianism and Polemic from Temple to Talmud and Beyond*, BRLJ 54 (Leiden: Brill, 2017), 208–16.

Christians concluded from this that worship in Jerusalem and Gerizim would be replaced by worship "in spirit," and then read Deuteronomy 12 in line with that belief.[66] For instance, Basil of Caesarea (329/330–379 CE) claims that the chosen "place" does not refer to a physical location at all, but rather to the Spirit, whose true home is in "the saints," that is, among Christians:

> This is the special and peculiar place of true worship; for it is said "Take heed to thyself that thou offer not thy burnt offerings in every place…but in the place the Lord thy God shall choose" [Deut. 12:13-14]. Now what is a spiritual burnt offering? "The sacrifice of praise" [Ps. 50:14; LXX: 49:14]. And in what place do we offer it? In the Holy Spirit. Where have we learnt this? From the Lord himself in the words "The true worshippers shall worship the Father in spirit and in truth" [Jn 4:23]. This place Jacob saw and said, "the Lord is in this place" [Gen. 28:16]. It follows that the Spirit is verily the place of the saints and the saint is the proper place for the Spirit, offering himself as he does for the indwelling of God, and called God's Temple.[67]

Thus, if the author(s) or editor(s) of Deuteronomy 12 present commitment to worship God at a single sanctuary as constitutive of Israelite identity (in contrast to "the nations" who must be driven out), Jews, Samaritans, and Christians have each read forms of this passage as commanding the distinctive practices of their own communities, in implicit and explicit contrast to those of Others. Their interpretations (and the variant forms of the text itself that they have transmitted) cannot therefore be separated from each group's self-perceptions of identity, as each sees itself as the true addressees of the command.

Yet just as we saw with regard to colonial England's self-justifications, Deuteronomy's redefinition of identity is not merely negative and contrastive. By fusing ancient Near Eastern legal codes, which embody a king's authority over his subjects as dispenser of justice, with covenantal language normally used to establish diplomatic relations between a king and his vassals, Deuteronomy depicts YHWH as addressing "you" as a community united under divine authority and justice, and not merely as

---

66. For an argument that John does not intend to replace the Jerusalem temple, but instead uses its imagery to portray Jesus as the embodiment of the God of Israel, see Ken Brown, "Temple Christology in the Gospel of John: Replacement Theology and Jesus as the Self-Revelation of God" (MA thesis, Trinity Western University, 2010), https://www.academia.edu/8870006/.

67. Basil, *De Spiritu Sancto* XXVI.62; translation from NPNF 2.8:39.

a land dominated by a king or foreign overlord.⁶⁸ In this way, the text establishes an "imagined community," in Benedict Anderson's words, that unites various clans, families, and peoples under one deity—presenting them all as "Israelites"—and thereby gives them a collective voice and agency.⁶⁹

In doing so, Deuteronomy explicitly and repeatedly ties its audience to the promises made to "your ancestors" or "our ancestors" in the wilderness (e.g., Deut. 12:1 et passim), and even denies any temporal distinction that might separate the present reader from the "original" audience. As the introduction to Deuteronomy's version of the Ten Commandments states: "Not with our ancestors did Y<small>HWH</small> make this covenant, but with us, all of us here who are alive today" (Deut. 5:3). This direct identification of the audience with "our" ancestors, who escaped slavery in Egypt, encourages solidarity not only among their "own" people, but also with the foreigners living among them: In the following passage, the Israelites are commanded to allow rest to their servants and "the immigrant in your towns, so that your male and female slave may rest as well as you," because "you were a slave in the Land of Egypt" (Deut. 5:14-15). Similarly, Deut. 26:5 urges its readers to remember that "My father was a wandering Aramean; he went down into Egypt and lived there as an immigrant, few in number, and there he became a great nation, mighty and populous." In context, this recollection is invoked to justify celebrating God's gifts "together with the Levites *and the immigrants who reside among you*" (Deut. 26:11).⁷⁰

---

68. Eckart Otto goes so far as to see the basic origin of Deuteronomy as a transfer of the Neo-Assyrian loyalty oath onto the relation between the Judean people and Y<small>HWH</small>, with a concomitant rejection of the centralized cult of Aššur in favor of a centralized cult of Y<small>HWH</small>; Otto, "Treueid und Gesetz: Die Ursprünge des Deuteronomiums im Horizont neuassyrischen Vertragsrechts," *ZABR* 2 (1996): 1–52; similarly, Levinson, *Hermeneutics*, 147; for additional bibliography and critique, cf. Reinhard G. Kratz, "The Idea of Cultic Centralization and Its Supposed Ancient Near Eastern Analogies," in Kratz and Spieckermann, eds., *One God—One Cult—One Nation*, 121–44, esp. 123–30.

69. Cf. Benedict Anderson, *Imagined Communities: Reflections on the Origin and Spread of Nationalism*, rev. ed. (London: Verso, 1991). See the discussion of Anderson and the community-producing function of particular technologies of discourse, including Deuteronomy's rhetoric, in Seth L. Sanders, *The Invention of Hebrew* (Urbana: University of Illinois Press, 2009), esp. 32–5; Sanders, "What Was the Alphabet For? The Rise of Written Vernacular and the Making of Israelite National Literature," *Maarav* 11 (2004): 25–56.

70. On these passages and their role within the development of the book of Deuteronomy, see Mark A. Awabdy, *Immigrants and Innovative Law: Deuteronomy's Theological and Social Vision for the* גר, FAT II/67 (Tübingen: Mohr Siebeck, 2014).

In all these cases, Deuteronomy was initially fashioned as a tool for identity-construction and maintenance, and it has continued to function in this role ever since. Precisely by addressing an imagined community as "you," the text remains structurally open to reading outside its initial context(s) of composition, which did not end with the formation of an ancient Israelite body politic.[71] Forms of Deuteronomy subsequently helped shape (and were in turn shaped by) the exilic Judahite community, the Persian-period community of Yehud, the Samaritan community, the wide variety of Second Temple Judaisms, early Christian communities, Rabbinic Judaism, and many later societies, nations, and empires, including the English. Each of these have embraced and adapted particular versions of the book as scripture, and interpreted them in light of their own beliefs and experiences. In doing so, numerous possibilities for building and denying identity have served both to promote religious and social cohesion, and to destroy it, to build up and tear down the distinctions that separate Us from Them, the self from the Other.

As the text has been granted an authoritative place within these traditions, it has continued to mediate the social dynamics of the communities that preserve and transmit it as their own. But this can become manifest in contrasting ways. As we have already seen, just as a text itself can emphasize or deny the commonality between people-groups, so also can interpretation serve either to emphasize *or* downplay the otherness of the text, its author(s) or its implied audience.

After all, not every self-identification leads to an embrace of the text; the opposite also occurs, when texts are rejected or reinterpreted in part due to their association with the Other. For instance, Martin Luther regularly identified Christians as the "true Israel," and applied countless biblical texts to his own community,[72] but he also famously rejected the

---

71. For "political" readings of Deuteronomy in conversation with modernity, see Bernard M. Levinson, "The First Constitution: Rethinking the Origins of Rule of Law and Separation of Powers in Light of Deuteronomy," *Cardozo Law Review* 27, no. 4 (2006): 1853–88; Rob Barrett, *Disloyalty and Destruction: Religion and Politics in Deuteronomy and the Modern World*, LHBOTS 511 (London: T&T Clark, 2009).

72. E.g., in the prologue to his 1523 translation of the Pentateuch, Luther states that "There are some who have little regard for the Old Testament. They think of it as a book that was given to the Jewish people only and is now out of date, containing only stories of past times.... But Christ says in John 5, 'Search the Scriptures, for it is they that bear witness to me'"; Martin Luther, "Preface to the Old Testament," in *Luther's Works*, vol. 35, ed. E. Theodore Bachmann (Philadelphia: Muhlenberg, 1960), 235–6; cited by Richard B. Hays, *Reading Backwards: Figural Christology and the Fourfold Gospel Witness* (Waco: Baylor University Press, 2014), 1.

continuing relevance of the Mosaic Law (including in Deuteronomy), in part through a denial of identity. As he puts it, with clear rhetorical exaggeration:

> It is true, God has commanded Moses and has therefore spoken to the people. But we are not the people to whom the Lord spoke. Beloved, God has also spoken to Adam; I am not therefore Adam. He commanded Abraham, [that] he should strangle his son; I am not therefore Abraham, that I [should] strangle my son.[73]

For Luther, Christian identity implies both continuity and distinction with the people described in the Bible. Early in his career, this led him to emphasize commonality with "the Jews" (e.g., in his 1523 book *That Jesus Christ Was Born a Jew*), in hopes of converting them. But by the end of his life, he concluded that widespread conversion was impossible and composed several violent denunciations of "the Jews" as enemies of humanity, such as his 1543 book, *On the Jews and Their Lies*.[74] For Luther, as for others, identity is a double-edged sword.

Thus, while Jews, Samaritans, and Christians have all identified themselves with the people of "Israel" referred to and addressed in Deuteronomy and elsewhere in the Hebrew Bible / Old Testament, these social identifications are varying and multifaceted. Each must ignore or deny the massive religious, cultural, social, and—in most cases—genetic differences between themselves and the earliest addressees of the text. The text is read *as if* it were addressed directly to each of these groups, not merely to some "other" people who lived long before them. In each case, perceptions of individual and corporate identity have been simultaneously driven by and justified through particular readings of "other peoples' texts," which are in turn interpreted based on that claimed identity.

---

73. WA 24:12 lines 3–7; from a 1527 sermon *Über das erste Buch Mose*. Elsewhere he makes a similar point: "For Moses is only given to the Jewish people and does not concern us pagans and Christians. We have our Gospel and New Testament.... If you want to make Jews out of us through Moses, we will not stand for it"; WA 18:76 lines 4–8, from a 1525 tract titled *Wider die himmlischen Propheten, von den Bildern und Sakrament* (both translations are the authors'). On Luther's complex embrace of and dissociation from the Old Testament, including these statements, see Heinrich Bornkamm, *Luther and the Old Testament*, trans. Eric W. and Ruth C. Gritsch (Mifflintown: Sigler, 1997).

74. On Luther's shifting perspectives towards the Jews, including his sharply aggressive turn towards the end of his life, see, e.g., Thomas Kaufmann, *Luthers Juden*, 2nd ed. (Stuttgart: Reclam, 2015); Isaac Kalimi, "Martin Luther, the Jews, and Esther: Biblical Interpretation in the Shadow of Judeophobia," *JR* 100 (2020): 42–74.

Summary and Synthesis

The following ten essays explore the ties between interpretation and identity through a focus on the reception of Jewish, Christian, and other ancient religious literature. The examples discussed range from the earliest editorial layers embedded within the biblical texts themselves, to the most recent contemporary interpretations. Yet in all of them, the guiding question has been: How have particular groups or individuals construed particular authoritative religious texts as "their own" or "other peoples'," in order to justify their reading, rewriting, reuse, or rejection of those texts? Though each essay takes its own individual approaches, shaped partly by the bodies of literature being studied, together they provide a broad range of perspectives on the phenomenon of reading "other peoples' texts."

The first three essays continue to explore the relation between reception and identity on a broad theoretical and methodological level. First, Musa Dube reflects on her own experience as a displaced person, its impact on her work as a New Testament scholar, and the need to reread the biblical texts in light of their postcolonial history.[75] She underlines the multiple-border crossings of the postcolonial world and the resulting global diaspora communities. Born within this modern colonial history herself, Dube maps the journey of reading a book that had colonized her, and the continuity of colonizing ideology in the academic study of the Bible. Proposing to decolonize biblical studies from its eurocentrism, she challenges the focus on the ancient Greco-Roman world in much of New Testament studies, since it brackets questions about modern colonialism. Instead, she investigates several biblical texts' attitudes towards the Other and towards the imperialism of their own time, explores the use of gender to articulate positions of inequality, and proposes alternative ways of reading the Bible. In a bid to profile both the colonizing and the colonized Bible reader of modern times, she reads letters from modern colonial contexts, seeking to identify strategies of domination, resistance, collaboration, and the emergence of hybridity in the modern colonial contact zone.

Next, Michael Satlow observes that much scholarship on biblical literature attempts to use a deductive method in order to prove a text's provenance or adduce its reuse and appropriation by others. By contrast,

---

75. This essay was first published by Musa W. Dube, "Boundaries and Bridges: Journeys of a Postcolonial Feminist Biblical Scholar," *Journal of the European Society of Women in Theological Research* 22 (2014): 139–56. We would like to thank Peeters Publishers for their generous permission to republish the essay.

he explores other methodological models for approaching these texts and argues that there can be no compelling interpretation outside of some implicit understanding of historical context. The chapter focuses on the book of *Jubilees* and the letters of Paul as test cases in order to argue that how people read, transform, adapt, and appropriate the texts of others is ultimately a historical rather than merely or even primarily a textual question. In other words: How an author appropriates another text cannot be demonstrated from the texts themselves; any such proposals need to be grounded in a wider historical narrative. Instead of *reading history out of texts* we need to *read texts within history*.

Next, Robert L. Brawley argues that reading is a constructive enterprise in which readers attempt to comprehend reality, even if the reality of the text is fictional. Although authorial intention is a will o' the wisp, attempts to comprehend texts ordinarily construe them as if one were recovering the mind of an author, or alternatively as if one were recovering a stable meaning expressed concretely in syntax and grammar. Against the notion of fixed stability, authors often produce texts and only later discover new perspectives in their own writing. In addition, every text is interpreted in the contingencies of a different context. This chapter demonstrates the inevitable variety of interpretations and illustrates the dialogical relationship between precursor texts and successor texts in terms of figurations. The precursor and successor play back and forth on each other. The very processes of comprehension produce "reflections" that shape the reader's perceptions of both the precursor and the successor, and these are in turn shaped by the reader's conceptions of identity, which are always socially mediated.

The next two essays explore the dynamic relation between interpretation and identity by considering the redaction history of the Pentateuch as a form of reception, with a focus on the ways this is shaped by the social identities of the redactors. First, Alison L. Joseph explores "Redaction as Reception," taking as an example the story of the "rape" of Dinah in Genesis 34. This is a tale that is deeply shaped by perceptions of identity and difference, on multiple levels. In the reconstructed base-text, the potential marriage of "Dinah, daughter of Jacob," with "Shechem, son of Hamor, the Hivite" is described as shameful and is rejected in the strongest possible terms: The sons of Jacob demand that Shechem become circumcised like them, but when he does so, they kill him. Joseph argues that several elements in this story appear to have troubled early readers, leading to a secondary revision that emphasizes that the essential problem with this marriage was not Shechem's individual unsuitability as a husband, but instead his foreignness. The marriage request is rephrased as an offer to intermarry between the two peoples more broadly, and in the end, not just Shechem, but all the men of his city are circumcised then killed. In this secondary edition of the story, the text is heavily revised without being replaced, as the editor draws authority from his source, even while transforming its story of illegitimate sexuality into a blanket renunciation of intermarriage.

Next, Ken Brown looks more specifically at how "inner-biblical" rewriting serves to link particular communities to the groups described within the texts. To show this, the chapter compares the ways in which the story of Moses bringing water out of a rock in Exodus 17 is rewritten within the Pentateuch itself (Numbers 20), in the apocrypha (Wisdom of Solomon 11), and in the New Testament (1 Corinthians 10). He argues that each of these rewritings implies distinct identifications between "the children of Israel" described in Exodus, and their contemporary audiences in the Persian and Greco-Roman periods. How these identifications are established, and who is included within them, changes substantially from one rewriting to the next, but all of them reflect an essential link between social identity and interpretation, as reflected in both the redaction *and* reception of the text.

In the next chapter, Kyle Wells notes that the question of Jewish identity was especially live and evasive during the turmoil of the late Second Temple period, when various Jewish communities were forced anew to validate for themselves and others that they were, in fact, the people of the Abrahamic covenant. This essay compares and contrasts how two writers, Paul and Pseudo-Philo, went about that complex task by adopting and appropriating authoritative traditions about the Abrahamic covenant in the light of their current circumstances. Among other things, Wells argues that the differences between how various Jews thought about "covenant" were, in part, driven by the need to reinforce group identity.

Continuing to explore early Jewish literature, Courtney Friesen focuses on an example of the reception of a non-biblical text and tradition, examining the literary appropriation and cultural subversion of Heracles legends. He notes that Heracles was widely revered as a semi-divine hero in the Greek and Roman world, honored with cult and celebrated in literature and art. Several early Christians mocked his extreme behaviors, deploying them in their attacks against paganism. By contrast, Philo of Alexandria takes the Greek demigod as a positive model of philosophical courage. Friesen argues that Philo does this ironically, by quoting several passages from a satyr play by Euripides, one of antiquity's most popular poets, in which the hero's comic excesses in eating and drinking demonstrate his true character. Thus, in his appropriation of an "authoritative" text of a cultural Other, Philo's admiration of this son of Zeus becomes indistinguishable from his ridicule. A form of this paper won the 2017 Paul Achtemeier Award for New Testament from the Society of Biblical Literature.

Next, Choon-Leong Seow compares the differing forms of the book of Job embraced by Jews and Christians in antiquity, and argues that there is no common text for this classic, and no single history of reception, only varied cultural histories of contested narratives. Jews and Christians do not in fact share a common "book of Job," and each grapples with whether to see the book and its protagonist as "their own" or "other peoples'," in different ways. Christians followed the Greek translation of Job, which attenuates or eliminates Job's critique of God found in the Hebrew version. Accordingly, Job himself was imagined as a kind of saint, or even a model of Christ. By contrast, Jews eventually rejected the Greek version as "other peoples' text," and disagreed among themselves over whether Job himself was an Israelite of exemplary character, or a gentile blasphemer. As a further illustration of the overlap between diverse textual forms and non-linear reception, the chapter compares the differing ways in which the figure of Leviathan has been portrayed among Christians and Jews.

The final two papers turn to the impact of social identity on contemporary reception of the Hebrew Bible / Old Testament. First, Sonja Ammann explores the ways in which contemporary interpretations continue to be shaped by the degree to which the text is perceived as the interpreter's "own" or "other peoples'." She argues that biblical scholars, despite being critical and historically informed readers, retain a particularistic relationship to the biblical texts they study. Focusing on scholarly readings of the polemic against idol worshippers in Isa. 44:9-20, she investigates how and to what extent the biblical text is perceived as "other peoples'" by biblical scholars themselves: Do interpreters take on or refuse the role the text invites them to perform? Drawing on the concepts of the "implied reader" and of the "ingroup / outgroup" distinction used in social identity theory, Ammann compares four commentators who read the text in differing social and confessional contexts (Claus Westermann, Angelika Berlejung, José Severino Croatto, and Dominic Sundararaj Irudayaraj). She argues that these commentators generally comply with the role of the implied reader and identify with the textual ingroup. However, their understandings of the text's message as well as their characterizations of the textual ingroup and outgroup differ considerably. The variety of interpretations highlights that the commitment to the text as "one's own" is prior to, and to a certain extent apparently independent of, the actual content of the text.

Finally, Brennan Breed notes that, in general, critical biblical scholars attempt to bracket their own commitments and presuppositions in order to objectively reconstruct the past contexts in which biblical texts originated, and then to discern the intended message of the text's author(s). Nevertheless, though many scholars frame this practice in terms of "respect" for the text and author(s) who were responsible for it, Breed argues that this hermeneutical theory in fact fails to "respect" the inherent open-endedness of the text. Using the book of Ecclesiastes / Qohelet and its reception as an example, he notes that the text has not called forth, and cannot be reduced to, a single interpretation. The text invites a wide range of potential readings, which are shaped in part by the reader's perceptions of identity and otherness. Ecclesiastes in particular holds together seemingly contradictory perspectives, allowing readers to see in it both a pious embrace of traditional religion, and a radical critique of it. Such readings cannot be separated from the contrasting ways that these readers have seen their own identity in relation to the text. Breed argues that such divergent readings should not be closed off in a misguided attempt at objectivity and offers an alternative understanding of how respect for the text might function in biblical scholarship.

Altogether, these essays open up a range of approaches to the social contexts of textual development and reception. Regarding methods: some focus on the historical embeddedness of the texts, others employ and refine literary theory, while others emphasize ideology. Regarding examples: some illustrate the roles of identity and reception in the earliest origins of the texts, others trace their divergent consequences across history, and still others elucidate their ongoing impact up to the most recent interpretations. Yet all of them highlight the relations between identity and otherness in the reception of biblical and other religiously authoritative literature. Despite the variety of approaches and examples they represent, these essays are more than just isolated reflections on a common theme. They participate in a shared conversation, which extends well beyond the texts themselves. While each essay highlights differing and complementary aspects of the social contexts of reception, they also challenge assumptions that are widely shared among biblical interpreters, including, in some cases, those presupposed by other essays in this same volume.

In the end, all interpretation raises the question: "Whose text is it?" and every answer to that question, even if left implicit, has significant consequences. From the earliest cross-cultural retellings of ancient myths, to the latest internet memes parodying political opponents, human beings have constantly reread, rewritten, and reused "other peoples' texts," either to minimize or exaggerate their differences, to embrace the authority, social identities, or interpellations they entail, or to reject them. Yet whether intended to build bridges or to burn them, every reading is shaped by the reader's own perceptions of identity and otherness, which have not only impacted the reception of the Bible across history, but continue to drive contemporary disputes about its meaning, relevance, and application.

BOUNDARIES AND BRIDGES:
JOURNEYS OF A POSTCOLONIAL FEMINIST
IN BIBLICAL STUDIES

Musa W. Dube

As a young girl, one of the derisive comments I frequently heard at our family retail shop was: "*Dilo ke lona le tsile le tlola melolwane le melolwane; dinoka le dinokana, le tsile go bapala kwano.*" That is, "you came crossing one boundary after another, one river after another to trade in our country." The subtext in the statement was that we were foreigners who did not deserve, or had merely been favored to access economic resources in Botswana. My parents and five of my eldest siblings were born in Zimbabwe, and the last five of us were born in Botswana. Before we migrated to Botswana, it had happened that the village where my parents lived was declared a white man's ranch. Indigenous people in the area were given two choices: to remain in their homes and assume the status of servants to the owner of the ranch, or to move to the reserves. The reserves were arid and crowded places, where black indigenous people of Zimbabwe were moved from their villages and resettled. My parents chose to remain. And so their status was redefined to servanthood. After a while they were restricted to ploughing only an acre and to owning a maximum of five cows. That is when my parents decided to move to Botswana, a semi-desert country that did not attract white colonial settlers due to its harsh temperatures.

I was thus born in Botswana due to this colonial experience. Yet even those of us who were born in Botswana bore Zimbabwean names and spoke Ndebele in our family, which immediately marked us as those who do not have roots among the indigenous ethnic groups of Botswana. As many diaspora narratives attest,[1] people living in diaspora contexts often

---

1. See Ps. 137:1-6, which reads, "By the rivers of Babylon, there we sat down and there we wept, when we remembered Zion, On the willows there we hung our harps…. How could we sing the Lord's song in a foreign land? If I forget you, O

permanently bear the stamp of being foreigners even when they have long settled in their host country, because their very existence is an unending process of crossing boundaries, living in between spaces, and continuous negotiation with the larger cultural, economic, and political community. One remains unsettled. And so recently a friend of mine told me that some people have remarked that I behave and carry myself as if I am foreigner in Botswana, even though I was born and bred in Botswana. Indeed I have no other country to call my own, save Botswana. If I were to return to Zimbabwe, as we occasionally return with my family, I would find myself even at a stranger place there. Describing this diasporic experience, Fernando Segovia, a Cuban American New Testament scholar, says it is tantamount to "having two places and no place on which to stand."[2] Edward Said, in his now classical book, *Culture and Imperialism*, points out that modern imperialism covered three quarters of our world. He holds that "the great imperial experience of the past two hundred years was global and universal (and) it has implicated every corner of the globe, the colonizer and the colonized together."[3] He also notes that it is a unique characteristic of this age "to have produced more refugees, migrants, displaced persons, and exiles than ever before in history."[4] I am part of this history.

In the past four centuries, most colonial travelers came from the western hemisphere in the form of traders, explorers, colonizers, and missionaries, or forced migration in the form of enslavement, indentured labor, or resettlements of indigenous people. In the contemporary era of the global economy,[5] the picture has become much more complex: the Empire does

---

Jerusalem, let my right hand wither!" This does not only express the exiled and diasporic Jewish communities' yearning for home, but has also become a popular language for many other contemporary diaspora communities expressing their unsettled identities. A good example is its use in Reggae music. See also Fernando F. Segovia, "Towards a Hermeneutics of the Diaspora: A Hermeneutics of Otherness and Engagement," in *Reading from the Place, Vol. 1: Social Location and Biblical Interpretation in the United States*, ed. Fernando F. Segovia and Mary A. Tolbert (Minneapolis: Fortress, 1995), 57–78.

2. Segovia, "Towards a Hermeneutics of the Diaspora," 68.

3. Edward Said, *Culture and Imperialism* (New York: Knopf, 1993; repr. New York: Vintage, 1994), 259.

4. Said, *Culture and Imperialism*, 332.

5. Sankaran Krishna, *Globalisation and Postcolonialism: Hegemony and Resistance in the Twenty-First Century* (New York: Rowman & Littlefield, 2009), explores the link between modern colonialism and contemporary globalization and some postcolonial forms of resistance that characterize this period.

not only write back,[6] it also travels back to the colonial mother countries—seeking a share in the commonwealth.[7] According to Avtar Brah:

> There has been a rapid increase in migrations across the globe since the 1980s. These mass movements are taking place in all directions. The volume of migration has increased to Australia, North America and Western Europe. Similarly, large-scale population movements have taken place within and between countries of the "South." Events in Eastern Europe and former Soviet Union have provided impetus for mass movements of people.... People on the move may be labor immigrants (both documented and undocumented), highly-qualified specialists, entrepreneurs, students, refugees and asylum seekers or the household members of the previous migrants.[8]

The intensity of movements across the borders has become a major feature among contemporary philosophers who have begun to theorize border-crossing, exile, and the diaspora as a framework of being, seeing, thinking, living, and doing scholarly work. Said, a Palestinian scholar who lived and died in the USA, holds that "Exile, far from being the fate of the nearly forgotten unfortunates who are dispossessed and expatriated, becomes something closer to the norm, an experience of crossing boundaries and charting new territories in defiance of the classic canonic enclosures."[9] Gloria Anzaldúa, the famed feminist Chicana scholar, drawing from the Mexican experience, theorized borderlands and border-crossing across cultures, sexualities, languages, and spiritualities.[10] Similarly, Homi Bhabha, one of the outstanding postcolonial thinkers of our time, advocates that we should regard ourselves as living

---

6. The statement evokes Bill Ashcroft, Gareth Griffiths, and Helen Tiffin, eds., *The Empire Writes Back: Theory and Practice in Postcolonial Literatures* (New York: Routledge, 1989), which was one of earliest literary expositions highlighting the centrality of the empire in commonwealth literary writers.

7. The global economy is a system noted for its policies of deregulation, privatization, and liberalization, which reduces social welfare, creates insecurity, and separates families, as increasingly people are forced to move in search for economic survival.

8. Avtar Brah, "Diaspora, Border and Transnational Identities," in *Feminist Postcolonial Theory: A Reader*, ed. Reina Lewis and Sara Mills (New York: Routledge, 2003), 613–34, here 613.

9. Said, *Culture and Imperialism*, 317.

10. Gloria Anzaldúa, *Borderlands/La Frontera: The New Mestiza* (San Francisco: Aunte Lute, 1999).

in-between spaces, and our identities should be constructed along a model of "hybridity."[11] He proposes that we should regard our homes as strange. The strangeness of home is a concept that invites us to be guests even in our own spaces, to occupy our own spaces with discomfort and to remain critical of the structures of what we call home. Bhabha also proposes a metaphor of the border, not as a place that brings us to the end, but one that invites us to look beyond our reality to another reality.[12] The border metaphor is a metaphor that places us in a migratory position, where we are all unsettled and where home is strange.

In her paper, "Diaspora, Border and Transnational Identities," Brah underlines the above positions when she challenges us to acknowledge that with current migrations we are experiencing "the homing of diaspora, the diasporising of home."[13] Given the massive movements that we have from all directions, Brah proposes that we should inhabit our homes and all spaces as "a diasporic space," which she describes as "the global condition of culture as a site of travel."[14] Brah describes the diaspora space as a conceptual category, "inhabited not only by those who migrated and their descendants, but equally by those who are constructed and represented as indigenous."[15] She proposes the diaspora space as "the site where the native is as much a diasporian as the diasporian is the native."[16] In short, we are all in the diaspora space, scattered; home is at the border where we encounter all sorts of cultures, where there is no settlement and where we are invited to look beyond our immediate homes and cultures to other realities that challenge and stretch our constructed realities. Home is indeed strange given the hybridity of our cultures and identities.

Biblical Studies at the Site of Travel

Biblical Studies is intertwined with these journeys of our world and the journeys of the word, both of the past and the present. According to Leticia Guardiola-Sáenz, the biblical text is a borderless text,[17] and Jesus

---

11. See Homi K. Bhabha, *The Location of Culture*, 2nd ed. (New York: Routledge, 2004).
12. Bhabha, *The Location of Culture*, 4–5.
13. Brah, "Diaspora, Border," 623.
14. Brah, "Diaspora, Border," 632.
15. Brah, "Diaspora, Border," 632.
16. Brah, "Diaspora, Border," 632.
17. Leticia A. Guardiola-Sáenz, "Borderless Women and Borderless Texts: A Cultural Reading of Matthew 15:21-28," *Semeia* 78 (1997): 69–81, here 71–2.

is a border crosser.[18] Arguing that the "the biblical story itself invites its readers to identify with it and to act it out in history," I have argued that the biblical story is an unfinished story: it invites its own continuation in history, it resists the covers of our Bibles, and writes itself on the pages of the earth. On these grounds, it is legitimate to hold that various biblical reader-actors from different moments in history should illumine the meaning and implications of the text for us.[19]

I wish it was all happy travel, where opportunities are available to all, boundaries open to all, bridges are laid for all, and the encounter with the Other is a justice-loving kiss. These journeys, however, are intertwined with the power relations that characterize our world—the so-called center and margins, developed and "underdeveloped," First and Two-Thirds Worlds, colonizer and colonized. Border-crossing theorists and readers thus tell stories of contested power and concerted struggles to survive—wrenching power from boundary keepers, who will have doors closed behind them. In her reading of the woman with a demon-possessed daughter, Guardiola-Sáenz says, "my reading is a story retold by the defeated, re-written from the inter-space of the postcolonial reader."[20]

For most contemporary Two-Thirds World biblical readers and Christians, Jesus and the Bible arrived within their borders with colonizers. The Kenyan theorist Ngugi wa Thiong'o thus holds that during the colonial era both Jesus and Shakespeare had brought light to the darkest Africa.[21] He insists that both the Bible and the needle were supposedly England's greatest gifts to Africa. He also points out that "the English, French, Portuguese came to the Third World to announce the Bible and the Sword."[22] In these statements, Ngugi wa Thiong'o makes connections between the Bible and colonial history—with its economic desires (needle), its literature (Shakespeare), its attack and suppression of the Other (sword). Ngugi wa Thiong'o connects the biblical texts with modern colonial movements. Indeed, when we study the 1884 Berlin Conference documents, where modern European colonialists gathered to slice the

18. Leticia A. Guardiola-Sáenz, "Border-Crossing and Its Redemptive Power in John 7:53–8:11: A Cultural Reading of Jesus and the Accused," in *John and Postcolonialism: Travel Space and Power*, ed. Musa W. Dube and John Staley (Sheffield: Sheffield Academic, 2002), 129–52.

19. Musa W. Dube, "Towards a Postcolonial Feminist Interpretation of the Bible," *Semeia* 78 (1997): 11–26, here 12.

20. Guardiola-Sáenz, "Borderless Women," 74.

21. Ngugi wa Thiong'o, *Decolonising the Mind: The Politics of Language in African Literature* (London: James Currey, 1986), 91.

22. Ngugi wa Thiong'o, *Decolonising the Mind*.

African continent among themselves without consulting or involving Africans, we realize that missionaries were acknowledged participants of the process.[23] Making connections between biblical texts and modern imperialism, in other words, does not need any special pleading. It is self-evident that biblical texts are entangled in this dance. According to Said: "Modern imperialism was so global and all-encompassing that virtually nothing escaped it…whether or not to look at the *connections between cultural texts and imperialism* is therefore to take a position already taken—either to study the connection in order to criticize it and think of alternatives for it, or not to study it in order to let it stand."[24]

In this paper, I seek to share my journeys with the "word" in biblical scholarship, as a child of modern colonialism, neo-colonialism, and the contemporary global economy, and as a black African woman scholar, who is mired within the continuous struggles for liberation, decolonization, and depatriarchalization. I seek to share some of the boundaries I have sought to cross, the in-between spaces I have inhabited, and still inhabit, and some bridges I have crossed or tried to weave as a Two-Thirds World Black African feminist scholar. I seek to share how I have been wrestling with the fact that the Bible was inseparably intertwined with the history of modern colonialism in Africa. This can only be a roughly summarized sketch tracing some of the journeys I have undertaken—for up to now, I am still trying to find a way through the maze. The sketches I wish to draw here, marking the questions I have borne as a Two-Thirds Worlds African feminist scholar, shall be addressed under the following sub-headings:

- Crossing the Greco-Roman Historical Boundaries
- Bridging the Boundaries of the Biblical Studies Curriculum
- Interrogating the Biblical Readers of Modern Colonial Times
- Interrogating the Ideological Boundaries of the Text
- Border-crossing the Academic Boundaries of Readers
- Entering the Borders of Colonized Bibles
- Bridging Biblical Methods

Crossing the Greco-Roman Historical Boundaries

The first thing I confronted in western academic biblical studies, where I did my postgraduate studies in the 1990s, was that the boundaries of

---

23. Musa W. Dube, *Postcolonial Feminist Interpretation of the Bible* (St. Louis: Chalice, 2000), 3–6.

24. Said, *Culture and Imperialism,* 68, emphasis added.

academic biblical studies excluded my questions. Whereas I was interested in doing biblical studies that engaged the modern colonial history and the biblical text's entanglement with this history, such a space was not readily available then. Instead as a biblical student, my historical space of engagement with the biblical text was neatly placed in the Greco-Roman context. I studied Greco-Roman history, culture, language, political structures, and economic systems, and read the biblical texts within such a background. I was expected to read the text "objectively," searching for the original or the author's meaning. This approach yielded many fruitful harvests for me and remains vital, yet it bracketed many of the questions I came bearing to the field. It bracketed other histories of the biblical text.[25] Instead, the travelling biblical text had come to me, and many Two-Thirds World communities of readers, marching with modern colonial travelers and garments. But because the standard historical context of studying the New Testament had been primarily defined as the ancient Greco-Roman context, and the reading method as historical criticism, my burning questions had no space of articulation.

At the core of my quest were the questions of: "How do I read the Bible as a *woman who was colonized through the Bible*?" "Why was it ethically acceptable for Bible readers, male and female, of modern colonialism to function hand-in-glove with colonizers of their countries?" For me, and other Two-Thirds World women, the colonial oppression was as equally significant as patriarchal oppression. Given the privileged status of the Greco-Roman context and historical criticism, my questions could pass as church history questions or history of interpretation. Yet, when I looked into the curriculum of church history in the western world, where I studied, church history seldom included the world-wide modern church history that brought Christianity to Two-Thirds World countries. Perhaps modern church history was studied under missions, if at all. I must say that given the daunting walls of historical criticism, it was very helpful that I entered biblical scholarship when minority readers from the Two-Thirds World and within the western metropolitan centers had begun to problematize the guild. The feminist framework of posting the personal as political, the narration of one's story, together with the reader-response theories, provided windows of hope.

Accordingly, many minority and postcolonial scholars have problematized the focus on the Greco-Roman context as the privileged history for studying philosophy, biblical studies, literature, democracy, politics, and other related issues, pointing out that it is a Eurocentric approach

---

25. Dube, "Towards a Postcolonial Feminist," 11–15.

that upholds the ideology of the superiority of the west.[26] In their book, *Unthinking Eurocentrism*, Ella Shohat and Robert Stam critique the academy for maintaining the colonizing Eurocentric heuristic posture that depicts Greece as the center of all knowledge.[27] Two-Thirds Worlds scholars have crossed the boundaries of this privileged academic framework of study by using their own cultural/historical contexts (Liberation Theologies) and histories of the encounter of the biblical text working hand in glove with modern colonies.[28] Diasporic African American scholars have challenged the construction and focus on the Greco-Roman context by, for example, highlighting ancient Egypt as another historical context for understanding biblical texts.[29] Others have pointed out that the historical critical approach in academic biblical studies was hewn in the Enlightenment period, which was also the height of modern imperialism; hence its assumptions perpetuate the same ideology.[30] Underlining the need to factor the entanglement of the biblical text with the "worldly" journeys, Guardiola-Sáenz points out that: "A cultural text is not confined to the borders of its written pages, but to the whole culture that embraces its interpretations.... A cultural text should be read not just for the history it reflects, but also for the history it has made: the political, moral, economic, and social consequences that the text has effected in the culture."[31]

My work still continues to investigate modern missionary letters, reports, and books, to study their biblical interpretations, their perspectives towards the colonial projects of their mother countries, and their construction of the Other. It investigates how colonial biblical readers translated indigenous cultures, religious spaces, gender, and their motivations. I have been reading Robert Moffat's *Missionary Labours and*

---

26. Ella Shohat and Robert Stam, *Unthinking Eurocentrism: Multiculturalism and the Media* (New York: Routledge, 1994), 55–94.

27. Shohat and Stam, *Unthinking Eurocentrism*, 55–8.

28. See Kwok Pui-lan, *Discovering the Bible in the Non-Biblical World* (Maryknoll: Orbis, 1995); Fernando F. Segovia, *Decolonizing Biblical Studies* (Maryknoll: Orbis, 2000); and Rasiah S. Sugirtharajah, ed., *The Postcolonial Biblical Reader* (New York: Blackwell, 2006).

29. See Vincent L. Wimbush, ed., *African Americans and the Bible: Sacred Texts and Social Textures*, with Rosamond C. Rodman (New York: Continuum, 2000), and more specifically the article by Randall C. Bailey, "Academic Biblical Interpretations among African Americans in the United States," 696–711.

30. Segovia, *Decolonizing*, 3–33 and Shawn Kelley, *Racializing Jesus: Race, Ideology and the Formation of Modern Biblical Scholarship* (New York: Routledge, 2002).

31. See Guardiola-Sáenz, "Borderless Women," 72.

Scenes in Southern Africa volume of 1842 and a collection of papers and letters of John Mackenzie. Both missionaries worked among the Batswana ethnic groups over a long time.[32] The experience of reading such books is tantamount to what was succinctly named by Phyllis Trible as reading "Texts of Terror."[33] For a black African reader, it is a walk in a haunted house, that features your very own "monsterfied" image, so that you do not want to look at yourself, you are afraid of yourself, you want to run away from yourself or simply despise yourself. To read such texts is a charring experience: a walk in a park of hellfire. The dilemma is whether to read or not read, and none of the choices is better. The challenge, for those who read, is how to read texts.[34] My advice is that one must enter such a colonizing literary jungle wearing the most efficient bullet proof armor of decolonization that one can make.

Bridging the Boundaries of the Biblical Studies Curriculum

Of course, the questions and the observations raised here interrogate the boundaries of academic biblical scholarship and its curriculum. The observations question how biblical studies programs are designed: what they exclude and include and the ideological purposes they serve.[35] It calls for interdisciplinary connections between various histories (ancient and modern) and various theological subjects (biblical studies with church histories, histories of interpretation, and missions) and non-theological studies (economics and politics) and the integrations of various readers of the Bible, missionaries, and academic readers. In a world where modern

---

32. My initial analysis is found in Musa W. Dube, "Decolonizing the Darkness," in *Soundings in Cultural Criticism: Perspectives and Methods in Culture, Power and Identity in New Testament*, ed. Francisco Lozada Jr. and Greg Carey (Minneapolis: Fortress, 2013), 31–44, and Musa W. Dube, "The Bible in the Bush: The First 'Literate' Batswana Bible Readers," *Translation* 2 (Spring 2013): 79–103.

33. See Phyllis Trible, *Texts of Terror: Literary-Feminist Readings of Biblical Narratives*, OBT (Minneapolis: Fortress, 1984).

34. See Dube, *Postcolonial Feminist*, 121–4, where I proposed a new reading strategy titled Rahab's Reading Prism. I defined the strategy as "a postcolonial feminist eye of many angles and of seeing, reading, and hearing literary texts through resisting imperial and patriarchal oppressive structures and ideologies" (123).

35. See Musa W. Dube, "Curriculum Transformation: Dreaming of Decolonization in Theological Education," in *Border Crossings: Cross-Cultural Hermeneutics*, ed. P. N. Premnath (Maryknoll: Orbis, 2007), 121–38, where I elaborate further on decolonizing theological education. See also Fernando F. Segovia and Mary Ann Tolbert, eds., *Teaching the Bible: The Discourses and Politics of Biblical Pedagogy* (Maryknoll: Orbis, 1998).

colonialism has created overlapping territories and intertwined histories,[36] academic biblical studies must endeavor to cross multiple boundaries and live in the crossroads—for the biblical texts have long crossed multiple boundaries. The biblical guild needs to own up to the fact that the biblical text and its readers have already travelled, and these journeys need to be factored into the curriculum and reading strategies. As a Two-Thirds World scholar who has sojourned in western academic halls, the exclusion of our contexts, histories, and questions makes academic biblical studies a lonely journey, if not torturous and traumatic. It silences, shutting down our participatory learning by dismissing our questions. As I described it, it is tantamount to a long walk in a hall of mirrors that refuse to acknowledge our images, underlining that one belongs to suppressed knowledges.[37] Something must give.

Interrogating the Biblical Readers of Modern Colonial Times

Growing up in the context of the struggle for independence, debating societies often invited me and my fellow members of the Student Christian Movement to explain why we follow the faith of our oppressors, the colonizer. As I have said elsewhere,[38] evidence was largely against us as historical documents indicated that missionaries, that is, Bible readers, were not an ethical voice of resistance against the colonial projects of their mother countries. Indeed, historical documents amply attest to missionaries as champions of colonialism. As Andrew Walls writes, "the missionary was spoken of in the vocabulary of the imperial pioneer."[39] Why did the modern colonial-time biblical reader fail to assume a prophetic and ethical role of resisting imperialism as an unacceptable economic and political system of exploiting Two-Thirds World populations? How about the western scholars of that time?[40] This has been a major question to me. As Bible readers, I assumed they should

---

36. Said, *Culture and Imperialism*, 3–63.

37. Musa W. Dube, "An Introduction: How We Come to 'Read With'," *Semeia* 73 (1996): 7–17, here 10.

38. Dube, *Postcolonial Feminist*, 4–6.

39. Andrew Walls, "British Missions," in *Missionary Ideologies in the Imperialist Era: 1880–1920*, ed. Torben Christensen and William Hutchinson (Aarhus: Aros, 1982), 8–24, here 12.

40. This question is best answered in Kelley, *Racializing Jesus*. Kelley's exploration highlights how modern scholar-thinkers did not escape from modern colonial ideology, and that their perspectives continue to inform contemporary academic biblical studies.

have provided the ethical and prophetic voice of resistance. Yet one is at pains to find it, if it exists at all. And so, by going with the faith of my colonizer, I could only be in the space of a collaborator, a betrayer. My agony brought me back to the biblical text. I sought to read again and to investigate the ideological angles of its travel narratives. I wanted to establish the reason for the failure of a prophetic voice among western modern biblical readers and scholars.

Interrogating the Ideological Boundaries of the Text

This investigation took three angles. First, I was eager to find out if the biblical texts sanctioned travel to foreign countries—if it is a borderless text—and if so, to assess the standards it provided for meeting the Other who is different. I also sought to investigate how gender is constructed in such texts. I used the case studies of the Exodus and mission-oriented texts, studying how they sanction travel, crossing borders, how they construct the indigenous people, their lands, and their cultures. In this investigation, I wanted to find out if the biblical text stood a better chance of providing a counter-colonial ideology. My findings were not encouraging. Mission texts constructed the Other negatively—as a blank slate awaiting divine teachers (Mt. 28:18-20)—as ethically or morally lacking and as women. The ideology of race was wrapped in gendered language. This is evident in the characters of Rahab (Joshua 2), the Samaritan woman (Jn 4:1-42), or the mother with a demon-possessed daughter (Mt. 15:21-28). Such characterization propounds an ideology that sanctions the suppression and oppression of the Other rather than encouraging relationships of liberating interdependence.

Second, I sought to analyze the biblical stance towards the imperialism of its time, to establish as much as I can, if it was a collaborative, resisting, or revolting text towards the colonial powers of its time.[41] Since biblical texts were written under various imperial powers, it was important to investigate how this history impacted the production and ideological stance of biblical texts towards the empire and how it may

---

41. Dube, *Postcolonial Feminist*, 127–55. Contemporary empire studies scholars in biblical studies have put up a spirited argument that biblical texts are anti-imperial. I just wish the modern missionary readers and scholars had interpreted the Bible from that perspective, then we would have a completely different story. Because they read it in resonance with imperialism of their time and countries, it begs the question why? Was the colonizing ideology in the text, the reader, or both? By and large, the function of the Bible as a colonizing book in modern colonialism is yet to be addressed by western empire studies scholars in biblical studies.

inform future readers. The findings to this second question were complex. Third, I also investigated the function of gender in the subjugation of the Other—both in the mission texts and colonizing narratives. As the above three cases highlight, female gender terminology was used to articulate the subjugation of the Other. Earlier feminist readers of these stories had sought to reconstruct the early Christian history as women's history, without problematizing the colonizing ideology embedded in these texts. My reading of feminist interpretations of mission texts[42] brought me in sharp conflict with my feminist community of readers as I argued that our commitment to liberation is wanting if it does not pay equal attention to imperialism and how imperialism is manifested in the texts.[43] In my conclusion, I suggested, among other things, that feminist biblical readers should endeavor to also become decolonizing readers given that patriarchal resistance does not always translate into a decolonizing reading.

Simultaneously, I sought to read colonial classics such as *The Aeneid*, Rudyard Kipling's poem, "The White Man's Burden," and Joseph Conrad's *Heart of Darkness* to assess how they construct the Other, who is the target of colonial desires.[44] In so doing, I was making connections between the Bible and Shakespeare. The latter assisted me to search for strategies of reading for decolonization, as suggested by Ngugi wa Thiong'o. The assessment enabled a comparison with biblical mission texts. There was much friendship here. I also analyzed texts of decolonizing writers, such as Torontle Mositi's *The Victims* and the Kenyan poet, Maina wa Kinyatti, whose title spoke loud and clearly, namely, "May Imperialism Perish Forever."[45]

Border-Crossing the Academic Boundaries of Readers

Taking a leaf from liberation readers who insisted on reading with base communities and from their contemporary contexts, I also sought to cross the boundaries of academic professional readers by reading with women from African Independent Churches in Botswana.[46] The latter were church communities that historically resisted colonial Christianity, by reading the

---

42. Dube, *Postcolonial Feminist*, 169–85.

43. See Laura E. Donaldson, *Decolonising Feminisms: Race, Gender, and Empire Building* (Chapel Hill: University of North Carolina Press, 1992), who points out that addressing patriarchy does not substitute addressing the empire.

44. Dube, *Postcolonial Feminist*, 81–95.

45. Dube, *Postcolonial Feminist*, 97–109.

46. Musa W. Dube, "Readings of *Semoya*: Batswana Women Interpretations of Matt 15:21-28," *Semeia* 73 (1996): 111–12.

Bible with and through African cultures, thus creating hybrid religions and cultures, and resisting colonial domination. They rejected the colonial approach that regarded their indigenous traditions as evil. I wanted to read mission passages with them in search of decolonizing feminist ways of interpretations. And so off I went to the field. I spent time with small house churches, where they read the text, narrated the text, sang the text, danced the text, and dramatized it, leaving me in a daze in my attempt to locate the interpretation of the passage. I had entered other boundaries of reading the text, outside the realm of western academic biblical halls. This approach was an attempt at shifting the voices of authority, by crossing the accepted academic boundaries of the reader, to hear Other interpretations. I am currently continuing this work by reading the letters of the first literate Batswana and studying their response to missionary biblical teaching and to the first Setswana Bible translation.[47]

Entering the Borders of Colonized Bibles

In taking this journey, I was not only forced to confront Other ways of reading, I was also forced to read the Bible in indigenous languages. The process opened a whole new area for me, in so far as reading for decolonization was concerned. I discovered that colonial ideology informed biblical translation in ways that I could never have imagined, without reading the translated Setswana Bible.[48] While reading the story of the woman with a demon-possessed daughter with women from African Independent Churches, many readers insisted on reading one of the oldest versions of the translation, done in 1903. I was forced to go shopping for the 1903 Wookey Bible to photocopy Mt. 15:21-28. Upon reading the passage, I discovered that the translator had used the Ancestors, Badimo, to translate the word demons. Badimo among Batswana and Bantu communities, stretching from Southern to Eastern Africa, are regarded as sacred figures, who represent the interests of their surviving members and communities before God. So sacred is the position of Badimo that they had more attention than the higher God. In the 1903 Wookey Bible, their position had been transposed from sacred to evil. It was shocking. My ground shook. This translation was a "text of terror." Here I was invited to spin back to 1857, when the first Setswana Bible was completed and placed in the hands of trusting believers. They discovered that according

---

47. Dube, "The Bible in the Bush," 79–103.
48. Musa W. Dube, "Consuming a Colonial Cultural Bomb: Translating *Badimo* into 'Demons' in Setswana Bible," *JSNT* 73 (1999): 33–59.

to their Setswana Bible, "Jesus went casting out Badimo!" What a perfect piece of evidence that Batswana, and all other Bantu people, were lost and in "darkness." It was written in the Bible! Translation theory cannot pretend that it is all about seeking dynamic or formal equivalences and staying faithful to the original meaning or source. For these reasons, I categorize such translations as "colonized Bibles."

Yet this translation was not only colonizing. It was also patriachalizing, for while the Ancestors (Badimo) were communities of the Living Dead that included both women and men, the Badimo were now relegated to the evil space. The colonizing ideology behind the translation sought to distance readers from their own cultural beliefs. Second, while the names of God are gender neutral in Bantu languages, in the Setswana Bible translation they assume male gender. Modimo, the Setswana name for God, becomes *"rara wa rona yo o ko legodimong,"* that is "our father who art in heaven." Jesus was also male—replacing the gender-neutral and communal role of Badimo. Through these translations, Batswana, Bantu peoples, and women had lost their place in the sacred space. The impact over the two centuries has been to intensify patriarchy in the sacred space as well as in the society.

Working with the Circle of Concerned African Women Theologians[49] and African biblical scholars in general,[50] we are continuing to re-read our colonized Bibles, to expose how modern colonialism informed indigenous translations, to rethink translation theory, and to consider how Bible translations could be enriched by our gender inclusive languages. This is one area where there could be an enriching project between African feminist scholars and the earlier western feminist research on gender inclusive translations of the Bible. This project of re-reading our colonized Bible

---

49. See Dora Mbuwayesango, "How Local Divine Powers Were Suppressed: A Case of Mwari of the Shona," and Gomang Seratwa Ntloedibe Kuswani, "Translating the Divine: The Case of Modimo in the Setswana Bible," in *Other Ways of Reading: African Women and the Bible*, ed. Musa W. Dube (Atlanta: SBL Press, 2000), 63–77 and 78–97, respectively.

50. Aloo Mojola, "How the Bible is Received in Communities: A Brief Overview with Particular Reference to East Africa," in *Scripture Community and Mission: Essays in Honor of Preman Niles*, ed. Philip L. Wickeri (Hong Kong: Christian Council of Asia, 2002), 1–17, is most instructive in this area. A summarized version of various other African scholars exploring colonized Bible translations can be found in Musa W. Dube, "The Scramble for Africa as the Biblical Scramble for Africa: Postcolonial Perspectives," in *Postcolonial Perspectives in African Biblical Interpretations*, ed. Musa W. Dube, Andrew Mbuvi, and Dora Mbuwayesango, Global Perspectives on Biblical Scholarship 13 (Atlanta: SBL, 2012), 1–29, here 11–15.

also calls for a shift in the pedagogical contents of biblical studies.[51] Whereas a good biblical studies program often required all postgraduate students to learn biblical languages and two European languages such as German, French, or Spanish, such a requirement was not only further colonization for most of us—it also did not enable Two-Thirds World biblical scholars to carry out the necessary research within their communities. Given that Christianity, and hence a large portion of Bible readers, has shifted toward the Two-Thirds World, a review of biblical programs is necessary. Then languages of the latter, which were first used to translate Bibles, can be featured. This will enable informed research and review of colonized Bibles that are still the daily bread of many African communities.

Bridging Biblical Methods

As said earlier, my paper does not seek to be exhaustive, but to give or provide a summarized sketch. In my conclusion, I want to describe the project, "Other Ways of Reading: African Women and the Bible,"[52] which became a book. In this volume, I worked with various members of the Circle of Concerned African Women Theologians to challenge and cross the theoretical and methodological boundaries of biblical studies. Bringing in African folktales, divination style, African storytelling techniques, poetry, enculturation, and histories of various colonial experiences, we sought to challenge the predominantly Eurocentric methods of biblical interpretation and gender-insensitive ways of reading among African male theologians. We were submitting other ways of reading. This project highlights that theories and methods of reading are themselves context-specific. Much as we learn methods of reading from the First World, the First World, too, can learn and apply our frameworks. Unless theoretical and methodological frameworks of reading are generated from various contexts, exclusively western methods maintain the Eurocentric colonial ideology.[53]

Yet by bringing African folktales to be read with biblical stories—not as inferior and lesser traditions—the volume also sought to challenge the colonizing ideology held in mission texts and practices that treat the Other

---

51. Dube, "The Scramble for Africa," 11–15.

52. Initially, the plan was to produce three volumes on methods, translation, and a commentary, but due to lack of sufficient human resources, the three areas were collated together into one volume.

53. Shohat and Stam, *Unthinking Eurocentrism*, 55–94.

as a blank slate. In the Christian reading of the Bible, all other cultures and religious beliefs were lacking, evil, and/or awaiting the pinnacle of salvation—namely the Christian gospel. Women and scholars from Two-Thirds Worlds are more often than not in multi-faith and multi-religious contexts.[54] They have embraced Christianity and the biblical texts through and within a historical context that dismissed and denigrated their indigenous beliefs, but they remain within multiple traditions. It is no longer possible for us to pretend that the biblical text has not done many rounds, slept around, and sired many mixed children. The biblical text has created many contact zones in modern colonial history. In my view, if we study that Bible alone, we come very close to asserting that it still has the right to annihilate other traditions and cultures. I also do not believe that studying the Bible through various methods and theories sufficiently counters the history of the biblical text that claimed the right to dismiss other religious and cultural beliefs.[55] A postcolonial feminist reading thus seeks to work at the crossroads of various traditions in a hybrid space.

It might seem logical for people in former colonial contexts to explore multi-faith hermeneutics. Yet if we take Brah's observation; namely, that the massive movements of people towards all directions place the contemporary world in a state of a diasporian identity for both those who have moved and those who have remained in their native homes (because one's neighborhood is now a hub of various cultures and religions), Brah's observation implies that all departments, including biblical studies, religion, and theology, should review their programs accordingly. Islam, Hinduism, African indigenous religions, and other religions are no longer found only in specific geographic-cultural spaces. Rather, they have journeyed into all directions with the contemporary movement of people. Thus if one wants to study African Indigenous Religions one may have to go to Cuba, Brazil, or the USA.[56] and if one wants to study African Pentecostalism, one may have go to London or Brussels.[57] This is what

---

54. Dube, *Postcolonial Feminist*, 31–4.

55. Canaan Banana, "The Case for a New Bible," in *"Rewriting the Bible": The Real Issues*, ed. Isabel Mukonyora, James O. Cox, and Frans J. Verstraelen (Gweru: Mambo, 1993), 17–32, who makes the argument that the current Bible must be extended to include sacred traditions and norms of communities where the Bible has journeyed and tabernacled.

56. See Jacob K. Olupona and Terry Rey, eds., *Òrìṣà Devotion as World Religion: The Globalization of Yorùbá Religious Culture* (Madison: The University of Wisconsin Press, 2008).

57. See J. Kwabena Asamoah-Gyadu, "From Prophetism to Pentecostalism: Religious Innovation in Africa and African Religious Scholarship," in *African*

constitutes "the global condition of culture as a site of travel," and "the site where the native is as much diasporian as the diasporian is the native," as posited by Brah.⁵⁸ Academic biblical studies should be true to this context by dancing with this complexity.

These sketches of journeys, border-crossings, and bridges described in this paper remain at the margins. They remain unsettled and unsettling energies between the boundaries, inviting more border-crossing towards relationships of liberating interdependence in the academic biblical guild.

Traditions in the Study of Religion in Africa: Emerging Trends, Indigenous Spirituality and the Interface with Other World Religions, Essays in Honour of Jacob Kehinde Olupona, ed. Afe Adogame, Ezra Chitando, and Bolaji Bateye (Surrey: Ashgate, 2012), 161–75.

58. Brah, "Diaspora, Border," 632.

Reading without History*

Michael L. Satlow

As a field within the modern secular academy, "biblical studies" is an odd beast. Emerging from theology, biblical studies most often begins with a text and moves outward to that text's interpretation or "meaning." The modes of interpretation might vary (e.g., ideological, theological, historical) but the starting point—a text—remains more or less constant.[1] The problem of translation into the secular academy is apparent: what, in a disciplinary perspective, is this? Literature? Philosophy? History? Most frequently such study tends to end up in "religious studies," which is itself a hodgepodge of approaches, many of which had their origins in theology.

Yet many of the questions that secular academics have that relate to the Bible are ultimately historical. Where, when, by whom, and why was a particular text produced? What function did it serve, and for whom? The questions at the heart of this volume, about the nature of and reasons for textual appropriation in antiquity, are historical questions.

The purpose of this essay is to step back and ask a more fundamental question: Using the methods that are typically deployed through biblical studies, can we ever adequately answer these questions? It is usually easy enough to identify textual appropriation and to highlight the changes made by the appropriator. It is much harder, however, to draw historical conclusions from such inferences.

In a recent essay, Benjamin D. Sommer has argued that most (although not all) historical criticism of biblical texts is so beset by methodological

---

* My thanks to the other contributors to this volume and to Bernard Levinson for their careful critiques of an earlier draft.

1. See also, James Barr, *History and Ideology in the Old Testament: Biblical Studies at the End of the Millennium: The Hensley Henson Lectures for 1997 Delivered to the University of Oxford* (Oxford: Oxford University Press, 2000).

flaws that the entire enterprise is largely futile.² Sommer trenchantly critiques attempts to date the constituent parts of the Torah by the ideas that they express. He warns of two related fallacies: (1) "the assumption that if an idea or text is especially relevant to a particular historical period, then the idea or text must have originated in that period," and (2) that scholars often "fail to acknowledge that the idea or text is equally appropriate for some other moment as well."³ He thus argues that while there is a place for historicism in biblical studies, given the relatively small yield of such study, scholars might better spend their time probing the eternal truths of ancient literature.

These kind of "pseudo-historical" (as Sommer calls them) fallacies are not the only problems found in many examples of historical criticism of biblical texts. Those in biblical studies also often tend to use deductive reasoning in ways that far exceed its capabilities. It is not unusual, for example, for a scholarly discussion in the field to begin with a long and involved exegesis only to end with a few short comments about what can then be deduced from the exegesis about the text's historical provenance and audience.

This essay will argue that this tendency to move from a text to history is backwards. In actuality, we base many of our exegeses on a robust conceptual apparatus that usually includes many implicit assumptions about history and human behavior. The point is simple and not particularly original, and yet continues to have significant ramifications for many areas of biblical studies. It is, moreover, particularly relevant for this volume: When we seek to know how and why ancient authors adapted and deployed for their own purposes "other people's texts," how do we go about our work?

This paper makes two related points. First, that there is no reading outside of history and our larger conceptual apparatus. That is, we cannot escape the well-known hermeneutical circle and psychological tendencies to try to reinforce that apparatus rather than challenge it. Second, following Hans-Georg Gadamer, I think that there is a way to move the field forward despite this problem (which is greatly exacerbated by the paucity and quality of our evidence) by being increasingly explicit about our assumptions while acknowledging, even embracing, the role that historical imagination (or speculation) plays in our work. After

2. Benjamin D. Sommer, "Dating Pentateuchal Texts and the Danger of Pseudo-Historicism," in *The Pentateuch: International Perspectives on Current Research*, ed. Thomas B. Dozeman, Konrad Schmid, and Baruch J. Schwartz, FAT 78 (Tübingen: Mohr Siebeck, 2011), 85–108.

3. Sommer, "Dating Pentateuchal Texts," 94.

developing the problem and the argument, I use two short case studies, the book of *Jubilees* and the Letters of Paul, to illustrate how this approach might work in practice.

Narratives and Facts

Some time ago, I conducted a classroom experiment in which I structured an entire undergraduate class on the history of Jews in the Second Temple period around primary sources. Through the course of the semester the students worked on a single, collaborative project in which they created their own narrative, in the form of a Wiki, of the history of the period using only these primary texts (with a little outside help).[4] As pedagogical experiences go, this one was mixed. The students learned quite a bit but really could not complete the central assignment; it was simply too difficult for them to create a narrative out of the complex and fragmentary evidence with which they were working. They needed a conceptual apparatus to make sense of the isolated bits of evidence.

Professional scholars, in theory, know this problem well and are trained to create their own narratives. In practice, though, that often means accepting an existing conceptual apparatus as a basis for contextualization and interpretation. That existing conceptual apparatus is the only thing that enables interpretation.

Let me illustrate this with a brief modern example. In an experiment conducted on history teachers, Sam Wineburg gave different history teachers a text that claimed that whites were racially superior to blacks, and which read in part, "There is a physical difference between the two [white and black races], which in my judgment will probably forever forbid their living together upon the footing of perfect equality." The teachers were given the additional information that the text was written in the United States in the nineteenth century.[5] Many of the teachers assumed that the writer was from the South. When told, however, that its actual author was the "Great Emancipator," Abraham Lincoln, their evaluation of the text changed sharply. The text does not give its context, it is instead interpreted by its context, and this example should encourage us to consider deeply the relationship between artifacts, interpretation, and our own conceptual apparatus.

---

4. Michael L. Satlow, "Narratives or Sources? Active Learning and the Teaching of Ancient Jewish History and Texts," *Teaching Theology and Religion* 15 (2012): 48–60.

5. Sam Wineburg, *Historical Thinking and Other Unnatural Acts: Charting the Future of Teaching the Past* (Philadelphia: Temple University Press, 2001), 89–112.

The issue has been extensively discussed from both philosophical and psychological perspectives. Philosophically, the idea that one understands only out of one's conceptual apparatus (or "anticipations") is known as the hermeneutic(al) circle. This is the notion that there is always an interpretive relationship between the whole and the parts. Although the roots of this philosophical debate go back to antiquity, today it is most associated with Martin Heidegger, Hans-Georg Gadamer, and (from a theological perspective) Rudolf Bultmann. In Heidegger's formulation, all understanding is founded on the "anticipatory structure" (*Vorstruktur*) that an agent brings to bear on interpreting new things (or events, ideas, etc.). There is no way to escape this circle, but for Heidegger there is a correct way to enter it:

> For Heidegger, this signifies that we have to acknowledge that there are indeed anticipations in every understanding; second, that we can sort them out through the self-understanding of understanding he calls *Auslegung* (interpretation, elucidation), and, third, that we should dismiss through "destruction" false anticipations which are imposed upon the things themselves in order to replace them by more authentic ones which would be assured by the things themselves. Some of our anticipations, we can surmise from this, are blindly taken over, say, from an unquestioned tradition or the prevailing chatter (*Gerede*), and impede an understanding of the things themselves.[6]

Whereas Heidegger encourages us to move toward "authentic" understandings by refining our anticipations—thus offering if not quite a way out of the circle, at least a vantage point provided by history—Gadamer embraces the circle as a simple condition of being. For Gadamer, the relationship between prejudices or "fore-meanings" (as he calls them) and understanding is always dynamic. Not only can an agent's encounter with a new thing cause one to modify one's prejudices, but so too, ideally, can the agent's efforts to locate the hermeneutical circle historically, tracing back the genealogy of prejudices and seeing them within earlier hermeneutical circles.

While a strain of this idea generated postmodern theories (e.g., all truth is relative and thus all narratives equal; all ideas have genealogies), neither Heidegger nor Gadamer gave up on the notion that there are better

---

6. Jean Grondin, "The Hermeneutical Circle," in *The Blackwell Companion to Hermeneutics*, ed. Niall Keane and Chris Lawn (Malden: John Wiley & Sons, 2015), 299–305, here 299. See also, C. Mantzavinos, "Hermeneutics," in *The Stanford Encyclopedia of Philosophy* (June 22, 2016), at https://plato.stanford.edu/entries/hermeneutics/.

and worse anticipations or prejudices. For Gadamer, the hermeneutical circle is in fact to be welcomed as an opportunity to constantly challenge and test our anticipations. As he writes:

> How do we discover that there is a difference between our own customary usage and that of the text?
> I think that we must say that generally we do so in the experience of being pulled up short by the text. Either it does not yield any meaning at all or its meaning is not compatible with what we had expected. This is what brings us up short and alerts us to possible difference in usage....
> But what another person tells me, whether in conversation, letter, book, or whatever, is generally supposed to be his own and not my opinion; and this is what I am to take note of without necessarily having to share it. Yet this presupposition is not something that makes understanding easier, but harder, since the fore-meanings that determine my own understanding can go entirely unnoticed.[7]

For Gadamer, it is precisely the encounter with the Other that continuously forces us to recognize, acknowledge, and grapple with our "fore-meanings" that often make us misinterpret the Other by putting their own opinions into our hermeneutical circles.

These philosophical observations may in fact have a psychological basis. Behavioral scientists have long been working on the problem of heuristics and biases. This research points to the tendency of humans to bias their opinions in certain predictable ways. We tend, for example, to let a more recent thought or event sway our opinion rather than an earlier, less "cognitively available" one.[8] For our purpose, the bias that is of most relevance is probably that of confirmation bias. People tend to selectively sort through evidence, shaping it to bolster their previously held beliefs.[9] This tendency can be so strong that when we encounter low probability events or facts that should challenge our conceptual apparatus (e.g.,

---

7. Hans-Georg Gadamer, *Truth and Method*, 2nd ed., trans. Joel Weinsheimer and Donald G. Marshall (New York: Crossroad, 1990), 268.

8. There is an enormous literature on these biases, which have been extensively studied by Daniel Kahneman and Amos Tversky among others. See their early articles, "On the Psychology of Prediction," *Psychological Review* 80 (1973): 237–51 and "Availability: A Heuristic for Judging Frequency and Probability," *Cognitive Psychology* 5 (1973): 207–32. The research is summarized in an accessible form in Daniel Kahneman, *Thinking, Fast and Slow* (New York: Farrar, Straus & Giroux, 2013).

9. Raymond S. Nickerson, "Confirmation Bias: A Ubiquitous Phenomenon in Many Guises," *Review of General Psychology* 2 (1998): 175–220.

"100-year floods" that happen every few years, or parallel lines that meet in a curved space), we often misinterpret them, instead fitting them into the account that we think we know.[10]

The outcome of the philosophical and psychological approaches are similar. We do have the ability to step back and to see our existing narratives and biases, and thereby to better understand how an input or piece of evidence might challenge rather than confirm them, but it requires effort. This is a self-reflective process that is well worth the effort.

Biblical Studies, Texts, and History

Generally speaking, academic historiography falls along two axes. The first is that of cause and meaning. A history might focus on the (diachronic) causes of a particular event, or it might instead wish to elucidate the meaning of it, putting it within a wider synchronic context and showing how it was understood by those impacted by it. The historian's story, though, is also plotted along a kind of causal axis, between individual agency and systemic forces. Do individuals and their decisions cause important events to occur, or do they arise from larger social forces that individuals do not (at least directly) control?[11]

Scholars in the field of biblical studies, to the extent that they engage in historical questions (which is more than they often admit), tend to cluster at the intersection of meaning and individual agency. They read their texts as produced by particular players, often assumed to be in positions of authority, seeking to influence (usually state) affairs. Their questions often begin with a text and, using sources thought to be contemporaneous (synchronic), they seek to provide a context that will unlock that text's meaning.

This scholarly process faces two interlocked problems. The first is that the meaning of a text is assumed to be fundamentally linked to history. The conditions of production of a text are seen as relevant to determining authorial intent. Yet, no matter how weighted a scholar might be toward the power of individuals to change history, no historian would say that social forces were completely irrelevant, and it is precisely this depiction of the deeper social forces that is so often absent from this scholarship.

---

10. John R. Anderson, *Cognitive Psychology and its Implications*, 8th ed. (New York: Worth, 2015), 253–7; Nassim Nicholas Taleb, *The Black Swan: The Impact of the Highly Improbable* (New York: Random House, 2007).

11. For more on these dichotomies, see Sarah Maza, *Thinking About History* (Chicago: University of Chicago Press, 2017), 157–98.

Lawrence Stone, in his history of the English Revolution, helpfully articulates a way for the historian to understand the dynamic relationship between these different kinds of forces. Stone distinguishes between the "preconditions," e.g., institutions, political factors, etc., that underlie an event; the "precipitants," which set the stage for the event; and the "trigger," which is its immediate cause.[12] Following Stone, we might think that a responsible discussion of the (historically based) "meaning" of a text must include all three of these levels.

This desire to create a rich context, or to use Clifford Geertz's language a "thick description," of a text or event runs straight into the other problem facing nearly all historians of premodern times: the methodology appropriate for sparse and eclectic evidence.[13] We engage in a necessarily circular process in which we use our limited evidence to construct our historical context against which we then interpret our text. The methodological circle creates a hermeneutical circle. So how can one break out of, or at least be more conscious of, the hermeneutical circle when one is trapped in the methodological circle?

We can only interpret our texts against a richer contextual background that describes both the preconditions and the precipitates for it, but those are frequently only reconstructed from the very same texts that we seek to interpret. And while the texts, together with other evidence, might provide some more or less obvious suggestions for those contexts, the judgment of which are plausible, which are likely, and which are neither often ends up being rather arbitrary.

I propose that we take a different approach that cannot remove us from the hermeneutical circle, but which does make us more aware of it and reduces our tendencies toward confirmation bias. I call this approach "if–then history." It begins not from a text but from a hypothetical context (the "if") about which we are explicit: What, in this case, are we assuming about the preconditions of textual production and consumption? Who were the scribes and what was their audience? How did texts work against the "preconditions" in which they circulated (or not)? These questions are not fully answerable from the evidence we have currently available, but at the same time textual interpretation without some theory about the answers is impossible. Explicitly articulating these answers—and acknowledging that they are largely

---

12. Lawrence Stone, *The Causes of the English Revolution, 1529–1642* (New York: Harper & Row, 1972), 9–10.

13. Clifford Geertz, *The Interpretation of Cultures* (New York: Basic Books, 1973), 3–30.

speculative—is thus the first step to interpretation. Whatever interpretation of a text we then offer is conditioned on whether there is agreement about this speculative context.

There are many potential advantages of such an approach. In many cases, it would lead to more important scholarly debates about the context rather than on isolated bits of evidence. It would sensitize us to the hermeneutical circles in which we frequently work, helping us, as Gadamer suggests, to find some perspective. It would also add more integrity to our work by forcing us to be more explicit about where speculation—which is a necessary part of our work—really does impact our conclusions.

A ramification of this approach involves the grounds for critique. It is no longer enough to critique an argument on the grounds that it is "speculative" because it, in fact, recognizes that all of our arguments are speculative. Legitimate critique could then focus on both the wider context (e.g., is the hypothetical context the best of all possible contexts) and, if so, then the details of the interpretation. I am not suggesting that scholars do not often do this in any case, but doing it with a bit more self-awareness can only help to drive scholarly discussion forward productively.

Such an approach may not be comfortable for many. We all like to think that our arguments are not built in the sand and that they can endure the ground being taken from under them. Nobody wants to come up for tenure with a book whose presuppositions have been rejected. But this discomfort, mitigated to some degree by our ability as professional colleagues to negotiate it and hold it in perspective, is a cost worth paying.

To this point I have been somewhat theoretical. In the following two short case studies, I hope to show how these considerations can significantly alter our understandings of textual appropriation in antiquity.

The Book of Jubilees

The book of *Jubilees* appears to rework the Torah while barely (or perhaps implicitly) acknowledging the latter's existence. Now in the voice of an angel (instead of the omniscient third person narrator of Genesis, or Moses, as in Deuteronomy), *Jubilees* retells the story of Genesis while splicing in other, usually legal, sections of the Torah, in order, it seems, to ground these revealed laws in the natural order and Israel's mythic history. These historical events are in turn embedded in a calendrical structure that revolved around the "weeks" of the jubilees that were formed around a 364-day solar calendar. Thus, the work also polemicizes against ritual use of the lunar calendar (*Jub.* 6:32, 36-37). *Jubilees* forges a relationship (that remains somewhat ambiguous) between it and the "heavenly tablets," suggesting at times that the book itself draws from them.[14]

Jubilees presents three interrelated problems that concern us here: genre, compositional history, and purpose. These issues have normally been considered separately and, in a certain technical sense, this is justified. Whereas compositional history, for example, is often seen as a matter of closely reading the text, looking for disturbances that would point toward reconstructing the text's history, a study of genre places the text within a larger, textual world, comparing and contrasting its formal characteristics. Yet at the same time, and despite a vast amount of excellent scholarship on each of these questions (which for reasons of space I make no attempt to treat fully), there is also a certain circularity to the way that they are normally approached. Reconstructing the compositional history of a text requires importing certain assumptions about the way a text "should" look in order to locate perceived seams and gaps, and the results reinforce the assumptions originally brought to bear. Identifications of genre are made based on a tiny library of texts that have themselves been carefully selected and preserved in antiquity for certain characteristics. And history is thought to emerge from these investigations rather than to ground them. My goal in this section is to draw out, in only the most schematic way, some of these issues and to suggest that a different approach might, at this point in the scholarship, be more fruitful.

The first debate about *Jubilees* is its genre. Given what seems to be its significant engagement with the Torah, *Jubilees* is often understood to be an example of "rewritten Scripture." The problems with this categorization, which include the possibility of an anachronistic understanding of "Scripture" and the incorporation into these works of material that has no basis in any extant versions of Scripture, have been well recognized.[15] Even so, many, probably most, scholars continue to consider *Jubilees* as a primary example of this genre.[16] Zahn, among the most sophisticated

---

14. See, for example, *Jubilees* 49. For an inventory and discussion of these passages, see Florentino García Martínez, "The Heavenly Tablets in the *Book of Jubilees*," in *Between Philology and Theology: Contributions to the Study of Ancient Jewish Interpretation*, ed. Hindy Najman and Eibert Tigchelaar (Leiden: Brill, 2013), 51–69.

15. See Moshe Bernstein, "'Rewritten Bible': A Generic Category Which Has Outlived Its Usefulness?" *Textus* 22 (2005): 169–96. The entire issue of *Dead Sea Discoveries* 17, no. 3 (2010) (entitled *Rethinking Genre: Essays in Honor of John J. Collins*) is devoted to this topic.

16. See especially Molly M. Zahn, "Genre and Rewritten Scripture: A Reassessment," *JBL* 131 (2012): 271–88 at, e.g., 277. Zahn's caveat is that assigning a work to a genre does not prevent seeing it as examples of other genres as well.

thinkers on this issue, categorizes *Jubilees* as "rewritten Scripture" by both (correctly, in my opinion) pointing out that a work can fall into more than one genre while at the same time clarifying how she understands the genre:

> I propose that we could profitably think of Rewritten Scripture as a genre that functions interpretively to renew (update, correct) specific earlier traditions by recasting a substantial portion of those traditions in the context of a new work that locates itself in the same discourse as the scriptural work it rewrites. From a rhetorical point of view, what these texts do is provide a version of past tradition that better reflects the concerns and ideology of their community. The genre, so defined, enables authoritative tradition to continue to speak to the present community directly; it provides a lens for reading existing tradition by expanding the contents of that tradition.[17]

One of Zahn's goals is to provide a definition that can include *Jubilees* while at the same time is part of a conceptual framework in which it can also be included in other genres, such as prophecy, as Hindy Najman has argued.[18]

It is worth reflecting briefly on the assumptions behind Zahn's proposal. Zahn seems to assume that there are relatively stable, written texts with which the new writer is familiar; that these rewritings have a goal that goes beyond the idiosyncratic understanding of the author, being rooted in contemporary "concerns"; that the new work is meant to be circulated within a "community" and claims some authority within that community; and that that community is literate enough to recognize how the new work fits into genre expectations and builds on previous texts. While Zahn assumes that there is a communal dimension to understanding a text's genre, the precise nature of the community is not relevant to her.

My point is not that Zahn's proposal and the assumptions upon which they are based are wrong. They may, in fact, be right. It is a simpler observation: that (1) there are assumptions that Zahn does not feel the need to justify and (2) that these assumptions are not, and cannot be, derived from the text alone. The assumptions are simply imported as part of the conceptual apparatus.

Imagine, however, if there was no community to speak of but only an idiosyncratic scribe drawing on a confused set of oral traditions and

---

17. Zahn, "Genre and Rewritten Scripture," 286.
18. Hindy Najman, "Reconsidering *Jubilees*: Prophecy and Exemplarity," in *Enoch and the Mosaic Torah: The Evidence of Jubilees*, ed. Gabriele Boccaccini and Giovanni Ibba (Grand Rapids: Eerdmans, 2009), 229–43.

writing only for her own amusement, or that of a small body of friends. This conceptual apparatus, which might also be applied to a large variety of ancient texts such as the Temple Scroll or even Deuteronomy, however unlikely (a position that would have to be argued), seems to me to be impossible to disprove, certainly from the text itself. Beginning from these assumptions, we would most likely arrive at a very different set of conclusions about the question of the genre of *Jubilees*.

Changing the conceptual apparatus has the potential to impact not just our evaluation of the text's genre, but also its purpose and compositional history. Later, some of the Dead Sea Scrolls attribute authority to *Jubilees* that is roughly on par with other texts that this collection considers "scriptural" (e.g., 4Q228), and many copies of *Jubilees* were found among them. What we do not know—and perhaps cannot know from the text itself—is the intention of its writers. Was it meant to supplement Scripture, to replace it, or did it originally have other functions altogether?[19] Did *Jubilees*' claim that this revelation was from the "Angel of Presence," rather than directly from God or through Moses, point to a communal stance about revelation?[20] What exactly has been appropriated and to what ends?

A similar set of issues makes it difficult to reconstruct the compositional history of the text, a question on which scholars have long been deeply divided. Most recently, the three major positions have been argued by James VanderKam (it is a unified text from a single author); James Kugel (the text is mostly unified but some passages are later interpolations); and Michael Segal (the text came about through continuous redaction).[21] Whatever the merits of each of these positions, all treat their conclusions

---

19. Cf. Bernard M. Levinson, *A More Perfect Torah: At the Intersection of Philology and Hermeneutics in Deuteronomy and the Temple Scroll*, Critical Studies in the Hebrew Bible (Winona Lake: Eisenbrauns, 2013), 43: "The Temple Scroll was the creation of a community engaged with a scriptural tradition and a scriptural language from which they were long distant and yet whose pristine, revelatory voice they sought, 'hand in hand, with wandering steps and slow,' to revivify and claim as their own."

20. See James C. VanderKam, "The Putative Author of the Book of Jubilees," in *From Revelation to Canon: Studies in the Hebrew Bible and Second Temple Literature* (Leiden: Brill, 2000), 439–47.

21. James [C.] VanderKam, "Jubilees as the Composition of One Author?," *RevQ* 26 (2014): 501–16; James L. Kugel, "The Contradictions in the *Book of Jubilees*," in *A Walk through* Jubilees: *Studies in the* Book of Jubilees *and the World of its Creation*, JSJSup 156 (Leiden: Brill, 2012), 227–96; Michael Segal, *The Book of Jubilees: Rewritten Bible, Redaction, Ideology, and Theology*, JSJSup 117 (Leiden: Brill, 2007).

as coming out of their reading of the text. A close reading of the text is thought to give up its compositional history, which in turn can be used to deduce its social location. For Segal, the final redaction was intended as an "inner-Jewish polemic," "redacted within the same stream of Judaism within which one can locate the Qumran sect…following the formation of the Essene sect or stream."[22] James VanderKam, relying on the content of the book, argues that "the author belonged to or was an immediate forerunner of the branch of Judaism that we know as Essene."[23] Kugel, to my knowledge, does not take a stand on the historical production of the text, apparently finding the issue irrelevant to his own exegetical project.

How does one adjudicate between the claims of VanderKam and Segal? Both have merit to them and represent different reconstructions that are consistent with the internal evidence of *Jubilees* itself. At the same time, though, both rely on thin references to wider historical contexts. An implicit historical model is brought to *Jubilees*, which then is used to generate its context. Neither VanderKam, or Segal help us to understand the social position of the author, the extent to which the book circulated, and how it might have functioned (or been intended to function). Since for both the answers to these questions are ideally deduced from the text, neither acknowledge how they actually play an a priori role in interpreting it.

In my book, *How the Bible Became Holy*, I attempted to show how reversing this process by putting history ahead of the text can provide a different leverage point for understanding a text and how and why it came into being. Readings of individual texts provide a range of *possible* meanings, but it is only when embedded in specific historical circumstances and narratives that some of those *possible* meanings become *plausible*. The proper test of such an analysis is not whether the data directly support the narrative, but whether the narrative helps to account for more of the extant evidence in a more comprehensive way than other accounts.

Let me illustrate how such an approach might play out for *Jubilees*.[24] Following the rise of the Hasmonean dynasty, beginning around 163 BCE, two politico-religious "factions" arose.[25] According to Josephus, one of

22. Segal, *The Book of Jubilees*, 322.
23. James C. VanderKam, *The Book of Jubilees* (Sheffield: Sheffield Academic, 2001), 143.
24. See Michael L. Satlow, *How the Bible Became Holy* (New Haven: Yale University Press, 2014), 124–52.
25. I use the term "faction" with some hesitation. Josephus, Philo, and New Testament writers label these groups in the first century CE, but the terms "Pharisees,"

the most distinguishing features of one, the Pharisees, was their reliance on "traditions of the ancestors." The other faction, the Sadducees, were distinguished by their reliance on Scripture to authorize their religious practices.[26] Ultimately, this disagreement had political stakes; whoever made the best claim to be following God's will in conduct of the sacrificial service also had power in the Jerusalem temple, a major source of wealth and political power. In the time of John Hyrcanus I, the Sadducees got the upper hand in their dispute with the Pharisees.[27]

Over time, as one would expect from any group in power, the Sadducees began to fray. *Jubilees* was authored, or probably more likely redacted, by one such break-away Sadducean group. For the editor/author of *Jubilees*, the Sadducees in power did not go far enough. *Jubilees* puts "Scripture"—here defined somewhat differently as the "heavenly tablets" dictated to Moses (but not identical with the Torah) by the Angel of Presence—at the pinnacle of religious authority. *Jubilees* drew from earlier Scripture but it did not draw its own authority from those texts; it was meant to replace them as new Scripture, much like, it would appear, the Temple Scroll. For the editor of *Jubilees*, the ruling Sadducees had gone astray in not following laws such as the 364-day calendar.

The author/editors of *Jubilees* were trained scribes, as shown by their command of Hebrew, a language that few outside of scribal circles would have understood at the time. They might be identified as extremist Sadducees on the fringe of power who broke off sometime between 150 and 100 BCE and who had affinities (perhaps even a stronger connection) to the emerging (Essene?) community, some of whom would ultimately retire to the Dead Sea.[28] The group could not have been large, and this text was written for and circulated among the elite, having some impact on those that broke away to live at Qumran (and who might be identical with Philo's and Josephus's "Essenes."). At the same time, though, it never

---

"Sadducees," and "Essenes" appear in no prior document. I do not know if such groups formally existed at this time (and what such group identity would have meant then) but I do think that there is some justification to using these group names at least heuristically, as umbrella terms for loose coalitions of groups that share similar outlooks.

26. Josephus, *A.J.* 13.10.6; A. I. Baumgarten, "The Pharisaic Paradosis," *HTR* 80 (1987): 63–77.

27. Josephus, *A.J.* 13.10.5-6.

28. The identification of this group with the Essenes is vexed. For a recent discussion, see Jonathan Klawans, "The Essene Hypothesis: Insights from Religion 101," *DSD* 23 (2016): 51–78. For the sake of this argument, it does not matter whether or not we call these authors Essenes.

did replace Scripture for this group. There was a gap, that is, between its intention and its reception.

Whether correct or not, this reconstruction provides a wider lens through which to consider claims of *Jubilees*' provenance and function. It is a bit harder, at least for me, to imagine a plausible historical reconstruction that dates *Jubilees* closer to 160 BCE and explains its authors, audience, and function. I would not claim that a richer reconstruction cannot be created, but only that it is needed in order to make a more convincing case for answering many of the most important historical questions that *Jubilees* raises. Deduction can provide a set of possibilities, but ultimately, those possibilities must be embedded in larger narratives for them to become more plausible and thus to adjudicate between them.

The Letters of Paul

The letters of Paul offer a different kind of example. Unlike *Jubilees*, Paul's letters explicitly accept and mark the authority of Scripture with citation formulae. Paul often uses Scripture—all from Jewish Scripture as it is known today—as prooftexts, explicitly prefacing their citation with words like "as it is written" or "Scripture says."[29]

In the context of this volume, Paul's letters raise an obvious question: is his use of Scripture that of "other people" or his own people? That is, are we to see Paul as falling somewhere within the spectrum that we call "Jewish," or is he outside of that spectrum and thus "appropriating" Jewish texts?

Many earlier scholars, explicitly or implicitly, assume the latter. According to this narrative, Paul was born a Hellenistic Jew, one trained in and comfortable with Scripture in Greek, before moving at some (early) point in his life to Jerusalem. After his training with the Pharisees, he became an "apostle to the Gentiles," preaching God's message as recorded in the Hebrew Bible to non-Jews outside of Judea and forming several nascent Christian communities. Paul, in a sense, appropriates Scripture in order to bring God's message to those who were not familiar with it and was largely successful in doing so.

---

29. This section summarizes Satlow, *How the Bible Became Holy*, 210–23 and Michael L. Satlow, "Paul's Scriptures," in *Strength to Strength: Essays in Honor of Shaye J. D. Cohen*, ed. Michael L. Satlow (Providence: Brown Judaic Studies, 2018), 257–73. On citation formulae in Paul, see E. Earle Ellis, *Paul's Use of the Old Testament* (Grand Rapids: Eerdmans, 1957), 22–5, 48–9; D. M. Turpie, *New Testament View of the Old: A Contribution to Biblical Introduction and Exegesis* (London: Hodder & Stoughton, 1872), 340–1.

This narrative, admittedly (even by its proponents) sketchy as it is, can certainly be justified with textual evidence. Acts (e.g., 22:2-5; 23) provides the backbone of the narrative, with some supplements from the very brief autobiographical passages in Paul's letters (e.g., Phil. 3:5). Moreover, it makes sense of Paul's knowledge of Greek and his use of versions of the Hebrew Bible that are closer to surviving Greek forms than they are to Hebrew ones.[30]

From the perspective of this volume, however, there are three central problems with this reconstruction. The first is that it never deals with the question of how the non-Jews to whom Paul is writing got to know, and accept the authority, of heretofore "Jewish" Scripture. Paul cites bits and pieces of Scripture in his letters (and, if Richard Hays is to be believed, alludes to a great deal more) as if it is authoritative.[31] Why should we assume that it was read as such? The second problem is methodological: it relies significantly on Acts, which is a tenuous historical source. The third problem is that it assumes that Jews in and out of Jerusalem would have received significantly different educations in language and Scripture. That is, it relies on a priori notions of Paul's social context.

Despite these problems, the basic narrative sketched above has been remarkably enduring, even in the scholarship that over the past few decades has taken more seriously Paul's Jewish context and identity.[32] What, however, if the assumptions behind it are wrong? What if the author of Acts was not working from independent sources but instead was a historian trying to make sense, as the modern historian, of limited data? What if the Jewish social context, and particularly what is assumed about Jewish education in Jerusalem, was quite a bit different? From that simple starting point a somewhat different narrative can be constructed.

Aside from the fragment in Acts, there is no direct evidence that Paul was not born and raised in Jerusalem.[33] He would thus have been a near

---

30. See E. P. Sanders, "Paul's Jewishness," in *Paul's Jewish Matrix*, ed. Thomas G. Casey and Justin Taylor (Mahwah: Paulist, 2011), 51–73. For a more nuanced presentation, see James Albert Harrill, *Paul the Apostle: His Life and Legacy in Their Roman Context* (Cambridge: Cambridge University Press, 2011), 23–45.

31. Richard B. Hays, *Echoes of Scripture in the Letters of Paul* (New Haven: Yale University Press, 1989).

32. The literature is vast. See especially E. P. Sanders, *Paul and Palestinian Judaism: A Comparison of Patterns of Religion* (Philadelphia: Fortress, 1977); James D. G. Dunn, *The New Perspective on Paul*, 2nd ed. (Grand Rapids: Eerdmans, 2008); Gabrielle Boccaccini and Carlos A. Segovia, eds., *Paul the Jew: Rereading the Apostle as a Figure of Second Temple Judaism* (Minneapolis: Fortress, 2016).

33. W. C. van Unnik, *Tarsus or Jerusalem: The City of Paul's Youth* (London: Epworth, 1962), 52. See also his rejoinder to critique in van Unnik, "Once Again:

contemporary of Josephus. His Greek rhetorical skills suggest, again *pace* Acts, that his family was well-enough off to hire him a tutor as a youth. There is no sign that he knew Hebrew, but there is also little evidence either that Josephus knew Hebrew or that Hebrew was commonly known, even by the upper class, in Jerusalem. In fact, it is possible that neither Paul nor Josephus even learned much Scripture in their youth.[34] The Scripture that they did learn might mainly have been conveyed as oral stories, embodied practices, and, if the Dead Sea Scrolls are a guide, prophecies.

Given the high level of engagement that both Paul and Josephus had with Scripture, this claim might seem to be counterintuitive. Yet it is also important to remember, perhaps more important than has been recognized, that Paul and Josephus traveled and spent time in Jewish communities outside of Judea. These communities accorded Greek Scripture a special kind of visible authority.[35] It was in this environment that both Paul and Josephus may have first encountered written Scripture, even if in Jerusalem they knew it existed and may have previously heard some of it orally recited in Aramaic translation. This reconstruction would help us to understand why both Paul and Josephus usually follow the Greek version of Scripture and, where the Greek and Hebrew versions diverge, almost never follow the Hebrew. It also makes better sense of the books that Paul prefers to cite and the purpose of his citations, both of which have strong parallels in the Dead Sea Scrolls.

Such a reconstruction opens intriguing issues about Paul's audience. Paul's letters are addressed by and large to "mixed" communities of Jews and non-Jews. Each of these groups may well have received Paul's use of Scripture differently. Jews would have shared Paul's assessment of Scripture as authoritative, although they may have been puzzled by both the Scripture he uses—much of which was from outside of the Torah—and how he uses it, that is, in the form of prophetic prooftexts, which in our extant literature seems more distinctive of Judean rather than "diaspora" use.[36] Would non-Jews, though, have made any sense of Paul's use of

---

Tarsus or Jerusalem," *Sparsa Collecta: The Collected Essays of W. C. van Unnik*, NovTSup 29 (Leiden: Brill, 1973), 321–7; Martin Hengel, "The Pre-Christian Paul," in *The Jews among Pagans and Christians*, ed. Judith Lieu, John North, and Tessa Rajak (London: Routledge, 1992), 29–52.

34. On Josephus's knowledge of Scripture, see Seth Schwartz, *Josephus and Judaean Politics* (Leiden: Brill, 1990), 22–57.

35. Michael Tuval, *From Jerusalem Priest to Roman Jew*, WUNT 357 (Tübingen: Mohr Siebeck, 2013).

36. See Satlow, "Paul's Scriptures."

Scripture? Would they have known the contexts of these citations and, if so, where and how did they learn them? If not, would they simply accept their authority on Paul's word and attribute some kind of numinous power to them? Or would they have been puzzled by them and skipped over them to get at what they would have seen as the more important issues contained in the letters? There is certainly some evidence, most clearly reflected in the strength of Marcion's followers, that many non-Jews were willing to accept both Paul and Christ but had little patience for Jewish Scripture.[37]

I do not know the answer to these questions. In fact, I do not know if this reconstruction is correct. My point is to emphasize two things. First, our reading of Paul's letters, and our interpretation of whether or how he appropriated "other people's texts," depends on a number of a priori assumptions: How did Paul learn Scriptures and in what language? Who was Paul writing to? How would these communities have understood Paul's use of Scripture? How well did Paul know his audience? The second point is that Paul's letters provide only a few clues to some of these answers. As in the case of *Jubilees*, a compelling reading must emerge from and be consistent with the historical context. Our readings of Paul's letters *rest upon* rather than *generate* the historical assumptions within which they function.

Conclusion

Throughout this paper, I have argued against a particular kind of reading of ancient texts that is largely distinctive to the field called "biblical studies." This form of reading assumes that a text can be interpreted independently of a wider consideration of its historical context. While such an approach frequently claims to follow "only the evidence," in truth it is almost always based on a set of unstated and unsupported contextual assumptions. Our assumptions about the composition of Paul's audience, for example, or even the language environment in which *Jubilees* was produced, can have a significant impact on our interpretations. Whether we explicitly acknowledge it or not, we all import these assumptions into the texts.

I have sought in this paper to begin to develop a methodological approach that steers around this problem. I suggest that we be more aware of the "pseudo-historicism" in our field, on the one hand, but on the other

---

37. See, among others, Judith M. Lieu, *Marcion: The Making of a Heretic* (Cambridge: Cambridge University Press, 2015).

that there is a path around it. We should begin, simply, by explicitly acknowledging the conceptual apparatus that grounds our readings, the implicit narrative and assumptions about human behavior that allow for the interpretation. And we should frankly acknowledge that since our evidence is so thin, nearly every act of exegesis ultimately is grounded in a conceptual apparatus that is speculative.

One pay-off to this approach (aside from what I believe is a higher level of intellectual honesty and integrity) is that it allows us more clearly to define our arguments. If we fundamentally disagree about the conceptual apparatus, for example, then that changes the nature of potential disagreements about a particular textual interpretation. At the same time, we are better able to clarify when we are advancing textual *possibilities* and when we are making wider claims that give those possibilities plausibility.

Finally, this approach also changes the nature of critique. Speculation—or in gentler language, historical imagination—is not "bad"; it is a necessary part of what we do. Critiques need to be focused less on what is not "proven" and more on how well the narrative does explaining a wide range of evidence.

An approach like this moves us away from the strange, non-disciplinary field of "biblical studies" to history. The investigation of "other people's texts" is at heart a historical one. While we might be able to make limited arguments about how individual authors read previous texts, anything beyond that—to, for example, a community—requires a fair bit of historical speculation. We should not denounce or ignore this. Instead, we should embrace it. At a time when the humanities in general and biblical studies in particular are increasingly questioned and defunded, it might be best to look toward creating a scholarly ethos that instead of retreating into the narrow confines of the chimera of certainty expands our intellectual lives with visions of possible worlds that challenge and engage us.

WHAT HAPPENS TO PRECURSOR TEXTS IN THEIR SUCCESSORS?

Robert L. Brawley

The question of reading other people's texts tacitly recognizes that once a text is written, it achieves a life of its own, a life that not even authorial intention can control. Nevertheless, texts may be written for groups that claim a corporate identity and assert propriety over such texts. Concretely, consider the collection of texts that Israel claimed as its Scriptures. Distinct Israelite subgroups highly disputed both the content and interpretation of the collection of texts, as attested by distinctions in surviving versions of their Scriptures: Qumran, the Masoretic Text, the Samaritan Pentateuch, not to mention the Septuagint, Aquila, Symmachus, and Theodotion. Simply put, proprietorship of Israel's Scriptures is not a simple matter.

Unavoidable Intertextuality

Under the umbrella of intertextuality, I turn first to the inevitability of reading other people's texts. Texts begin with the irreducible complexity of intertextuality, due to the fact that all language incorporates precursors. All texts emerge from an enormous reservoir of potential: vocabulary; structure; modes of communication; figurations; temporal, spatial, and personal points of view; varying rhetorical moves of logic, humor, affections; and so forth. Charles Taylor launches his investigation of the *Sources of the Self* with the simple but insightful observation that the very language that we manipulate into spoken and written texts is composed of antecedents that are transmitted to us by communal networks in which we are socialized.[1] Every utterance is constructed from antecedent utterances,

---

1. Charles Taylor, *Sources of the Self: The Making of the Modern Identity* (Cambridge: Harvard University Press, 1989), 46–52.

and without the antecedents, no language exists for producing texts. This, of course, implicates an immeasurable pool of linguistic prototypes upon which we draw in order to communicate. In addition, like Taylor's location of the capacity for communication in socialization, both Roland Barthes and Julia Kristeva think of the move from the reservoir of antecedents to actualization in terms of an influence from culture on culture, a power move if you will, to which I will return.[2]

And yet language also holds immense potential for creativity beyond antecedents. We know that in early stages of learning language, children formulate sentences they have never heard. Patently, this means that the positivistic view that language conveys a stable, definitive concept from an originator to a receptor hardly holds. Martin Heidegger's claim to a transformation in approaching language reflects this very creativity of language. He moves away from logical-grammatical productions of propositions, in which a meaning that exists apart from language is then expressed in language.[3] Heidegger focuses instead on the "appropriating event" (*Ereignis*).

On the one hand, a language event does not produce permanent meaning. Rather, in giving itself, meaning withdraws and remains unrestricted. Language makes something "appear,"[4] but then it disappears, even as it creates something that abides, that is, as something is appropriated as event.[5] Without producing one definitive meaning, language still bears fruit; it is creative—even creative in an inverted sense in which words do not contain meanings but accrue meanings.[6]

A significant element of creativity, however, is that texts draw on a cultural repertoire to such an extent that texts alone never express the fullness of meaning because implied assumptions lie unexpressed behind verbal expressions. Wolfgang Iser refers to the unexpressed aspect of communication as the unbounded text, which always greatly exceeds

---

2. Cf. Roland Barthes, *S/Z: An Essay*, trans. Richard Miller (New York: Hill & Wang, 1974); Julia Kristeva, *Desire in Language: A Semiotic Approach to Literature and Art*, ed. Leon S. Roudiez, trans. Thomas Gora, Alice Jardine, and L. Roudiez (New York: Columbia University Press, 1980).

3. Theodore Kisiel, "The Language of the Event: The Event of Language," in *Martin Heidegger: Critical Assessments*, vol. 3, ed. Christopher Macann (London: Routledge, 1992), 151–67, esp. 152.

4. Martin Heidegger, *Sein und Zeit*, 7th ed. (Tübingen: Max Niemeyer, 1953), 32–4.

5. Martin Heidegger, *Unterwegs zur Sprache* (Pfullingen: Neske, 1960), 196; *Sein und Zeit*, 46–9, 54–66; Kisiel, "Language of the Event," 157, 163.

6. Heidegger, *Sein und Zeit*, 161: "Den Bedeutungen wachsen Worte zu."

the written or spoken text.[7] Barthes identifies unexpressed presumptions underlying texts as the "cultural voice."[8] Kristeva speaks of texts as a part of the culture and the culture as a part of them.[9] For instance, a simple schedule for an airline departure at 10:00 am leaves unexpressed the entire cultural artifice of dividing a day into twenty-four hours of 60 minutes each.

Rather than concentrate on the creativity of language, however, Kristeva adopts the term "ideologeme" to focus on a function that involves an ideological impulse in the incorporation of a textual pattern in the cultural repertoire external to the successor text on the level of what makes communication possible.[10] Expressing something in language involves some ideological purpose, an element of evaluation if you will, which also involves both power and identity (more on power and identity below). A shift on the level of what makes communication possible occurs when an external textual pattern is incorporated into a new text. And this brings us a bit closer to the issue of reading other people's texts. An external textual pattern takes on a transformed possibility of communicating in a text into which it is incorporated.

A concrete case of transformation by means of incorporating a pattern from another text is Jesus's words according to Mk 15:34, where he expresses his own situation in his crucifixion by incorporating a textual pattern from a psalm of lament, Psalm 22, but indeed in an Aramaic transliteration without any reference to the psalm. Such cases of direct relationships between two texts differ from the kind of intertextuality that Kristeva describes, which operates at the level of the very possibility of communication, rather than parsing the nuances of the language in the precursor and successor text. But as Daniel Boyarin points out, there is no reason why we cannot discern dimensions for communicating in *particular* cases of the incorporation of a precursor text in a successor.[11]

---

7. Wolfgang Iser, *The Act of Reading: A Theory of Aesthetic Response* (Baltimore: Johns Hopkins University Press, 1978), 69. Jonathan Culler specifies that this includes everything that depends on a shared view of reality; *Structuralist Poetics: Structuralism, Linguistics and the Study of Literature* (Ithaca: Cornell University Press, 1975), 203.

8. Barthes, *S/Z*, 18, 100.

9. Kristeva, *Desire in Language*, 36.

10. Compare Kristeva's ideologeme with Harold Bloom's revisionary ratios, discussed below.

11. Daniel Boyarin, *Intertextuality and the Reading of Midrash*, Indiana Studies in Biblical Literature (Bloomington: Indiana University Press, 1990), 135 n. 3.

So the question becomes simpler when we reduce the complexity by considering the use of precursor texts in successor texts irrespective of claims of proprietorship. Boyarin points out convincingly: "Intertextuality may therefore comprise a *specific* identifiable discursive space which makes a *specific* text intelligible."[12] In order to illustrate both the manner in which the cultural repertoire of a text is presumed but unexpressed and the manner in which a precursor text is used in a successor, I turn to William Faulkner's *The Sound and the Fury*. I first saw the 1959 film when I was a teenager, before I had studied either Shakespeare or American literature, and I had no idea that Faulkner's title is in intertextual interplay with Macbeth's remarks upon the death of Lady Macbeth in Shakespeare's play. I did not yet know the cultural repertoire (Act V, Scene V, lines 23–28):

> Out, out, brief candle!
> Life's but a walking shadow, a poor player
> That struts and frets his hour upon the stage
> And then is heard no more. It is a tale
> Told by an idiot, full of sound and fury,
> Signifying nothing.

Shakespeare's lines are in Macbeth's mouth upon the suicide of Lady Macbeth, who has spurred Macbeth to hasten his accession to the throne of Scotland by murder. And Faulkner's novel is in intertextual interplay with these lines. Indeed, the intertextual interplay runs deeper than Faulkner's title, as we will see. His story is about the demise of the aristocratic Compson family in early twentieth-century Mississippi. Benjy, who is characterized by his arrested mental development (corresponding to Shakespeare's idiot), and whom his family often brutalizes with punishing blows, does indeed tell a story. Not until I studied Shakespeare in college and then read Faulkner's *The Sound and the Fury* did I see that the purported normal siblings in the Compson family think of Benjy as the idiot full of sound and fury signifying nothing (Faulkner makes him bellow a lot). But Benjy, with his arrested mental development, is one of Faulkner's narrators, and so from Benjy's point of view, he is the idiot who tells his story, which is about the sound and the fury of the rest of the family that for him signify nothing.

---

12. Boyarin, *Intertextuality and the Reading of Midrash*, 135 n. 2 (emphasis original).

In Kristeva's terms, Shakespeare's tale told by an idiot full of sound and fury has therefore taken on a different function. But, as she would put it, Faulkner's appropriation acknowledges the existence of the external text "only to the extent that it makes it *its own*."[13]

The Dialogical Character of Intertextuality

I turn now to the dialogical character of embedding an external text in a new text. I take the notion of dialogicality from Mikhail Bakhtin, who demonstrates how Dostoevsky does not control his characters by means of his authorial perspective but allows them to speak with their own equally authoritative voices, thereby producing a combination of pluralistic consciousnesses and worldviews in one text.[14] I suggest that something similar occurs with intertextuality. Faulkner's appropriation of Shakespeare does not silence the Bard's voice. It still speaks on its own. In fact, unless Faulkner's readers recall the larger context of Macbeth's murderous path to the throne and the suicide of Lady Macbeth, they will not catch the import of Faulkner's allusions. And yet Shakespeare is pulled into interplay with Faulkner's voice, or I should say voices, because there are four narrators in his novel. Although Bakhtin is speaking about different characters in one novel, he cites L. P. Grossmann, who likens the multiplicity of voices to counterpoint in music harmonizing variously on a single theme.[15] From this perspective intertextuality is also dialogical.

Expanding Intertextuality

I expand the interrelationship of precursor and successor texts in terms of both Kristeva's notion of an ideological shift in function and Bakhtin's dialogical nature of intertextuality by turning to two other theorists, John Hollander and Harold Bloom. The key to both of these literary critics is their perception that in relation to each other precursor and successor texts form a figuration. First of all, the successor text inevitably offers a revisionary perspective on the precursor. Take the bumper sticker, "A fool and his money are soon partying." This successor text evokes an external text that remains an unexpressed textual pattern, which Michael

---

13. Kristeva, *Desire in Language*, 46 (emphasis original).
14. Mikhail Bakhtin, *Problems of Dostoevsky's Poetics*, trans. Caryl Emerson, intro. by Wayne Booth, Theory and History of Literature 8 (Minneapolis: University of Minnesota Press, 1984), 18–22.
15. Bakhtin, *Problems of Dostoevsky's Poetics*, 42.

Riffaterre calls the "hypogram."[16] Although on the bumper sticker itself the hypogram remains unexpressed, it is nonetheless present in the cultural repertoire in the adage "A fool and his money are soon parted."

But the relationship of the two texts is reciprocal, and this reciprocity is the heart of the figuration. On the one hand, the precursor and the successor texts obviously have a diachronic relationship—one predates the other. Further, the precursor has an established place in the cultural repertoire. But when a successor text incorporates a precursor, the two stand together in a synchronic relationship. Hollander likens this to reverberations in which sounds echo back and forth, and this reciprocity produces a figuration in which there are new twists on the meaning of the independent parts.[17] "A fool and his money are soon partying" evokes a retrospective view of "a fool and his money are soon parted," but the old adage also provides a lens through which to view the new variation. On the one hand, "a fool and his money are soon partying" turns the negative consequence of "a fool and his money are soon parted" into something pleasurable and positive; on the other, it ignores that the partying likely still drains the fool of his wherewithal. Finally, however, the two together form the reverberating figuration, and the reverberations never stop.

In noting the way a successor produces a revisionary perspective on the precursor, Bloom emphasizes discontinuity even as he recognizes continuity. With discontinuity in mind, he calls every successor text a "misinterpretation."[18] Hollander by contrast accentuates continuity, but this distinction between the two theorists is merely a matter of emphasis. The amalgam of discontinuity and continuity is actually a way in which we "make contemporary sense out of messages that were intended for other ears."[19] The twist in meaning produces an additional way in how one understands reality.[20] But the interaction is complex, because intertextual allusions may generate striking similarities while ignoring divergences or even contradictions, or may conjure up combinations of these

---

16. Michael Riffaterre, *Semiotics of Poetry*, Advances in Semiotics (Bloomington: Indiana University Press, 1978), 12–13. See Robert L. Brawley, *Text to Text Pours Forth Speech: Voices of Scripture in Luke-Acts*, Indiana Studies in Biblical Literature (Bloomington: Indiana University Press, 1995), 7.

17. John Hollander, *The Figure of Echo: A Mode of Allusion in Milton and After* (Berkeley: University of California Press, 1981), ix, 31, 43, 111.

18. Harold Bloom, *The Anxiety of Influence* (New York: Oxford University Press, 1973), 94.

19. Julian Pitt-Rivers, *The Fate of Shechem or the Politics of Sex* (Cambridge: Cambridge University Press, 1977), 146.

20. Hollander, *Figure of Echo*, 31, 43, 111.

simultaneously.[21] Further, every diachronic relationship of earlier and later texts in a synchronic relationship of simultaneity produces what Bloom calls "a lie against time."[22] Intertextuality turns diachrony into synchrony.

Moreover, when we speak of intertextuality as a figuration, it is possible to understand the relationship between precursor and successor texts as comparable to classical figures of speech. Bloom does this by associating six shifts of function in intertextuality, which he calls revisionary ratios, with irony, synecdoche, metonymy, hyperbole, metaphor proper, and metalepsis.[23] A caveat is that these analytical categories separate functions that often bleed over into one another. In addition, Bloom gives them intriguing titles, which I take to be elaborations of Aristotle's basic description of figures of speech (*Poetics* 1457b). On the one hand Bloom's titles more than complicate understanding. What he calls *clinamen* corresponds to irony, that is, the figuration bends meaning toward another nuance so that the precursor and successor texts offer two levels of meaning, which can only be discerned ironically because the mind inevitably installs one meaning over the other as superior. And two levels of meaning, one of which is superior to the other, is the essence of irony. *Tessera* corresponds to synecdoche, where a part stands for the whole, or the whole for a part. *Kenosis* corresponds to metonymy, a figuration that uses one term to name another. Aristotle gives examples where "bronze" stands for a "knife" or in another case "bronze" stands for a "bowl" (*Poetics* 1457). *Kenosis* of course means to empty out, but it is a strange emptying because the figuration works only when what is supposedly emptied stands in a tensive relationship with what is named anew. *Daemonization* corresponds to hyperbole, as in the case of Acts 21:20 where James says to Paul, "See, brother, how many tens of thousands there are among the Jews who have believed," whereas he actually implies a large number (no one could have counted). *Askesis* corresponds to metaphor proper, which involves an implicit analogy as when a poet refers to "evening" as "the old age of a day" (*Poetics* 1457b). Finally, *apophrades* corresponds to metalepsis, which makes a figuration on a figuration, such as leaving the baby in the bath water. Significantly, Bloom describes this as coming back from the dead. To clarify, I understand these enigmatic designations as Bloom's attempt to speak of these

---

21. Bloom, *Anxiety of Influence*, 14; Michael Fishbane, *Biblical Interpretation in Ancient Israel* (New York: Oxford University Press, 1985), 421.

22. Harold Bloom, *The Breaking of the Vessels* (Chicago: University of Chicago Press, 1982), passim.

23. On Bloom's revisionary ratios see Brawley, *Text to Text*, 10–13.

figurations figuratively, and my experience is that the attempt to decipher them leads to deeper perceptions of what is going on in the revisionary relationships between successor and precursor texts.

Cases in Point from Biblical Texts

Clinamen, Tessera, and Daemonization

The prophet Jonah has a divine mandate to proclaim destruction to his arch enemies, the Ninevites. He ultimately does, but they repent, and instead of the destruction that he predicted, God likewise repents and spares the Ninevites. Result: Jonah is angry, and he explains why he is angry. He did not want to go in the first place, and he tried to flee to Tarshish, because he says (regretfully), "I knew what kind of God you are. I already knew that you are a gracious God and merciful, slow to anger, and abounding in steadfast love, and ready to relent from punishing" (Jon. 4:2). The question arises: How did he know? He knew from a precursor text. He is citing part of Exod. 34:6-7. Let me underscore that he is quoting only a part of God's revelation to Moses, and in this sense Jonah's citation has the character of what Bloom calls *tessera*, not so much like the individual tiles in a mosaic, but more like a shard that completes a larger piece of pottery. What Jonah quotes is thus a synecdoche, a part that evokes the whole, because Jonah's citation is enough to recognize the place of Exod. 34:6-7 in Israel's cultural heritage.

But something quite different occurs as well. Exodus 34:6-7 is God's revelation to Moses for the sake of Israel. When Jonah cites it, the characterization of God takes on a new slant (*clinamen*) inasmuch as it now pertains to Israel's arch enemy—disarmingly ironic. It is true that Jonah is angry, angry enough to die because of what he already knows about God. In fact, God's nature to "relent from punishing" motivates his attempt to evade the divine mandate.[24] But certainly for the readers of Jonah, when this revelation comes back a second time around with respect to the Ninevites, the characterization of God rises to a higher level. This also corresponds to Bloom's *daemonization*, which he takes in the original sense of a *daemon* as a higher power, semi-divine, transcending ordinary experience, and which he associates with hyperbole. The figuration climbs to a higher level. Or to choose another figuration, as Michael Fishbane puts it, there is "a theological deepening of the notion that YHWH 'relents of the evil.'"[25]

---

24. Michael Fishbane, *Biblical Interpretation in Ancient Israel* (New York: Oxford University Press, 1985), 347.

25. Fishbane, *Biblical Interpretation in Ancient Israel*, 346.

Tessera

In the third beatitude in Mt. 5:5, Jesus asserts that the "meek" will inherit the earth, and in so doing he cites Ps. 36:11 LXX (MT 37:11). Readers who are immersed in the cultural encyclopedia of Scripture know beyond the citation alone that the entire psalm centers on the distribution of land, which is the eventual implication of the promise of land in the Abrahamic covenant. But in the case of Psalm 36 LXX, equitable distribution of the land is out of balance.[26] To this point, in vv. 9, 11, 22, 29, 34, the Psalm repeats the notion of "inheriting the land," which is formulaic for the Abrahamic covenant. Incidentally, the same term that the NRSV translates as "earth" in Mt. 5:5 also appears in the Septuagint in both Ps. 36:11 LXX and in Genesis (e.g., 15:7, 18 LXX) with reference to what the NRSV translates as "land," that is, the Greek in Mt. 5:5 is the same as in Ps. 36:11 LXX.[27]

Without recognizing the intertextual relationship between Mt. 5:5 and Psalm 36 LXX, interpreters conventionally take the "meek" to be humble in spirit. But beyond the citation alone, the psalm repeatedly protests the wicked who plot, use violence, turn to murder, or employ deceptive economic practices and oppression to confiscate land. This of course violates the equitable distribution of the land among Abraham's descendants who are the recipients of the promise that they will inherit the land. On the basis of the psalm, the meek (οἱ παρεῖς) in Mt. 5:5 are those who have lost their land at the hands of the unjust, and the beatitude is an affirmation of God's fidelity to the promises in the Abrahamic covenant.[28] The loss of access to land was increasingly the plight of subsistence farmers in Jesus' time who, for instance, incurred debt by using land as collateral to secure seed for planting, then suffered crop failure, and thereby lost their access to land.[29]

Psalm 36 LXX and Mt. 5:5 together form a figuration because together they say more than either text alone. To be sure, the socio-political context

---

26. The citation implies a context far beyond the citation itself. So Gerhard von Rad, "Typological Interpretation of the Old Testament," in *Essays on Old Testament Interpretation*, ed. Claus Westermann (London: SCM, 1963), 17–39, esp. 20.

27. Both the Greek γῆ and the Hebrew ארץ can mean a plot of ground such as a garden or a homeland such as Canaan or even the entire earth.

28. Robert Brawley, "Evocative Allusions in Matthew: Matthew 5:5 as a Test Case," in *Literary Encounters with the Reign of God*, ed. Sharon Ringe and H. C. Paul Kim (New York: T & T Clark, 2004), 127–48, esp. 139–48.

29. Ekkehard Stegemann and Wolfgang Stegemann, *The Jesus Movement: A Social History of Its First Century*, trans. O. C. Dean, Jr. (Minneapolis: Fortress, 1999), 108, 126.

of Jesus's beatitude involves elite collaborators of the Ἰουδαῖοι in Roman imperial systems, which Josephus identifies primarily as the high priestly party.[30] Moreover, as indicated above, the first century of our era was a perilous time for people living at the subsistence level to lose access to land. Therefore, an aspect of the revisionary ratios of these texts is what Bloom calls *tessera*. The two texts reflect off of each other and fit together like shards of pottery that together form a whole. In order to do this, however, the figuration commits Bloom's "lie against time." That is, it turns a diachronic relationship into a synchronic one.

Kenosis and Apophrades

Bloom's idea of *kenosis* is straightforward. The successor text empties the meaning of the precursor. An equally straightforward case in point is the proverb in Ezek. 18:2 that is repeated in Jer. 31:29-30. The proverb itself has an intertextual relationship with the notion of the consequences of sin, as in Exod. 20:5 where idolatry incurs divine punishment to children for the iniquity of their parents for three and even four generations: "The parents have eaten sour grapes and the children's teeth are set on edge." But both Ezekiel and Jeremiah controvert the proverb to emphasize personal consequences for iniquity. Both prophets spell out this personal responsibility, but Jeremiah also revises the proverb: "The teeth of everyone who eats sour grapes will be set on edge" (Jer. 31:30). His revision first of all empties the meaning of the original proverb (*kenosis*), but the revision also is a trope that plays off of another trope. That is, Jeremiah restates the figurative proverb of eating sour grapes, with the consequence that his revisionary proverb requires interaction with the original trope. The *kenosis* so to speak kills the original proverb, but the potency of Jeremiah's successor text depends on bringing the original trope back to life. This bringing back to life is what Bloom calls *apophrades*. To give this additional names, this is also transumption or metalepsis—the intertextuality makes a figuration on what is already a figuration.

The parable of the Tenants in the Vineyard in Mk 12:1-9 is also such a figuration on what is already a figuration, a parable on a parable. In the Parable of the Vineyard in Isaiah 5, the vineyard is a stock image

---

30. Josephus, *A.J.* 20.251. The typical pattern for Roman imperial systems in the provinces involved client kings such as the Herodian tetrarchs, governors such as the procurator Pilate, and regional elite collaborators such as the high priestly party. See K. C. Hanson and Douglas E. Oakman, *Palestine in the Time of Jesus: Social Structures and Social Conflicts*, 2nd ed. (Minneapolis: Fortress, 2008), 59–60, 137–42.

for Israel, which Mark takes over. Mark's dependence on Isaiah 5 is especially evident in the details of digging a pit for a wine press and building a watchtower (Mk 12:1 = Isa. 5:2). But the revisionary ratio is most evident in that in Isaiah the vineyard is destroyed, whereas in Mark the vineyard is not destroyed but transferred to other tenants. The tenants who are problematic in Mark are the high priestly coterie (11:27; 12:12), but emphatically Israel remains Israel so that anti-Jewish interpretations "cannot be tolerated."[31]

Askesis

This figuration is like a metaphor itself that gives those who perceive it a new way of viewing reality by taking away the meaning of a precursor, like an ascetic withdrawing from society. For this case in point, I take one aspect of Gabriel's interpretation of the Davidic covenant in Lk. 1:33. Gabriel asserts that Mary's son will reign over the house of Jacob forever and his kingdom will have no end. The Davidic covenant in 2 Sam. 7:12 promises that one of David's descendants (σπέρμα, "seed") will reign "forever" (εἰς τὸν αἰῶνα). Gabriel's revision repeats this but adds that the kingdom will have no end (τέλος). In the context of Luke and Acts, it is clear that τέλος is taken both temporally and spatially. Not only will the kingdom last forever, but its dimensions will be universal, as reflected in the enthronement of Jesus in Acts 2:29-36, "...until I put all your enemies under your feet." But this happens only with the withdrawal of the meaning of a political restoration of Israel. This is *askesis*.

I end these cases in point by recalling the caveat above that these revisionary ratios or figurative categories are analytical and cannot be restricted to the subheads that I have assigned to them. They may bleed over into each other, and because catching figurations is inevitably a matter of construal in the mind of the beholder, they may be perceived in entirely different, even contradictory ways.

Identity and Legitimation[32]

I wish now to blend in with these revisionary ratios a little more from Kristeva. Earlier, I anticipated returning to the issue of how intertextuality is infused with cultural potency. By this I mean that the move from

---

31. Ruben Zimmermann, *Puzzling the Parables of Jesus: Methods and Interpretation* (Minneapolis: Fortress, 2015), 206.

32. See in this volume, "Social Identity and Scriptural Interpretation: An Introduction."

a cultural reservoir of potentialities to actualization inevitably carries the weight of cultural influence. We can speak of Kristeva's emphasis on the function of embedding an external text into a new text in terms of a kind of power of identity and legitimation.

But before I speak of legitimation and identity, I need to mention two different ways external texts are embedded in new texts. One way is like the case of Jonah where textual patterns of a precursor text are repeated, cited, quoted. But it is also possible to refer to an external textual system that does not appear in the new text. At the end of the Gospel of Luke, Jesus appears to eleven disciples after his resurrection and says: "This is what I said to you while I was still with you, that everything written about me in the law of Moses and the prophets and the psalms must be fulfilled." This "everything" is then summarized as the suffering of the messiah, the resurrection on the third day, and the preaching of repentance in his name (Lk. 24:46-47). The external system of Israel's Scriptures makes an appearance here without any repetition of a textual pattern, no allusion, no citation.

The function of embedding a reference to Israel's Scriptures in the new text is obviously a move to influence the impact of a communication. Authors appropriate texts for their own purposes,[33] one of which is always to assure themselves of who they are both in the eyes of others and in their own eyes.[34] This view belongs to an extended philosophical tradition, including Martin Heidegger, that identity is socially mediated.[35] Such social identity is always at issue in the public dissemination of texts that appropriate other texts. In the case of Luke, Jesus' reference to the textual system of Israel's Scriptures without citing any text supports the legitimation of a virtually incongruous belief in an executed messiah. Luke's last three chapters about Jesus' arrest, crucifixion, and resurrection are filled with two basic conflicting views of his story.

One side is identified predominantly with the high priestly party, which as indicated above in the first century CE was by necessity in collaboration with imperial systems. As elsewhere in provinces of the Empire, local elites were charged with maintaining order among their own

---

33. Susan Rubin Suleiman, "Pornography, Transgression, and the Avant-Garde: Bataille's *Story of the Eye*," in *The Poetics of Gender*, ed. Nancy Miller; Gender and Culture (New York: Columbia University Press, 1986), 117–36, esp. 122.

34. Julia Kristeva, "Psychoanalysis and the Polis," *Critical Inquiry* 9, no. 1 (1982): 77–92, esp. 78.

35. Taylor, *Sources of the Self*, 46–52; Martin Heidegger, *Identity and Difference*, trans. Joan Stambaugh (New York: Harper & Row, 1969), 41.

people (Josephus, *A.J.* 20.251).[36] Collaboration means both resistance and compliance. Resistance expresses some sense of autonomy; compliance is necessary for local leadership to remain in office at all, otherwise the Empire would depose the local leaders and turn the land into occupied territory. And this produces what Homi Bhabha describes as "less than one and double."[37] Ruling local elites are less than an autonomous nation, but ruling leaders who are also accountable to Rome mean that economic and political systems are doubled.

The other side in conflicting views about the executed Jesus is an appeal for a way of life that is an alternative to imperial systems. "Belief in a Jew as Son of God, as Messiah, crucified by the Romans, is in itself a fact of resistance in a world dominated by the Romans...."[38] For example, whereas traditionally Israelite village life had allocative economic systems in which distribution of goods among families in the village was based on need, imperial systems imposed extractive economic systems.[39] Among other emphases, Luke supports the social life of groups of Jesus's followers with distribution of the resources of the earth based on need (see Lk. 6:30, 35; Acts 4:34-35). But much more is in the air, because the identity of a group who are followers of Jesus is at stake. Indeed, as indicated above, any time an external text is taken over into a successor text, cultural issues are involved. Or as Wayne Booth puts it insightfully, "All actual works of art are loaded with ideology."[40] On a macro scale, there is an appeal either for continuity or discontinuity. Intertextuality is either about finding resources to strengthen ideologies or trying to expunge deficiencies in ideologies. Taking up a precursor text in a new text by citation or by reference to a textual system that the new text does not contain is either about finding angel voices or exterminating devils. But this is also taken up in the evaluative perspective of the implied author, and it is designed to shape the readers' construals of reality.

---

36. Peter Garnsey and Richard Saller, *The Roman Empire: Economy, Society and Culture* (Berkeley: University of California Press, 1987), 152.

37. Homi K. Bhabha, *The Location of Culture*, 2nd ed. (London: Routledge, 2004); the expression is repeated on 139, 142, 166, 169, 170, 171.

38. Luise Schottroff, "'Give to Caesar What Belongs to Caesar and to God What Belongs to God': A Theological Response of the Early Christian Church to Its Social and Political Environment," in *The Love of Enemy and Nonretaliation in the New Testament*, ed. Willard Swartley (Louisville: Westminster John Knox, 1992), 223–57, esp. 223.

39. Roland Boer, *The Sacred Economy of Ancient Israel*, Library of Ancient Israel (Louisville: Westminster John Knox, 2015), xii, 1–2, 102–45.

40. Wayne Booth, "Introduction," in Bakhtin, *Problems of Dostoevsky's Poetics*, xiii–xxvii, esp. xiv.

So Jesus' reference to Israel's Scriptures at the end of Luke is a move to nourish the identity of followers of Jesus. Marcion was entirely wrong when he used a form of the Gospel of Luke that he cut off from Israel's Scriptures, because Luke cannot be understood in any other way than as an appeal for continuity with the history of Israel. In fact, at the heart of Luke's narrative is the memory of God's promises to Israel in the Abrahamic, Mosaic, and Davidic covenants. But this does not occur without Bloom's revisionary ratios, which from the perspective of the implied author mean that there are new developments both as expansions and restrictions. For Dostoevsky, every character has equal rights with the hero,[41] and in an analogous way for Luke the equal rights of the dialogical relationship of precursor and successor texts would be violated either by Marcionism or by closed and guardedly controlled canonicity. Bloom refers to artistic uses of intertextuality as "the anxiety of influence," as if authors wished to be perceived as so original as to deny intertextual continuity. I rather expect that an author like Luke would be scandalized if the continuity with Israel's Scriptures were to be denied.

Conclusion

As indicated above, Bloom calls every use of a precursor text in a successor a "misinterpretation." This is to say that the precursor text inevitably appears in an ideological system that revises interpretation. In fact, I would be so bold as to claim that the same is true for any interpretation of other people's texts. Every interpretation pays attention to certain features of a text at the expense of others, and so inescapably interpretation is always a misinterpretation. This kind of misinterpretation, however, is especially obvious in the conscious type of intertextuality that is the concern of this essay. The citation of or an allusion to a precursor text in a successor inexorably locates it in a different context that cannot avoid putting a new slant on it. That is, in the eyes of the beholder a view of reality that comes to expression in a word event from the precursor text becomes part of a different view of reality when it appears in a successor text.

New visions of reality are filled with cultural significance, and therefore play important roles in identity and legitimation, which is another way of speaking about power moves. Perhaps I can speak only personally, but my own conviction is that power moves involved in reading other people's text inevitably involve the ethics of interpretation. This raises a problem toward which up to this point I have given only a slight nod. I

41. Bakhtin, *Problems of Dostoevsky's Poetics*, 49–50.

have mentioned what Bloom calls *kenosis*, and noted that it can attempt to obliterate the precursor, and I called attention to Kristeva's discernment that intertextuality involves a power move, a power move that can enable views of reality to rise to a higher level. On the other hand, the power move can be viciously destructive in silencing precursors. Bernard Levinson astutely detects just such a move in the Deuteronomistic revision of the Covenant Code and in the Chronicler's revision of the Deuteronomistic History. But in what he calls the "final irony" the canonicity of Israel's Scriptures has kept both the Covenant Code and the Deuteronomistic revision alive.[42]

In the history of interpretation, such power moves have even taken the form of supersessionism. Supersessionists have murderously (deplorably sometimes literally) attempted to silence their precursor. But supersessionists have hardly been any more successful at silencing than Cain who murdered his brother (Gen. 4:8-10), because Abel's blood cried out to God from the ground. Again thanks to another stage of canonicity Abel still speaks (Heb. 11:4): *apophrades*.

---

42. Bernard Levinson, *Deuteronomy and the Hermeneutics of Legal Innovation* (New York: Oxford University Press, 1997), 144–57, esp. 155.

Redaction as Reception: Genesis 34 as Case Study

Alison L. Joseph

Traditionally reception is seen as the afterlife of a text: what happens to a biblical text after it is written, canonized, or made authoritative in some other way. In John Barton's recent collection of essays on methodologies in biblical studies, Alison Gray states that reception "pertains to the ways in which the texts and *all* that is related to them—their beliefs, characters, ideas, motifs, stories, underlying traditions—have been understood, used, transmitted, translated, interpreted, expressed, and retold within any medium since their conception. How the HB/OT has been 'received'— that is, understood or interpreted, in different cultures and at different times…"[1] This definition seems to presume some moment of completion of one text and the beginning of another. This volume explores many ways that biblical texts have been read and received. In this chapter, I will consider reception during the process of composition and redaction, when the biblical text itself is still quite fluid. The redactors were essentially readers, who received traditions, either written or oral, responded to them, and often revised and/or rewrote them. Rather than Gray's definition, we should, with Brennan Breed, "understand the biblical text as a series of processes—text, reading, transmutations, and nonsemantic impact— whose nature it is to change over time."[2]

I will deconstruct the story of Dinah in Genesis 34, as a case study, to demonstrate a way that redaction can be seen as an act of reading. In its canonical form, Dinah, daughter of Jacob and Leah, walks out among the

---

1. Alison Gray, "Reception of the Old Testament," in *The Hebrew Bible: A Critical Companion*, ed. John Barton (Princeton: Princeton University Press, 2016), 405–30, here 405 (italics in original).

2. Brennan W. Breed, *Nomadic Text: A Theory of Biblical Reception History* (Bloomington: Indiana University Press, 2014), 205.

women of the land. Shechem, son of Hamor, prince of the local city, sees her and has sex with her. Following their sexual union, Shechem urges his father to enter into negotiations with Jacob so that he can marry Dinah. With deceit, the sons of Jacob agree to Hamor's proposal that Shechem and Dinah marry and that their families continue to intermarry with one another. The sons counter that they can only give their sister or sisters to circumcised men. Hamor and Shechem agree and all the men are circumcised. While they are recovering, Simeon and Levi massacre the town, "by the sword," activating the laws of holy war and demonstrating that the prospect of intermarriage is unconditionally offensive to them.

The story of Dinah in Genesis 34 is presumed to be about her and the vengeance her brothers take on her behalf, but instead this is a story in which Dinah does not speak, is named only once, after which she is referred to only as an object and never as a subject. The text instead is focused on the perspectives of the men, the wrongs done to them. It is possible to see two competing versions of the same story, neither of which is about Dinah as anything more than a commodity. The two stories, identified early on by Hermann Gunkel, John Skinner, and August Dillmann, when separated can be read almost independently. The first version is a clan-saga focused on the shame and honor of Jacob and his sons, while the second version, which ends with a call for mass extermination, highlights the offense of intermarriage. The differences in these two versions illustrate a powerful example of not only the existence of competing perspectives, but also the process of reading and rewriting by the redactors.

Redaction of Genesis 34

Scholars have long debated the compositional history of the Dinah story in Genesis 34. For more than a century, they have divided the chapter into two sources. Gunkel (1901) and Skinner (1910) identified them as E and J, but with some hesitation. Gunkel and Skinner focused on competing reports of similar events and recognizing them as doublets, identifying what they called the "Hamor variant" and the "Shechem recension," divided according to the lines of the marriage negotiations undertaken by each character. Hamor proposes a "national" marriage alliance while Shechem only wants Dinah.[3]

---

3. Hermann Gunkel, *Genesis*, trans. Mark E. Biddle (Macon: Mercer University Press, 1997), 358. According to Skinner, "There are grave *material* difficulties in assigning either recension to J or E." John Skinner, *A Critical and Exegetical Commentary on Genesis*, ICC (Edinburgh: T. & T. Clark, 1969), 418. While these

While Dillmann (1882) breaks down the Dinah narrative to J and P,[4] Rofé (2005), building on Kuenen (1880), highlights a postexilic context with features of priestly diction and marks of Late Biblical Hebrew.[5] I agree that Genesis 34 reflects two levels of redaction, one preexilic and a second postexilic.[6]

An Earlier Version

The first version, often attributed to J, can be considered within the genre of "clan sagas."[7] It deals with issues of identity of the young nation—the children of Israel—and their existence among the foreign inhabitants of the land. There is some anxiety about who this generation will marry and how such marriages will take place. The honor of the people, in a culture of honor and shame, is largely at stake. Shechem, the eponymous ancestor of the city, sees Dinah the daughter of the patriarch Jacob, and sleeps with her. It is only after taking her and treating her as a wife

---

doublets are important in identifying two independent components to the narrative, Gunkel and Skinner were warranted to have reservations about their source designations.

4. August Dillmann, *Genesis: Critically and Exegetically Expounded*, trans. William B. Stevenson, 2 vols. (Edinburgh: T. & T. Clark, 1897), 2:287–301; Dillmann, *Die Genesis* (Leipzig: S. Hirzel, 1882).

5. Alexander Rofé, "Defilement of Virgins in Biblical Law and the Case of Dinah (Genesis 34)," *Biblica* 86, no. 3 (2005): 369–75; Abraham Kuenen, "Beiträge zur Hexateuchkritik: VI. Dina und Sichem (Gen. 34)," in *Gesammelte Abhandlungen zur biblischen Wissenschaft* (Freiburg i.B: Mohr, 1894), 255–76. My own reconstruction most closely parallels theirs (see below).

6. There has been immense debate in recent scholarship about the dating (and even the existence) of J, and about whether the non-P material in the Pentateuch is pre-Priestly or post-Priestly. It is not necessary to my argument here to take a stand on any of these theories, except to argue that the earlier version of Genesis 34 is likely preexilic and a secondary version is likely postexilic with priestly interests. For more on the current trends in this discussion, see Thomas B. Dozeman and Konrad Schmid, eds., *Farewell to the Yahwist? The Composition of the Pentateuch in Recent European Interpretation*, SymS 34 (Atlanta: Society of Biblical Literature, 2006). And, more recently, Friedhelm Hartenstein and Konrad Schmid, eds., *Abschied von der Priesterschrift? Zum Stand der Pentateuchdebatte* (Leipzig: Evangelische Verlagsanstalt, 2013). Also, Konrad Schmid, "Post-Priestly Additions in the Pentateuch: A Survey of Scholarship," in *The Formation of the Pentateuch: Bridging the Academic Cultures of Europe, Israel, and North America*, ed. Jan C. Gertz et al., FAT 111 (Tübingen: Mohr Siebeck, 2016), 589–604.

7. Lyn M. Bechtel, "What If Dinah Is Not Raped? (Genesis 34)," *JSOT* 62 (1994): 19–36, here 22–3.

(both bringing her to his household and having intercourse with her) that Shechem approaches her family to participate in marriage negotiations. This is not the normal order of things, but it is not illegal. Laws in Exodus and Deuteronomy, as well as other ancient Near Eastern laws, provide penalties and precedent for what to do in this situation.[8] Dinah's brothers counter-offer that Shechem (alone) must be circumcised, to which he agrees in order to attain the "blessing" of the family and maintain their honor, but the brothers want revenge and kill him after his circumcision, taking Dinah from his house.

I offer here my reconstruction of the earlier edition of this story. It focuses on the one son and the one daughter, not all the sons of Hamor and all the daughters of Jacob. My reconstruction is based on separating doublets, such as the repetition of marriage negotiations by both Shechem and Hamor. It attributes anything about defilement, a term of priestly categories, to a later redaction.[9] As such, Gen. 34:1-26*[10] can be reconstructed as follows:[11]

> [1] And Dinah, daughter of…Jacob, went out to see the daughters of the land. [2] And Shechem son of Hamor, the Hivite,…saw her and he took her, lay with her, and debased her. [3] And his self clung[12] to Dinah daughter of Jacob and he loved the young woman and he spoke to the heart of the young woman…
> [7] But the sons of Jacob came from the field upon their hearing and the men were vexed and they were very angry because an insult [נבלה] had been done to lie with the daughter of Jacob, for such is not done…
> [11] And Shechem said to her father and her brothers, "I will find favor in your eyes, and that which you will say to me I will give. [12] Make great upon me the bride price and the gift. And let me give what you say to me. And give to me the young woman as a wife." [13] And the sons of Jacob answered Shechem and with deception they spoke[.]…

---

8. Exod. 22:15-16; Deut. 22:28-29. Cf. Middle Assyrian Laws 55–56.

9. Defilement, in the sense of moral (vs. ritual) impurity, appears in the Holiness Code (roughly Leviticus 17–27). Jonathan Klawans, "Idolatry, Incest, and Impurity: Moral Defilement in Ancient Judaism," *JSJ* 29 (1998): 391–415, esp. 396.

10. In my reconstruction, I have included the assigned verse numbers so you can see where the later additions are removed. The footnotes give explanations for why I made some redactional decisions. The reconstruction is intended to be read through.

11. My reconstruction most closely parallels that of Kuenen ("Beiträge zur Hexateuchkritik," 255–76).

12. The use of this verb דבק is the same one used in Gen. 2:24. These texts are likely related compositionally (traditionally identified as J). This may be this narrator's way of understanding and explaining male/female coupling.

¹⁴ And they said to them, "We are unable to do this thing, to give our sister to a man who is 'with foreskin'¹³ because it is a shame [חרפה] for us."...
¹⁹ And the young man did not tarry to do the thing because of his desire for the daughter of Jacob. And he was honored of all the house of his father....
²⁶ But...Shechem they killed...and they took Dinah from the house of Shechem and went out.

The reconstructed text reads pretty smoothly with internal narrative coherence, except for the last verse, which is a somewhat surprising turn of events. Crucial to understanding the original narrative as one of social shame is the accurate translation of Shechem's actions. I have argued elsewhere that the verb ענה (*piel*), which is often translated "rape" in this context and others,¹⁴ does not mean rape, but instead indicates some kind of social debasement, frequently associated with sex.¹⁵ This verb should be understood as "lower, debase, dishonor, humiliate," similar to its use in Gen. 16:6: "And Abram said to Sarai, 'Behold, your handmaid is in your hand, do to her as seems fit in your eyes,' and Sarai debased her [ותענה], and she fled from before her." It is a verb that deals with social status rather than forced sexual intercourse. In contexts involving sex, the coupling is problematic in some way, usually involving illicit sexual activity, but not necessarily coercive. The most important prooftexts that lead to the proper translation of the verb, but likely also contribute to its misunderstanding as "rape," are found in laws in Deuteronomy 21 and 22 that outline various illicit and licit sexual couplings, and the punishments for illegal activity. Several of these laws include acts of ענה.¹⁶

13. I.e., "uncircumcised." Literally, "has foreskin." This is a different expression from the later narrative, where it uses *niphal* forms of √מול.

14. Such translations of ענה in Gen. 34:2 include NJPS, NRSV, NAB "by force"; KJV "defiled"; NIV "violated"; NJB "forced"; Vulgate, *opprimens* "ravishing."

15. Alison L. Joseph, "Understanding Genesis 34:2: *'Innâ*," *VT* 66 (2016): 663–8. For contextual uses of ענה in the *piel* with a woman as object that indicate "debasement," see: Gen. 16:6, 9; Deut. 21:11-14; 22:23-24, 28-29; significantly, it is not used in Deut. 22:25-27, a clear example of coercive sex, in which only the man is punished. Also see Hilary Lipka, *Sexual Transgression in the Hebrew Bible* (Sheffield: Sheffield Phoenix, 2006), 87, and Erhard Gerstenberger, "ענה," *TDOT* 11:230–52.

16. Deut. 21:11-14, the law of the captive: A man may marry a captive of war, but cannot enslave her because he has already *'innâ*-ed ("lowered, dishonored") her; Deut. 22:23-24: If a man has sex with (שכב עם) a virgin betrothed to another man in a city, they are both punished (stoned) because she did not cry out (implying consent), and he "debased" (ענה) another man's wife. This is not about forced sex, but adultery; Deut. 22:25-27: If a man meets a virgin betrothed to another in an open field, and takes hold of her (החזיק ב) to have illicit sex with her (שכב עם), only he is punished by death for rape. In this verse, a case of rape, ענה is not used.

In this society, Dinah's voice in extending consent is not important, or even necessary. She does not have sexual autonomy. The shame is not Dinah's shame, but the shame of her male protectors. Without their consent, Shechem acts as if no man speaks for her or protects her virginity. This is not uncommon, as Hilary Lipka argues: "in cultures in which women do not have any legal agency or autonomy[,] sexual assault against women is viewed as the violation of the rights of possession held by the woman's guardian…. [S]anctions [are often] in the form of repayment of property damages."[17] Such a situation would seem culturally applicable to ancient Israel.

While the brothers burn with anger (ויחר), they are not enraged because of rape, abduction, or any kind of violence, but "because an insult [נבלה] had been done…to lie with the daughter of Jacob, for such is not done [וכן לא יעשה]" (Gen. 34:7). The term נבלה, as Anthony Phillips argues, is "not a term reserved for sexual offences of a particularly abhorrent kind. Rather *nebalah* is a general expression for serious disorderly and unruly action resulting in the breakup of an existing relationship whether between tribes, within the family, in a business arrangement, in marriage or with God."[18] This is an offense of "crossing the line," threatening a relationship status quo.

When the brothers describe Shechem's actions as something that "is not done," they suggest not a legal but a social violation. Other contexts where לא יעשה appears as a reference about custom include Abimelech accusing Abraham of passing off Sarah as his sister, because perhaps they might have done something to her that must not be done (Gen. 20:9), Laban in giving Leah to Jacob before Rachel, because it is not done to marry the younger before the elder (Gen. 29:26), and even in 2 Sam. 13:12, when Tamar protests such a thing is not done—her objection does not seem to be to rape or to incest, but to premarital (negotiation) sex. Her next sentence is that she would be shamed and the king, their father, would certainly agree to the match.[19] While analogizing the custom of not marrying a younger daughter before the elder to what happens to Dinah may be incongruent to our modern sensibilities, these words are spoken by the brothers, highlighting their perception of the act and its ramifications.

---

17. Lipka, *Sexual Transgression*, 24.
18. Anthony Phillips, "Nebalah: A Term for Serious Disorderly and Unruly Conduct," *VT* 25 (1975): 237–42, here 241.
19. Phillips, "Nebalah," 238.

The offense that ought not be done is ambiguous. Perhaps it is that no one should sleep with the daughter of Jacob without their permission or that Shechem is uncircumcised, and it would be reprehensible, as in verse 14, to marry their sister to an uncircumcised man. Given the resolution to the story, it is unclear whether their objection to an uncircumcised man is a legitimate concern, or whether, from the beginning, it is part of their ruse to weaken Shechem so that it will be easier to kill him. Shechem seems to understand their shame and request, as he complies, but it is unclear if their "shame" were ever their real motivation, or just an excuse to set their plan in motion.[20]

The language of shame and honor is used throughout the narrative (Gen. 34:2, 7, 19). It is shameful for the brothers not to be able to control and choose the sexual partner of their sister. Sexual norms were not governed by concepts of virginal purity as modern sexual values often are, but instead, "If the sexual act is prohibited…it is because of the danger it poses to society at the level of cooperation within the community, in that the sexual act is perceived as highly destructive to the bonds necessary to hold the community together."[21] Culturally speaking, sanctions are imposed to avoid conflicts, in order to prevent sexual transgression and resolve situations when they occur.[22] Here, the threat posed is to their societal boundaries. Tikva Frymer-Kensky argues that "Israel acts to ensure that sexuality serves the purpose of the polis; that it be a force for the preservation of the social order, and that it be prevented from disturbing social relationships."[23]

---

20. Yitzhaq Feder highlights "the phallic justice linking Shechem's crime to his retribution…. [T]he only other source which refers to a מהר ('bride-price') aside from Genesis 34 and the law of seduction in Exod. 22:15-16[, is] 1 Sam. 18:25-27, [where] King Saul devises a ploy to kill off David at the hands of Philistines by demanding a bride-price of a hundred Philistine foreskins to become a suitor for the king's daughter…. [W]hereas the bride-price of Philistine foreskins was taken by force (after their killing, one presumes), Shechem in his naïve enthusiasm voluntarily agrees to pay any מהר Jacob's sons may require. For this lack of foresight, he not only pays with his foreskin but also leads his fellow villagers to the same demise as David's Philistine victims." Yitzhaq Feder, "The Defilement of Dina: Uncontrolled Passions, Textual Violence, and the Search for Moral Foundations," *BibInt* 24 (2016): 281–309, here 292–3.

21. Lipka, *Sexual Transgression*, 39.

22. Lipka, *Sexual Transgression*, 24.

23. Tikva Frymer-Kensky, *In the Wake of the Goddesses: Women, Culture, and the Biblical Transformation of Pagan Myth* (New York: Ballantine, 1992), 189.

As such, control of women's sexuality was important to maintaining honor and even safety, so Jacob and his sons were rightly upset (Gen. 34:7) at the denial of their ability to consent to the sexual coupling of Dinah, yet honor could be restored. The law in Deut. 22:28-29 (and Exod. 22:15-16), sometimes called "The Law of the Rapist," provides for such situations: "If a man comes upon a virgin who is not engaged and he seizes her and lies with her, and they are discovered, the man who lay with her shall pay the girl's father fifty shekels of silver, and she shall be his wife. Because he has debased her, he can never send her away."[24] This law may have been an option in Dinah's situation, a way of rectifying the fallen honor of the family. The man (Shechem) would be obligated to pay the father (Jacob) and marry the woman (Dinah) without the ability to divorce her.

While socially acceptable and perhaps even advantageous, the sons of Jacob do not believe that any price can rehabilitate the honor taken from them and their damaged reputations. This is not concern that Dinah would gain a reputation as sexually promiscuous, but that they are unable to protect their women/clan. Instead, they take it upon themselves to restore honor in an act of "flexing their muscles." They kill Shechem, sending the message to his city that they will not be put into a position that does not allow them to control the sexuality of their women, where they are forced to accept as husbands men who have sex with their women and ענה them, as per the law of Deut. 22:28-29. The issue at hand is one of clan safety and well-being. Dinah's mating with Shechem was a great danger to Jacob's family because it threatened the ability of the men to control the sexuality of their women.

What is at stake in reading this earlier version and how might it have functioned, without the later rewrite, as in the MT? The wrong done them is mostly social. They have been *'innâ*-ed, "debased" because of this act against their sister. In this version, Jacob's hesitation to act is missing and the brothers are the ones who look bad. Without the language of holy war, the brothers' deception is nefarious; they appear to renege on what seemed to be a negotiation in good faith, for a resolution that would have been culturally appropriate. While their duplicity is indicated before they speak, they are culpable for it. They make an agreement, and Shechem complies

---

24. Similarly, in Exod. 22:15-16, the father can refuse the man, but he must still pay the 50 shekels of silver: "If a man seduces a virgin for whom the bride-price has not been paid, and lies with her, he must make her his wife by payment of a bride-price. If her father refuses to give her to him, he must still weigh out silver in accordance with the bride-price for virgins."

post-haste. In this version, Shechem is almost sympathetic, especially when read with the parallels in 2 Samuel 13, contrasting his response to that of Amnon.[25] The brothers violate the agreement, killing Shechem anyway and taking Dinah from his house. The disjunctive syntax in verse 26 is telling, especially if it originally followed directly after Gen. 34:19: "And the young man did not tarry to do the thing because of his desire for the daughter of Jacob… But Shechem…they killed" (Gen. 34:19, 26). Shechem held up his side of the bargain, *but* they killed him anyway.

In this version, while not necessarily supportive of it, the issue is not intermarriage. There is some shame expressed towards an uncircumcised husband, but this can be rectified by performing circumcision. The issue is not ethnic/racial. This is consistent of the collection of non-Priestly texts. In the early narratives, there seems to be a silent acceptance of intermarriage, but at the same time the inheritors of the promise are only the products of endogamous or like marriages.[26]

---

25. Feder, "The Defilement of Dina," 286. While after the sex act, Shechem's "self clung to" Dinah and "loved" her (ותדבק נפשו...ויאהב; Gen. 34:3), Amnon is disgusted by Tamar (וישנאה אמנון שנאה גדולה מאד כי גדולה השנאה אשר שנאה מאהבה אשר אהבה, "And Amnon hated her with a great hatred, for greater was the hatred with which he hated her than the love with which he had loved her"; 2 Sam. 13:15).

26. After the death of Sarah, Abraham takes another wife, Keturah. We know nothing of her background, but assume, since it is not mentioned, that she is not part of the family. There is no judgment against Abraham or Keturah for this marriage. Similarly, any concern with the appropriateness of Hagar as a second wife has nothing to do with her Egyptian-ness, but only of the drama that ensues between her and Sarah. Yet, in the case of the offspring of both these matches, the children are considered separate from, and less than, Isaac, the product of Abraham's endogamous marriage to Sarah. Similarly, Judah in Genesis 38 takes a Canaanite wife. Unless you consider the merit of the offspring of that union, Ur who was רע, and is struck down, and Onan, who does not fulfill his levirate obligation and is also struck down, as implicit critique of Judah's Canaanite wife, the text reserves negative judgment on the union. Still, the inheritor of the promise, and ancestor of King David, does not derive from Judah's Canaanite wife. Instead, he is the product of Judah's union with Tamar, whose origin is unspoken, but she is not explicitly Canaanite. Similarly, Joseph marries an Egyptian woman, Asenath daughter of Potiphera. There is no critique and perhaps there is even praise. Following the statement that Pharaoh gave Asenath to Joseph, the text reports that Joseph gained authority over the land of Egypt. In Gen. 41:45, the *waw*-conversive construct, at least implicitly, hints at the causative connection between Pharaoh giving him Asenath (ויתן לו את אסנת) and Joseph gaining authority over the land (ויצא יוסף על ארץ מצרים). So while in the early version of the patriarchal narratives there is no explicit celebration of exogamous marriages, censure of them is limited.

A Postexilic Response

A reader of this early text may have had concerns about Jacob's behavior. He does not speak or act. The characters of the story, Dinah and the brothers, are identified as the daughter (Gen. 34:3, 7, 19) and sons of Jacob (vv. 7, 13), but Jacob is silent. Did he agree with the brothers' plan—either genuinely or also with duplicity? Does he enter into marriage negotiations as recommended in Deut. 22:28-29, to marry his daughter to the man who deflowered her? Was this his attempt to renew honor? And especially, a later reader would have a serious concern with a text that allows or even advocates for intermarriage.

I am suggesting that postexilic scribes, associated with the priestly class,[27] would have had major difficulties with this text and attempted to rewrite it to align with their theological perspectives, which would see exogamy as a serious offense. In late biblical literature, particularly the Ezra tradition, intermarriage and group identity are central themes.[28] In particular, Ezra 9–10 and Nehemiah 13 speak out strongly against exogamy. The returnees from exile are to divorce their foreign wives, and going forward, the people should be careful as not to give their sons and daughters to *their* daughters and sons. Status and belonging are primary. Outsiders should not be included. Similarly, Deuteronomy 7 bans intermarriage and calls for a genocide of the people of the land: "And Yahweh your God will set them before you and you will smite them, utterly destroying them, do not cut a covenant with them and do not be merciful to them. And do not intermarry with them, do not give your daughters to their sons and do not take their daughters for your sons" (Deut. 7:2-3).

In order to answer some of these questions and to clear up ambiguities, another layer is added to the earlier text. The later rewrite of the text is somewhat coherent independently, but it does rely on a few details from the earlier version, like the sex act in Gen. 34:2 and the brothers' deceitful speech in verse 13. I indicate that in italics, but the rest can mostly stand alone and still make sense. Most of the linguistic evidence supporting my redactional decisions is in the footnotes. I am not sure whether this circulated on its own. My intuition is that it is a corrective, but it does read well enough independently. Yet, it is also possible that the stories could have existed independently, based on a shared *Vorlage* or tradition.[29]

---

27. I am not advocating a particular author but am referring to a larger school of thought. This version reflects the traits and interests of priests.

28. Klawans, "Idolatry, Incest, and Impurity," 398–401.

29. If the two versions did circulate independently that would still imply that both reflect, in some way, a common story, which they represent in differing ways. The

¹ [*And Dinah, daughter of*] Leah whom she bore to³⁰ [*Jacob*]...
² [*And Shechem son of Hamor, the Hivite,*] prince³¹ of the land, [*saw her and he took her, and he lay with her, and he debased her...*]
⁴ And Shechem said to Hamor his father, saying "acquire for me this girl³² as a wife." ⁵ (When Jacob heard that he had <u>defiled</u> [טמא] Dinah his daughter, his sons were in the field with his flocks but Jacob remained quiet until they came [back].) ⁶ And Hamor, father of Shechem, went out to Jacob to speak with him... ⁸ And Hamor spoke with them, saying: "Shechem, my son, is in love with your [pl.] daughter. Give [pl.] her to him as a wife. ⁹ And intermarry with us. You shall give us your daughters and you will take our daughters. ¹⁰ And you will dwell with us and the land will be before us. Settle and pass through it as shepherds and take possession³³ of it."...
¹³ [*And sons of Jacob answered Shechem and*] Hamor [*and with deception they spoke*] because he <u>defiled</u> Dinah their sister... ¹⁵ "Only on this [condition] will we agree³⁴ with you. If you will become like us, circumcising yourselves every male. ¹⁶ And then we will give our daughters to you and we will take for ourselves your daughters. And we will dwell with you and we will be as one people. ¹⁷ And if you do not heed us to circumcise, then we will take our daughter³⁵ and go." ¹⁸ And their words seemed good in the eyes of Hamor...

possibility that the Priestly or post-Priestly form of the story might have circulated independently of the non-Priestly form would not affect whether it is a product of reception, but only whether the text received by the later redactor is the same one that it has been combined with or something no longer extant.

30. Priestly writers like this kind of genealogical detail, especially in the Jacob cycle, cf. Gen. 35:23-25; 36:2-5, 12-15, 17. It also connects Dinah more closely with Simeon and Levi, also borne by Leah, who figure prominently later in the narrative.

31. נשיא is a priestly word. Found also in Gen. 23:6, Lev. 4:22, many times in Numbers 7, 25, 34, and elsewhere (Rofé, "Defilement of Virgins," 373).

32. This is the singular use of ילדה in the narrative. Everywhere else she is referred to as נערה. ילדה, as "young woman" rather than "girl" as indicated here, is expected in LBH, cf. Zech. 8:5, and Joel 4:3 (Rofé, "Defilement of Virgins," 373).

33. The *niphal* of √אחז is priestly diction. Also found in Gen. 47:27 and Num. 32:30, also priestly-related texts, and Josh. 22:9, 19 (Rofé, "Defilement of Virgins," 373).

34. This word, the *niphal* of √אות, meaning "to consent, be agreed," is a late word. It appears only in Gen. 34:15, 22 and 2 Kgs 12:9 but is common in post-biblical literature (Rofé, "Defilement of Virgins," 373).

35. Here in direct speech, the brothers refer to Dinah as "daughter." In v. 14, part of the early story, they speak of her as "sister." Can this be an indicator of the different hands that wrote the direct speech and put it in the mouths of the brothers?

²⁰ And Hamor…came to the gate of [the] city, and [he] spoke to the men of [the] city, saying: ²¹ "These men are peaceful with us. Let them settle in the land, and pass through it as shepherds and behold, the land is wide before them, and their daughters, let us take for ourselves as wives, and our daughters, let us give to them. ²² But, only on this [condition] will the men agree with us to dwell with us, to become one nation, by circumcising every male for ourselves, because they are circumcised. ²³ Their flocks and their possession and all their animals—will they not be for us, only let us agree with them and they will live with us." ²⁴ And all who went out to the gate of his city heeded Hamor…³⁶ and every male was circumcised, all who went out to the gate of his city. ²⁵ And it came to pass on the third day, when they were in pain,…brothers of Dinah, each man took his sword and came to the city undisturbed, and they killed every male. ²⁶ …by the sword…
²⁷ The sons of Jacob came upon the slain and they plundered the city because they had <u>defiled</u> their sister. ²⁸ Their flocks and oxen and donkeys and all that was in the city and in the field they took. ²⁹ And all their wealth and their children and their wives they captured and they plundered and all that was in the house. ³⁰ And Jacob said to [them]…"You have brought ruin upon me and disrepute among the inhabitants of the land, the Canaanites and Perizzites.³⁷ But as for me, I am few in number and they will gather upon me and smite me, and I will be annihilated, me and my house." ³¹ And they said, "Should he make our sister like a prostitute?"

In this version, rather than an individual marriage negotiation of Shechem for Dinah, Hamor negotiates for the communal inter-marrying of the two clans, a request of connubium (marriage connections) that would be used to create (or prevent) alliances between tribal groups. The text's response to this suggestion is serious. The coupling of Shechem and Dinah is not a "debasement" (Gen. 34:2) or even an "insult," that overturns the social order (Gen. 34:7), but one of טמא, "defilement," a legal and religious category of improper sexual behavior that carries the penalty of death. This is a term that belongs exclusively to priestly diction.³⁸ In verses 5, 13, and 27, the narrator categorizes the sexual act as טמא, "defilement."

---

36. The final text says they "heeded Hamor and Shechem, his son." I wonder if "Shechem" is added here at an even later moment, as a gloss attempting to integrate the two versions. Just as the two men, Hamor and Shechem, appear at the negotiations with Jacob and his sons, they go together to speak with the men at the gate.

37. The inclusion of the Canaanites and Perizzites is somewhat awkward and may be a gloss of the "inhabitants of the land" (Gunkel, *Genesis*, 365).

38. Rofé, "Defilement of Virgins," 369; Lipka, *Sexual Transgression*, 250–1; Klawans, "Idolatry, Incest, and Impurity," 391–402; G. André, "טמא," *TDOT* 5:330–42.

טמא, when connected to illicit sexual acts, is a capital crime. "Defilement" occurs in both ritual impurity (mostly in P) and impurity brought on by willful transgressive acts (mostly H).[39]

The example of the *Sotah* in Num. 5:11-31, where the root טמא is used no fewer than seven times, is a serious accusation of adultery. A woman who has committed adultery is considered to have "defiled herself." Also, in Leviticus 18 and 20, the long list of illicit sexual acts and couplings are also considered acts that make one טמא. The punishment is death. Adultery is included on this list. These acts are also connected with the sexual practices of the nations (Lev. 18:24) who have "defiled" the land, resulting in their removal from it by Israel. The people of Israel are warned that if they defile themselves, they too will be "vomited out" of the land (Lev. 18:27-28). Similarly, in Ezekiel (also priestly related) illicit sex acts are defiling and are considered capital crimes. These specifically refer to defiling a neighbor's wife (adultery, Ezek. 18:6), and other improper matches (Ezek. 22:11). The ideology is clear; intermarriage is not to be ignored and should be punished with death. According to Feder, "The rejection of intermarriage is unconditional. Ultimately, the rejection of intermarriage is explainable only in terms of pollution, by the fact that Shechem *defiled* Dinah."[40]

Unlike the earlier version, the narrator seems to silently admonish Jacob. In Gen. 34:5, Jacob hears what happened to Dinah, but the brothers are out and he "remains quiet until they came [back]." While not an explicit rebuke, Jacob's inaction does not speak well of him. This is coupled with his objection at the end of the narrative (Gen. 34:30), when he accuses the brothers of having brought ruin on his house and making him vulnerable to neighboring tribes. The negative portrayal of the passive and self-concerned Jacob contributes to the positive picture of the brothers. They are extremely active, taking steps to respond to Shechem's illicit sexual coupling.

This rewrite is not just about Shechem and Dinah, but also all the children of Jacob and Hamor. In this version, Hamor, on his son's behalf, initiates and controls the marriage negotiations. While he addresses both Jacob and his sons, as indicated by the plural אתם and בבתכם and the verb תנו in verse 8, this is a conversation "patriarch to patriarch." Hamor's request in verse 8 is almost verbatim to Shechem's request in the end of verse 12: "Give [pl.] her to him as a wife." But Hamor continues, not only negotiating for his biological son, but also for all the sons of the city.

---

39. Lipka, *Sexual Transgression*, 49.
40. Feder, "The Defilement of Dina," 298.

Hamor offers connubium, an alliance that will make them as one people. It is significant that Hamor speaks the same words in Gen. 34:9 that were used in the prohibition in Deut. 7:2-3,[41] triggering in the mind of the reader the necessity of the brothers' response.

Given the suggestion of connubium, it makes sense that the brothers respond that to become one people, mixing together, they must not retain any individualizing characteristics, including physical ones. In this way, the brothers offer one condition, "become like us, circumcising yourselves every male. And then we will give our daughters to you and we will take for ourselves your daughters. And we will dwell with you and we will be as one people" (Gen. 34:15-16). The alternative is that they will take Dinah and leave.

Intermarriage is not the only offense that calls for mass annihilation. The later narrator adds into the killing of Shechem the words לפי חרב, "by the sword." This is the language of war. This term is used in Deuteronomy, Joshua, and elsewhere in the laws of extermination, both in wiping out idol worshippers and in war against enemies who do not submit peacefully. To put a town "*to the sword*, [meant] utterly destroying it and everything in it—even putting its livestock to the sword" (Deut. 13:16). This is ideological, not just retaliation for a personal (or communal) wrong.

The later revision uses a vocabulary of sexual defilement punishable by death, mass genocide, and the laws of war to rewrite the Dinah story. By continually naming Shechem's sexual intercourse (or planned marriage) with Dinah as defilement (Gen. 34:5, 13, 27), this reader transforms an offense to the honor of the house of Jacob into an illicit sex act that demands capital punishment. Shechem should be killed for defiling their sister as the adulterer is killed for defiling the wife of another man (Lev. 18:20). The term טמא is used throughout the priestly corpus to refer to a state of impurity.[42]

The defilement here is largely a moral issue, relying on the role of disgust and notions of pollution, which Yitzhaq Feder highlights as "mechanisms for distinguishing the 'pure' in-group from the 'polluting' out-group."[43] Circumcision, beginning in Genesis 17, is a mark of identity, of being part of the in-group. The uncircumcised are set up as Other. Yet, in this narrative, the act of circumcision is not enough to erase the differences between Us (the Jacobites) and Them (the Shechemites).

---

41. The identical language may be an indicator that the text is post-Priestly, presuming knowledge of Deuteronomy.
42. Lipka, *Sexual Transgression*, 250.
43. Feder, "The Defilement of Dina," 297.

Redaction as Reception

A later, likely postexilic, priestly influenced audience read the early version. It was uncomfortable with, or better, disturbed by, the possibility of intermarriage that social convention might support (as in Deuteronomy 22/Exodus 22). Also, Jacob looked good while the brothers who opposed intermarriage looked bad. These readers, in their historical context, were concerned with defining Jewish identity with strong prohibitions against intermarriage, similar to Ezra and Nehemiah.[44] Intermarriage is not just a social offense that can be rectified by post-consummation bridal negotiations and marriage, or even circumcision, but instead is an act of defilement, one which calls for capital punishment. In this version, Jacob is censured for his lack of action; when he rebukes the brothers' deeds, they accuse him of a willingness to make Dinah like a prostitute, trading her sexually for an alliance with Hamor and his people.[45]

The scholarly trend to move away from focus on the "final form" leads us to consider the process of reception and composition. In *Seconding Sinai*, Hindy Najman argues that "to rework an earlier text is to update, interpret and develop the content of that text in a way that one claims to be an authentic expression of the law already accepted as authoritatively Mosaic."[46] Her suggestion that "by reworking and expanding older traditions through interpretation, a new text claims for itself the authority that already attaches to those traditions"[47] is applicable here. By reworking and expanding this earlier tradition about the potential marriage of Dinah and Shechem, the postexilic readers/(re)writers/redactors make clear their stance against intermarriage, "Don't do it!," with the most explicit and extreme consequences. The issue is not resolvable, as in the earlier version. The potential coupling with a non-Jacobite is polluting. The Otherness of Shechem is inviolable.

---

44. Rofé, "Defilement of Virgins."

45. Some readers will argue that the rebuke of Simeon and Levi in Gen. 49:5-7 is an implicit judgment against the brothers and their actions, but we do not need to read Genesis 34 with Genesis 49. Furthermore, I view the singling out of Simeon and Levi among the brothers in Gen. 34:25 as an even later addition to the text, likely a literary response to their treatment in Jacob's blessing in Gen. 49:5-7, and therefore did not include it in my reconstruction of the postexilic version.

46. Hindy Najman, *Seconding Sinai: The Development of Mosaic Discourse in Second Temple Judaism*, JSJSup 77 (Leiden: Brill, 2003), 13.

47. Najman, *Seconding Sinai*, 16.

Similarly, in his *Deuteronomy and the Hermeneutics of Legal Innovation*, Bernard Levinson argues that the authors of the deuteronomic law code "drew on and transformed earlier literary sources in order to mandate a major transformation of religion and society in ancient Israel."[48] This was the innovation of centralization. He describes the work of the Deuteronomist as "transformative exegesis": in reading and interpreting, he attempts to "reform" and innovate.[49] This is, in part, what is happening in Genesis 34.

The value of considering redaction as reception highlights different questions from a traditional redactional approach. Specifically: Why would a redactor include more than one text, especially if the goal is to subvert the earlier text? The Pentateuch especially is filled with doublets or even triplets of the same or similar stories. Levinson suggests, in the case of the Deuteronomist, that even while Dtr wanted to replace the Covenant Code with his own law code, he was still a little uncomfortable with such a revolutionary enterprise. As such, Dtr's work "suggests an extraordinary ambivalence on the part of the authors of Deuteronomy."[50] Najman critiques Levinson by challenging, "If one intends to *replace* an earlier code, why should one exert so much effort to incorporate and preserve its wording? Why should one constantly remind the reader of the earlier text, already accepted as authoritative, which one wishes to supplant? Would these constant reminders not be self-defeating?"[51]

This seems a relevant challenge for the compositional history of Genesis 34. The postexilic readers are troubled by elements of the narrative, and rewrite it to resolve some of their unease, as well as to promote their own theological perspectives, including the strict prohibitions against intermarriage. This is not unique to Genesis 34. There are other intermarriage stories in Genesis where the perspective is doubled. In many cases, the doublets stand together. For example, in Genesis 27, there are two reasons given for the flight of Jacob to Paddan-Aram following his theft of Esau's blessing. The two motives reflect two source traditions that are integrated at a later stage of redaction. The first impetus is to seek refuge from Esau's blood lust, expressed in verses 41-45. The second is articulated in Rebekah's fear that Jacob will marry a local Hittite woman in verse 46. In these stories, the later narratives function as a counter-memory or

---

48. Bernard M. Levinson, *Deuteronomy and the Hermeneutics of Legal Innovation* (New York: Oxford University Press, 1997), vii.
49. Levinson, *Hermeneutics*, 6.
50. Levinson, *Hermeneutics*, 46.
51. Najman, *Seconding Sinai*, 22–3 (italics in original).

alternative to the non-Priestly narrative. In the earlier period, exogamous marriages may have been tolerated, but not so in the exilic and postexilic periods. You may have thought that Jacob travels to Paddan-Aram to escape his brother's anger, but no, the priestly writers tell us, it is so that he can find a proper, endogamous wife.[52] Yes, we see a conflict in answering the question, Why does Jacob flee Canaan: to escape Esau or find a proper bride? But these two reasons are not mutually exclusive.

The tendency of a double explanation happens frequently in Kings, where a theological explanation is juxtaposed with a historical-political account of an event (e.g., the rationale for the split of the kingdom: Solomon's apostasy in 1 Kings 11 and Rehoboam's refusal to lessen the corvée labor in 1 Kings 12).[53] But we have to ask: Why does the redactor of Genesis 34 preserve the earlier version of the story, if the goal was to subvert it? I do not have a good answer to this question. One possibility is that the redactor is a third party, an inheritor of two independent traditions, who attempts to preserve both, but this undermines the overall argument of reception. This would lean toward a theory that the two versions were originally independent. A second option is one I explore in my work on Kings, that this has something to do with the collective memory, an anticipation of what the audience expects to be included (e.g., how could you have a history of David that did not include the giant slaying, even if it were viewed as mythic?). But I am not sure how relevant this is for Genesis 34, because the unique perspective of the early version of the narrative is only clear when you deconstruct the chapter. Also, the details are not really in conflict, prompting a redactor to integrate and preserve both, for example whether the flood lasted 40 or 150 days (Gen. 7:12, 24), or whether Noah took one pair or seven pairs of animals into the ark (Gen. 6:19-20; 7:2-3).

---

52. The desire for in-marriage is so strongly expressed by these writers that even Esau, who later becomes an outsider, is included. In Gen. 28:6-9, Esau sees that Isaac sent Jacob to Paddan-Aram and that his parents do not like the Canaanite women, so he takes it upon himself to find a wife among the daughters of Ishmael, "keeping it in the family." It is likely that this part of the narrative belongs to the same compositional strata as 27:46–28:5, and it is only in a later redaction that Esau is "excluded" from the line by marrying the Hittite women who "made life bitter for Isaac and Rebekah" in Gen. 26:34.

53. Alison L. Joseph, *Portrait of the Kings: The Davidic Prototype in Deuteronomistic Poetics* (Minneapolis: Fortress, 2015), 50–3, 71–4; Yairah Amit, "The Dual Causality Principle and its Effects on Biblical Literature," *VT* 37 (1987): 385–400.

A possible resolution may be that this is not really a helpful question. Instead, we should consider, as Breed suggests, the value of reception criticism: "Reception history can lead biblical scholars to ask instead, 'How might this text function? What can it do? What powers does it have, and how might these powers function in various settings?'"[54] The rewriting of this text responds to the needs of the postexilic community, similar to the narratives in Ezra and Nehemiah, offering an example to the returnees of the seriousness of intermarriage. It also offers an alternative to the entirety of the patriarchal narratives. In case the Israelites thought they could intermarry like Abraham, Judah, and Joseph, this text serves as a powerful corrective.

Some of the difficulties in the text for readers remain, even within the revised version. Genesis 34 has an active "afterlife." These concerns and others are taken up in the interpretation of some of the Second Temple literature. The story is again rewritten in *Jubilees* 30, the *Testament of Levi*, and elsewhere. These texts respond to some of the same issues and questions as those of the postexilic reader—the attitude towards intermarriage, Jacob's role/position, with additional concerns about using the sign of the covenant as a murder weapon, the primacy of Levi over Simeon, and the ethical concern of whether the Shechemites as a collective deserved such a harsh punishment.[55] More frequently, these are the texts that are seen as biblical "reception history," "rewritten" Bibles like *Jubilees* and the Temple Scroll, but, just as Najman describes, these texts

> responded to both the demand for interpretation and the demand for demonstration of authority: On the one hand, they retold biblical stories in ways that resolved apparent inconsistencies or solved puzzles for their readers. On the other hand, they wove their own versions of law, temple ritual, calendrical system and covenant, along with the words of already authoritative traditions, into a single seamless whole. Thus they claimed, for their interpretations of authoritative texts, the already established authority of the texts themselves.[56]

---

54. Brennan W. Breed, "Nomadology of the Bible: A Processual Approach to Biblical Reception History," *BibRec* 1 (2012): 299–320, here 313.

55. James [L.] Kugel, "The Story of Dinah in the *Testament of Levi*," *HTR* 85 (1992): 1–34; Michael Segal, "Rewriting the Story of Dinah and Shechem: The Literary Development of Jubilees 30," in *The Hebrew Bible in Light of the Dead Sea Scrolls*, ed. Norá Dávid et al., FRLANT 239 (Göttingen: Vandenhoeck & Ruprecht, 2011), 337–56; Louis H. Feldman, "Philo, Pseudo-Philo, Josephus, and Theodotus on the Rape of Dinah," *JQR* 94 (2004): 253–77.

56. Najman, *Seconding Sinai*, 45.

This seems to be what happens in Genesis 34. It is possible to apply this same enterprise that Najman describes at an earlier level of composition.

In conclusion, while the reconstruction of earlier stages of textual production is necessarily speculative, the questions of reception history can be fruitful for redactional studies. When we separate a text into its redactional layers and conjecture what kind of base-text may stand behind them, we can gain new insights into the meaning and development of the text by paying closer attention to the ways in which perceptions of identity and Otherness might have shaped the redactor's work. In the case of Genesis 34, growing opposition to "foreign" intermarriage in the postexilic period appears to have motivated a secondary rewriting of the text in order to more clearly emphasize the contrast between Us and the Other. The success of the corrective, the polluting power of Otherness as transmitted through the defilement of Dinah, is clear in the evaluation of Dinah in the subsequent reception of the story in the midrash. For example, *Gen. Rab.* 80:11 identifies Dinah as the "Canaanite woman" who mothered a son for Simeon in Gen. 46:10.[57] Dinah, the daughter of Jacob, through her defilement, has become completely Othered, so much so that she has become a Canaanite herself.

---

57. Alison L. Joseph, "Who Is the Victim in the Dinah Story?," *TheTorah.com*, 30 November 2017, http://thetorah.com/who-is-the-victim-in-the-dinah-story/.

Between Our Ancestors and the Other: Negotiating Identity in the Early Reception of the Water from the Rock

Ken Brown

There is an organic continuity between the development of the biblical texts and their reception, reflected in comparable compositional and editorial methods employed in each.[1] This essay explores one aspect of that continuity: the ways in which the rewriting and retelling of earlier biblical texts forge links between the characters the texts describe, and the (social) identities of later audiences. It will focus on the postexilic and Second Temple periods (ca. sixth century BCE through the first century CE), during which questions of identity formation and maintenance played a major role in shaping "Jewish" as well as "Christian" culture and literature.[2]

---

1. Molly Zahn has challenged the distinction between "biblical" and "non-biblical" in Second Temple period Judaism, suggesting that a more relevant distinction should be drawn between "revision" and "reuse"; Molly M. Zahn, "Innerbiblical Exegesis: The View from Beyond the Bible," in *The Formation of the Pentateuch: Bridging the Academic Cultures of Europe, Israel, and North America*, ed. Jan C. Gertz et al., FAT 111 (Tübingen: Mohr Siebeck, 2016), 107–20; cf. also Zahn, *Rethinking Rewritten Scripture: Composition and Exegesis in the 4QReworked Pentateuch Manuscripts*, STDJ 95 (Leiden: Brill, 2011). But "revision" and "reuse" cannot always be cleanly distinguished either, and both continued long after the end of antiquity; cf. Hindy Najman, "The Vitality of Scripture Within and Beyond the 'Canon'," *JSJ* 43 (2012): 497–518; Brennan W. Breed, *Nomadic Text: A Theory of Biblical Reception History* (Bloomington: Indiana University Press, 2014); Eva Mroczek, *The Literary Imagination in Jewish Antiquity* (Oxford: Oxford University Press, 2016); Ken Brown, *The Dynamic Development of the Bible: Revision and Reception* (forthcoming).

2. These terms are to a certain degree anachronistic, in part because there was no single, unified "Judaism" during these periods, and no separate "Christianity" until near the end of them; in addition to the bibliography cited in the Introduction, n. 17,

In the aftermath of the conquest and partial exile of the kingdoms of Israel and Judah, in the eighth through the sixth centuries BCE, their survivors were forced to adapt to life under foreign rule. Both among those who remained in or eventually returned to their homelands, and among those who settled elsewhere in the diaspora, this resulted in lasting transformations in their culture and religion, and a diversification of perspectives. Sharp disputes arose over the identity of the people(s) of "Israel" and "Judah," and how they should associate with "the nations" or "the Gentiles" (i.e., others, or the Other).

One way such disputes were negotiated was through telling and retelling stories concerning "Israelites," which project the experiences and concerns of their present audiences back into the situations of "our ancestors." To illustrate that phenomenon, this essay will compare three texts that retell the story in Exodus 17 about Moses striking water from a rock in the wilderness: in Numbers 20, the Wisdom of Solomon 11, and 1 Corinthians 10. Each retells the story in distinctive ways, which draw connections between "the children of Israel" or "our ancestors" and their present audiences. Yet they reflect sharply differing assumptions about who those audiences are, which have significant consequences for how each of these texts retells the story.

Water from the Rock in Exodus and Numbers

We begin with two accounts of the water from the rock within the Pentateuch, in Exod. 17:1-7 and Num. 20:1-13. Though they appear in two different books, these passages are set within an overarching narrative in the Pentateuch as we have it, so that nearly the same story is told twice: In each, "the whole congregation" of "the children of Israel" are in or near "the desert of Sin" or "Zin," where there is no water (Exod. 17:1 // Num. 20:1-2a). In each, they complain to Moses, who goes to YHWH for

---

cf., e.g., Christine E. Hayes, *Gentile Impurities and Jewish Identities: Intermarriage and Conversion from the Bible to the Talmud* (Oxford: Oxford University Press, 2002); Lynn LiDonnici and Andrea Lieber, eds., *Heavenly Tablets: Interpretation, Identity and Tradition in Ancient Judaism*, JSJSup 119 (Leiden: Brill, 2007); Gary N. Knoppers and Kenneth A. Ristau, eds., *Community Identity in Judean Historiography: Biblical and Comparative Perspectives* (Winona Lake: Eisenbrauns, 2009); Daniel C. Harlow et al., eds., *The "Other" in Second Temple Judaism: Essays in Honor of John J. Collins* (Grand Rapids: Eerdmans, 2011); Rainer Albertz and Jakob Wöhrle, eds., *Between Cooperation and Hostility: Multiple Identities in Ancient Judaism and the Interaction with Foreign Powers*, JAJSup 11 (Göttingen: Vandenhoeck & Ruprecht, 2013).

help (Exod. 17:2-4 // Num. 20:2b-6a). In each, Yhwh tells Moses to take a staff, and bring water out of a rock (Exod. 17:5-6a // Num. 20:6b-8). To that point, the stories are essentially parallel, with a great deal of similar or identical language. But then there is a twist: In Exodus, Yhwh *commands* Moses to strike the rock, and it is simply stated that "Moses did so, before the eyes of the elders of Israel" (Exod. 17:6). But in Numbers, Moses is not explicitly told to strike the rock, and when he does so anyway— twice—he and his brother Aaron are condemned, "because you did not trust in me, to show my holiness before the eyes of the children of Israel" (Num. 20:9-12).

This surprising combination of closely parallel stories with contrasting conclusions has led to numerous theories, both ancient and modern, regarding how they could be related. Many have seen them either as distinct accounts of two separate events,[3] or as (independent) versions of the same story.[4] The similarities are too close to be coincidental, however, including a virtually identical structure, and much parallel or verbatim wording. For instance, in both "the people quarreled with Moses" (וירב העם עם־משה; Exod. 17:2a // Num. 20:3a), and ask "why did you bring us up from Egypt?" (למה [זה] העליתנו ממצרים; Exod. 17:3c // Num. 20:5a). In both, Moses is told to "take the staff" (קח...[ה]מטה; Exod. 17:5c // Num. 20:8a), then he strikes (נכה; *hiphil*) the rock, and water pours out (ויצאו... מים; Exod. 17:6 // Num. 20:11). Finally, both refer to "Meribah" (מריבה) and conclude that "the Israelites quarreled with Yhwh" (רבו בני־ישראל את־יהוה, Num. 20:13b; cf. Exod. 17:7b, ומריבה על־ריב בני ישראל ועל נסתם את־יהוה).

---

3. This was assumed by most premodern readers, and is sometimes still defended; e.g., Timothy R. Ashley, *The Book of Numbers*, NICOT 4 (Grand Rapids: Eerdmans, 1993), 377–9.

4. Among source critics, Exod. 17:1-7* has most often been assigned to the Yhwhistic and/or Elohistic source(s), and Num. 20:1-13* to the Priestly source; cf. e.g., William H. C. Propp, *Exodus 1–18: A New Translation with Introduction and Commentary*, AB 2 (New York: Doubleday, 1998), 603–4; Baruch A. Levine, *Numbers 1–20: A New Translation with Introduction and Commentary*, AB 4 (New York: Doubleday, 1993), 483–4; Joel S. Baden, *J, E and the Redaction of the Pentateuch*, FAT 68 (Tübingen: Mohr Siebeck, 2009), 173–9, 259–61; Herbert Specht, "Die Verfehlung Moses und Aarons in Num 20,1-13* P," in *Torah and the Book of Numbers*, ed. Christian Frevel, Thomas Pola, and Aaron Schart, FAT II/62 (Tübingen: Mohr Siebeck, 2013), 273–313; see also the bibliography in Christoph Berner, "Das Wasserwunder von Rephidim (Ex 17,1-7) als Schlüsseltext eines nachpriesterschriftlichen Mosebildes," *VT* 63 (2013): 193–209, esp. 193–4 nn. 3, 6.

In light of such verbal and structural parallels, it is most likely that one of these texts has been written or edited in light of the other, and a comparison of the *differences* makes clear that the version in Numbers is more likely to be later.[5] In particular, Numbers includes several significant elements absent from Exodus that suggest secondary elaboration, including the death of Miriam (Num. 20:1), the role of Aaron (20:2, 6, 8-12), a fuller account of the Israelites' complaint (20:5) and, especially, an explicit account of Moses carrying out the miracle, followed by his and Aaron's unexpected condemnation (20:9-12).

Significantly, Numbers also adds several details that allude to the Promised Land: First, in contrast to Exod. 17:1, which states that the Israelites "camped" (חנה) at Rephidim, indicating a temporary halt, Num. 20:1 states that the Israelites "settled" (ישב) at Kadesh, using a term employed elsewhere in Numbers primarily to describe the inhabitants of the Land.[6] Most notably, it appears eleven times in the story of the spying out of the Land in Numbers 13–14, which is *also* set at Kadesh (Num. 13:26). Numbers 13–14 culminates in the Israelites' refusal to enter the Promised Land, resulting in their condemnation to die in the wilderness, so their being "settled at Kadesh" in Num. 20:1 is a direct consequence of that earlier refusal, and its mention reminds the reader of that fact.

It is therefore highly significant that when Num. 20:5 repeats nearly verbatim the Israelites' complaint from Exod. 17:3, "Why did you bring us up from Egypt?," it also adds "to bring us to this *bad* place, this is no place for seed, or *figs*, or *vines* or *pomegranates*, and there is no *water*

---

5. Accepted by, e.g., Philip J. Budd, *Numbers*, WBC 5 (Waco: Word, 1984), 216–17; Reinhard Achenbach, *Die Vollendung der Tora: Studien zur Redaktionsgeschichte des Numeribuches im Kontext von Hexateuch und Pentateuch*, BZABR 3 (Wiesbaden: Harrassowitz, 2003), 302–17; Ludwig Schmidt, "Der Stab des Mose in der vor- und nach-priesterlichen Redaktion des Pentateuch," in *Post-Priestly Pentateuch: New Perspectives on its Redactional Development and Theological Profiles*, ed. Federico Giuntoli and Konrad Schmid, FAT 101 (Tübingen: Mohr Siebeck, 2015), 253–76, esp. 261–71; Rainer Albertz, "Das Buch Numeri jenseits der Quellentheorie: Eine Redaktionsgeschichte von Num 20–24 (Teil 1)," *ZAW* 123 (2011): 171–83. Roy E. Garton argues for a partially independent process of development, but still accepts that the "final form" of Numbers has been expanded based on Exodus; see *Mirages in the Desert: The Tradition-Historical Developments of the Story of Massah-Meribah*, BZAW 492 (Berlin: de Gruyter, 2017), esp. 157–235. Specht, "Die Verfehlung Moses," 288; and Berner, "Das Wasserwunder von Rephidim," 193–209, argue that Exodus 17 is dependent on Numbers 20 rather than vice versa.

6. Cf. esp. Num. 13:18, 19, 28, 29, 32; 14:14, 25, 45; noted by Specht, "Die Verfehlung Moses," 285–8.

to drink." This alludes to the characteristic fruits of the Promised Land in Num. 13:23, where grapes, pomegranates, and figs are the three fruits brought back from the Land. It probably also alludes to Deut. 8:7-8, which offers an even closer parallel in its promise that

> YHWH your God is bringing you to a *good* land, a land with streams of *water*, with springs and underground waters welling up in valleys and hills, a land of wheat and barley, of *vines* and *figs* and *pomegranates*, a land of olive trees and honey.

By inverting this description, Num. 20:5 transforms the Israelites' complaint into a denial of the promise of the Land. Following the statement that the Israelites *settled* in the wilderness, this implies a demand that God provide them the fertility of the Land *now*, outside it.

It is in that light that the end of the story should be understood, which has also been dramatically expanded, again in direct connection with the promises concerning the Land: In Exod. 17:6, the execution of God's command is indicated only by the statement that "Moses did so" (ויעש בן משה), a standard expression for obedience.[7] By contrast, in Numbers Moses is said to have struck the rock *twice*, and is condemned for failing to "trust in me, to show my holiness..." (Num. 20:11-12). The precise nature of his (and Aaron's) sin is unclear, and has been endlessly debated,[8] but the punishment is unambiguous: to be barred from entering the Promised Land: "Therefore, you shall not bring this assembly into the land that I have given them" (Num. 20:12b). This is precisely the same punishment that the rest of the exodus generation received for refusing to enter the Land in Numbers 13–14 (cf. 14:21-23, 27-30).

Thus, if Numbers 20 is indeed a retelling of the same event reported in Exodus 17, the character of the story has been radically altered. Where Exodus focused on God's provision for his people in the wilderness, and presented Moses as the faithful servant of God, Numbers presents the Israelites' complaint as an attempt to secure the promised fertility of the Land outside it (Num. 20:5), and even condemns Moses and Aaron themselves as part of the Israelites' rebellion (Num. 20:10, 12; cf. 20:24).

---

7. Cf. Gen. 6:22; Exod. 40:16; Num. 8:3; 17:26 (ET 17:11); Judg. 6:20; 1 Kgs 20:25; Isa. 20:2; Est. 2:4.

8. Cf. Jacob Milgrom, *The JPS Torah Commentary: Numbers* במדבר (Philadelphia: Jewish Publication Society, 1990), 448–56 (Excursus 50); Jonathan P. Burnside, "Why Was Moses Banned from the Promised Land? A Radical Retelling of the Rebellions of Moses (Num 20:2-13 and Exod 2:11-15)," *ZABR* 22 (2016): 111–59.

But who would rewrite the story in this way, and why? Is all this redactional manipulation purely an intellectual exercise, or could it be meant to speak to the *present* situation of its audience, and if so, to what end? In order to gain some perspective on these questions, let us briefly consider two other rewritings of this story, which employ similar methods in retelling it, but are more explicit about why they do so.

Rewriting and Identity in the Wisdom of Solomon 11

The Wisdom of Solomon is a Greek pseudepigraphal work attributed to Solomon, though it was actually written during the late Second Temple period. The story of the water from the rock is retold in chapter 11, where it appears as the first of a series of seven antitheses in Wisdom of Solomon 11–19, each contrasting the punishments of the Egyptians at the exodus with God's provision for the Israelites in the wilderness.[9] In this case, the water from the rock is contrasted with the tainting of the Nile (Wis. 11:4-10; cf. Exod. 7:14-24; 17:1-7 LXX):

> [4] They were thirsty [διψάω], and they called upon you,
> and water [ὕδωρ] was given [δίδωμι] to them out of sharp rock [ἐκ πέτρας ἀκροτόμου],
> and quenching for their thirst [δίψος] out of hard stone.
> [5] For through that by which their enemies were punished,
> through these they received benefit in their distress.
> [6] Instead of the spring [πηγή] of an everlasting river [ποταμός],
> defiled and stirred up with blood
> [7] in rebuke for the command to slay children,
> you gave [δίδωμι] them abundant water [ὕδωρ] unexpectedly,
> [8] showing by their thirst [δίψος] at that time
> how you punished their adversaries.
> [9] For when they were tested [πειράζω],
> although they were being disciplined in mercy,
> they learned how the ungodly were tormented when judged in wrath.
> [10] For you tested these like an admonishing father,
> but you examined those [others] like a stern king passing judgment.

---

9. On the seven antitheses, see below, n. 14. On the overall structure of the Wisdom of Solomon see, e.g., David Winston, *The Wisdom of Solomon: A New Translation with Introduction and Commentary*, AB 43 (Garden City: Doubleday, 1979), 4–12; Samuel Cheon, *The Exodus Story in the Wisdom of Solomon: A Study in Biblical Interpretation*, JSPSup 23 (Sheffield: Sheffield Academic, 1997), 24–6; Sonja Ammann, *Götter für die Toren: Die Verbindung von Götterpolemik und Weisheit im Alten Testament*, BZAW 466 (Berlin: de Gruyter, 2015), 193–6.

This passage draws several terms from the Greek translation of the story in Exodus 17.[10] There is also a close verbal parallel between Wis. 11:4b (ἐκ πέτρας ἀκροτόμου ὕδωρ) and Deut. 8:15b (LXX; ἐκ πέτρας ἀκροτόμου πηγὴν ὕδατος); the one term missing, πηγή, appears in Wis. 11:6.[11] The version in Numbers 20 is apparently ignored, as no significant vocabulary is drawn from it that is not also used in Exodus 17, and there is no allusion to the punishment of Moses and Aaron.[12] On the contrary, Wisdom 11 does not condemn any of the Israelites, who are not even presented as complaining, but instead "[When] they were thirsty,…they called upon you" (Wis. 11:4). This is similar to the allusions to the story in Pss. 81:8 (LXX 80:8; ET 81:7) and 107:5-6 (LXX 106:5-6).[13] Yet Wisdom goes further, explicitly contrasting the Israelites' positive response with the wicked behavior of the Egyptians, who acted with violence and suffered unquenchable thirst. The principle is summarized in Wis. 11:5 (and cf. 11:8-10):

> For through that by which their enemies were punished,
> through these they received benefit in their distress.

10. Cf. διψάω (Wis. 11:4, 14; Exod. 17:3); ὕδωρ (Wis. 11:4, 7; Exod. 17:1, 2, 3, 6; Num. 20:2, 5, 8, 10, 11, 13; cf. Deut. 8:15); δίδωμι (Wis. 11:4, 7; Exod. 17:2; Num. 20:8); πέτρα (Wis. 11:4; Exod. 17:6; Num. 20:8, 10; cf. Deut. 8:15); δίψος (Wis. 11:4, 8; Exod. 17:3; cf. Deut. 8:15); ποταμός (Wis. 11:6; Exod. 17:5); πειράζω (Wis. 11:9; Exod. 17:2, 7). There are also verbal parallels to the tainting of the Nile in Exod. 7:14-24, including ὕδωρ (Wis. 11:4, 7; Exod. 7:15, 17, 18, 19, 20, 21, 24); λίθος (Wis. 11:4; Exod. 7:19); ποταμός (Wis. 11:6; Exod. 7:15, 17, 18, 19, 20, 21, 24, 25); αἷμα (Wis. 11:6; Exod. 7:17, 19, 20, 21); γινώσκω (Wis. 11:9; Exod. 7:17).

11. Cf. also Deut. 32:10-14, which uses similar language; e.g., παιδεύω in Wis. 11:9; Deut. 32:10; and cf. Deut. 8:5. The rock is also called ἀκρότομος in Ps. 114:8 (LXX 113:8); Ps. 135:16b (LXX; the half-verse is not present in MT 136:16); Philo, *Leg.* 2.84; *Mos.* 1.210; *Decal.* 1.16.

12. The only notable expression that could be drawn from Numbers 20, but not Exodus 17, is δαψιλὲς ὕδωρ ("abundant water") in Wis. 11:7, which would be a plausible translation of מים רבים in Num. 20:11, though it differs from the LXX (ὕδωρ πολύ). This is unlikely to be due to any ignorance of Numbers 20, however, as Wisdom retells other stories from Numbers elsewhere (e.g., Num. 21:4-9 in Wis. 16:5-14).

13. Parallels noted by Winston, *Wisdom of Solomon*, 227; Cheon, *The Exodus Story in the Wisdom of Solomon*, 32–3; the former also notes similarly positive depictions of the wilderness period in Deut. 32:10-14; Jer. 2:1-3; Hos. 2:16-17 (ET 2:14-15); 11:1; 13:4-5, but all of the latter serve merely to set up condemnations of the audience for failing to live up to those noble beginnings. In Wisdom the reversal never comes.

The principle is repeated in Wis. 18:8, and seems to form the backbone for Wisdom of Solomon 16–19 as a whole, where six more antitheses are reviewed:[14]

> For by that which you punished the enemies,
> By these you called and glorified us.

In that framework, Wisdom of Solomon 11–19 is a highly selective retelling of the early history of Israel, loosely based on the Pentateuchal texts and related traditions, in order to contrast God's punishment of "our enemies" with his provision for "us."[15] Note, however, that the expressions "our enemies" and "us" are used to refer *both* to the people in the time of Moses, *and* to the work's contemporaries, implying an identification between the two (cf., e.g., Wis. 12:18-22; 15:2, 4; 18:8).

Who, then, is the implied audience of this text? Who is included in Us? According to its first verse, the book is explicitly addressed to "those who judge the earth" (Wis. 1:1; cf. 6:1, 9, 21). James Reese argues that this address is fictional, since Wisdom makes no attempt to convince foreign rulers of its claims, but instead polemicizes against them.[16] This is likely, as fictive addresses are common in biblical literature, including the Oracles against Nations found in many of the prophets.[17] But fictive

---

14. Note the prominent use of ἀντί in 11:6; 16:2, 20; 18:3; 19:10. After the first antithesis in 11:1-14, there is a lengthy digression regarding the punishment of idolaters in 11:15–15:19, then the antitheses continue in 16:1-4; 16:5-14; 16:15-29; 17:1–18:4; 18:5-25; 19:1-17 (or 19:1-8); followed by a conclusion in 19:18-22 (or 19:9-22). The division of sections follows Winston, *Wisdom of Solomon*, 8–9; Cheon, *The Story of the Exodus in the Wisdom of Solomon*, 25. It remains disputed why such a long digression separates the first two antitheses.

15. See further Cheon, *The Exodus Story in the Wisdom of Solomon*, 108–16 et passim, who notes, "Pseudo-Solomon supplements the biblical narratives (11.7-9; 16.6, 11; 18.5), suppresses whatever would interfere with his own account and embellishes the tradition to suit his arguments (16.2; 17; 18.2-3, 20; 19.7). Moreover, he rearranges the biblical events and gives them a new meaning (11.6-7; 17.7-8; 18.5)" (110).

16. See James M. Reese, *Hellenistic Influence on the Book of Wisdom and Its Consequences*, AnBib 41 (Rome: Pontifical Institute, 1970), 148–9; followed by Andrew T. Glicksman, *Wisdom of Solomon 10: A Jewish-Hellenistic Reinterpretation of Early Israelite History through Sapiential Lenses*, DCLS 9 (Berlin: de Gruyter, 2011), 24–30.

17. Cf., e.g., Amos 1; Isaiah 13–23; Jeremiah 46–51 (cf. LXX 25–31); Ezekiel 25–32, all of which describe or address foreign peoples, but "were not primarily spoken or written to be heard or acted upon by the nations mentioned in the texts";

or not, this introduction still formally invites (non-Israelite) rulers to hear themselves addressed by the text, including its references to Us.

Nor do the references to the Israelites as "our ancestors" (Wis. 12:6; 18:6, 22) exclude such an audience, since they are never explicitly named. In fact, *none* of the groups or individuals referred to in the book are directly named: The Israelites are "a holy people" (Wis. 10:15), Moses is "a holy prophet" (11:1), and the Egyptians are "our enemies," "their enemies," or "the enemies" (e.g., 11:3, 5, 8; 12:22; 16:8; 18:8, 10). Various explanations have been offered regarding this avoidance of proper names,[18] but I would suggest that one reason may be to facilitate the identification between these ancient groups and contemporary ones, which is stressed by the frequent use of first person plural forms. That is, despite the book's opening verse, the implied audience is a community that identifies itself with the ancient Israelites, in contrast to the "enemies" who surround them, but it leaves open-ended precisely who may be included in those identifications.

Who, then, is this community? Though it cannot be determined with certainty, most commentators have concluded that the Wisdom of Solomon was probably composed in Alexandria during the Roman period.[19] Descendants of the former kingdom of Judah had been living in Egypt since at least the sixth century BCE (cf. Jeremiah 42–44), and in Alexandria since the late fourth century, where they enjoyed a degree of self-governance.[20] In that context, they were able to maintain a measure

---

John H. Hayes, "The Usage of the Oracles against Foreign Nations in Ancient Israel," *JBL* 87 (1968): 81–92, here 81; cf. Reese, *Hellenistic Influence*, 148–9; Glicksman, *Wisdom of Solomon 10*, 25–6.

18. See the summary by Winston, *Wisdom of Solomon*, 139–40.

19. This is supported by the book's focus on Egypt, and many conceptual parallels with other Alexandrian Jewish literature, most notably the writings of Philo of Alexandria, who may have been a contemporary of its author; see Winston, *Wisdom of Solomon*, 12–18; Hans Hübner, *Die Weisheit Salomons: Liber Sapientiae Salomonis*, ATD Apokryphen 4 (Göttingen: Vandenhoeck & Ruprecht, 1999), 15–19; Glicksman, *Wisdom of Solomon*, 6–13.

20. Cf., e.g., Josephus, *B.J.* 2.487; *A.J.* 12.8; 19.281; *C.Ap.* 2.35, 42. On the Jewish communities in Alexandria and Egypt, cf. E. Mary Smallwood, *The Jews Under Roman Rule: From Pompey to Diocletian: A Study in Political Relations*, SJLA 20 (Leiden: Brill, 1976), 220–55; John M. G. Barclay, *Jews in the Mediterranean Diaspora: From Alexander to Trajan (323 BCE–117 CE)* (Edinburgh: T. & T. Clark, 1996), 19–228; Donald Redford, "Some Observations on the Traditions Surrounding 'Israel in Egypt,'" in *Judah and the Judeans in the Achaemenid Period: Negotiating Identity in an International Context*, ed. Oded Lipschits, Gary N. Knoppers, and Manfred Oeming (Winona Lake: Eisenbrauns, 2011), 279–364; Nathalie LaCoste, *Waters of the Exodus: Jewish Experiences with Water in Ptolemaic and Roman Egypt*, JSJSup 190 (Leiden: Brill, 2018), 1–64, cf. 148–51.

of cultural and communal distinctiveness, but not without change: They began to speak, read, and write in Greek, adapted to Hellenistic culture, and some even obtained citizenship in the city.[21] Through most of the Ptolemaic and early Roman periods, the Alexandrian community enjoyed relative peace, but there were exceptions. The most significant was during the reign of the Roman emperor Gaius Caligula (37–41 CE), when the Roman Prefect in Alexandria, Aulus Avilius Flaccus, abolished Jewish self-governance and sparked a series of attacks against the Jewish community in 38 CE.[22] Whether this specific incident is in view is uncertain, but the book does seem to reflect a period of tension, or even crisis, between the community and its neighbors: There are allusions to persecution (especially in Wis. 5:16-23), and the book sharply condemns the (unnamed) Egyptians as those who "justly suffered because of their own wickedness, for they practiced a more bitter hatred of foreigners. While others did not receive strangers who came to them, these enslaved [their] foreign benefactors" (Wis. 19:13b-14).

In that context, the book's purpose appears to be to urge contemporary readers to trust in God's protection and provision, not to abandon the traditions of "our ancestors" by assimilating to the practices of their "foreign" neighbors. Wisdom accomplishes this by drawing an extremely sharp contrast between Us and Them: We are wise, faithful, and blessed, while the Other is wicked, idolatrous, and doomed. The boldness of this dichotomy should not be overlooked: The Wisdom of Solomon has been written to a community that had lived in Egypt for generations, spoke an entirely different language than that in which the biblical texts were originally composed, and had developed religiously and culturally into a very different kind of society from the nomadic lifestyle described in the book of Exodus.[23] Yet they still identified themselves with those Israelites, still claimed God's election for themselves, and still retold these stories

---

21. Cf. Smallwood, *The Jews Under Roman Rule*, 227–35, with examples of the latter.

22. Cf. Philo, *In Flaccum*; Richard Alston, "Philo's 'In Flaccum': Ethnicity and Social Space in Roman Alexandria," *Greece and Rome* 44 (1997): 165–75; Sandra Gambetti, *The Alexandrian Riots of 38 CE and the Persecution of the Jews: A Historical Reconstruction*, JSJSup 135 (Leiden: Brill, 2009); many commentators link the book to this period, cf., e.g., Winston, *Wisdom of Solomon*, 20–5; Cheon, *The Exodus Story in the Wisdom of Solomon*, 125–49; Glicksman, *Wisdom of Solomon 10*, 12–24. By contrast, Hübner prefers an earlier dating, either under Augustus or (he thinks more likely) under Ptolemaic rule; *Weisheit Salomons*, 16–19.

23. Indeed, Wisdom's rewriting of the biblical traditions is deeply shaped by Greek culture and philosophy, especially Platonism and Stoicism; cf. Reese, *Hellenistic Influence*, 146–52 et passim; Winston, *Wisdom of Solomon*, 3–4, 14–20,

of "our ancestors" in order to support a contrast between themselves and their "enemies," who were in fact their own neighbors. As we now turn to 1 Corinthians, we find that the apostle Paul did much the same, but with a very different audience in view.

Rewriting and Identity in First Corinthians 10

Paul's first preserved letter to the church he founded in the Greek city of Corinth, probably written in the mid-50s CE,[24] tackles a range of practical and theological issues that had arisen in the community. Among these is the question of whether Christ-followers may participate in the cultic practices of their non-believing neighbors. In 1 Corinthians 10, Paul addresses one part of that question through an appeal to Israel's experiences in the wilderness (1 Cor. 10:1-6):

> I do not want you to be ignorant, brothers [and sisters], that our ancestors were all under the cloud, and all passed through the sea, ² and all were baptized into Moses in the cloud and in the sea, ³ and all ate the same spiritual food, ⁴ and all drank [πίνω] the same spiritual drink. For they drank [πίνω] from the spiritual rock [πέτρα] that followed them—and the rock [πέτρα] was Christ. ⁵ But with most of them God was not pleased, and they were cast down in the wilderness. ⁶ These things are examples for us, so that we might not desire evil as they did.

Here Paul directly affirms that "our ancestors" drank from the rock, using two terms from the Greek translation of the Pentateuchal accounts, πίνω (Exod. 17:1, 2, 6; Num. 20:5, 11) and πέτρα (Exod. 17:6; Num. 20:8, 10, 11).[25] Yet in doing so he makes several significant modifications to

---

25–58; Hübner, *Weisheit Salomons*, 13–14. In this, Wisdom is closely aligned with the perspective of Philo of Alexandria; see esp. Winston, *Wisdom of Solomon*, 59–63.

24. See Gordon D. Fee, *The First Epistle to the Corinthians*, NICNT (Grand Rapids: Eerdmans, 1987), 4–5; Joseph A. Fitzmyer, *First Corinthians: A New Translation with Introduction and Commentary*, AB 32 (New Haven: Yale University Press, 2008), 48–53. 1 Cor. 5:9 refers to an earlier letter, but this has not survived.

25. Despite the brevity of these allusions, there is little doubt that Paul is referring to these two passages. The rest of 1 Cor. 10:1-22 echoes many stories from Exodus and Numbers, especially Numbers 11–25; see, e.g., Fitzmyer, *First Corinthians*, 379; Andrew J. Bandstra, "Interpretation in 1 Corinthians 10:1-11," *CTJ* 6 (1971): 5–21; Wayne Meeks, "'And Rose Up to Play': Midrash and Paraenesis in 1 Corinthians 10:1-22," *JSNT* 16 (1982): 64–78, esp. 72; James W. Aageson, "Written Also for Our Sake: Paul's Use of Scripture in the Four Major Epistles, with a Study of 1 Corinthians 10," in *Hearing the Old Testament in the New Testament*,

the story: He describes the water in 1 Cor. 10:4 as "spiritual drink" from a "spiritual rock," which *followed* the Israelites. The idea that the rock moved through the wilderness is not original to Paul; something like it is reflected in other retellings of the story, including Pseudo-Philo's *Liber Antiquitatum Biblicarum* 10.7; 11.15, and *t. Suk.* 3.11-13, in which the rock is described as a supernatural well that followed the Israelites wherever they went.[26]

What sets Paul's use of this notion apart is his conclusion that "the rock was Christ."[27] It is not entirely clear what he means by this, but certainly more than just that the rock can be *compared* with Christ. As Gordon Fee emphasizes, Paul does not say "the rock *is* Christ," as he does in similar constructions elsewhere (e.g., 2 Cor. 3:17; Gal. 4:25), but rather "the rock *was* [ἦν] Christ," implying that Christ was somehow actually present in or as the rock.[28] This might assume an identification of Christ with the Lord/God of the Exodus, in line with Deuteronomy 32 and several other texts that had already identified God himself as "the Rock" (הצור; Deut. 32:4, 15, 18, 30, 31, 37; cf. Exod. 17:6; Deut. 8:15), who provides the Israelites "with honey from the crags, with oil from the sharp rock" (Deut. 32:13).[29]

---

ed. Stanley E. Porter (Grand Rapids: Eerdmans, 2006), 152–81; Matthew Thiessen, "'The Rock Was Christ': The Fluidity of Christ's Body in 1 Corinthians 10.4," *JSNT* 36 (2013): 103–26.

26. For many other examples of this tradition, see Louis Ginzberg, *The Legends of the Jews*, trans. Henrietta Szold, Paul Radin, and Boaz Cohen (Philadelphia: Jewish Publication Society of America, 1909–1938), 3:50–4 and 6:20–2; Peter E. Enns, "The 'Moveable Well' in 1 Cor 10:4: An Extrabiblical Tradition in an Apostolic Text," *BBR* 6 (1996): 23–38 (with earlier bibliography, 26 n. 9); James L. Kugel, *Traditions of the Bible: A Guide to the Bible As It Was at the Start of the Common Era* (Cambridge: Harvard University Press, 1998), 613–21, 628–30. This background is accepted by Fee, *First Epistle to the Corinthians*, 448. Fitzmyer notes the tradition, but cautions against reading Paul in light of such "later" texts (*First Corinthians*, 382–3), even though *Liber Antiquitatum Biblicarum* probably derives from the first century CE as well, and (like Paul) takes the idea for granted, rather than introducing it as something new; cf. Daniel J. Harrington, "Pseudo-Philo," in *OTP* 2:297–377.

27. A similar identification is probably also implied in Jn 7:37-39 and 19:34; cf. Mary B. Spaulding, *Commemorative Identities: Jewish Social Memory and the Johannine Feast of Booths*, LNTS 396 (London: T&T Clark, 2009), 130–1.

28. Fee, *First Epistle to the Corinthians*, 448–9, who contrasts this with Philo, *Leg.* 2.86, where the present tense is used: "the sharp rock is the Wisdom of God" (cf. also *Det.* 1.115).

29. However, in the LXX, all the references to God as הצור are translated simply as θεός ("God"); but it is still affirmed that God provides sustenance from the rock in Deut. 32:13. That 1 Corinthians 10 has Deuteronomy 32 specifically in view is

That Paul places Christ in this role appears to be confirmed by 1 Cor. 10:9, where he warns that "We must not put Christ[30] to the test [ἐκπειράζω], as some of them tested [πειράζω; implicit direct object: him or God], and were destroyed by serpents." The verse alludes to Num. 21:5-9, but it uses the same verb for testing (πειράζω) as in Exod. 17:2, 7 (and Wis. 11:9). This equates Corinthian believers testing Christ to the Israelites testing God (or Christ) in the wilderness, and in the rest of the passage as well, Paul draws a very close link between the ancient Israelites and his Corinthian audience.

For instance, just as the Israelites drank "spiritual drink" and ate "spiritual food" from the rock that was Christ, so also "The cup of blessing that *we* bless, is it not a participation in the blood of Christ? The bread that *we* break, is it not a participation in the body of Christ?" (1 Cor. 10:16).[31] Yet this continuity is remarkable, because Paul is explicitly addressing a Gentile audience.[32] His whole argument in 1 Corinthians 8–10 focuses on whether it is permissible to participate in pagan temple feasts *as they used to do*. As he puts it in 1 Cor. 8:7, "some [implied: of you] have been

---

supported by the parallels between 1 Cor. 10:20, 22 and Deut. 32:17, 21, respectively; cf. Meeks, "'And Rose up to Play,'" 66, 72; Fee, *First Epistle to the Corinthians*, 442, 448–9; Thiessen, "'The Rock Was Christ'," 103–26, who emphasizes that many other texts also refer to Israel's God as the Rock; e.g., 1 Sam. 2:2; 2 Sam. 22:3, 32, 47 // Pss. 18:3, 32, 47 (LXX 17:3, 32, 47; ET 18:2, 31, 46); Isa. 17:10; 26:4; 30:29; 44:8; Hab. 1:12; Pss. 78:35 (LXX 77:35); 89:27 (LXX 88:27; ET 89:26). All of these are translated non-literally in the LXX.

30. There is a textual variant here: Sinaiticus, Vaticanus, and some other manuscripts read "Lord"; while Alexandrinus and a few others read "God," but "Christ" is attested in the earliest and widest range of surviving manuscripts, including P[46], and it is the *lectio difficilior*; cf. Fitzmyer, *First Corinthians*, 386; Anthony C. Thiselton, *The First Epistle to the Corinthians: A Commentary on the Greek Text*, NIGTC (Grand Rapids: Eerdmans, 2000), 740. Regardless of which form is original, the textual variant itself underscores the fluid overlap between "Christ," "Lord," and "God" in this passage and its reception.

31. Again, a similar link is seen in John 6, which affirms that the "bread from heaven" given to "our ancestors" in the wilderness came from the same Father who sends Jesus (Jn 6:25-40), then goes on to speak of eating Jesus' "flesh" and drinking his "blood" (6:41-58); cf. Ken Brown, "Temple Christology in the Gospel of John: Replacement Theology and Jesus as the Self-Revelation of God" (MA diss., Trinity Western University, 2010), 86–91, https://www.academia.edu/8870006/.

32. Fee, *First Epistle to the Corinthians*, 6–15; Ben Witherington III, *Conflict and Community in Corinth: A Socio-Rhetorical Commentary on 1 and 2 Corinthians* (Grand Rapids: Eerdmans, 1995), 19–36; Fitzmyer, *First Corinthians*, 37–47.

accustomed to idols until now, and [still] eat meat as though sacrificed to an idol." Later Paul even states that, "You know that when you *were* Gentiles [ὅτε ἔθνη ἦτε], you were led astray by mute idols…" (1 Cor. 12:2), implying that they were Gentiles at one time, but no longer are.[33] In that context, Paul's appeal to "our ancestors" does not urge them to *maintain* a traditional identification, but to take up a new one, setting aside their earlier ethnic, national, and religious identities in order to join themselves to "Israel."[34]

How, then, should we understand Paul's reference to "Israel according to the flesh" in 1 Cor. 10:18? Such expressions have often played a role in supporting Christian supersessionism, and raise deep questions about how Paul saw the relation between Jews and Gentiles.[35] For instance, Joseph Fitzmyer asserts that "Israel according to the flesh" refers to "the ethnic or historical-empirical Israel of old, which Paul will distinguish in Rom. 9:6 from those who are truly 'Israel'."[36] It is not likely, however, that 1 Cor. 10:18 is intended to contrast "Israel according to the flesh" with "Israel according to the spirit." Instead, the chapter emphasizes *continuity* between those who belong to "Israel" by descent, and those who join

---

33. Emphasized by Richard B. Hays, *Echoes of Scripture in the Letters of Paul* (New Haven: Yale University Press, 1989), 96, cf. 84–121.

34. Cf. Gal. 3:6-9, 29; 6:16; Phil. 3:3; Rom. 2:28-29; 9:3-6; 11:17-24. That Paul includes his non-Jewish audience in this reference to "our ancestors" is generally accepted; e.g., Fee, *First Epistle to the Corinthians*, 444; Thiselton, *First Epistle to the Corinthians*, 723–4; Eckhard J. Schnabel, *Der erste Brief des Paulus an die Korinther*, HTANT (Wuppertal: Brockhaus, 2006), 526; Fitzmyer, *First Corinthians*, 380.

35. This issue is highly controversial, and cannot be resolved here; cf., e.g., E. P. Sanders, *Paul and Palestinian Judaism: A Comparison of Patterns of Religion* (Minneapolis: Fortress, 1977); Sanders, *Paul, the Law, and the Jewish People* (Minneapolis: Fortress, 1983); Daniel Boyarin, *A Radical Jew: Paul and the Politics of Identity*, Contraversions 1 (Berkeley: University of California Press, 1994); Terence L. Donaldson, *Paul and the Gentiles: Remapping the Apostle's Convictional World* (Minneapolis: Fortress, 1997); D. A. Carson, Peter T. O'Brien, and Mark A. Seifrid, eds., *Justification and Variegated Nomism*, 2 vols., WUNT 140, 181 (Tübingen: Mohr Siebeck, 2001, 2004); James D. G. Dunn, *The New Perspective on Paul*, 2nd ed. (Grand Rapids: Eerdmans, 2008); Robert B. Foster, *Renaming Abraham's Children: Election, Ethnicity, and the Interpretation of Scripture in Romans 9*, WUNT II/421 (Tübingen: Mohr Siebeck, 2016).

36. Fitzmyer, *First Corinthians*, 392. Fee, *First Epistle to the Corinthians*, 470 n. 38, also states that Paul "seems to imply that there is another Israel κατὰ πνεῦμα," but that is not a point Paul ever makes in this letter.

to "Israel" through faith. After all, it was "Israel according to the flesh" (literally, "our ancestors") who first received the "spiritual food" and "spiritual drink" from the rock that was Christ (1 Cor. 10:1-4).[37]

Accordingly, Paul emphasizes that believers who eat of "the blood" and "body of Christ" are participants with Christ, and therefore dare not join themselves to idols (1 Cor. 10:14-22), *just as* "Israel according to the flesh" participated in the Lord's altar, and were warned not to join themselves to idols (10:6-11, 18). As Richard Hays notes, "It is no accident that Paul never uses expressions such as 'new Israel' or 'spiritual Israel.' There always has been and always will be only one Israel. Into that one Israel Gentile Christians such as the Corinthians have now been absorbed."[38] Throughout the passage as a whole, the Other against whom Paul warns is *not* "Israel according to the flesh," but rather the idolaters, with whom both the Corinthians and "our ancestors" are warned not to join themselves.

Nevertheless, by appealing to "our ancestors" while writing to an audience who were not genetically related to the ancient Israelites, Paul implies a drastic redefinition of his readers' own perceived identities, cutting themselves off from the cultural practices to which they had been accustomed. Simultaneously, he radically redefines "Israel" as well, broadening it to include Christ-followers of any background. For Paul, this is no mere metaphor: Not only are the Corinthians included in the identity of "Israel," but the old stories concerning the "Israelites" are also read in light of Christ, who is asserted to have himself been present with them in the wilderness. Thus, for Paul, interpretation cannot be separated from identity, and together they reshape his understanding of both the present and the past.

The Children of Israel and the Implied Audience of Numbers 20

Both the Wisdom of Solomon and 1 Corinthians explicitly identify their audiences with the descendants of the Israelites, despite the massive religious, cultural and—at least in the latter case—genetic differences between them and their purported "ancestors." Each substantially rewrites their sources in order to speak to the contemporary situations of these audiences. What then of Numbers 20? In turning Moses from an obedient hero into a condemned rebel, it is no less radical in its rewriting of

---

37. A similar continuity with the wilderness generation is implied by the claim that the Israelites were "baptized into Moses" (1 Cor. 10:2; cf. Gal. 3:27; Rom. 6:3).
38. Hays, *Echoes of Scripture in the Letters of Paul*, 96–7, cf. 95–102.

Exodus 17 than Wisdom of Solomon 11 and 1 Corinthians 10 are. Does it also assume a link between its contemporary readers and the ancient "Israelites," and if so, what implications does such a connection have?

The clearest sign of an identification between the Israelites and the implied audience of Numbers 20 is its use of direct speech: As in the Wisdom of Solomon and 1 Corinthians, and indeed already in Exodus 17, "the children of Israel" speak in the first person plural: "Why have you brought *us* up out of Egypt, to bring *us* to this bad place?" (Num. 20:5a). In this way, the text invites its audience to read this complaint in their own voices, and thus to include themselves in "the children of Israel." But unlike in Wisdom, here "the children of Israel" are not praised; they are condemned as "rebels," in a verse in which even Moses and Aaron speak as "we": "Listen, *you rebels*, shall *we* bring water for *you* out of this rock?" (Num. 20:10). And in the end, Moses and Aaron are also condemned, "because *you rebelled* against my command at the waters of Meribah" (Num. 20:24). Like 1 Corinthians, therefore, the use of the first person plural by the author or editor of Numbers 20 can be read as an implicit warning *not* to follow in the footsteps of those earlier "children of Israel."

That this is intended is supported by consideration of the probable historical background of the book of Numbers. The compositional history of Numbers is sharply disputed in recent scholarship, but one thing at least is clear: The book only reached its present form sometime after the exile.[39] It is most likely that the present form of Numbers 20 represents one of the later stages of the book's development, as it combines language and ideas from a range of earlier sources, traditions, or layers. This is evident from the close links to Exodus 17, Numbers 13–14, and Deuteronomy 8, generally assigned to three different sources or layers, and from a comparison with other biblical texts that use the imagery of the water from the rock to speak explicitly about the return from exile.

---

39. In older source-critical scholarship, which still has its advocates, the Pentateuch is primarily seen as a weaving together of earlier, largely independent, compositions, but the final combination was dated to the postexilic period; a recent advocate of this approach is Baden, *J, E, and the Redaction of the Pentateuch*. In redaction-critical scholarship, much more of the text has been seen as the result of intentional rewriting and expansion of earlier sources, which continued throughout the Persian and possibly even the Hellenistic periods; see, e.g., Achenbach, *Vollendung der Tora*; Albertz, "Das Buch Numeri jenseits der Quellentheorie," 171–83; cf. also Theodore E. Mullen, *Ethnic Myths and Pentateuchal Foundations: A New Approach to the Formation of the Pentateuch*, SemeiaSt 35 (Atlanta: Scholars Press, 1997). For further bibliography, see above, nn. 4–5.

Most notable is Isaiah 40–55, which uses this imagery repeatedly. For example, Isa. 48:20-21 includes a clear play on the language of Exod. 17:2-6 in order to call its audience to flee Babylon and return to the Land:

> [20] Come out [יצא] from Babylon, flee from Chaldea!
> With a shout of joy announce this news! Proclaim it!
> Bring it forth [יצא; *hiphil*] to the ends of the earth!
> Say, "YHWH has redeemed his servant Jacob!"
> [21] They were not thirsty [צמא]
> when he led them through the deserts [בחרבות];
> he brought out water from the rock [מים מצור],
> he made it flow for them;
> he split open the rock [צור] and the water [מים] flowed out.

Each of the highlighted terms parallels the language of Exodus 17,[40] while מים מצור echoes Deut. 8:15. By contrast, Isaiah draws no distinctive term from Numbers 20 that is not shared with Exodus, nor does it include any hint of the punishment Numbers describes. Instead, this allusion serves as a clear encouragement to its exilic audience to follow in the footsteps of their ancestors and "come out" of Babylon. If they do so, Isaiah implies, God will provide for them along the way just as he did for the ancient Israelites (lit. "Jacob") who "came out" of Egypt. Indeed, this is just one of several passages in Isaiah that describes the return from exile with imagery drawn from Exodus, including water in the wilderness. In some, the motif is even further exaggerated, so that entire "rivers" will pour through the desert, bringing it to life: "I will open rivers on the barren heights, and springs in the midst of the valleys; I will make the wilderness a pool of water, and the dry land springs of water" (Isa. 41:18).[41]

How different does Numbers 20 sound? Here the Israelites have decided to *settle* in the wilderness, refusing to enter the Land itself. Then, in direct

---

40. יצא (Isa. 48:20; Exod. 17:6; Num. 20:8, 10, 11); צמא (Isa. 48:21; Exod. 17:3); מים (Isa. 48:21; Exod. 17:1, 2, 3, 6; Num. 20:2, 5, 8, 10, 11, 13; cf. Deut. 8:15); צור (Isa. 48:21; Exod. 17:6; cf. Deut. 8:15); and compare the use of בחרבות (Isa. 48:21) with בחרב (Exod. 17:6). The parallel with Exodus 17 is noted by Benjamin D. Sommer, *A Prophet Reads Scripture: Allusion in Isaiah 40–66* (Stanford: Stanford University Press, 1998), 276 n. 19.

41. Cf. also Isa. 11:15–12:3; 35:1-7; 41:18-20; 43:20; 51:3; 58:11-14. Other exilic prophets use similar imagery; e.g., Ezekiel 40–48. Jeremiah and Ezekiel also compare God's judgment against their generation with that of "your ancestors" in the wilderness, e.g., Jer. 21:5-6 (cf. Exod. 6:6; Deut. 4:34); Ezek. 9:4-6; 11:9; 20:34-38; cf. Dalit Rom-Shiloni, "Facing Destruction and Exile: Inner-Biblical Exegesis in Jeremiah and Ezekiel," *ZAW* 117 (2005): 189–205.

contradiction to Isaiah's predictions of fertility in the desert, "the children of Israel" (also called "the people") complain that the desert has *not* been turned into paradise, using language drawn from descriptions of the Promised Land itself. Moses calls them "rebels," but when he strikes the rock and "abundant water" pours out, both he and Aaron are condemned with the rest of Israel, and barred from entering the Land as well. Since their sister Miriam also dies in this same passage (Num. 20:1), Numbers 20 signals the death of the entire leadership of the exodus generation, and implicitly ties this to the rebellious desire for paradise outside the Land.

Why would anyone retell the story in this way? I would suggest that it could be a direct response to the reality of the postexilic period: Despite the prophets' grand promises of a joyful return to Zion, the fact is that most did *not* return, even once they were given permission by the Persian emperor to do so.[42] Despite Isaiah's command to "Come out from Babylon!," many chose to stay. Read in that context, Numbers 20 becomes a stark warning: By adding a complaint that God has not provided the fertility of the Land *in the wilderness*, and concluding that even Moses and Aaron were barred from the Land for failing to "trust in me [= YHWH]," Numbers transforms the story into a repudiation of any attempt to secure the promises of the Land outside it. Insofar as its audience is expected to identify with the ancient Israelites as Us, they too are urged not to abandon God's promises by "settling" in the wilderness.

---

42. "The returnees were only a small portion of a much larger Yahwistic community in the east of the Empire, notably in Elam and Babylonia"; John Kessler, "Persian's Loyal Yahwists: Power Identity and Ethnicity in Achaemenid Yehud," in *Judah and the Judeans in the Persian Period*, ed. Oded Lipschits and Manfred Oeming (Winona Lake: Eisenbrauns, 2006), 91–121, here 95; cf. also Hans M. Barstad, *The Myth of the Empty Land: A Study in the History and Archaeology of Judah during the 'Exilic' Period*, SO 28 (Oslo: Scandinavian University Press, 1996); Lester L. Grabbe, ed., *Leading Captivity Captive: "The Exile" as History and Ideology*, JSOTSup 278 (Sheffield: Sheffield Academic, 1998); Bob Becking, "'We All Returned as One!' Critical Notes on the Myth of the Mass Return," in Lipschits and Oeming, eds., *Judah and the Judeans in the Persian Period*, 3–18; Jill Middlemas, *The Templeless Age: An Introduction to the History, Literature and Theology of the 'Exile'* (Louisville: Westminster John Knox, 2007). As these note, many never left the Land in the first place, but most of those who did never returned. On the continued hope for a mass return in the late Second Temple period and beyond, see Esther G. Chazon, "'Gather the Dispersed of Judah': Seeking a Return to the Land as a Factor in Jewish Identity of Late Antiquity," in *Heavenly Tablets: Interpretation, Identity and Tradition in Ancient Judaism*, ed. Lynn LiDonnici and Andrea Lieber, JSJSup 119 (Leiden: Brill, 2007), 159–73; and cf. also Betsy Halpern-Amaru, *Rewriting the Bible: Land and Covenant in Post-Biblical Jewish Literature* (Valley Forge: Trinity Press International, 1994).

The allusions to Numbers 13–14 fit with this, since there as well the great sin of the exodus generation was their refusal to "trust" in God by entering the Land (Num. 14:11; cf. also Deut. 1:31-36).

Therefore, much as Wisdom and 1 Corinthians use retellings of the story to warn their own audiences not to adopt or continue the practices of their "foreign" neighbors, this retelling in Numbers can be read as a warning to those living after the exile: Any hope of securing paradise outside the Land is false, and choosing to "settle" there is a rebellion of the highest order. "You" may receive the water you request—as the text concludes, God will show himself holy even if Moses himself fails to do so (Num. 20:13)—but you will die in the wilderness, a fate not even Moses and Aaron could escape.

Yet the message is not only negative. Notably, while Moses calls the Israelites rebels, Yhwh does *not* confirm that charge, even when he turns it back against Moses and Aaron (Num. 20:24; 27:14). After Miriam, Aaron, and Moses all die in the wilderness, the remnant of the next generation does enter the Land, under the new leadership of Joshua and Eliezer (Num. 27:12-23; cf. Joshua 1–4). For an audience reading these texts after the exile, the message would seem to be this: To seek God's provision outside the Land means death, but the promises still stand, and await fulfillment for all those "children of Israel" ready to complete the journey that "our ancestors" began, but did not complete.

Conclusions

Each of the texts reviewed here reflects irreversible changes in the social situation between the nomadic tribes of "Israelites" Exodus describes, and those communities that have continued to retell their stories about "our ancestors" in later periods. Each adds to, omits from, paraphrases, and recontextualizes the story of the water from the rock in comparable ways, apparently for similar reasons. Each uses it to warn their audiences against integration into their surrounding societies, and to encourage faithful obedience to the God of Israel.

Such retellings assume an identification between their implied audiences and the "children of Israel" in Exodus, which inherently stretches the designation of "Israel" to encompass new communities. Paul and the author of the Wisdom of Solomon may have been contemporaries, who both wrote in Greek to audiences influenced by Hellenistic culture and religion, but each speaks of the Israelites as "our ancestors" in such a way that a broad range of potential readers could identify themselves with Us. For Paul, this includes not only the literal descendants of "Israel," but also the Gentile Christ-followers in Corinth. For the author of Wisdom, the group referred to as Us is not explicitly named, but might even include "those who judge the earth." Numbers 20 is not as explicit about its intended audience, but its own use of first person plural speech similarly invites a range of potential readers to see themselves as part of Us. In fact, even Exodus 17 is probably not the "original" form of the story either, but has itself been written or revised on the basis of still earlier traditions concerning water in the wilderness.[43] It also projects a concept of national unity as "the children of Israel" back into the Mosaic period, in order to tell *its* story of rebellion and divine provision in the wilderness (i.e., in exile). Whatever the ultimate origins of the story, each of the forms that survive have been retold to address the situations of later audiences, who are invited to identify themselves with "the children of Israel."

At the same time, however, these identifications are not all-inclusive. Both Wisdom and 1 Corinthians retell the story as part of a broader argument not to participate in the religious practices of their neighbors— the idolatrous Other which is presented as the counterpoint to Us. Wisdom contrasts God's plagues against the Egyptians with provision for the Israelites, in order to discourage assimilation to foreign religious practices. First Corinthians recalls both God's provision for the Israelites, and their own idolatry, to warn against continued participation in pagan sacrifice. Numbers 20, like Exodus 17, only alludes to the Other briefly (in the question "why did you bring us up from Egypt?"), but it may serve a broadly similar purpose, warning "the children of Israel" against attempting to "settle" in the wilderness, as a metaphor for remaining among the nations in the diaspora. Presupposing an identification of their audiences with the Israelites as "our ancestors," each of these texts demands that We dissociate from the society and cultic practices of Them, the Other.

Nevertheless, these examples differ among themselves in many important ways: Numbers 20 is a direct rewriting of the story from Exodus (or something very like it), using the same prose narrative form as its *Vorlage*, with the same overall structure and a substantial amount of identical

---

43. See, e.g., Propp, *Exodus 1–18*, 609–13; Nathan MacDonald, "Anticipations of Horeb: Exodus 17 as Inner-Biblical Commentary," in *Studies on the Text and Versions of the Hebrew Bible in Honour of Robert Gordon*, ed. Geoffrey Khan and Diana Lipton (Leiden: Brill, 2012), 7–19; cf. Berner, "Das Wasserwunder von Rephidim," 193–209, though his conclusion that Exodus 17 is later than Numbers 20 is unconvincing.

wording. By contrast, Wisdom of Solomon 11 is a poetic recombination of the story with another passage from Exodus, following a different structure and only repeating isolated words. Finally, 1 Corinthians 10 merely alludes to the story within a letter, sharing only a couple of words. Regarding content, while all three urge some kind of separation from the Other, the manner in which this is expected to take place differs: For Numbers, it means leaving the wilderness/exile/diaspora and entering the Land; for Wisdom and 1 Corinthians, it means refusing to participate in the religious practices of their neighbors *outside* the Land (in Alexandria and Corinth respectively), with no indication that they should leave these places.

Similar diversity is reflected in the broader reception history of this story. When Numbers turns Moses' faithfulness into rebellion, this leads to numerous further rewritings in later literature, such as the medieval Jewish commentaries of Rashi, ibn Ezra, and others, who debated what sin Moses could have committed that even he—like them—was barred from the Promised Land.[44] Similarly, when Wisdom of Solomon 11 (like Isaiah) omits this rebellion to emphasize God's abundant provision for his people, this anticipates numerous similar elaborations, such as *t. Suk.* 3.11-13 (also written in a time of ongoing exile), which describes twelve rivers flowing from the rock to provide the Israelites "all necessary goods" in the wilderness.[45] Likewise, when Paul identifies the rock with Christ, he sets the stage for further Christian usage along the same lines, such as when Martin Luther asserts that Catholics, Muslims, and Jews die "inwardly" of thirst because they do not recognize Christ.[46] These rewritings are no less creative than Numbers 20, Wisdom of Solomon 11, or 1 Corinthians 10, and they are no less dependent on an assumed identity between their contemporary audiences and those peoples described in the texts. They too add details that are not explicit or intended by their sources, to address situations in the later lives of various groups who self-identified with the "Israelites."

Therefore, rewriting the biblical texts, even writing ourselves *into* them, is not some unusual indulgence of a few Second Temple period scribes. It is characteristic of the Bible's entire history of revision and reception.

---

44. Cf. Michael Carasik, ed., *The Commentators' Bible: The JPS Miqra'ot Gedolot, Numbers* במדבר (Philadelphia: Jewish Publication Society, 2011), 146–9.

45. Jacob Neusner, *The Tosefta: Translated from the Hebrew with a New Introduction*, 2 vols. (Peabody: Hendrickson, 2002), 1:576–7.

46. Cf., e.g., Martin Luther, *Sämtliche Schriften*, ed. Johann G. Walch (Groß Oesingen: Harms, 1987), 8:77–89, esp. 78–9, §174.

Jews, Christians, and others have continued to read these texts precisely *because* they have seen themselves in them, and they have continued to rewrite the texts to make those identifications explicit. All interpretation is rewriting, and all rewriting reflects the perceived or projected identities of its authors and audiences.

Abrahamic Identity in Paul and
*Liber Antiquitatum Biblicarum**

Kyle B. Wells

Introduction

David Novak opens his book, *The Election of Israel*, by observing how "[f]rom the very beginning of our history until the present time, we Jews have been involved in a continuing process of self-definition. We have never stopped asking ourselves the most fundamental question of our identity: Who is a Jew?"[1] The process to which Novak refers is on particular display during the vicissitudes of the Second Temple period. The cultural, social, and geographic diversity of Jews made Jewish identity especially unstable. How could one justify claims to Jewishness in the face of competing claims and counterfactuals? How were the various and diverse communities making such claims to relate to one another? Many Jews looked to the patriarchal narratives in Israel's scriptures for answers. The adoption and interpretation of these texts thus played an essential role in the identity-construction process.

But this process was not straightforward, nor could it be. For one, these foundational narratives were developed in and describe a religious and cultural landscape that is distinct from the Second Temple period. That is, the narratives of Genesis were initially produced by and for communities "other" than those utilizing them to construct and confirm their sense of self in the Second Temple period. This fact renders any engagement with

---

* Along with all those already mentioned who made the colloquium possible, I would like to thank the Bridwell Library at the Perkins School of Theology, whose fellowship and abundant resources allowed me to conduct much of the research for this article.

1. David Novak, *The Election of Israel: The Idea of the Chosen People* (Cambridge: Cambridge University Press, 1995), 1.

these texts for the purpose of identity formation an inherently imaginative and creative act. Moreover, the diverse social locations of various Jewish communities meant that not only could Jews appropriate texts in a variety of ways to construct and confirm their sense of self, they must.

In this essay, I would like to probe how two Jewish authors from that period, Paul and the author of *Liber Antiquitatum Biblicarum* (henceforth *LAB*), adopted and interpreted narratives about the origin of the Abrahamic covenant in order to validate the identities of those for whom they wrote. Whether it is responding to the crisis of 70 CE or the discord leading up to it, *LAB* gives a protracted "treatise on the irrevocability of Israel's covenant promises" in order to console a people for whom God's covenant seemed to have failed.[2] Though Paul barely uses the term covenant and shows little to no interest in the land of Israel, as a self-described Jew-by-birth (Gal. 2:15) and descendant of Abraham (Rom. 11:1; cf. Phil. 3:5), he also wrestles with the question of Jewish identity and the faithfulness of God, but for altogether different reasons. What drives Paul to these questions is his conviction that God has sent Israel's Messiah, and the fact that God has done so in an unexpected manner and with unprecedented results (Rom. 1:2-4; 3:1-9; 9:1–11:36; Gal. 4:4).

By setting these two authors' utilizations of the Abrahamic covenant side by side, we gain a sharper picture of how this foundational story could support the identities of (at least) two very distinct groups of people. In what follows, I first investigate the role the covenant with Abraham performs in *LAB*, with special attention to how it relates to the covenant made with Israel at Sinai. Then I will tease out how Abrahamic covenant-making narratives function in Paul's letters to the Romans and Galatians.

Abraham in Pseudo-Philo

In *LAB*'s interpretive retelling of Genesis through 2 Samuel, Abraham, and the promises God makes to him, play a dominant role. We are first

---

2. So Bruce N. Fisk, *Do You Not Remember? Scripture, Story and Exegesis in the Rewritten Bible of Pseudo-Philo*, JSPSup 37 (Sheffield: Sheffield Academic, 2001), 45. See also Frederick J. Murphy, "The Eternal Covenant in Pseudo-Philo," *JSP* 3 (1988): 43–57. Though there is no consensus on the question of whether *LAB* was written before or after the destruction of the temple, most conclude that it was written "to people who suppose that they may have been totally rejected by God," "in fear of their existence as a nation"; see George W. E. Nickelsburg, "Good and Bad Leaders in Pseudo-Philo's *Liber Antiquitatum Biblicarum*," in *Ideal Figures in Ancient Judaism: Profiles and Paradigms*, ed. John J. Collins and George W. E. Nickelsburg (Chico: Scholars Press, 1980), 49–65, esp. 64.

introduced to Abraham in the midst of a genealogy about the sons of Noah. That Abraham enters the narrative in *LAB* so much earlier than in the Genesis account gestures to the primary role the patriarch plays in our author's hermeneutic.³ Though Abraham remains nameless, we learn that:

> From him [= Serug] there will be born in the fourth generation one who will set his dwelling on high and will be called perfect and blameless; and he will be the father of nations, and his covenant will not be broken, and his seed will be multiplied forever. (*LAB* 4.11)⁴

LAB announces Abraham through the lens and language of Genesis 17. Themes of "blamelessness" (תמים; Gen. 17:1), multinational paternity (אב המון גוים; Gen. 17:4), seed-multiplication (וארבה אותך במאד מאד; Gen. 17:2), and an enduring covenant (ברית עולם; Gen. 17:7) come from the first half of that chapter. The utilization of these themes is not straightforward, however. Our author turns God's prescriptive command to Abraham—"walk before me and be blameless" (התהלך לפני והיה תמים; Gen. 17:1)—into a descriptive prophecy about Abraham's character: Abraham "will be called perfect and blameless" (*et perfectus vocabitur et inmaculatus*; *LAB* 4.11).⁵ Abraham's blamelessness is then set within the context of a godly lineage. When the other inhabitants of the earth began to dabble in astrology and child-sacrifice, Abraham's forefathers "did not act as these did" (*LAB* 4.16).

The depiction of Abraham as a paragon of virtue is unsurprising in the Second Temple milieu (cf. Sir. 44:19-21; 1 Macc. 2:52; *Jub.* 23:10; CD 3.2). More notable is how *LAB* describes Abraham's covenant as one that "will not be broken" (*LAB* 4.11). To speak of the covenant's perpetuity is not in and of itself significant. Genesis 17:7 calls the covenant "everlasting" (עולם) and says that it will succeed "for generations" (לדרתם). But the specific phrase—"cannot be broken"—is suggestive in

---

3. On the role birth announcements play in *LAB*, see John R. Levison, "Torah and Covenant in Pseudo Philo's *Liber Antiquitatum Biblicarum*," in *Bund und Tora: Zur theologischen Begriffsgeschichte in alttestamentlicher, frühjüdischer und urchristlicher Tradition*, ed. Friedrich Avemarie and Hermann Lichtenberger, WUNT 92 (Tübingen: Mohr, 1996), 111–27, esp. 112–13.

4. D. J. Harrington, "Pseudo-Philo," *OTP* 2:297–377, here 308–9. Except where otherwise noted, all subsequent translations from *LAB* are from Harrington. For a critical edition of the Latin Text (by D. J. Harrington), see C. Perrot and P.-M. Bogaert, *Pseudo-Philon: Les Antiquités Bibliques*, SC 229, 230 (Paris: Gabalda, 1976).

5. While the LXX has ἄμεμπτος, *perfectus et inmaculatus* gives a fuller accounting of תמים.

light of Gen. 17:14, where God tells Abraham that "Any uncircumcised male who is not circumcised in the flesh of his foreskin shall be cut off from his people; he has broken my covenant" (בריתי הפר).[6]

An initial reading of Genesis 17 indicates that the everlasting covenant can be broken, at least from the human side. In a subtle move, our author subverts language that introduces contingency in the Genesis narrative in order to underline the covenant's durability. The twin themes of the founding father's fidelity and the covenant's finality in 4.11 lay the foundational planks for *LAB*'s covenantal framework.

The Immutable Covenant of Promise

If there is a dominant lens through which *LAB* views God's covenant with Abraham, it is that of promise. Against the backdrop of Babel, God announces his election of Abraham: "And before all these I will choose my servant Abram, and I will bring him out from their land and will bring him into the land.... For there I will have my servant Abram dwell and will establish my covenant with him and will bless his seed and be Lord for him as God forever" (7.4). Though Jacobson and Levison are correct to note how *LAB* is drawing off Gen. 17:6-8,[7] reverberations of Gen. 12:1-3 can also be heard in 7.4, particularly with its mention of "blessing" (*bendicam*) and its focus on displacement, all against the backdrop of Babel. Genesis 17 is invaluable to our author as it is the only place in the Abraham cycle that describes the covenant as eternal.[8] But there are features of Genesis 17 that do not sit well with his theology.

Our author's unease with Genesis 17, with its talk of covenant-breaking, started to manifest at 4.11 and resurfaces again at 8.3:

---

6. *LAB*'s *dissolvō* (*et non dissolvetur testamentum eisus*) most likely reflects the LXX's surprising decision to render פרר with διασκεδάζω. Under διασκεδάζω, T. Muraoka, *A Greek-English Lexicon of the Septuagint* (Leuven: Peeters, 2009), 158, gives LXX Gen. 17:4 as an example of the use "to reject, throw away as unimportant, unacceptable," but gives an asterisk, indicating an unprecedented meaning in the LXX. A more common meaning of διασκεδάζω is "to cause to disintegrate," which comes closer to *dissolvō*. On the text critical issues in Gen. 17:14, see further Matthew Thiessen, *Contesting Conversion: Genealogy, Circumcision, and Identity in Ancient Judaism and Christianity* (New York: Oxford University Press, 2011), 18–31.

7. Howard Jacobson, *A Commentary on Pseudo-Philo's Liber Antiquitatum Biblicarum, with Latin Text and English Translation*, AGJU 31 (Leiden: Brill, 1996), 383; Levison, "Torah and Covenant," 112.

8. Murphy, "The Eternal Covenant in Pseudo-Philo," 45.

> And God appeared to Abram, saying, "To your seed I will give this land, and your name will be called Abraham, and Sarai, your wife, will be called Sarah. And I will give to you from her an everlasting seed, and I will establish my covenant with you."

When God appears to Abraham, instead of the command "walk before me and be blameless so that I may establish my covenant with you" (Gen. 17:1-2a), we find a promise: "To your seed I will give this land" (see Gen. 12:7; 15:18; cf. 17:8). Once again our author has written out the command of Gen. 17:1, this time to foreground God's unrelenting commitment to give the land to Abraham's seed. The perpetuity of God's commitment to the Abrahamic promise is further seen when God tells Abraham that through Sarah he will give him not "a son" (בן; Gen. 17:16), but an "everlasting seed" (*semen sempiternum*).[9] As we saw with the repurposing of the word "broken" in 4.11, so here Pseudo-Philo fortifies his strong sense that God's commitment to Abraham's collective descendants is unalterable.

Given the author's focus on Genesis 17, it is remarkable that there is absolutely no mention of circumcision in the Abrahamic cycle. In fact, the only mention of circumcision in the entire work is a cryptic reference to Moses, who "was born in the covenant of God and the covenant of the flesh" (*LAB* 9.13). "Covenant of flesh," a circumlocution for circumcision, alludes to Gen. 17:10 (cf. *LAB* 9.15). While the relationship (*et*) between "the covenant of God" and "the covenant of the flesh" is obscure, to intimate that Moses was born circumcised is in keeping with our author's prioritization of promise over command. As Levison comments: "This circumcision is no product of human hands, of obedience to the stipulations of the covenant with Abraham, for Pseudo-Philo omits reference to circumcision in his portrayal of Abraham; rather, Moses was miraculously 'born in the covenant of God and of the flesh'."[10] If our author downplays the emphasis on circumcision in Genesis 17, it is because circumcision might well undermine the covenantal story that he is trying to tell, a story of a covenant that emphatically "cannot be broken" (*LAB* 4.11), established as it is on God's inviolable promise.

LAB reinforces the idea that God's covenant with Abraham is immutable in various ways. Perhaps the strongest statement to this effect occurs in chapter 9, when Amram, the father of Moses, flaunts Egyptian oppression, declaring: "It will sooner happen that this age will be ended forever

---

9. Jacobson, *A Commentary*, 388, notes how the author "elaborates Gen. 17:16 in order to emphasize God's guarantee of the eternity of the Jewish people."

10. Levison, "Torah and Covenant," 113.

or the world will sink into the immeasurable deep or the heart of the abyss will touch the stars than that the race of the sons of Israel will be ended" (*LAB* 9.3). Confidence that God will sustain Israel is then rooted in the Abrahamic covenant. Twice in 9.4, Amram states that neither the Abrahamic family nor the Abrahamic covenant are "in vain" (*in vanum*), drawing on one of *LAB*'s favorite expressions for communicating the immutability of God's purposes (e.g., *LAB* 12.4, 9; 15.5; 18.11; 23.13). What assures the author that God will fulfill his promises is his more general conviction that God does not lie and that his purposes cannot fail.[11] In fact, even the plight under Egyptian rule serves to confirm God's word to Abraham (*LAB* 9.3; cf. Gen. 15:13).[12]

Not only do the covenant promises withstand threats from Israel's enemies, they also withstand Israel's own self-sabotaging tendencies. Many have noted the deuteronomistic scheme of sin–punishment–restoration emphasized in *LAB*'s telling of Israel's story, especially with the space it gives to the time of the Judges (*LAB* 25–48).[13] Even so, it is clear that the durability of the covenant is not contingent upon Israel's faithfulness. For the author, the covenant's distinction is that it operates in the face of Israel's rebellion.[14] If the people's repentance plays a role in this scheme (*LAB* 26.1; 33.2, 5), that role is not determinative.[15] The judges

---

11. See *LAB* 14.2; 18.3; 21.9; 23.11; 27.13; 46.1; 47.2, 12; 51.6; 53.12; 56.1; 61.3; 62.2, 4. See further Frederick J. Murphy, "Divine Plan, Human Plan: A Structuring Theme in Pseudo-Philo," *JQR* 77 (1986): 5–14; Murphy, "God in Pseudo-Philo," *JSJ* 19 (1988): 1–18, esp. 12–13, 17–18; Eckart Reinmuth, "'Nicht vergeblich' bei Paulus und Pseudo-Philo, *Liber Antiquitatum Biblicarum*," *NovT* 33 (1991): 97–123.

12. See also *LAB* 15.5.

13. The seminal work on this theme is Nickelsburg, "Good and Bad Leaders." See also Odil Hannes Steck, *Israel und das gewaltsame Geschick der Propheten: Untersuchungen zur Überlieferung des deuteronomistischen Geschichtsbildes im Alten Testament, Spätjudentum und Urchristentum* (Neukirchen-Vluyn: Neukirchener Verlag, 1967), 173–6.

14. On this theme, see John M. G. Barclay, *Paul and the Gift* (Grand Rapids: Eerdmans, 2015), 270–3.

15. Important here are the arguments of Murphy, "The Eternal Covenant in Pseudo-Philo," 43–57. See further Betsy Halpern-Amaru, *Rewriting the Bible: Land and Covenant in Post-Biblical Jewish Literature* (Valley Forge: Trinity Press International, 1994), 91; Barclay, *Paul and the Gift*, 271; and Preston M. Sprinkle, "The Hermeneutic of Grace: The Soteriology of Pseudo-Philo's *Biblical Antiquities*," in *This World and the World to Come: Soteriology in Early Judaism*, ed. Daniel M. Gurtner, LSTS 74 (London: T&T Clark, 2011), 50–67, esp. 60–1: "Even in instances where the people do repent, the author is quick to show that their repentance is not the basis of God's restorative action…. The covenant with the fathers is" (60).

illustrate the point. Deborah, in the face of serial disobedience, assures that God will have mercy "not because of you but because of his covenant that he established with your fathers and the oath that he has sworn not to abandon you forever" (*LAB* 30.7; cf. 32.14).[16] Similarly, the Angel of the Lord tells Gideon that God will have mercy on Israel "not on account of you but on account of those who have fallen asleep" (*LAB* 35.3). What becomes overwhelmingly clear from *LAB* is that the covenant is unbreakable not for any virtue in Israel, but because of God's unwavering commitment to fulfill his promise to Abraham.

Promise and Law, Abraham and Sinai in LAB

Having looked at how our author takes up God's covenant with Abraham, it is important to consider how that covenant functions in relationship to the other covenants God makes with Israel, especially the covenant at Sinai. Through a focused analysis on the birth announcements of Abraham and Moses (*LAB* 4.11; 9.7-8), alongside the speeches of Joshua (21.9-10; 23.1-14), Levison notes how *LAB* construes "disparate covenants into a single strand, stretching from ancestral promise to future fulfillment at the dwelling place of God."[17] Each covenant, Levison concludes, serves a subsequent one so that "the telos of the covenants of Noah and Abraham...is the covenant established through Moses."[18] Horeb thus "becomes the centerpiece of covenant history, the focal point of God's actions...."[19]

Levison's thesis regarding the unity of the covenants appears fundamentally sound. While *LAB* can present future covenants as distinct from previous ones—as when God declares that he will show Moses "my covenant that no one has seen" (9.8)—it is also clear that when an additional covenant is added to a previous covenant, the two become one. For this reason *LAB* will often speak of God's single covenant, and any reference to "covenants" refers to the promises made to the patriarchs (see, e.g., 10.2; 13.10).[20] The singularity of the one eternal covenant administered to Abraham and then mediated through Moses is expressed in a variety of ways, not least when Torah is styled "the law of his eternal covenant" (*legem testamenti sempiterni*; 11.5). Like the Abrahamic promises, the commandments of Torah are "everlasting"

---

16. That "fathers" refers specifically to the patriarchs is clear from 9.4, 7; 10.2.
17. Levison, "Torah and Covenant," 114.
18. Levison, "Torah and Covenant," 113.
19. Levison, "Torah and Covenant," 114–15.
20. *LAB* 13.10 is somewhat ambiguous, however, as it could include Sinai.

(*precepta eterna*; 11.5).²¹ Such unity is present in Joshua's speeches, where the land settlement is a fulfillment both of "every word of his [= God's] Law" spoken at Horeb (21.9) and of the "covenant that I [= God] promised to the fathers" (23.11; cf. 21:9).²² These examples confirm not only the essential unity that our author reads into the various divine covenants, but also how law is an integral feature of covenant.²³

It is crucial to understand the fundamental role the Abrahamic promises continue to play in this unified, covenantal structure. Significant in this regard is that throughout *LAB* the durability of the covenant is rooted not in the eternal law given at Sinai, but in the eternal promises given to the patriarch(s).²⁴ It is precisely for this reason that *LAB* continually situates the deuteronomistic pattern of judgment and reconciliation—and the conditional blessing and curses of Sinai—within the context of God's larger unconditioned commitment to fulfill his pledge to Abraham. A prime example of this dynamic is seen in *LAB*'s portrayal of the golden calf incident. *LAB* writes out any threat of annihilation found in his ancestral *Vorlage* (Exod. 32:9-10) and replaces the divine threat with a reminder of God's promise to Abraham from Gen. 12:7 (*LAB* 12.4). As Fisk comments: "Having suppressed the scandalous message of Exod. 32:10, including its echo of antecedent Scripture, Pseudo-Philo has given voice to the larger covenant context to which that text alluded, in order to protect, rather than undermine, Israel's secure status as chosen heir to the land."²⁵ Here the narrative of Sinai must yield to the Abrahamic promises.

This is not an isolated incident. Indeed, it seems that a primary aim in *LAB* is to endow its readers with a covenantal hermeneutic whereby Sinai and its laws are always filtered through the Abrahamic promises. Thus if the author takes up the conditional language of Lev. 26:3-4, 9-10, he will then recast such language in light of God's omniscience and patriarchal promise: "I surely know that they will corrupt their ways and I will abandon them, and they will forget the covenants that I have established with their fathers; but nevertheless I will not forget them

---

21. On the eternal nature of Torah in *LAB*, see Eckart Reinmuth, "Beobachtungen zum Verständnis des Gesetzes im *Liber Antiquitatum Biblicarum* (Pseudo-Philo)," *JSJ* 20 (1989): 151–70.

22. Astutely noted by Levison, "Torah and Covenant," 123.

23. Levison, "Torah and Covenant," 122–3.

24. Conversely, Gideon believes that if God has abandoned Israel it is because he has "forgotten the promises that he told our fathers" (*LAB* 35.2; cf. 49.6).

25. Fisk, *Do You Not Remember?*, 161

forever" (*LAB* 13.10).²⁶ Deuteronomy 31:16-29 is likewise reframed so that it is read in light of God's patriarchal promises; as certain as Moses is that the Israelites will abandon the stipulations that he gave at Sinai, so he is certain that God will restore Israel "because he will remember the covenant that he established with your fathers" (*LAB* 19.2). When Balaam asks God if he should curse Israel, God implies a negative by reminding Balaam of the Abrahamic promise (*LAB* 18.5; cf. Gen. 15:5; 22:17).²⁷

A similar rationale lies behind the excision of circumcision from the Abrahamic covenant. Thus while the book may employ strategies "to counteract a tendency to remove the Law from its privileged place,"²⁸ this concern is suspended when it comes to the command of circumcision. Our author risks such a counterproductive strategy because he wants to protect something he privileges more than any demand associated with the covenant—the promises on which the covenant was founded.

The fastidious degree to which our author guards against seeing anything other than the Abrahamic promises as the covenant's basis delimits what we mean when we say that Sinai "becomes the centerpiece of covenant history, the focal point of God's actions," as Levison concludes. It is not that *LAB* has no place for laws—it does! But life in the law is only as secure as the Abrahamic promise on which it stands. If Sinai provides the walls in *LAB*'s covenant architecture, then the Abrahamic promises provide the foundation. Without a foundation that is constructed solely on the non-contingent promise of God, the house collapses.

This way of structuring the covenant lends some support to the thesis of David Noel Freedman and David Miano, who suggest that the unconditional promise with Abraham was understood by pre- and postexilic Jews to make the conditional covenants eternally renewable.²⁹ Yet this way of putting it sounds like the promises made to Abraham give the covenant a latent potential—the covenant is available for renewal if the people will just avail themselves of it. In *LAB*, however, there is a much stronger sense that God will fulfill his covenant promises, and the only question is whether or not the people will participate.

---

26. Translation from Jacobson, *A Commentary*, 114. See further Sprinkle, "The Hermeneutic of Grace," 55; Murphy, "The Eternal Covenant in Pseudo-Philo," 47; Halpern-Amaru, *Rewriting the Bible*, 85–6.

27. On the conflation of Gen. 15:5 and 22:17 here, see Jacobson, *A Commentary*, 582.

28. Levison, "Torah and Covenant," 123.

29. David Noel Freedman and David Miano, "People of the New Covenant," in *The Concept of the Covenant in the Second Temple Period*, ed. Stanley E. Porter and Jacqueline C. R. De Roo, JSJSup 71 (Leiden: Brill, 2003), 7–26.

Father Abraham and the Origin of God's Covenant Promise

To a certain degree, our author grounds God's faithfulness to his promises in Abraham's exemplary character, which is evident as soon as he comes on the scene. His name initially appears as the first among a group of twelve men who refused to contribute to the building of the tower at Babel and are thrown in prison as a result of this fidelity to the Lord (*LAB* 6.3-4). A leader named Joktan sympathizes with the twelve and so devises a plan to rescue them. Upon reaching the prison, Joktan encourages the twelve to make their escape in the steadfast confidence that "the God in whom you trust is powerful, and...he will free you and save you" (*LAB* 6.9). While eleven of the men react positively to Joktan's instructions (*LAB* 6.10), Abram is singled out by his silence (*LAB* 6.11). When questioned, Abraham protests that to leave would constitute a lack of trust in the providence, power, and justice of God: "And now as he in whom I trust lives, I will not be moved from my place where they have put me. If there be any sin of mine so flagrant that I should be burned up, let the will of God be done" (*LAB* 6.11). In various ways, the text emphasizes the distinctiveness of Abraham's response: "Eleven of the men said..." (*LAB* 6.10); "Abram alone was silent" (*LAB* 6.11); Abraham was then locked up "by himself." He was not only faithful; his fidelity was without parallel.

It is against this backdrop that we read about Abraham's election and the covenant that God intends to make with him: "And before all these I will choose my servant Abram, and I will bring him out from their land and will bring him into the land.... For there I will have my servant Abram dwell and will establish my covenant with him and will bless his seed and be lord for him as God forever" (*LAB* 7.4). With the words "before all these," our author sharpens the juxtaposition between the call of Abraham and the catastrophe of Babel. Though Chris VanLandingham probably goes too far when he reads election as a reward for Abraham's obedience,[30] it is difficult to see how the narrative is not providing some rationale for God's choice of Abraham "before all these," especially given the fact that Abraham has just been extolled for his exemplary faith and his refusal to participate in the tower-building program.

This is not the last time *LAB* correlates Abraham's initial fidelity with God's covenant promises. The Lord reminds the people through Joshua how "when all those inhabiting the land were being led astray after their own devices, Abraham believed in me and was not led astray with them.

---

30. Chris VanLandingham, *Judgment & Justification in Early Judaism and the Apostle Paul* (Peabody: Hendrickson, 2006), 29.

And I rescued him from the flame and took him and brought him over all the land of Canaan and said to him in a vision, 'To your seed I will give this land'" (*LAB* 23.5). Significant here is that Joshua's speech fails to mention the idolatry of Terach (cf. Josh. 24:2), as such a depiction would go against *LAB*'s earlier presentation of Abraham's impeccable lineage (*LAB* 4.17).

Deborah's song provides another witness to Abraham's character at Babel:

> Behold the LORD has shown us his glory from on high, as he did in the height of the heavenly places when he sent forth his voice to confuse the languages of men. And he chose our nation and took Abraham our father out of the fire and chose him over all his brothers and kept him from the fire and freed him from the bricks destined for building the tower. And he gave him a son at the end of his old age and took him out of a sterile womb. (*LAB* 32.1)

While the song is overwhelmingly concerned with God's action, the mention of Abraham being "kept from the fire" metaleptically draws its reader's attention back to his exceptional fidelity.[31] The various references to the Akedah sprinkled throughout *LAB* serve to confirm that God made a fitting choice (18.1-6; 32.1-4; 40.2).[32] It is the memory of Abraham, and particularly his offering of Isaac, which incites God to keep all the promises he has made (*LAB* 18.5; 32.4).

If Abraham is presented as an exemplar, he is nevertheless a passive one.[33] There is no mention of Abraham's keeping the commandments, and Abraham's protest presents a narrative of trust (*LAB* 6.11; cf. 6.9). In the recollection of this event at *LAB* 23.5, God highlights that Abraham believed in him (*credidit Abraham mihi*). This focus on faith can also be seen in the story of Amram. Amram's non-conformity to Egyptian oppression is of a piece with Abraham's non-conformity at Babel: both men demonstrate trust in the utter reliability of God's character. Amram's action develops what such trust would look like now that God's character is focused in the promise made to Abraham. And it is this act that is met with the Lord's favor (*LAB* 9.7), just as Abraham's act was met with the Lord's favor (*LAB* 6.11, 17-18; 7.4). What makes Abraham a suitable

---

31. So Murphy, "The Eternal Covenant in Pseudo-Philo," 45, and Frederick J. Murphy, *Pseudo-Philo: Rewriting the Bible* (New York: Oxford University Press, 1993), 244.

32. On this theme in *LAB*, see Tavis A. Bohlinger, "The Akedah in Pseudo-Philo: A Paradigm of Divine–Human Reciprocity," *JSP* 25 (2016): 189–227.

33. So Sprinkle, "The Hermeneutic of Grace," 57–8.

choice to bear the covenant is that he, and he alone, possessed wholehearted trust in the character of God. This is not to conclude that Israel's salvation is somehow merited by Abraham's obedience,[34] but neither is it to conclude that God's choice is arbitrary.[35]

In sum, for *LAB* the story of God's covenant is the story of the triumph of the promises made to Israel's trusting founder. As history progresses, the covenant builds until it reaches its climax at Sinai, when the eternal law is revealed. The eternal law is an integral aspect of the eternal covenant in so far as it provides the unalterable ground rules for relating to God (16.5; 19.6). While cycles of judgment and renewal will play out over the surface of the narrative, what grounds Israel's history and secures its future are the promises God made to Abraham.

This reading of the Abrahamic covenant would have significant implications for the identity-construction of Jews facing the turbulence of first-century Judea. To be a Jew was to be Abraham's seed, an irreducible aspect of God's irrevocable promise. This renders Israel's existence as secure as God's own, for the two are bound together (9.3). Thus whatever sins Israel may have committed to contribute to its current situation, Israel must remain. Moreover, God's commitment to Israel's future was rooted in the faithfulness of the patriarch. History's consistent pattern reaches back to God's dealing with Abraham and forward into the future. In the center stands Sinai, the climatic event in the history of God's covenant dealings with Abraham's seed.

---

34. See Murphy, "The Eternal Covenant in Pseudo-Philo," 56 n. 14: "This is not the same as the doctrine of the merits of the fathers (*zekut 'abot*), which is explicitly contradicted in 33.5. The usual formulation in Pseudo-Philo is salvation because of the promises to or covenant with the fathers, and not because of their merit (but see 62.5)."

35. *Pace* Sprinkle, "The Hermeneutic of Grace," 57–8, and Bohlinger, "The Akedah in Pseudo-Philo: A Paradigm of Divine–Human Reciprocity," 209, the latter of whom refers to God's choice of Israel as "arbitrary," citing 28.4, 31.5, and 39.7, along with the fact that Israel's election is mentioned "before Abraham's fidelity at the tower" at 32.1. To be sure, 28.4 roots God's choice of Israel in his eternal plan. But all that is said of God's plan is that he will choose a plant. Even if we assume that God had Israel in mind, 28.4 still does not specify why God would choose Israel. A rationale for election is also missing from 31.5 and 39.7. These absences do leave open the possibility of an arbitrary choice. But it proves too much to conclude that because these specific texts fail to mention a rationale for election, one does not exist. While 32.1 does mention Israel's election prior to Abraham's fidelity, such a conclusion must be balanced against the evident desire earlier in *LAB* to establish Abraham's exemplary character independently of God's call.

Abraham in Paul

We begin our investigation of Paul's appropriation of the Abrahamic covenant narratives in the highly contested terrain of Romans 4. Paul frames this chapter with a reference to the covenant-making narrative of Genesis 15 (Rom. 4:3, 22-23). He also interprets the significance of Genesis 17 for his auditors.[36] Given that Genesis 15 and 17 are the only places where God explicitly makes a covenant with Abraham, Paul clearly has this covenant narrative in mind, even if he does not use the word "covenant." But how does Paul read these chapters in Israel's history? And how does this reading work to establish the identities of his readers?

The Fulfillment of the Promise and the Faith of Abraham

Like the author of *LAB*, the characteristic that interests Paul most about the patriarch is his trust in God, which is evidenced in Romans 4 by his use of Gen. 15:6 (Rom. 4:3, 22-23), and by his frequent employment of πιστεύω (Rom. 4:3, 5, 17, 18, 24) and πίστις (Rom. 4:5, 9, 11, 12, 13, 14, 16 [2×], 19, 20). Paul is not interested in "faith" as a generic human quality. Rather, the Abrahamic narrative specifies the object of such "trust" as God's fidelity to his promises.[37] The clearest mention of these promises occurs in Rom. 4:17-18, when Paul makes reference to Gen. 17:5 ("for I have made you the father of a multitude of nations") and to

---

36. Genesis 17 is quoted or alluded to at Rom. 4:11, 17, 19, and possibly 13. On the importance of Genesis 17 for Romans 4, see Francis Watson, *Paul and The Hermeneutics of Faith* (Edinburgh: T. & T. Clark, 2004), 215–19.

37. Caroline Johnson Hodge, *If Sons, then Heirs: A Study of Kinship and Ethnicity in the Letters of Paul* (New York: Oxford University Press, 2007), rightly critiques construals of πίστις in Paul that are "abstract," "private," and "disconnected from resulting behavior" (82–83). She wrongly concludes from this, however, that what interests Paul is Abraham's faithfulness/trustworthiness; so too Richard B. Hays, *The Faith of Jesus Christ: An Investigation of the Narrative Substructure of Galatians 3:1–4:11* (Grand Rapids: Eerdmans, 2002), 175–7, 290; Lloyd Gaston, *Paul and the Torah* (Vancouver: University of British Columbia Press, 1987), 61. The verbal form πιστεύω in Rom. 4:3, 18 and Gal. 3:6 specifies πίστις as "faith" or "trust"; see further R. Barry Matlock, "Detheologizing the ΠΙΣΤΙΣ ΧΡΙΣΤΟΥ Debate: Cautionary Remarks from a Lexical Semantic Perspective," *NovT* 2 (2000): 1–23. While Johnson Hodge correctly renders πιστεύω as "trust" in Romans 4 and Galatians 3, she consistently interprets those passages to be about Abraham's trustworthiness/faithfulness (see, e.g., *If Sons, then Heirs*, 83, 84, 87, 88, 89). But "trust" and "trustworthiness" are quite distinct conceptually, even though they elide in Johnson Hodge's work. To be trustworthy is to merit someone's trust: one trusts a trustworthy person or thing. Trustworthiness has to do with dependability; trust with dependence.

Gen. 15:5 ("so shall your offspring be"). But an allusion to the promises of the Abrahamic covenant appears as early as Rom. 4:4-5:

> τῷ δὲ ἐργαζομένῳ ὁ μισθὸς οὐ λογίζεται κατὰ χάριν ἀλλὰ κατὰ ὀφείλημα. τῷ δὲ μὴ ἐργαζομένῳ πιστεύοντι δὲ ἐπὶ τὸν δικαιοῦντα τὸν ἀσεβῆ λογίζεται ἡ πίστις αὐτοῦ εἰς δικαιοσύνην
>
> To the one who works the reward is not reckoned according to gift but according to due. But to the one who does not work, but who trusts in the one who justifies the ungodly, this trust is reckoned as righteousness.

With this analogy Paul continues to explicate the significance of Genesis 15 for his Roman auditors. In Gen. 15:1 LXX, God tells Abraham: ὁ μισθός σου πολὺς ἔσται σφόδρα ("your reward will be exceedingly great"). As N. T. Wright has argued, Paul interprets μισθός as the fulfillment of God's promise to give Abraham an heir, a reasonable interpretation given Abraham's complaint that he does not have a son to serve as his heir in Gen. 15:2-3.[38] According to Genesis 15, God confirms his promise to give Abraham a son (15:4) and then expands the promise by insisting that his offspring will be as numerous as the stars (15:5). Abraham responds to this promise with trust (15:6).

What interests Paul about this story is not only the specific content of the promise, but *how* the promise is fulfilled. In Rom. 4:4-5, Paul uses an analogy that draws a distinction between "the one who works" and "the one who trusts" (τῷ δὲ ἐργαζομένῳ...τῷ δὲ μὴ ἐργαζομένῳ πιστεύοντι). Since the one who trusts is also described as "not working," it is clear that Paul understands the two dispositions antithetically. To the worker, the reward occurs κατὰ ὀφείλημα ("according to due"). To the believer, the reward occurs κατὰ χάριν ("according to gift"). The forefather is ὁ πιστεύων, and therefore the fulfillment of God's promise to him (i.e., his reward) necessarily runs along the lines of gift (κατὰ χάριν).

Paul reiterates this point at Rom. 4:16: "Therefore, the promise is by faith [ἐκ πίστεως], so that it may be according to gift [κατὰ χάριν] and may be guaranteed to all Abraham's offspring." Though advocates of the so-called Old Perspectives on Paul tend to lend greater weight to verses 1-8, while advocates of the New Perspectives instead emphasize verses

---

38. See N. T. Wright, "Paul and the Patriarch: The Role(s) of Abraham in Galatians and Romans," in *Pauline Perspectives: Essays on Paul, 1978–2013* (Minneapolis: Fortress, 2013), 558–63. The other plausible contextual explanation is that the "reward" is righteousness; see Francis Watson, *Paul, Judaism, and the Gentiles: Beyond the New Perspective*, rev. ed. (Grand Rapids: Eerdmans, 2007), 262.

9-17 in the interpretation of this chapter, the obvious parallels between 4:4 and 4:16 demand that the sections be interpreted together. What binds 4:4 and 4:16 at a linguistic level is the phrase κατὰ χάριν, a phrase which only appears in these two verses.³⁹ What is the significance of this phrase and how does it relate to the guarantee (βέβαιος) of the promise?

To answer this question, we must begin with the recognition that, for Paul, χάρις is now concentrated in and redefined by the "gift" of God in Jesus Christ (2 Cor. 8:9; 9:15). This shades the meaning of χάρις in two important ways, both of which can be seen here. First, χάρις concerns a gift given through the miraculous agency of God (Rom. 5:15, 21; 11:5; 2 Cor. 4:15). The patriarch's story is prototypical. With language from Jesus' death and resurrection, Paul focuses on elements of the Genesis narrative—Abraham's "dead" body and Sarah's "dead" womb—which require that the promise be fulfilled by the God "who gives life to the dead and calls into existence that which did not hitherto exist" (Rom. 4:17, 19). Abraham's story thus demonstrates the necessity of relying on God's power to effect the miracle that realizes the promise (Rom. 4:18-22).

The second way in which the Christ-event shades the meaning of χάρις is that Paul now understands God's χάρις to be a gift given without regard to worth. While Paul came to this conviction experientially (Gal. 2:15; 3:2-5; 1 Cor. 15:9-10), and now understands it theologically (Rom. 5:6, 8, 10), in Romans 4 he traces it ancestrally, back to Israel's founding father. The fact that Gen. 15:6 (LXX) says that "Abraham believed God" signals to Paul that God's promise to Abraham was neither given nor fulfilled "according to works" (Rom. 4:2-3; cf. 3:27). As John Barclay notes: "Nothing Abraham did made him worthy of the favor of God."⁴⁰ In Rom. 4:6-8, Paul presses the point further; but rather than taking an episode from the Abrahamic material, Paul quotes Ps. 32:1-2 (LXX 31:1-2), which declares a "blessing" (μακαρισμός) over those, like Abraham, whose sin the Lord overlooks (i.e., sinners). The blessing overlooks criteria of worth.

To describe the fulfillment of the Abrahamic promise as κατὰ χάριν, then, is to say that it is fulfilled by the miraculous power of God and without regard to worth. Correspondingly, the promise is not contingent upon circumstances in the history of the world. On the contrary, the Abraham story establishes that the promise operates according to the purpose and power of God, an idea Paul pushes to extremity in Romans 9–11.⁴¹ There Paul initially traces the fulfillment of the promise in Isaac

---

39. Compare κατὰ τὴν χάριν, which Paul uses to speak of the gifts of roles in the church (Rom. 12:6; 1 Cor. 3:10; cf. Eph. 4:7; 2 Thess. 1:12).

40. Barclay, *Paul and the Gift*, 484.

41. See especially Rom. 9:6-18; 11:2, 32.

(not Ishmael, Rom. 9:7-9), in Jacob (not Esau, Rom. 9:10-13), and finally in idolatrous Israel (not idolatrous Egypt, Rom. 9:15-18) to show how fulfillment does not operate according to normal or natural means.[42] Instead, from beginning to end, God fulfills his promise through his newly creative call (οὐκ ἐξ ἔργων ἀλλ' ἐκ τοῦ καλοῦντος, Rom. 9:12; cf. 4:17; 9:7) and this "so that God's purposes in election might remain" (ἵνα ἡ κατ' ἐκλογὴν πρόθεσις τοῦ θεοῦ μένῃ, Rom. 9:11).[43] That the promise runs κατὰ χάριν, and not according to anything else, is what guarantees its fulfillment (Rom. 4:16).

Abraham, the Father of us All

At this point we can see substantial overlap between Paul and the author of *LAB*'s adoption of the Abrahamic narrative. For both, the Abrahamic covenant is a covenant of promise. And both call for their communities to trust that God will fulfill his word in the face of counterfactuals. But for the Apostle to the Gentiles, the payoff of the fact that God's promises run κατὰ χάριν is precisely that it means that God can and does fulfill his promises among circumcised and uncircumcised alike (Rom. 4:9, 11; 9:24-26), so that Abraham can rightfully be deemed "the father of us all" (4:16), with the cosmos as his inheritance (τὸ κληρονόμον αὐτὸν εἶναι κόσμου, 4:13; cf. Gen. 22:17).[44]

These same features of the Abraham story emerge in Galatians 3, a context where Paul seeks to establish how the Abrahamic promises, here called εὐλογία τοῦ Ἀβραάμ, are given to Gentiles through Christ Jesus (Gal. 3:14).[45] Paul opens the chapter by tracing a direct correspondence between the Galatians' and Abraham's faith:

42. On this line of interpretation, see further Barclay, *Paul and the Gift*, 529–32.

43. On the newly creative call of Israel in Paul, see Beverly Roberts Gaventa, "On the Calling-Into-Being of Israel: Romans 9:6-29," in *Between Gospel and Election: Explorations in the Interpretation of Romans 9–11*, ed. Florian Wilk, J. Ross Wagner, and Frank Schleritt, WUNT 257 (Tübingen: Mohr Siebeck, 2010), 255–69.

44. On the globalization of the land-promise in the Second Temple period, see also Sir. 44:19-21; *Jub.* 17:3; 19:21; 22:14; 32:18, Mek. Exod. 14:31; Philo, *Mos.* 1.155; Heb. 2:5; Mt. 5:5. I am appreciative to Robert Brawley for passing along these references.

45. On the centrality of Abrahamic paternity in Galatians 3–4, see J. Louis Martyn, *Galatians: A New Translation with Introduction and Commentary*, AB 33A (New York: Doubleday, 1997), 117–26, 302–6; Gordon D. Fee, "Who are Abraham's True Children? The Role of Abraham in Pauline Argumentation," in *Perspectives on Our Father Abraham: Essays in Honor of Marvin R. Wilson*, ed. Steven A. Hunt (Grand Rapids: Eerdmans, 2010), 126–37, esp. 128–31.

> Let me ask you only this: Did you receive the Spirit from a position of adherence to Torah or from a position of trusting the preached word [ἐξ ἔργων νόμου τὸ πνεῦμα ἐλάβετε ἢ ἐξ ἀκοῆς πίστεως]?... did he who supplies the Spirit to you and works miracles among you do so when you were relating to him from a position of adherence to Torah or relating to him from a position of trusting the preached word [ἐξ ἔργων νόμου τὸ πνεῦμα ἐλάβετε ἢ ἐξ ἀκοῆς πίστεως]? So also Abraham believed God and it was reckoned to him as righteousness. (Gal. 3:2, 5-6; cf. Rom. 4:23-24)

With rhetorical punch, Paul reminds the Galatians that they received the Spirit—here closely related to the Abrahamic blessings (Gal. 3:14)—according to the miraculous agency of God (ἐνεργῶν δυνάμεις, 3:5).[46] This event did not occur when the Galatians were in a state of adhering to Torah (ἐξ ἔργων νόμου), and thus not according to worth, but when they were responding to God's life-giving message with trust (ἐξ ἀκοῆς πίστεως, Gal. 3:2).[47] It is this event which constituted Paul's Gentile auditors as children of Abraham and the recipients of the Abrahamic promise (3:7-9, 26-29).

This reading strategy re-emerges in the next chapter. As in Romans 9, so also in Galatians 4, Paul compares the births of Ishmael and Isaac in order to highlight the unique means through which God's promise to Abraham was initially fulfilled (Gal. 4:21-31). He observes how Ishmael was born κατὰ σάρκα and thus a product of human ingenuity and agency (Gal. 4:23, 29). Isaac, however, was born δι' ἐπαγγελίας (4:23) or, put differently, κατὰ πνεῦμα (4:29). Here δι' ἐπαγγελίας and κατὰ πνεῦμα provide a functional equivalent to κατὰ χάριν in Rom. 4:4 and 16. Juxtaposed to κατὰ σάρκα, these phrases signal how Isaac was born through the miraculous agency of God, which did not take account of the worthiness of his parents. Unsurprisingly, Paul equates his Gentile,

---

46. On the appositional relationship between the two purpose clauses in Gal. 3:14, see Watson, *Hermeneutics of Faith*, 192. For connections between faith and the reception of the Spirit in Jewish literature, see Matthew Thiessen, *Paul and the Gentile Problem* (Oxford: Oxford University Press, 2016), 109.

47. Johnson Hodge, *If Sons, then Heirs*, 80, has shown how ἐκ often denotes genealogical lineage in Greek literature and suggests that οἱ ἐκ πίστεως in places like Gal. 3:7 is shorthand for "those whose line of descent springs from Abraham's faithfulness." But it is difficult to imagine how one could interpret the parallel phrase ἐξ ἀκοῆς πίστεως in 3:2, 5 in this light (cf. 1 Thess. 1:4-5; 2:13; Rom. 10:17), which makes Johnson Hodge's thesis less attractive. More likely is Thiessen's suggestion that Paul uses the phrase to mean "those born out of faith" (*Paul and the Gentile Problem*, 110–11); cf. 1 Pet. 1:23.

Christ-followers at Galatia with "Isaac"; they too were created through God's power (Gal. 4:28).⁴⁸

If Paul associates the Galatians with Isaac, the child of promise and freedom, he at the same time differentiates them from Esau, the natural born child who remains enslaved (οὐκ ἐσμέν…ἀλλά; Gal. 4:31). This act of disassociation is significant precisely for its contemporary relevance. With the words "so also now" (οὕτως καὶ νῦν; Gal. 4:29), Paul subtly casts his opponents in the role of Esau, thus distinguishing himself and his hearers as children of promise (Gal. 4:28, 31) from those who promote circumcision (4:30–5:2).⁴⁹ He thus fortifies the Galatians' identities over against competing claims.

The Relationship between Promise and Demand, Abraham and Sinai

Paul's reading of the Abrahamic covenant is radical and aggressive: radical in its assertion that uncircumcised Christ-followers are children of promise; aggressive in its insistence that those who promote Gentile circumcision are not. How could Paul maintain this position in the face of Genesis 17 and its demand to circumcise Isaac? In *LAB*, we saw how material from Genesis 17 both served and threatened to undermine the author's purposes. On the one hand, the description of an eternal covenant supports Pseudo-Philo's conviction that the covenant is inviable. On the other hand, the command to circumcise, along with its attendant curse on

---

48. I thus agree, at this point, with Thiessen's recent observation that Paul's utilization of this passage hinges on the fact that "the narrative of Genesis 16 emphasizes human activity" and that, in contrast, "the narrative of the birth of Isaac stresses divine activity" (*Paul and the Gentile Problem*, 88–9), though I fail to see how this differs from what he calls "anti-legalistic" interpretations, since these interpretations are primarily concerned with precisely the agency dynamics he highlights (cf. 75, 87). Thiessen's larger thesis is less convincing. He believes that Paul utilizes this story to show that "not all circumcisions were of covenantal value" (88), and that what Paul rejects in particular is Gentile circumcision because it was not the eighth-day, covenantal circumcision (91–2). Yet Paul never explicitly mentions the temporal stipulation of circumcision in his arguments Gentile circumcision. Further, while Thiessen's proposal provides a rationale for why Ishmael was not a child of promise, it runs into serious problems in the case of Esau (see Rom. 9:10-13), who presumably would have undergone 8th day circumcision. For Paul, children of promise are created only through God's miraculous call, a call which operates irrespective of all criteria, including the criteria of 8th-day circumcision.

49. On the allegorical relevance of this story for Paul, see Steven Di Mattei, "Paul's Allegory of the Two Covenants (Gal 4.21-31) in Light of First-Century Hellenistic Rhetoric and Jewish Hermeneutics," *NTS* 52 (2006): 102–22.

those who do not, introduces the possibility of covenant failure. If parts of Genesis 17 did not sit well with the theology of *LAB*, its command to circumcise would appear even more problematic for Paul. How does Paul deal with this command in Genesis 17?

Due to the nature of Paul's controversial proposal and the obvious objections it raises, he does not have the option of suppressing the command to circumcise in the same way that the author of *LAB* does. Paul must deal with the requirement directly. His tactic is to relegate circumcision's significance. He does this by noting how Abraham was deemed righteous (i.e., worthy to have the covenant promises fulfilled through him) before he was circumcised (Rom. 4:9-10),[50] and because he trusted the miraculous agency of God to fulfill his promise in one as good as dead (Rom. 4:2, 18-22); that is, in one who had no intrinsic qualification (Rom. 4:2-4). What this does, in effect, is to make Abraham the forefather not of those who are merely circumcised (Rom. 4:12),[51] but of all those who believe in the miraculous agency of God to fulfill his promise in those who possess no intrinsic suitability (Rom. 4:11, 16, 24-25).

---

50. Wright's argument that to reckon righteous means "to establish a covenant" based on Phinehas, while suggestive, is inconclusive ("Paul and the Patriarch," 566–8). In every example Wright mentions to support his point, one could also translate "to reckon righteous" as "to reckon worthy," with the context specifying the sense of "worthy to establish a covenant." That Phinehas was reckoned righteous from generation to generation (Ps. 106:31-32, LXX 105:30-31) may simply indicate how future generations regarded him, not covenant succession.

51. The placement and doubling of τοῖς in Rom. 4:12 is notoriously difficult. The majority of interpreters believe Paul is referring to one group, and see here a grammatical or scribal error; so, e.g., James D. G. Dunn, *Romans 1–8*, WBC 38A (Dallas: Word, 1988), 196; C. E. B. Cranfield, *A Critical and Exegetical Commentary on the Epistle to the Romans* (Edinburgh: T. & T. Clark, 1975), 237; Richard B. Hays, *The Conversion of the Imagination: Paul as Interpreter of Israel's Scripture* (Grand Rapids: Eerdmans, 2005), 76. Others believe that Paul's placement of τοῖς before στοιχοῦσιν indicates that he is referring to two groups, whether believing Gentiles and believing Jews, or more likely, unbelieving Jews and believing Jews; so, e.g., Joseph A. Fitzmyer, *Romans: A New Translation with Introduction and Commentary*, AB 33 (New York: Doubleday, 1993), 382; Thomas H. Tobin, "What Shall We Say that Abraham Found? The Controversy behind Romans 4," *HTR* 88 (1995): 437–52, esp. 447. But Love L. Sechrest, *A Former Jew: Paul and the Dialectics of Race*, LNTS 410 (New York: T&T Clark, 2009), 120–3, has now demonstrated that grammatical parallels actually favor interpreting "the circumcised" as a single group (the circumcised who are qualified by faith). Importantly, if Sechrest is correct, it is hard not to conclude that Paul has called the Abrahamic paternity of his unbelieving compatriots into question, at least at this point and in certain respects (but cf. Rom. 4:1; 9:5).

With the importance of circumcision's timing firmly established, Paul then rewrites Gen. 17:11 to make circumcision a sign of "righteousness of faith" (δικαιοσύνης τῆς πίστεως) rather than a "sign of the covenant" (Rom. 4:11). While this may indicate that Paul believed that "the righteousness of faith" constitutes the Abrahamic covenant,[52] at the very least, it further prioritizes the covenant episode of chapter 15 over that of Genesis 17.

Paul is not always obliged to marginalize Genesis 17, of course. In Rom. 4:17, he strengthens this point about the inclusion of Gentiles into Abraham's family by capitalizing on the articulation of the promise in Gen. 17:5: "For I have made you the father of a multitude of nations." There "many nations" colors God's promise of countless offspring in Gen. 15:5 (Rom. 4:18). Thus when Genesis 17 supports Paul's identity-constructing purposes, he will amplify its voice over that of Genesis 15.[53] Nevertheless, what takes precedent is that "Abraham believed God and it was reckoned to him as righteousness." The temporal priority of this declaration rules out the possibility that God deemed Abraham a suitable bearer of the promises for any reason other than his recognition that God would do it. Otherwise Abraham would be "justified by works" and therefore have something about which to boast (Rom. 4:2-3). Paul thus relativizes any sense of obligation, including the obligation to circumcise, to the role of sign.

Paul gestures that he is thinking more globally than circumcision when he reminds his readers that "the promise was not through Law" (Οὐ γὰρ διὰ νόμου ἡ ἐπαγγελία; Rom. 4:13). While νόμος can refer to Israel's national covenant in Paul's writings, the γάρ suggests that here circumcision is primarily envisioned.[54] But the shift to νόμος does generalize Paul's discourse, the purpose of which is to establish a principle. In fact, Paul applies this principle explicitly to the whole of Torah in Galatians 3–4. Paul again makes much of the promises' antiquity, how they came 430 years prior to the institution of Torah at Sinai (Gal. 3:17). Whereas the Torah is temporary (Gal. 3:23-24; cf. 4:1-3, 7), "promise" forms the essence of the Abrahamic covenant and is fundamental to God's dealing with the world (Gal. 3:18).[55]

52. See Wright, "Paul and the Patriarch," 566–8.
53. See further Watson, *Hermeneutics of Faith*, 215.
54. Thus it is best not to take "law" and "promise" to refer to Sinai and Abraham as representing two types of covenants. Rather, law and promise refer to two aspects of the covenant relationship, here with the Abrahamic covenant at the forefront.
55. The absence of διαθήκη in Romans 4 is striking in this regard, when you consider that Paul quotes from the only two chapters in the Abrahamic narrative which explicitly describe God making covenant with Abraham—Genesis 15 and 17.

As with the author of *LAB*, Paul has structured God's promises to Abraham so that they are not contingent on demands. But, quite unlike the author of *LAB*, he has exploited their temporal relationship to do so. For Paul, the promises are not fulfilled through law, neither because law would confine the promise to one nation, nor because law was given only to one nation, but because a promise that was contingent on demand would allow transgression to bring wrath and thereby compromise its fulfillment (Rom. 4:14-15). In other words, the promises are not fulfilled through law because that would undermine Paul's most fundamental conviction—that the promises run κατὰ χάριν (Rom. 4:16).

The Christological Promise: Abraham's Seed and the Gentiles

Paul reads the Abrahamic promises christologically. In Gal. 3:16, he stresses how the promises were directed towards Abraham and to his singular messianic offspring: οὐ λέγει· καὶ τοῖς σπέρμασιν, ὡς ἐπὶ πολλῶν ἀλλ' ὡς ἐφ' ἑνός· καὶ τῷ σπέρματί σου, ὅς ἐστιν Χριστός. Paul is initiating an interpretive debate over the phrase καὶ τῷ σπέρματί σου and what scripture does and does not "say" (οὐ λέγει). His specificity would suggest that he has a particular text in mind, even if it is not transparent about which text it is.[56]

In the context of the Abrahamic narrative, the exact phrase καὶ τῷ σπέρματί σου appears only at Gen. 13:15, 17:8, and 24:7 (LXX). If we allow for the pronominal adjustment, we can add Gen. 17:19 (LXX). But it is difficult to make sense of how Paul would be utilizing any of these passages, which all focus on the giving of the land. There is a near parallel to Paul's καὶ τῷ σπέρματί σου in Gen. 22:18 (LXX, καὶ [ἐνευλογηθήσονται ἐν] τῷ σπέρματί σου), which C. John Collins has argued is the more likely source.[57] What makes this passage so promising is precisely that it concerns the seed's inheritance and the nations' blessing.[58] In fact, the

---

Elsewhere Paul's consistent focus is on the promises made to the patriarchs (ἐπαγγελίας τῶν πατέρων; Rom. 15:8). When Paul does mention the Abrahamic arrangement as a covenant, he quickly glosses this as "the promises made to Abraham" (τῷ δὲ Ἀβραὰμ ἐρρέθησαν αἱ ἐπαγγελίαι καὶ τῷ σπέρματι αὐτοῦ, Gal. 3:15-16).

56. Compare Thiessen, *Paul and the Gentile Problem*, 122; Hans Dieter Betz, *Galatians: A Commentary on Paul's Letter to the Churches in Galatia*, Hermeneia (Philadelphia: Fortress, 1979), 156.

57. C. John [Jack] Collins, "Galatians 3:16: What Kind of Exegete Was Paul?," *TynBul* 54 (2003): 75–86.

58. Compare καὶ κληρονομήσει τὸ σπέρμα in Gen. 22:17 LXX with κληρονομία in Gal. 3:18, and καὶ ἐνευλογηθήσονται ἐν τῷ σπέρματί σου πάντα τὰ ἔθνη in Gen. 22:18 LXX with ἐνευλογηθήσονται ἐν σοὶ πάντα τὰ ἔθνη in Gal. 3:8.

remaining words in Gen. 22:18 are nearly identical to the gospel that Paul says was preached beforehand to Abraham only eight verses earlier: προευηγγελίσατο τῷ Ἀβραὰμ ὅτι ἐνευλογηθήσονται ἐν σοὶ πάντα τὰ ἔθνη (Gal. 3:8).

Galatians 3	Genesis 22:18 LXX
v. 8: <u>ἐνευλογηθήσονται ἐν σοὶ πάντα τὰ ἔθνη</u>	καὶ <u>ἐνευλογηθήσονται ἐν</u> τῷ σπέρματί <u>σου πάντα τὰ ἔθνη</u> τῆς γῆς
v. 16: <u>καὶ τῷ σπέρματί σου</u>	

Given that Gal. 3:8 is the last time that Paul has mentioned the Abrahamic narrative, it would make sense that Paul has the same scriptural source in mind when he comes back to that narrative in 3:16. But how does Gen. 22:18 support Paul's christological reading?

Interpreters of Paul often assume that זרע ("seed" or "offspring") refers unambiguously to a collective in Genesis, and have struggled to make sense of Paul's assertion.[59] It is possible, however, that Paul saw a justification for his approach in Genesis' own grammar. Even though זרע does not have distinctive singular and plural forms, syntactical features, such as verb inflections, adjectives, and pronouns, that surround any instances of זרע lend themselves to either the singular or plural understanding of the noun.[60]

In Gen. 22:17-18a, the angel of the Lord confirms God's promise to Abraham, saying:

> I will surely bless you, and I will surely multiply your seed [והרבה ארבה את־זרעך] as the stars of heaven and as the sand that is on the seashore. And your seed shall possess the gate of his enemies [וירש זרעך את שער איביו] and in your seed [בזרעך] shall all the nations of the earth be blessed.

---

59. For various suggestions, see Hans-Joachim Schoeps, *Paul: The Theology of the Apostle in the Light of Jewish Religious History*, trans. Harold Knight (Philadelphia: Westminster, 1961), 181, 234; Martyn, *Galatians*; E. Earle Ellis, *Paul's Use of the Old Testament* (Grand Rapids: Eerdmans, 1957), 70–3; N. T. Wright, *The Climax of the Covenant: Christ and the Law in Pauline Theology* (Edinburgh: T. & T. Clark, 1991), 162–8. Wright's proposal that Christ is collective is updated in his "Messiahship in Galatians?," in *Galatians and Christian Theology: Justification, the Gospel, and Ethics in Paul's Letter*, ed. Mark W. Elliott, Scott J. Hafemann, N. T. Wright, and John Frederick (Grand Rapids: Baker Academic, 2014), 3–23.

60. For a survey of the grammatical contexts of זרע in Genesis, see C. John (Jack) Collins, "A Syntactical Note (Genesis 3:15): Is the Woman's Seed Singular or Plural," *TynBul* 48 (1997): 139–48.

The first reference to זרע is an indisputable collective; זרע is multiplied like stars and sand. As such, it is often assumed that the second זרע is also a collective. Yet Desmond Alexander has pointed out how the Hebrew grammar of verse 17 opens up another reading.[61] First, he observes how the syntax of the final clause in this verse is disjunctive, thus allowing for זרע to have a different referent. Second, and more importantly, the seed possesses the gate of "*his* enemies" (איביו). The masculine, singular pronoun invites inclined interpreters to construe this second זרע as an individual descendant of Abraham, who would conquer Gentiles. The next pronouncement—that in Abraham's seed (בזרעך) all the nations of the earth will be blessed—could then be interpreted as describing a singular seed also: through a single descendant of Abraham the Gentile nations would be conquered and blessed.

Psalm 72 provides us with one example of Gen. 22:17-18 being read in this manner. The Psalm concerns the eternal and world-wide reign of a royal Son (Ps. 72:1, 5, 7-8), who defeats "his enemies" (איביו; Ps. 72:9; cf. Gen. 22:17). "All nations" (כל־גוים/πάντα τὰ ἔθνη) not only serve him (Ps. 72:11 [LXX 71:11]; cf. Gen. 22:18) but are blessed in him (ויתברכו בו כל־גוים; Ps. 72:17; cf. והתברכו בזרעך כל גויי הארץ in Gen. 22:18).[62] At both a thematic and verbal level, all this sounds strikingly similar to the promise made to Abraham about his seed in Gen. 22:17-18, and yet here this promise is applied to an individual king, a royal son.[63] It seems likely that Paul is exegeting Gen. 22:18 in a similar manner at Gal. 3:16, but specifies that this promised descendant is the Messiah (ὅς ἐστιν Χριστός).[64] The likelihood of Paul reading Genesis in line with Psalm 72 is increased when we turn to the book of Romans.

Paul bookends his letter to the Romans with statements to the effect that, as Messiah, Jesus is the realization of God's ancient promises (Rom. 1:2-4; 15:7-12). In Rom. 1:2-4, Paul introduces his gospel as the fulfillment of promises God made through his prophets. As with Psalm 72, these promises concern God's Son (περὶ τοῦ υἱοῦ αὐτοῦ), who comes

---

61. T. Desmond Alexander, "Further Observations on the Term 'Seed' in Genesis," *TynBul* 48 (1997): 363–7, esp. 365.

62. Compare πᾶσαι αἱ φυλαὶ τῆς γῆς in Ps. 71:17 LXX.

63. In its initial setting, Psalm 72 concerned Solomon (72:1).

64. For another proposal for how Paul links the seed-promise with the Messiah, see Matthew V. Novenson, *Christ among the Messiahs: Christ Language in Paul and Messiah Language in Ancient Judaism* (Oxford: Oxford University Press, 2012), 141–2, building on the arguments of Richard B. Hays, *Echoes of Scripture in the Letters of Paul* (New Haven: Yale University Press, 1989), 85.

out of David's genealogical lineage (ἐκ σπέρματος Δαυὶδ). Here Paul is drawing on 2 Sam. 7:12-14 and Psalm 2. In 2 Samuel 7, God promises David, through the prophet Nathan: "I will raise up your offspring after you, who shall come from your body" (ἐκ τῆς κοιλίας σου; 2 Sam. 7:12b; cf. Rom. 1:3a). This offspring is then called God's "son" (2 Sam. 7:14). Being appointed God's Son "in power" (Rom. 1:4) corresponds to the enthronement language of Ps. 2:7.[65] It is clear from this that Paul understood the promises about the Messiah made through the prophets to concern the Davidic covenant.

Yet we can see by the end of the letter that these promises about a messianic Son are integrally linked to the Abrahamic covenant. For Paul writes in Rom. 15:8-9:

> ...for Christ became a servant of the circumcised concerning the truthfulness of God, in order to guarantee the promises to the patriarchs [εἰς τὸ βεβαιῶσαι τὰς ἐπαγγελίας τῶν πατέρων], or [in other words] in order that the Gentiles might glorify God for mercy [τὰ δὲ ἔθνη ὑπὲρ ἐλέους δοξάσαι τὸν θεόν].

Since elsewhere Paul's focus is on the patriarchal promises given to Abraham, it is best to take the plural, "patriarchs," as the reiteration of these promises to Abraham's children. And Paul says that the Messiah's ministry had a two-fold purpose: to fulfill the promises to the patriarchs and to cause the Gentiles to worship. But if the specific patriarchal promises that Paul has in mind are those he developed in chapter 4—namely that Abraham would "inherit the world" and become "the father of many nations" (Rom. 4:13, 17-18)—then these are one and the same. The Davidic Messiah fulfills the Abrahamic promises precisely because those promises concern a Messiah through whom the Gentiles would become Abraham's children and receive Abraham's blessings (Gal. 3:29).[66] So it would appear that, like the author of Psalm 72, Paul reads the Abrahamic and Davidic "seed" promises together. But his christological reading of

---

65. That 2 Sam. 7:12-14 and Ps. 2:7 are in Paul's mind can be deduced from the fact that these are the only two texts in the LXX in which the prophetic voice of God calls the Davidic king his "son" (cf. Ps. 72:1-2). Furthermore, combinations of 2 Samuel 7 and Psalm 2 were common in Jewish literature (4QFlor 1:10-13, 18-19; *Pss. Sol.* 17:4, 23; Heb. 1:5).

66. For a creative suggestion on how exactly Paul saw these Gentiles being related to Abraham through the *pneuma* of the Messiah, see the work of Johnson Hodge, *If Sons, then Heirs*, 93–197, which has now been developed by Thiessen, *Paul and the Gentile Problem*, 115–60, in relation to Gen. 15:5-6.

the Abrahamic and "seed-promise" is marshaled to support the identity of his messianic, Gentile communities. "They" are what the promises of the Abrahamic covenant were always about (Gal. 3:7-9, 16-18).

Conclusion

Paul and the author of *LAB* converge at many places in their reading and utilization of the Abrahamic narrative. Setting these authors' reception of Abrahamic traditions side by side has allowed us to tease out and sharpen similarities and differences between them. We have also been able to see how these similarities and differences arise, in large measure, from the need to reinforce the identities of their respective communities in various ways.

The author of *LAB* is writing to assure an anxious community that God will fulfill his promises in the future, and that whatever the present bleakness of the situation, they can rest assured that, to borrow Paul's words, they really are loved on account of the fathers; for the gifts and calling of God really are irrevocable. The author's focus on God's abiding promise causes him to depict "trust" as Abraham's most quintessential attribute, even if Abraham's exemplary, covenant-establishing piety is manifest in other ways. Abraham's life is significant in two identity-forming respects. First, since Abraham's life secures the covenant, the community of *LAB* is to see themselves as the beneficiaries of his life. But as his seed, the community of *LAB* is to mimic their forefather's trust and to remain faithful to God in the midst of the present crisis.

As the Apostle to the Gentiles, Paul is trying to make sense of God's faithfulness to the Abrahamic promises in light of the fact that so many Gentiles have responded positively to his message, while so many of his fellow Jews have responded negatively. To meet this crisis, felt by himself and his communities, Paul re-reads the Abrahamic covenant in a christological manner. This reading strategy gives his Gentile congregations ownership of Abraham's story and assures them that God's promises to Abraham were in fact about them. It is precisely because the fulfillment of God's promises run κατὰ χάριν and not κατὰ σάρκα that Paul's Gentile communities can see themselves as children of promise, even over against those promoting circumcision (Rom. 4:1, 4, 11-12, 16; 9:8; Gal. 4:21-31; Phil. 3:2-3).

Like the author of *LAB*, Paul also values Abraham's trust as his most significant attribute. But because of Paul's unique identity-forming purposes, Abraham's trust performs a different function in his writings than it does in *LAB*. The fact that Gen. 15:6 (LXX) says "Abraham believed God and it was reckoned to him as righteousness" before he was circumcised, indicates that Abraham can be the father of those who share his faith while uncircumcised. Faith in the miraculous agency of God is the demarcating attribute of Abraham's children.[67]

Noteworthy in this respect is that Paul's exposition makes no mention of Abraham's life before God's election, but is only concerned with Abraham's life as a response to God's call. Presumably this is because Paul saw Abraham's call as an act of new creation (2 Cor. 4:6). While this is in harmony with Genesis' silence, it looks odd when compared to other Second Temple authors who obsess over Abraham's history and heritage. If *LAB* is exceptional for the sparse attention it pays to these features, Paul is uncanny. For Paul, the only backdrop to the call of Abraham is the plight of Adam and the reign of Sin (Rom. 5:12-21; Gal. 3:22).

If certain features of the Abraham story serve Paul's purposes, others do not. Among them is God's confirmation in Gen. 15:4 that Abraham's heir would come from his own body. Such a detail could potentially subvert his purposes in helping Gentiles see themselves as children of promise. This purpose also leads him, by necessity, to distance the covenant promises not only from the instructions about covenant circumcision in Genesis 17, but also from the law given at Sinai. Unlike the author of *LAB*, Paul does not view each new covenant as that which includes, perfects, and supersedes the previous one. The Torah is temporary, an overlay, to be dispensed with at the proper time (Gal. 3:19-26; 4:1-5).

To the author of *LAB*, Paul's conclusions must have appeared scandalous. It would have been unfathomable for our author to conceive of someone claiming participation in the covenant promise without standing in positive relationship to the covenant's Torah, since in *LAB*, promise and law are as inseparable as they are eternal, connected to the very structure of the universe, and an extension of the eternal God himself.[68] To be sure,

---

67. Erin M. Heim, *Adoption in Galatians and Romans: Contemporary Metaphor Theories and the Pauline* huiothesia *Metaphors*, BibInt 153 (Leiden: Brill, 2017), 172, is correct to insist that Paul makes Christ the focus of Abrahamic descent. It is perhaps too sharp of a dichotomy, however, to insist that Paul does this "rather than appealing to [the Galatians] sharing of their characteristic 'faith' with Abraham." Faith is a family trait to which Paul can appeal (Gal. 3:9); cf. Debbie Hunn, "Galatians 3:6-9: Abraham's Fatherhood and Paul's Conclusions," *CBQ* 78 (2016): 500–514, whose focus on metaphorical patronage through the imitation of Abraham's faith seems to overlook Paul's christological argument altogether.

68. Reinmuth, "Beobachtungen zum Verständnis des Gesetzes im *Liber Antiquitatum Biblicarum* (Pseudo-Philo)," 153.

the author of *LAB* will distance the covenant promises from the covenant demand of circumcision, but this is emphatically not out of a concern to downplay the distinction between Israel and the nations as heirs of the Abrahamic promise. He has no interest in the fate of the nations (*LAB* 9.5; cf. 18.13-14; 43.5, 7). As one writing to a people worried about the extinction of their identity, the author assures his community that the world was created for Israel. God would destroy the world before he would destroy Israel (*LAB* 18.10).[69] To blur the lines between the identity of Israel and that of the nations would undermine his very purposes.

In sum, Paul and the author of *LAB* share an intense focus on the unconditioned saving agency of God. If other Jews in the Second Temple period believed in grace, to most readers *LAB* and Paul would stand out for their dogged commitment to the triumph of grace in the face of human sin.[70] We have seen that one feature of this commitment is how, for both authors, the primary import and essential nature of the Abrahamic covenant is that it is an immutable covenant of promise. This promise marches forward in the face of human conditions to the contrary. And thus for neither author are the Abrahamic promises finally contingent on human fidelity. Nevertheless, the authors take the import of their promise hermeneutic in radically divergent directions to construct and maintain the particular identities of their respective communities. If two authors could place so much hermeneutical priority on the Abrahamic promises and yet construe Israel's covenant in such a fundamentally different fashion, then it is probable that no shared or set "covenant theology" existed by which Second Temple Jews could identify.

---

69. On the importance of Israel in *LAB*, see further Barclay, *Paul and the Gift*, 275–8; Murphy, "The Eternal Covenant in Pseudo-Philo," 49.

70. Of the numerous works related to this topic in Paul, see, more recently, Barclay, *Paul and the Gift*. On *LAB*, see Sprinkle, "The Hermeneutic of Grace," 50–67.

Heracles between Slavery and Freedom: Subversive Textual Appropriation in Philo of Alexandria

Courtney J. P. Friesen

Introduction

Roman Alexandria afforded new opportunities, arguably unparalleled in the ancient world, to read other peoples' texts. Indeed, with the creation of its celebrated library in the third century BCE, the Ptolemies had fashioned themselves as curators of the world's literatures. Jews living in this context wrote themselves into the legendary origins of the Library, imagining that Ptolemy II Philadelphus (283–246 BCE), at the urging of his chief librarian Demetrius, commissioned the Greek translation of Hebrew scripture. Populated by Greeks, Jews, Egyptians, and governed by Romans, the city was a complex nexus of political and religious forces. Not infrequently, cultural contestations were fought out in the realm of textual appropriation, as various communities would stake their identities upon different, sometimes conflicting, literary authorities.

Philo of Alexandria offers an especially useful window into the role of authoritative texts in constructing social identity. While he is best known for his innovative interpretations of Jewish scriptures, he was at the same time closely engaged with classical Greek literature. This essay takes as a starting point one particularly striking instance of Philo's deployment of a text from classical Athens. In *That Every Good Person Is Free*, he quotes extensively—17 lines in 5 fragments—from Euripides' satyr play, the *Syleus*, interspersed with plot summary and commentary. The play's heroic protagonist, Heracles, functions for Philo as a paradigm of true virtue. In a perhaps surprising turn, Heracles' divine freedom is displayed through his persistence in prolific eating and drinking, even amidst his temporary guise as a slave.

Philo's evocation of this text problematizes our conceptions of what, or who, qualifies as "other," and which texts function as "authoritative." To the extent that modern scholarship divides up the ancient world into cultural and religious categories of Jews and Christians on the one hand, and "pagan" Greeks and Romans, on the other, a Euripidean play will be seen as "other" with respect to Philo. It is less clear, however, that in his ancient milieu Philo perceived things in these terms. In fact, he cites this text and takes its divine hero as a model for emulation without qualification. At the same time, however, I argue that his choice of this satyr drama as an authority in moral instruction, portraying as it does Heracles acting as a buffoon, has a potentially ironic effect.

Hellenistic Jews, in general, and Philo, in particular, exhibit well the complexity of boundaries between social and ethnic identities.[1] In recent years, scholars of Greek culture under the Roman Empire have grown more attentive to Judaism as a productive site for exploring cultural hybridity. Under the rubric of the so-called Second Sophistic,[2] Tim Whitmarsh proposes a reevaluation of the classical canon, and he places Jewish literature at the center of this task. Whereas standard histories of Greek literature in the Roman period focus on authors such as Plutarch, Dio Chrysostom, and Lucian as the true intellectual heirs of the classical tradition, Whitmarsh seeks out "lateral engagement with other peoples' cultures, poetics and imaginative literature, the continuity with Hellenistic Greek culture."[3] In this regard, he observes that classicists, himself

---

1. For a discussion of relevant social theory, see, e.g., Richard Jenkins, *Social Identity*, 4th ed. (London: Routledge, 2014), 120–33.

2. Conventionally, the term "Second Sophistic" has been applied to the literary movement connected with Greek orators beginning during the reign of Nero. This temporal framework was established by the ancient biographer, Philostratus, in his *Lives of the Sophists*. Standard historical and literary treatments include Glen W. Bowersock, *Greek Sophists in the Roman Empire* (Oxford: Clarendon, 1969); B. P. Reardon, *Courants littéraires grecs des IIe et IIIe siècles après J.-C.*, Annales littéraires de l'Université de Nantes 3 (Paris: Les belles lettres, 1971); Graham Anderson, *The Second Sophistic: A Cultural Phenomenon in the Roman Empire* (London: Routledge, 1993); Simon Swain, *Hellenism and Empire: Language, Classicism, and Power in the Greek World AD 50–250* (Oxford: Clarendon, 1996); Thomas Schmitz, *Bildung und Macht: Zur sozialen und politischen Funktion der zweiten Sophistik in der griechischen Welt der Kaiserzeit*, Zetemata 97 (Munich: Beck, 1997); Tim Whitmarsh, *Greek Literature and the Roman Empire: The Politics of Imitation* (Oxford: Oxford University Press, 2001); Whitmarsh, *The Second Sophistic*, Greece and Rome: New Surveys in the Classics 35 (Oxford: Oxford University Press, 2005).

3. Tim Whitmarsh, *Beyond the Second Sophistic: Adventures in Greek Post-classicism* (Berkeley: University of California Press, 2013), 4.

included, have largely neglected Hellenistic Judaism. But, in fact, it "offers a much better expression of what many critics seek in the Greek Second Sophistic, namely a coherent articulation of subaltern resistance through literature." This can be seen, Whitmarsh argues, in the ways Jewish authors studied and adapted classical poetic genres in their own compositions, particularly epic by Theodotus and Philo (the poet) and tragedy by Ezekiel.[4] While Whitmarsh does not include Philo of Alexandria in his analysis, Erich Gruen's recent contribution to *The Oxford Handbook to the Second Sophistic* places him at the head of his survey of Jewish literature.[5] Gruen draws attention, above all, to the treatise *That Every Good Person Is Free* due to the extent to which Philo deploys Greek and Roman exempla in support of a Stoic moral paradox: "All of this shows Philo comfortable, quite unselfconsciously so, in the culture of the Hellenes."[6] The inclusion of Judaism in this *Oxford Handbook* is itself evidence that the disciplines of classics and Jewish and Philonic studies are poised for new directions of cross-disciplinary engagement. And this is precisely the sort of methodological coordination suited for the present project concerned with "Reading Other Peoples' Texts."

This study proceeds, first, with a brief survey of the role of Heracles in comedy and satyr drama as relevant background to Philo's engagement with the *Syleus* discussed in the subsequent section. Then, under the remaining two headings, I aim to situate Philo's use of this satyr play within a larger context, arguing that his valuation of Euripides as an authoritative text is consistent with the sentiment of many contemporary intellectuals, while at the same time being subversive of the status of Heracles, especially as he was valorized at Rome and deployed in imperial propaganda.

Heracles on the (Alexandrian) Scene

Philo's use of the *comic* Heracles as a *positive* model of moral virtue sets him apart from several other ancient Greeks and Romans.[7] By contrast, Christian critics of traditional religion, especially, found in Heracles

---

4. Whitmarsh, *Beyond the Second Sophistic*, 211–27, 239–47 (at 213).

5. Erich S. Gruen, "Jewish Literature and the Second Sophistic," in *The Oxford Handbook to the Second Sophistic*, ed. Daniel S. Richter and William A. Johnson (Oxford: Oxford University Press, 2017), 639–54.

6. Gruen, "Jewish Literature and the Second Sophistic," 488–92, at 490.

7. The standard survey treatment of Heracles remains G. Karl Galinsky, *The Herakles Theme: The Adaptations of the Hero in Literature from Homer to the Twentieth Century* (Oxford: Blackwell, 1972); see also Abraham J. Malherbe,

striking proof of the debauchery innate to paganism. Origen observes that the polytheists "possess stories concerning [their deities] in which much licentiousness of Heracles is reported and his womanly enslavement to Omphale" (φέροντες τὰς περὶ αὐτῶν ἱστορίας, ἐν αἷς ἀναγέγραπται πολλὴ Ἡρακλέους ἀκολασία καὶ ἡ πρὸς τὴν Ὀμφάλην γυναικείως δουλεία, *Cels.* 3.22).[8] By contrast, in Christian scriptures, "no intemperance of [Jesus] is contained" (οὐδεμία τούτου φέρεται ἀκολασία, *Cels.* 3.23). That Heracles' enslavement to Omphale should have a distinctly feminizing (γυναικείως) effect is similarly emphasized by Tertullian. He asserts that it was on account of "sexual desire" (*libido*) that Heracles donned "a woman's clothing" (*muliebris cultus*). In exchange, while he dressed in her silk (*sericum*), she wore his lion skin (*Pall.* 4.3; cf. Lactantius, *Inst.* 1.9).

For these Christian writers, fixation on the gender reversal inherent in Heracles' temporary slave status evidenced in his wearing female garb and, conversely, her wearing the attributes of Heracles, has a clear apologetic function. While these features of Heracles' mythological biography may have been common cultural knowledge, it is particularly on the comic stage that the exchange of costume would have left a vivid impression upon audiences. According to Dio Chrysostom, this was a distinctly Alexandrian obsession: "They think it hilarious when they see such a Heracles carried about and, as customary, dressed in saffron" (τὸν δὲ Ἡρακλέα τοιοῦτον ὁρῶσι γελοῖον δοκεῖ, παραφερόμενον, καὶ καθάπερ εἰώθασιν, ἐν κροκωτῷ, *Alex.* [*Or.*] 32.94).[9]

Dio's enslaved, cross-dressing Heracles is broadly attested in comedy and satyr drama, and thus not limited to any one play in particular. In a fragmentary satyr play by Ion, *Omphale*, for instance, the queen orders the Lydian women to "adorn our guest" (τὸν ξένον κοσμήσατε), insisting that on his body there should be "ointment, perfume, and a garment of Sardis" (βακκάρις δὲ καὶ μύρα καὶ Σαρδιανὸν κόσμον), and "dark kohl powder as eyeliner" (τὴν μέλαιναν στίμμιν ὀμματογράφον, *TrGF* 1.22, 24-25).[10]

"Heracles," in vol. 2 of *Light from the Gentiles: Hellenistic Philosophy and Early Christianity*, 2 vols., ed. Carl R. Holladay et al., NovTSup 150 (Leiden: Brill, 2014), 651–74.

8. All translations are mine throughout.

9. On this passage, see Dimitri Kasprzyk and Christophe Vendries, *Spectacles et désordre à Alexandrie: Dion de Pruse, Discours aux Alexandrins*, Histoire ancienne (Rennes: Presses Universitaires de Rennes, 2012), 78, 137–8. That saffron was assoe ciated with women is especially well attested in comedy; see Aristophanes, *Lys.* 44, 47; *Thesm.* 138; *Eccl.* 879; *Ran.* 46.

10. For discussion, see Monica Silveira Cyrino, "Heroes in D(u)ress: Transvestism and Power in the Myths of Herakles and Achilles," *Arethusa* 31 (1998): 207–41, esp.

Moreover, it is not just Heracles and Omphale who exchange attire; other *dramatis personae* could don the hero's attributes in order to impersonate him. Perhaps the best-known instance of this occurs in Aristophanes' *Frogs*, where Dionysus undertakes a journey to the underworld carrying a club and wearing a lion skin in the hopes of retaking the recently deceased Euripides to the land of the living. Heracles is, of course, an expert in such endeavors, so Dionysus visits his home in order to learn the most effective route. Seeing him at the door, Heracles declares,

ἀλλ' οὐχ οἷός τ' εἴμ' ἀποσοβῆσαι τὸν γέλων,
ὁρῶν λεοντῆν ἐπὶ κροκωτῷ κειμένην.
τίς ὁ νοῦς; τί κόθορνος καὶ ῥόπαλον ξυνηλθέτην;

Indeed, I am unable to keep from laughter seeing a lion skin resting upon a saffron robe. What's the idea? Why have a buskin and club joined together? (Aristophanes, *Ran.* 45–47)

Dionysus' characteristically effeminate appearance, here represented in his robe (κροκωτός) and boots (κόθορνος, translated "buskin" above), is incongruent with the hyper-masculinity of the Heraclean disguise, much to the latter's amusement. The function of the heroic costume and its interchangeability underlie much of the comic action in the subsequent scenes. Having arrived in the underworld, when Dionysus approaches the abode of Aeacus, his slave Xanthias, sensing his master's fear, wonders whether he has merely "the form as Heracles" (καθ' Ἡρακλέα τὸ σχῆμα) but not also "the resolve" (τὸ λῆμ', *Ran.* 463). Upon learning that Heracles had made numerous enemies who were all now eager to exact vengeance, Dionysus immediately insists that Xanthias take over the disguise, while conversely he assumes the role of slave (*Ran.* 495–97). Later, however, when it appears that the lion skin and club would provide admittance to the inn where there was a feast and dancing girls, Dionysus demands to trade back (*Ran.* 522–28), only to reverse course again when he learns that Heracles had racked up debts that would result in severe punishment (*Ran.* 579–88).

These memorable comic scenes in Aristophanes' *Frogs* highlight the manner in which slave and heroic status could be exchanged by means of the Heraclean attributes of a lion skin and club, which functioned

---

218–19. For fragments of Greek tragedy and satyr drama, see Bruno Snell et al., *Tragicorum graecorum fragmenta*, 5 vols. (Göttingen: Vandenhoeck & Ruprecht, 1971–2004), hereafter abbreviated *TrGF*.

as convenient stage props to represent this.[11] These theatrical tropes, especially well-suited for comedy and satyr drama, are largely absent from other Greek genres. Thus, for instance, in Sophocles, *Trachiniae* 248–53, when Heracles' enslavement to Omphale is described there is no hint of it. Similarly, later historians and mythographers omit this detail (e.g., Diodorus Siculus 4.31.5-8; Apollodorus 2.6.3; Hyginus, *Fab.* 32).[12]

Heracles as Exemplum in Philo's That Every Good Person Is Free

In his philosophical treatise *That Every Good Person Is Free*, Philo takes up a popular Stoic paradox that a person of genuine virtue is truly liberated even if enslaved.[13] His argument unfolds broadly in two stages. In the preliminary section of the treatise (*Prob.* 1–61), he defines freedom as that which concerns the soul rather than the body and emphasizes that it is consequently not primarily external constraints but the passions that make one a slave (*Prob.* 17–18). Following these theoretical considerations, he proceeds with an extensive list of exempla to illustrate and establish the thesis (*Prob.* 62–160). These are diverse and wide ranging, and, significantly, only one derives from Judaism—the Essenes (*Prob.* 75–91). The rest are drawn from "Greeks and barbarians" (*Prob.* 98), among which classical tragedians figure prominently in Philo's sources. The first involves the actions of Heracles in Euripides' satyr play, the *Syleus*:

> ἴδε γοῦν οἷα παρ' Εὐριπίδῃ φησὶν ὁ Ἡρακλῆς·
> πίμπρα, κάταιθε σάρκας, ἐμπλήσθητί μου
> πίνων κελαινὸν αἷμα· πρόσθε γὰρ κάτω
> γῆς εἶσιν ἄστρα γῆ τ' ἄνεισ' εἰς αἰθέρα,
> πρὶν ἐξ ἐμοῦ σοι θῶπ' ἀπαντῆσαι λόγον.

---

11. For a discussion of the history and standardization of the costume of Heracles in drama, see Rosie Wyles, "Heracles' Costume from Euripides' *Heracles* to Pantomime Performance," in *Performance in Greek and Roman Theatre*, ed. George W. M. Harrison and Vayos Liapis, Mnemosyne Supplements 353 (Leiden: Brill, 2013), 181–98.

12. For this point, see esp. Cyrino, "Heroes in D(u)ress," 217–19.

13. The same paradox is addressed with similar arguments by Cicero (*Parad.* 5) and Epictetus (*Diatr.* 4.1). On Philo's treatise, see Madeleine Petit, *Quod omnis probus liber sit: introduction, texte, traduction et notes*, Les oeuvres de Philon d'Alexandrie 28 (Paris: Cerf, 1974), 17–132; Maren R. Niehoff, *Philo of Alexandria: An Intellectual Biography*, Anchor Yale Bible Reference Library (New Haven: Yale University Press, 2018), 81–4.

See, then, what kinds of things Heracles says in Euripides:
> Ignite and burn up my flesh, be filled with drinking my dark blood;
> for the stars will come down to earth, and the earth ascend to the sky
> before a flattering word from me meets you. (*Prob.* 99; *TrGF* 5.687)

In the dramatic context, Heracles finds himself in a state of temporary slavery to Syleus as a ploy to destroy the tyrant. Even so, the hero rejects any expectation that he should engage in "flattery" (θωπεία) which is "most befitting a slave" (δουλοπρεπέστατα, *Prob.* 99). Not only does he refuse to speak as a slave, he proves incapable of effectively disguising himself as one. In a scene set in the slave market, Hermes presents the hero for sale, and the comic effect arises from the trope of the Heraclean costume. Whereas in Aristophanes' *Frogs* taking on or off the lion skin and club were immediately successful means of establishing one's identity as Heracles or not, the hero in the *Syleus* seems unable or unwilling to shed his attributes or conceal his impressive visage. Not only does he appear as "honorable and not humble in form" (πρὸς σχῆμα σεμνὸς κοὐ ταπεινός), it seems he was still wielding his club: "to an observer he is splendid in garment and effective with a club" (στολὴν ἰδόντι λαμπρὸς καὶ ξύλῳ δραστήριος, *Prob.* 101; *TrGF* 5.688).[14]

Thus, in his manner of both speech and appearance, Heracles proves incapable of conforming to the expectations of servitude. But, for Philo, the conclusive proof of his genuine freedom comes later. With his master off in the fields, Heracles, "after sacrificing the best of the bulls there to Zeus as a pretense, was feasting, and when he had plundered much wine, consumed it unmixed all at once after reclining very happily" (τὸν μὲν γὰρ ἄριστον τῶν ἐκεῖ ταύρων καταθύσας Διὶ πρόφασιν εὐωχεῖτο, πολὺν δ' οἶνον ἐκφορήσας ἀθρόον εὖ μάλα κατακλιθεὶς ἠκρατίζετο, *Prob.* 102). Returning from the fields, Syleus is outraged by these actions. Rather than backing down, however, Heracles challenges him to a drinking competition:

κλίθητι καὶ πίωμεν, ἐν τούτῳ δέ μου
τὴν πεῖραν εὐθὺς λάμβαν᾽, εἰ κρείσσων ἔσῃ.

Lie down, and let us drink; take the test at once to see whether in this you are stronger than I. (*Prob.* 103; *TrGF* 5.691; cf. Athenaeus, *Deipn.* 10.411e-412b)

---

14. He was possibly also wearing a lion skin; while the precise nature of splendid garment remains unspecified in the *Syleus*, elsewhere Euripides uses στολὴ θηρός for the lion skin of Heracles (Euripides, *Herc. fur.* 465). Wyles argues that this latter play was especially influential in establishing a standardized Heraclean costume for subsequent theatrical productions ("Heracles' Costume," 181–98).

That Heracles' divine heroism expressed itself in comedy through prolific eating and drinking was a well-known trope. This was already a cliché in fifth-century plays (Epicharmus, frag. 18 K.-A.; Aristophanes, *Pax* 741–42; *Vesp.* 60; *Ran.* 503–48; *Av.* 1604; Euripides, *Alc.* 747–72), and, as suggested by Dio Chyrsostom (*Alex.* [*Or.*] 32.94), remained an especially beloved feature in Alexandrian theater even beyond the time of Philo.[15] Philo argues that the hero's persistence in these stereotypical actions even amidst his temporary slave status is precisely what establishes his genuine freedom and virtue.

Euripidean Drama as an Authoritative Text?

Philo's use of a text from Euripides as an authority in a philosophical treatise is consistent with his practices elsewhere, and reflects the literary culture of contemporary Greek elites living in the Roman world. While Homer was the most popular and frequently quoted poet, and his epics functioned as foundational and in some sense authoritative texts within Hellenistic culture, Euripides was by far the most prominent of the tragedians.[16] He earned a reputation for innovative, even radical, religious

---

15. On the comic Heracles, see esp. Radislav Hošek, "Herakles auf der Bühne der alte attischen Komödie," in *GERAS: Studies Presented to George Thomson on the Occasion of his 60th Birthday*, ed. Ladislav Varcl and Ronald F. Willetts, AUC Philosophica et historica 1, Graecolatina Prasgensia 2 (Prague: Charles University, 1963), 119–27; Galinsky, *The Herakles Theme*, 81–100; Courtney J. P. Friesen, "Gluttony and Drunkenness as Jewish and Christian Virtues: From the Comic Heracles to Christ in the Gospels," in *Envisioning God in the Humanities: Essays on Christianity, Judaism, and Ancient Religion in Honor of Melissa Harl Sellew*, ed. Courtney J. P. Friesen, Westar Seminar on God and the Human Future (Eugene: Wipf & Stock, 2018), 243–61, esp. 245–8.

16. Philo's preference for Euripides coheres with broader trends of popularity. Throughout Philo's corpus he is quoted some 21 times where there are only six quotations from Aeschylus and one from Sophocles. For these statistics, see David Lincicum, "A Preliminary Index to Philo's Non-Biblical Citations and Allusions," *SPhiloA* 25 (2013): 139–67. This ratio is roughly comparable to that of the surviving papyri—176 for Euripides; 38 for Sophocles; and 35 for Aeschylus—as calculated by Robert Garland, *Surviving Greek Tragedy* (London: Bloomsbury, 2004), 53. Philo was also closely acquainted both with Homer, whom he quotes 25 times, and contemporary interpretive methods applied to the epics; see Katell Berthelot, "Philon d'Alexandrie, lecteur d'Homère: quelques éléments de réflexion," in *Prolongements et renouvellements de la tradition classique*, ed. Anne Balansard, Gilles Dorival, and Mireille Loubet (Aix-en-Provence: Publications de l'Université Provence, 2011),

ideas, which he seems to have adopted from contemporary philosophers. Thus, he was later dubbed "philosopher of the stage" (Clement, *Strom.* 5.11.70.2; Origen, *Cels.* 4.77; Vitruvius, 8 praef. 1), and the biographical tradition invented legendary connections with Anaxagoras, of whom he was a student (Vitruvius, 8 praef. 1), and with Socrates, who collaborated with him on certain plays (*TrGF* 5 T A.1.IA.3; also Diogenes Laertius 2.18; cf. Aristophanes, *Ran.* 1491–99; Diogenes Laertius 2.22; Aelian, *Var. hist.* 2.13).

That Philo took Euripides to be a philosophical authority is evident in numerous places. For instance, in order to corroborate his interpretation of the days of creation in Genesis, he quotes lines from the *Chrysippus*:

ἀληθὲς εἶναι τὸ λεγόμενον ὅτι
　　θνήσκει δ' οὐδὲν τῶν γιγνομένων,
　　διακρινόμενον δ' ἄλλο πρὸς ἄλλο
　　μορφὴν ἰδίαν [var.: ἑτέραν] ἀπέδειξεν.

The saying is true that
　　None of the things coming to be dies,
　　but as one thing dissolves into another, it displays its own form.
　　　　　　　　　　　　　　(*Leg.* 1.7; *TrGF* 5.839.12-14)

This very same fragment was frequently quoted by others in philosophical writings, as with Philo, for its metaphysical content when detached from its original dramatic setting (Sextus Empiricus, *Math.* 6.17; Lucretius 2.991-1006; Vitruvius 8 praef. 1; Heraclitus, *All.* 22.11; Marcus Aurelius 7.50; Clement, *Strom.* 6.2.23).[17] It is not only in matters of metaphysical speculation; Euripides provides gnomic wisdom on a range of topics. This is especially evident in *That Every Good Person Is Free*, where Philo quotes Euripides ten times. Sometimes he deploys a common proverbial saying without attribution (*Prob.* 145; *TrGF* 5.893.1, also quoted in Athenaeus, *Deipn.* 4.158e).[18] Once, he claims to have attended a play

---

145–57; Maren R. Niehoff, "Philo and Plutarch on Homer," in *Homer and the Bible in the Eyes of Ancient Interpreters*, ed. Maren R. Niehoff, Jerusalem Studies in Religion and Culture 16 (Leiden: Brill, 2012), 127–53.

17. Philo also quotes the same fragment three times in *On the Eternity of the World* (5, 30, 144) where the introductory formulae explicitly identify the source as tragedy, though without naming Euripides: καὶ ὁ τραγικός (5); κατὰ γὰρ τὸν τραγικὸν (30); κατὰ τὸ φιλοσοφηθὲν ὑπὸ τοῦ τραγικοῦ (144).

18. Similarly at *Prob.* 22: "The author of the following trimeter is praised by some: 'Who, while taking no thought of dying, is a slave?'" (ἐπαινεῖται παρά τισιν ὁ τὸ

of Euripides in the theater and recalls the gnomic lines he heard on that occasion (*Prob.* 141; *TrGF* 5.275.3–4; also in Stobaeus 4.8.3). In one case (in addition to the *Syleus*), he is interested in the plot of the play for the heroic actions of its leading protagonist (*Prob.* 116; Euripides, *Hec.* 548–51).[19]

Clearly, therefore, Philo held Euripides in high esteem as a source of philosophical wisdom, and toward the end of this treatise he offers a programmatic justification for his use of not only Euripides, but poetry in general: it is "fitting to heed poets" (ποιηταῖς προσέχειν ἄξιον), because "they are educators through our entire life, just as parents train their children in moderation privately, so also they do for their cities publicly" (παιδευταὶ γὰρ οὗτοί γε τοῦ σύμπαντος βίου, καθάπερ ἰδίᾳ γονεῖς παῖδας καὶ οὗτοι δημοσίᾳ τὰς πόλεις σωφρονίζοντες, *Prob.* 143).

Philo's preference for Euripides and the manner in which he deploys his poetry is consistent with the opinion of Dio Chrysostom, who a few decades later offers the following advice to aspiring orators:

ἥ τε Εὐριπίδου προσήνεια καὶ πιθανότης τοῦ μὲν τραγικοῦ ἀναστήματος καὶ ἀξιώματος τυχὸν οὐκ ἂν τελέως ἐφικνοῖτο, πολιτικῷ δὲ ἀνδρὶ πάνυ ὠφέλιμος, ἔτι δὲ ἤθη καὶ πάθη δεινὸς πληρῶσαι, καὶ γνώμας πρὸς ἅπαντα ὠφελίμους καταμίγνυσι τοῖς ποιήμασιν, ἅτε φιλοσοφίας οὐκ ἄπειρος ὤν.

Although the smoothness and persuasiveness of Euripides may not happen to reach completely the worthiest condition of tragic majesty, it is nevertheless entirely useful to the political man; he is clever at filling his works with characters and incidents and he mixes gnomic wisdom into his poetry that is useful for all occasions, being that he is not inexperienced in philosophy. (*Dic. excercit.* [*Or.*] 18.7)

Not all philosophers, however, shared such opinions about Euripides, or concerning poetry more broadly. Plato famously proposed the banishment of Homer and the tragedians from his ideal society, arguing that they were a morally destructive influence (e.g., *Resp.* 10.603c-606b).[20]

τρίμετρον ἐκεῖνο ποιήσας "τίς δ' ἐστὶ δοῦλος τοῦ θανεῖν ἄφροντις ὤν;" *TrGF* 5.958). The verse quoted here is also found in Plutarch, *Adol. poet. aud.* (*Mor.*) 34b; *Cons. Apoll.* (*Mor.*) 10.106d; Cicero, *Att.* 9.2a.2; Clement, *Strom.* 4.7.49.4.

19. See Courtney J. P. Friesen, "Dying Like a Woman: Euripides' Polyxena as Exemplum between Philo and Clement of Alexandria," *GRBS* 56 (2016): 623–45, esp. 630–9.

20. See Stephen Halliwell, "Plato's Repudiation of the Tragic," in *Tragedy and the Tragic: Greek Theatre and Beyond*, ed. M. S. Silk (Oxford: Clarendon, 1996), 332–49; Martha C. Nussbaum, "Tragedy and Self-Sufficiency: Plato and Aristotle on Fear and Pity," *Oxford Studies in Ancient Philosophy* 10 (1992): 107–59, esp. 123–8.

Many Romans, likewise, were critical of theater on ethical grounds.[21] Nevertheless, by the time of Philo, philosophers of various schools advocated for the use of poetry as a source of wisdom and developed sophisticated strategies for navigating its potential threats to the moral education of youth. Stoics, for example, are especially known for their focus on etymological and allegorical interpretations of Homer.[22] Different tactics are outlined by Plutarch in his treatise *How a Young Person Should Listen to Poetry*, which functions as a manual for deploying poetry in education; with proper oversight from a tutor, good and useful insights could be extracted.[23] Regarding tragedy, Epictetus instructed his students how to understand a play; for the true sage, tragedy teaches that misfortune can only befall those who overvalue external things (*Diatr.* 1.24.15-16). Jewish authors also could look to dramatic texts as sources of divine revelation. In *De monarchia*, a brief treatise attributed by Eusebius to Justin Martyr but apparently dependent on a Jewish anthology, several quotations from drama are compiled (fifteen of tragedy, twelve of comedy, a few of which are clearly spurious). Within the context of the author's apologetic agenda, his compilation of dramatic verses is aimed at demonstrating that genuine divine revelation is available even among ancient Greek poets.[24]

In his use of Euripides, therefore, throughout this treatise and elsewhere, Philo treated the poet as an intellectual authority on a range of issues and endowed him with a cultural value in a manner consistent with many of his contemporaries. Nevertheless, his choice of a satyr play stands out. Although Philo does not identify it as such, its content clearly differentiates it from tragedy. Like comedy, satyr drama had as a central objective to amuse and to provoke laughter.[25] This is not to say that these plays

---

21. See Jonas Barish, *The Antitheatrical Prejudice* (Berkeley: University of California Press, 1981), 98–136; Catharine Edwards, *The Politics of Immorality in Ancient Rome* (Cambridge: Cambridge University Press, 1993), 98–136.

22. See esp. Phillip De Lacy, "Stoic Views of Poetry," *AJP* 69 (1948): 241–71; Martha C. Nussbaum, "Poetry and the Passions: Two Stoic Views," in *Passions and Perceptions: Studies in Hellenistic Philosophy of Mind: Proceedings of the Fifth Symposium Hellenisticum*, ed. Jacques Brunschwig and Martha C. Nussbaum (Cambridge: Cambridge University Press, 1993), 97–149.

23. See David Blank, "Reading between the Lies: Plutarch and Chrysippus on the Uses of Poetry," *Oxford Studies in Ancient Philosophy* 40 (2011): 237–64.

24. See Miroslav Marcovich, *Pseudo-Iustinus: Cohortatio ad Graecos, De monarchia, Oratio ad Graecos*, PTS 32 (Berlin: de Gruyter, 1990), 81–4.

25. On satyr drama, see Dana F. Sutton, *The Greek Satyr Play*, Beiträge zur klassischen Philologie 90 (Meisenheim: Anton Hain, 1980); Carl A. Shaw, *Satyric Play: The Evolution of Greek Comedy and Satyr Drama* (Oxford: Oxford University

lacked any serious content.²⁶ Nevertheless, as early as Aristotle, whose categorization of dramatic forms in the *Poetics* ignores satyr play, the genre had been marginalized. It remained so throughout antiquity and up to the present. While there is evidence for its ongoing performance in ancient theaters, its relatively limited textual survival (only one complete play is extant) is suggestive of its lesser status.²⁷

The *Syleus* is illustrative of these trends. It was a largely unknown play aside from one fragment, that is, the first in the sequence quoted by Philo (*Prob.* 99; *TrGF* 5.687, see above), which appears to have had an independent gnomic currency. It occurs earlier in the same treatise (*Prob.* 25), as well as in two other of Philo's works (*Leg.* 3.202; *Ios.* 78), each time without reference to its dramatic context. Similarly, the very same lines are attested in Artemidorus (*Onir.* 4.59), Eusebius (*Praep. ev.* 6.6.2), and Michael Psellus (*Poemata* 21.275-76).²⁸ By contrast, the additional thirteen lines excerpted by Philo in four fragments are completely unattested elsewhere. Given that this play was otherwise obscure, it is all the more surprising to find Philo quote from it to such an extent in conjunction with detailed knowledge of the plot. While it is impossible to be certain by what means Philo gained access to this material, it seems clear that he must have engaged in additional research.²⁹ This heightens

---

Press, 2014). Generically, comedy and satyr play were distinct. Most obviously, they belonged to different categories in dramatic festivals; and the latter involved its characteristic chorus of satyrs and costumes including tails and erect phalloi. Nevertheless, there was considerable overlap, not least in the frequency with which Heracles appears as a character; on this, see Ian C. Storey, "But Comedy Has Satyrs Too," in *Satyr Drama: Tragedy at Play*, ed. George W. M. Harrison (Swansea: Classical Press of Wales, 2005), 201–18, esp. 203.

26. For this point, see Sutton, *Greek Satyr Play*, 120–33.

27. On the reception and performance of satyr drama in the Roman period, see George W. M. Harrison, "Positioning of Satyr Drama and Characterization in the *Cyclops*," in *Satyr Drama: Tragedy at Play*, ed. George W. M. Harrison (Swansea: Classical Press of Wales, 2005), 237–58, esp. 252–3; Fritz Graf, "Comedies and Comic Actors in the Greek East: An Epigraphical Perspective," in *Athenian Comedy in the Roman Empire*, ed. C. W. Marshall and Tom Hawkins (London: Bloomsbury, 2015), 117–29, esp. 118 n. 5.

28. In addition to the five fragments in Philo, three additional fragments from the *Syleus* of two lines each are preserved in later authors (*TrGF* 5.692–94).

29. While it is plausible that Philo owned a small collection of books, for Greek literature this will have been mostly limited to philosophical texts; see David Lincicum, "Philo's Library," *SPhiloA* 26 (2014): 99–114. One might speculate that he visited the celebrated Library, though he only makes one passing reference to

the significance of its inclusion, given that Philo appears to have gone out of his way to feature the comic Heracles acting as a buffoon. There were, of course, numerous more dignified examples of the heroism of Heracles available—indeed, moral philosophers often deployed these as models for emulation. Why Philo foregrounded the behaviors of the comic hero must remain a matter of speculation; relevant insights emerge, however, when viewed within the political atmosphere of Rome.

Hercules On and Off the Roman Stage

Philo's *That Every Good Person Is Free* is best understood within a Roman context. As noted above, this particular Stoic paradox concerning freedom is addressed within the framework of Roman philosophical discourse (by Cicero and Epictetus), and, as Maren Niehoff has recently noted, Philo's discussion "has no parallel in Alexandria."[30] Moreover, Niehoff demonstrates the extent to which the exempla deployed by Philo are characteristically Roman. For instance, the Xanthians, known from recent Roman history, took their own lives rather than fall as subjects to Brutus (*Prob.* 118–20). Calanus, the Indian philosopher who killed himself rather than become enslaved to Alexander, is presented as a champion of Roman values over against Greek (*Prob.* 92–96). Even Philo's valorization of the Essenes as "athletes of virtue" (ἀθλητὰς ἀρετῆς, *Prob.* 88) suggests a Roman audience; their rigorous and austere lifestyle was also celebrated by the Roman historian Pliny the Elder, who characterized them as "a solitary tribe and remarkable beyond the rest in the entire world" (*gens sola et in toto orbe praeter ceteras mira, Nat.* 5.73).[31]

In view of the distinctly Roman casting of Philo's exempla in the treatise, his Heracles stands out more sharply. Significantly, this hero was absent from comedy at Rome. As Karl Galinsky notes, *gravitas* was the

---

"libraries" (βιβλιοθῆκαι) at the Sebasteum (*Legat.* 151). Regarding this silence, see Emmanuel Friedheim, "Quelques notes sur la signification historique du silence philonien à propos de la Bibliothèque d'Alexandrie," in *The Library of Alexandria: A Cultural Crossroads of the Ancient World*, ed. Christophe Rico and Anca Dan, Proceedings of the Second Polis Institute Interdisciplinary Conference (Jerusalem: Polis Institute, 2017), 245–55.

30. Niehoff, *Philo of Alexandria*, 83.

31. Niehoff, *Philo of Alexandria*, 85–8. As she notes, similar emphases are evident in Philo's depiction of the Therapeutae in *On the Contemplative Life*. In particular, this community conducted their common meals with rationality and sobriety in contrast with the excess and sensuality commonly associated with Greek symposia.

central trait of the Roman Hercules, and the burlesque actions prevalent in Greek comedy are almost entirely lacking.[32] The Roman Hercules was, as such, a compelling model for emulation by statesmen (and also philosophers in the Stoic or Cynic mode). To be sure, this was already an established trope in the Hellenistic world. Isocrates, for example, had urged Philip of Macedon to follow the lead of his heroic ancestor in his manner of establishing peace for Greeks and civilizing the barbarian realm (*Phil.* [*Or.*] 5.105-14). Subsequently, at Alexandria, Heraclean lineage was claimed by Theocritus for both Alexander and Ptolemy (*Id.* 17.26-27). In the Roman context and in closer proximity to Philo, at the funeral of Augustus, according to Cassius Dio, Tiberius delivered an encomium in which he likened his predecessor to Hercules. First, he proposes a comparison with Alexander or Romulus (*Hist.* 56.36.3) but then notes that unlike these men, Augustus, *while still a youth*, performed remarkable achievements in order to secure the State. For a more fitting equivalent, therefore, one must look "to Heracles alone and his deeds" (πρὸς μόνον δὲ δὴ τὸν Ἡρακλέα καὶ τὰ ἐκείνου ἔργα, *Hist.* 56.36.4), because he is known to have warded off serpents as an infant. Moreover, Tiberius adds, Augustus in fact outdid the hero, because the latter's achievements concern merely beasts, whereas the emperor, "by conducting war and establishing laws, rescued the commonwealth with precision" (πολεμῶν καὶ νομοθετῶν τό τε κοινὸν ἀκριβῶς ἔσωσε, *Hist.* 56.36.5).

Building on this mode of propaganda, several subsequent Roman emperors actively promoted a Herculean self-image.[33] Dio Chyrsostom, in an address to Trajan, exploits the emperor's well-known fondness for Hercules, using it as a means of both flattery and instruction for the recently ascendant ruler. Contrary to popular perception, in accomplishing his labors, Heracles was not a solitary wanderer, moving between the tasks beset upon him by Eurystheus. Instead, he commanded a vast army and ruled over an extensive kingdom (*1 Regn.* [*Or.*] 1.59-63). It is not

---

32. Galinsky, *The Herakles Theme*, 126–52. However, according to Macrobius, Heracles was apparently a character in a Pantomime of the Augustan period (*Sat.* 2.7.16–17); see Wyles, "Heracles' Costume," 193.

33. In addition to Trajan and Gaius discussed below, there were, among others, Nero (Suetonius, *Nero* 21.1) and Commodus (Athenaeus, *Deipn.* 12.537f); see Olivier Hekster, "Propagating Power: Hercules as an Example for Second-Century Emperors," in *Herakles and Hercules: Exploring a Graeco-Roman Divinity*, ed. Louis Rawlings and Hugh Bowden (Swansea: Classical Press of Wales, 2005), 205–21; Andrew Runni Anderson, "Heracles and His Successors: A Study of a Heroic Ideal and the Recurrence of a Heroic Type," *HSCP* 39 (1928): 7–58.

primarily as a slayer of beasts that he is to be celebrated, but because "wherever he would see tyranny or a tyrant, he would punish and destroy them, both among Greeks and barbarians [...] Indeed, it is because of this that he is savior of the earth and people, not because he repelled beasts for them" (τοιγαροῦν ὅπου μὲν ἴδοι τυραννίδα καὶ τύραννον ἐκόλαζε καὶ ἀνῄρει παρά τε Ἕλλησι καὶ βαρβάροις [...] καὶ διὰ τοῦτο τῆς γῆς καὶ τῶν ἀνθρώπων σωτῆρα εἶναι, οὐχ ὅτι τὰ θηρία αὐτοῖς ἀπήμυνεν, 1 Regn. [Or.] 84).[34]

Philo deploys the same trope in addressing Gaius, another emperor with known Heraclean aspirations. As with Dio Chrysostom, Philo redirects the focus of the demi-god's labors, emphasizing that these involve not merely that "he purged land and sea" (ἐκάθηρε γῆν καὶ θάλατταν, Legat. 81) but also that he laid down "good law and justice, plenty and thriving, and the abundance of all other good things, which enduring peace produces" (εὐνομίας καὶ εὐδικίας εὐθηνίας τε καὶ εὐετηρίας καὶ τῆς τῶν ἄλλων ἀγαθῶν ἀφθονίας, ὧν ἡ βαθεῖα εἰρήνη δημιουργός, Legat. 90). In contrast to Tiberias' encomium of Augustus cited above, the achievements of Gaius, Philo stresses, fall well short of the hero, and as such his claims to Heraclean status are illegitimate (Legat. 90–91). Moreover, Philo emphasizes that Gaius' Heraclean self-fashioning was distinctly theatrical: "as in a theater, he took up different apparel at different times, sometimes a lion skin and a club, both gold-gilded, adorning himself as Heracles" (ὥσπερ ἐν θεάτρῳ σκευὴν ἄλλοτε ἀλλοίαν ἀνελάμβανε, τοτὲ μὲν λεοντῆν καὶ ῥόπαλον, ἀμφότερα ἐπίχρυσα, διακοσμούμενος εἰς Ἡρακλέα, Legat. 79; also Cassius Dio, Hist. 59.26.7).[35] Here, the comic trope of the Heraclean costume discussed above is unmistakable. That is, like Dionysus in Aristophanes' Frogs, for example, Gaius donned the attributes of the demi-god, but in doing so only revealed the extent to which his own strength and valor missed the mark. The result is laughter and amusement, not honor and reverence.

Thus, for a Roman audience, the evocation of Hercules as a model for virtue had an established political resonance. Conversely, his boorish behavior, known from the comic stage in the Greek world, could function as a mode of polemic. For instance, Mark Antony, another aspiring ruler

---

34. On the function of Heracles in this oration, see Joy Connolly, "Like the Labors of Heracles: Andreia and Paideia in Greek Culture under Rome," in *Andreia: Studies in Manliness and Courage in Classical Antiquity*, ed. Ralph M. Rosen and Ineke Sluiter, Mnemosyne: Bibliotheca Classica Batava (Leiden: Brill, 2003), 287–318, esp. 307–10.

35. Cassius Dio likewise reports that Gaius at various times wore these attributes (*Hist.* 59.26.7).

with claims of Heraclean lineage (Appian, *Bell. civ.* 3.2.16), is said by Plutarch to have "appeared like paintings and sculptures of Heracles" (ἐδόκει τοῖς γραφομένοις καὶ πλαττομένοις Ἡρακλέους, *Ant.* 4.1), and that Antony imagined that he "confirmed [his Heraclean descent] in his form of body and his garment" (τῇ τε μορφῇ τοῦ σώματος [...] καὶ τῇ στολῇ βεβαιοῦν, *Ant.* 4.2 [4.3]).[36] But what stood out to Plutarch were the more "vulgar" (φορτικά) aspects of Antony's Heraclean manners, particularly at table: "boasting, jesting, [with] visible drinking vessel, sitting next to the person eating and standing while eating at the soldiers' table" (μεγαλαυχία καὶ σκῶμμα καὶ κώθων ἐμφανὴς καὶ καθίσαι παρὰ τὸν ἐσθίοντα καὶ φαγεῖν ἐπιστάντα τραπέζῃ στρατιωτικῇ, *Ant.* 4.2 [4.4]).[37]

Even though Hercules is not attested in comic drama at Rome, related themes occasionally arise in Latin literature. Cross-dressing and costume exchange, in particular, are exploited by Ovid in *Heroides* 9, a fictional epistle from Deianira to Hercules. She laments the recent reports concerning her husband, which have revealed that his true enemy was not Juno but Venus: "Juno was unable to conquer [you], but love did" (*non potuit Iuno vincere, vincit amor, Her.* 9.26). She proceeds to complain about his extended absence and his numerous mistresses ("you have multiplied foreign loves," *peregrinos addis amores, Her.* 9.47). The most shameful of these, however, was the most recent, Omphale, in whose case the distinctly feminine nature of his enslavement was utterly incongruent with the masculinity of his past achievements. Deianira received reports that he was wearing a *mitra*, that is, a specifically effeminate headdress (*Her.* 9.63), and female belt (*zona*) "in the manner of a licentious girl" (*lascivae more puellae, Her.* 9.65). Conversely, Omphale wore the lion skin (*Her.* 9.111-12), "and she furnished her hand with the club, tamer of beasts" (*instruxitque manum clava domitrice ferarum, Her.* 9.117).

Ovid's report of costume exchange and feminine garb involved in Hercules' enslavement to Omphale are most closely associated with Greek comedy. Moreover, it is precisely these demeaning and shameful behaviors that the Christian apologists (cited above) later highlight. Indeed, in Tertullian's observation that Hercules accepted "a woman's clothing" (*cultus mulierbri*), he appears to echo Deianira's question from Ovid:

36. On Antony's kinship with Heracles, see Anderson, "Heracles and His Successors," 42–4.
37. While his opponents regarded this as uncouth, it apparently met with approval among the soldiers. That Antony had a reputation for heavy drinking is widely attested; see also Cicero, *Phil.* 2.104; Pliny, *Nat.* 14.28.148; Athenaeus, *Deipn.* 4.148c.

Haec tu Sidonio potes insignitus amictu
dicere? non cultu lingua retenta silet?

Are you able to describe these things [your labors] while clothed in Sidonian garb? Is not your tongue held silent by your attire? (*Her.* 9.101-2)

For their part, Tertullian and Origen evoke the comic feminization of Hercules within their wider religious polemic. Ovid, on the other hand, is more closely concerned with the politics of Augustan Rome, and given the position of Hercules within imperial propaganda, his emphasis on the feminization of the hero is potentially subversive. While the poet does not make this explicit, when read in comparison with the imperial valorizations of the hero discussed above, his comic depiction by Ovid undercuts Roman ideals of masculine valor.[38]

Philo's treatise *That Every Good Person Is Free*, though immersed as it is in Roman philosophical discourse, adopts a version of Heracles very much at odds with the hero as celebrated at Rome. His Heracles is a comic buffoon, the stock character well-loved among Alexandrian audiences, where attempted exchanges of Heraclean costume and the hero's prolific appetites for food and wine were standard theatrical tropes. Such pillories of the demi-god, however, were not featured on the Roman stage. Romans seem to have been more reticent in this regard, and perhaps in part due to the potential conflict with imperial propaganda.

Conclusions

In Roman Alexandria, conflicting religious and political interests intersected with various modes of textual appropriation. As a Hellenistic Jew, Philo maintained an allegiance to scripture, while embracing the values of a Greek intellectual and navigating the complexities of Roman imperial power. The Bible was not his only authoritative text, however; he also drew on Greek poets as sources of truth and wisdom. Among them, Philo deploys verses of Euripides, the most popular of classical playwrights, in support of his metaphysical and ethical arguments.

This study analyzed one striking instance of Philo's engagement with Euripides—the *Syleus* in *That Every Good Person Is Free*. One may be inclined to view this play as "other" with respect to Philo, featuring, as it does, a demigod, popular in Greek and Roman mythology and cult.

---

38. As Cyrino suggests regarding Ovid, "to represent Hercules in a ridiculous posture is to undermine a conspicuous Augustan symbol" ("Heroes in D[u]ress," 220).

Nevertheless, Philo quotes it without qualification as evidence of the genuine freedom of a virtuous person. On closer inspection, however, his evocation of Heracles is not as straightforward as it seems. While the manner in which Philo draws on Euripides appears to be in common with his contemporaries who likewise viewed the playwright as an authority on numerous topics, this particular satyr play was not well known, apart from one gnomic fragment. And Philo goes well beyond that single fragment to review the wider plot of the drama, which displays the hero in his stereotypically comic mode, costumed as a slave and indulging his prolific appetites. This aspect of Heracles' behavior, though popular among audiences of comic theater especially in Alexandria, was later ridiculed by Christians, and stands in striking contrast to those features of his mythological biography emulated by philosophers and statesmen. At Rome in particular, Heracles is completely unattested in comedy; rather, it was his *gravitas* that was foregrounded, especially by emperors who evoked the hero within their programs of propaganda. Thus, whereas on the surface Philo's use of Euripides appears serious and straightforward, on closer inspection its effect is subversive and ironic.

Like the dramatic hero, Philo's own identity exhibited ambiguities, positioned between the commitments of Judaism and the cultural milieu of Hellenism. He aimed to embody the ideals of genuine divine freedom, even if he found himself momentarily under the constraints of tyranny.

Perspectives on a Pluriform Classic

C. L. Seow

The book of Job is widely recognized as a classic in world literature. As Victor Hugo once said: "Job is one of the greatest masterpieces of the human mind. It is, perhaps, the greatest masterpiece."[1] It is not simply its longevity, nor its captivating content, nor the near-universality of praise for its artistry that cements its status as a classic. Rather, the ongoing conversations that the story of Job instigates is the clearest evidence. Italo Calvino once explained: "A classic is a book which has never exhausted all it has to say to its readers."[2] The story of Job has produced and continues to produce deep and lasting effects in visual arts, music, film, and even dance.[3] Its global reach, not merely its origins in the ancient Near East nor its esteemed importance within the canon of Western Literature, is what makes it a classic of *world* literature.[4]

The fact that readers have struggled with, contested, and continually reused the book of Job in myriad ways across diverse cultural, spatial, and temporal contexts testifies to its unending relevance. Tenaciously

---

1. Octave Uzanne, "Conversations and Opinions of Victor Hugo," *Scribner's Magazine* 12 (1892): 558–76, esp. 570. This quotation comes from his daughter Adèle Hugo's unpublished notes.

2. Italo Calvino, *The Literature Machine: Essays*, trans. Patrick Creagh (repr., London: Vintage, 1997).

3. On the status of Job as a classic, see Freddie Rokem, "The Bible on the Hebrew/Israeli Stage: Hanoch Levin's *The Torments of Job* as a Modern Tragedy," in *The Book of Job: Aesthetics, Ethics, Hermeneutics*, ed. Leora Batinsky and Ilana Pardes, Perspectives on Jewish Texts and Contexts 1 (Berlin: de Gruyter, 2015), 185–212; see also C. L. Seow, *Job 1–21: Interpretation and Commentary*, Illuminations (Grand Rapids: Eerdmans, 2013), 110–248.

4. According to David Damrosch, "world literature is not an infinite, ungraspable canon of works but rather a mode of circulation and of reading," Damrosch, *What Is World Literature?* (Princeton: Princeton University Press, 2003), 5.

divergent interpretation is an ineluctable, even distinguishing, feature of a classic. John Coetzee argues that criticism, and even conflict, is "what the classic uses to define itself and ensure its survival."[5] That the classic survives implies that it has, in some way, escaped death, and enjoys a literary *Nachleben*. As T. S. Eliot suggests, "it is only by hindsight, and in historical perspective, that a classic can be known as such."[6]

While Ankhi Mukherjee notes the Anglocentrism and colonial power that undergirds Eliot's and Coetzee's conceptions of both classics and the canon of world literature, she agrees that the status of classic implies both conflict and that the readers of a classic *per se* must be Other to the text and its presumed context of origin: "In the end, the question and concept of the classic is perhaps always that of the outsider."[7] Throughout her study of the reception of Shakespeare's plays in contemporary India, Mukherjee argues that a classic is defined by its potential to engage readers from a wide variety of contexts over a long span of time and to provoke reimagining, rewriting, and critique.[8] In order for it to become a classic, many "other people" must engage a text, and even participate in re-creating it.

In this regard, I have often used the analogy of classical Chinese paintings to describe the consequences of a biblical text. A Chinese landscape artist who completed a painting would regularly leave at least a stamp with a name and often an epigram. Yet that is only the beginning of the life of that work, for others would come along and add their perspectives, an endorsement, or another epigram, or perhaps a poem that

---

5. John Coetzee, "What Is a Classic? A Lecture," *Stranger Shores: Essays, 1986–1999* (London: Vintage, 1992), 1–19, esp. 19.

6. T. S. Eliot, *What Is a Classic? An Address Delivered Before the Virgil Society on the 16th of October 1944* (London: Faber & Faber, 1945), 10. Because a classic can only be named as such after the language has been exhausted, Eliot claimed that "there is no classic in English." *What Is a Classic?*, 25. Colleen Lamos also emphasizes the connection between the production of a classic and the death of a culture: the classic "must come from the dead, from the tomb." Lamos, *Deviant Modernism: Sexual and Textual Errancy in T. S. Eliot, James Joyce, and Marcel Proust* (Cambridge: Cambridge University Press, 1998), 49.

7. Ankhi Mukherjee, *What Is a Classic? Postcolonial Rewriting and Invention of the Canon* (Stanford: Stanford University Press, 2014), 49. See Mukherjee, "'What Is a Classic?' International Literary Criticism and the Classic Question," *PMLA* 124 (2010): 1026–42. For other postcolonial perspectives on the question of the classic, see Barbara Goff, ed., *Classics and Colonialism* (London: Duckworth, 2005); Lorna Hardwick and Carol Gillespie, eds., *Classics in Post-Colonial Worlds* (Oxford: Oxford University Press, 2007).

8. Mukherjee, *What Is a Classic?*, 182–213, 215.

hints at another way of viewing the work, and each interpreter adds their personal stamp. As Maxwell Hearn notes, "a painting was not finalized when an artist set down his brush, but it would continue to evolve as later owners and admirers appended their own inscriptions or seals."[9] Over time, a renowned painting might accumulate multiple annotations, even conflicting points of view, all of which contribute to the painting's value and meaning. One classic painting, Han Gan's *Night Shining White*, "was embellished with a record of its transmission that spans more than a thousand years."[10] Viewers of a Chinese painting are thus drawn into the conversation that the image generates, even if one may never know who an artist was or what the artist intended. It is impossible for a viewer to insist on a pristine original and ignore all the voices that make the painting what it is in the present.

Likewise, the impact of the story of Job—not necessarily the book, which is only its best-known literary manifestation—extends beyond Jewish, Christian, and Muslim traditions. Yet, there is no single version of it and no single history of its reception, only varied cultural histories of contested versions. There is also no single point of origin and certainly no end to those histories. Thus, the book of Job's pluriform and contested nature is a testament to its status as a classic of world literature. In this essay, I will briefly explore aspects of two characters in the book of Job—namely, Job and Leviathan—focusing on the ways their differing identities are shaped by, and shape, the communities who interact with the book of Job as a classic of world literature.

No Beginning

Classics never emerge out of thin air. Like every text, they necessarily refer to cultural products that preceded them, and often draw heavily from these predecessors. Many classics are rewritten forms of already well-known stories. For example, T. S. Eliot's famous meditation on the concept of the classic focuses on the *Aeneid*, which Virgil based on a character from Homer's *Iliad* and other Greco-Roman legends and myths. For Eliot, a true classic like the *Aeneid* can only be composed as the culmination of a long succession of cultural products, and thus the classic has no clear beginning.[11]

---

9. Maxwell K. Hearn, *How to Read Chinese Paintings* (New Haven: Yale University Press, 2008), 5.
10. Hearn, *How to Read Chinese Paintings* 5–9, here 5.
11. Eliot, *What Is a Classic?*, 25–7.

Ancient texts are no different, Job included. A tradition concerning Job existed before the Hebrew book that most modern scholars date to the postexilic period. Already in the sixth century BCE, the prophet Ezekiel invoked Noah, Daniel, and Job as paragons, whose righteousness saved their children, though the prophet warned his contemporaries not to assume that they too would be saved by the righteousness of their parents (Ezek. 14:14, 20).[12] If this account of the story was a source used in the composition of the book of Job, it must have been reworked, because in the canonical book Job was not able to save his children by his righteousness.[13] Unfortunately, the terseness of these tantalizing allusions leaves much to speculation.[14] Nonetheless, the tradition of Job as an example of virtue would resurface in later manifestations of the story. Whether these later iterations are direct descendants of an exemplary-Job tradition that was an alternate to the Hebrew version, or if they are consequences of the prologue of the Hebrew version, is not entirely clear. What does seem clear is that the Hebrew composition is a consequence of earlier traditions. Indeed, issues that modern historical-critical scholars raise regarding the compositional history of the book, its traditional sources, and the processes of transmission and redaction, belong to a complex hermeneutical history.

Despite the literary affectations that contribute to the book's Transjordanian setting,[15] there is no question that the biblical version has been shaped by various Israelite traditions, as evident in the many intra-biblical intertextualities.[16] As for intertextualities with other cultures, among the most compelling are the several "pious-sufferer texts" from Western Asia, beginning with the so-called "Sumerian Job" (*Man and His God*),

---

12. See Paul M. Joyce, "'Even if Noah, Daniel, and Job were in it…' (Ezekiel 14:14): The Case of Job and Ezekiel," in *Reading Job Intertextually*, ed. Katharine Dell and Will Kynes, LHBOTS 574 (New York: Bloomsbury, 2013), 118–28.

13. See Shalom Spiegel, "Noah, Danel and Job: Touching on Canaanite Relics in the Legends of the Jews," in *Louis Ginzberg Jubilee Volume on the Occasion of his Seventieth Birthday* (New York: The American Academy of Jewish Research, 1945), 305–55; Bruce E. Zuckerman, *Job the Silent: A Study in Historical Counterpoint* (New York/Oxford: Oxford University Press, 1991), 29–33.

14. Joyce ("'Even if Noah, Daniel, and Job were in it,'" 127) notes that there is not enough for one to conclude that "the author of Job is dependent on Ezekiel."

15. For instance, there are elements in the Hebrew that in some ways mimic languages in the Transjordan, the friends of Job have names that are at home in the Transjordan, the divine names Eloah and Shaddai appear with exceptional frequency, and so forth.

16. See Dell and Kynes, eds., *Reading Job Intertextually*.

the earliest extant copy of which dates to the eighteenth century BCE.[17] This text was already known in the third millennium, for it is listed in a catalogue of literary texts compiled around 2000 BCE, which suggests that it was already a classic by that time.[18] Yet, even the "Sumerian Job" adapts earlier materials and conventions.[19] Thus, the earliest known source for pious-sufferer tradition is already a product of reception.

Alongside the Sumerian *Man and His God*, similar accounts of righteous sufferers are found in an Old Babylonian version of *Man and His God* (from the seventeenth century BCE), an Akkadian Hymn of Thanksgiving to Marduk from Ugarit (from the late thirteenth century or early twelfth century BCE), and *Ludlul Bēl Nēmeqi* ("I will Praise the Lord of Wisdom"; probably from the late twelfth century BCE).[20] *Ludlul* is among the texts that scribes called *iškaru*, "standard," that is, having an acknowledged authority.[21] Its status as a classic is corroborated by the fact that manuscripts, school texts, and commentaries on it have been found in seven cities, including in the library of the Assyrian king Ashurbanipal (reigned 668 to ca. 627 BCE), who famously boasted of having studied what we might call the classics, including even "the inscriptions on stone from before the flood."[22]

---

17. Samuel Noah Kramer, "Man and His God: A Sumerian Variation on the 'Job' Motif," in *Wisdom in Israel and the Ancient Near East Presented to Harold Henry Rowley by the Editorial Board of Vetus Testamentum in Celebration of his 65th Birthday, 24 March 1955*, ed. Martin Noth and D. Winton Thomas, VTSup 3 (Leiden: Brill, 1960), 170–82; Jacob Klein, "'Personal God' and Individual Prayer in Sumerian Religion," in *Vorträge gehalten auf der 28. Rencontre assyriologique Internationale in Wien 6.-10. Juli 1981*, ed. Hermann Hunger and Hans Hirsch, AfOB 19 (Austria: Ferdinand Berger & Sons, 1982), 295–306; Klein, "*Man and His God*: A Wisdom Poem or a Cultic Lament?" in *Approaches to Sumerian Literature: Studies in Honor of H. L. Vanstiphout*, ed. Piotr Michalowski and Niek Veldhuis, CM 35 (Leiden: Brill, 2006), 123–43.

18. Samuel Noah Kramer, "The Oldest Literary Catalogue: A Sumerian List of Literary Compositions Compiled about 2000 B.C.," *BASOR* 88 (1942): 10–19, line 46.

19. Klein, "*Man and His God*," 139.

20. For a critical edition of the latter, see Amar Annus and Alan Lenzi, *Ludlul bēl Nemeqi: The Standard Babylonian Poem of the Righteous Sufferer*, SAACT 7 (Helsinki: Neo-Assyrian Text Corpus Project, 2010); for additional details and bibliography for all of these texts, see Seow, *Job 1–21*, 51–6.

21. See Simo Parpola, "Assyrian Library Records," *JNES* 42 (1983): 1–29; Francesca Rochberg-Halton, "Canonicity in Cuneiform Texts," *JCS* 36 (1984): 127–44.

22. Natalie Naomi May, "'I Read the Inscriptions from before the Flood…' Neo-Sumerian Influences in Ashurbanipal's Royal Self-Image," in *Time and History*

All these texts assume that the suffering of the pious is due to sin, even if the precipitating offense is unknown or, as the poet of *Ludlul* implies, perhaps unknowable, because the values of the gods are utterly mysterious (*Ludlul* II.33-38). As the Sumerian *Man and His God* has it, no one is perfect and no sinless person has ever existed.[23] The inevitable sinfulness of every human is a manifestation of the fragility of humanity. These texts, whatever their precise genres, are all doxological, for they point to the restoration of the sufferers, either already experienced or anticipated (cf. *Ludlul* I.33-34).[24] As William Moran argues, these pious-sufferer texts suggest that "one may make the problem of the mind a problem of the heart, and solve it with reasons of the heart. Instead of wisdom, belief; instead of reflection and argument, a hymn to paradox and contradiction. *Credo quia absurdum*."[25] This is precisely the perspective that the friends of Job represent, as best exemplified by Eliphaz in his first speech. Eliphaz contends that no human being is without sin (Job 4:17-19), the proper response to suffering is doxology (5:8-16), suffering is not the final will of God, who wounds but heals (5:17-18), and one should look forward to restoration (5:19-26).

Alongside this traditional response is the *Babylonian Theodicy*,[26] which survives in nine manuscripts from the first millennium, including copies in the library of Ashurbanipal, though the composition is earlier, probably from the end of the second millennium BCE. Like Job, but unlike the pious sufferer in the other texts, the sufferer in the *Babylonian Theodicy* insists on his innocence, and the name of the author implies the same: Saggil-kīnam-ubbib ("O [E]Saggil, Clear the Just"). Also in literary form,

---

in the Ancient Near East: Proceedings of the 56th Rencontre Assyriologique Internationale at Barcelona, 26–30 July 2010, ed. L. Feliu et al. (Winona Lake: Eisenbrauns, 2013), 199–210, esp. 206.

23. Kramer, "Man and His God," lines 102–3.

24. See Moshe Weinfeld, "Job and Its Mesopotamian Parallels: A Typological Analysis," in *Text and Context: Old Testament and Semitic Studies for F. C. Fensham*, ed. W. T. Claassen, JSOTSup 48 (Sheffield: JSOT, 1988), 217–26; Karel van der Toorn, "Theodicy in Akkadian Literature," in *Theodicy in the World of the Bible: The Goodness of God and the Problem of Evil*, ed. Antti Laato and Johannes C. de Moor (Leiden: Brill, 2003), 57–89.

25. William L. Moran, "Rib-Hadda: Job at Byblos?" in *Biblical and Related Studies Presented to Samuel Iwry*, ed. Ann Kort and Scott Morschauser (Winona Lake: Eisenbrauns, 1985), 173–81, esp. 177.

26. See Wilfred G. Lambert, "The Babylonian Theodicy," in *Babylonian Wisdom Literature* (Oxford: Oxford University Press, 1960), 63–91; Takayoshi Oshima, *The Babylonian Theodicy*, SAACT 9 (Helsinki: The Neo-Assyrian Text Corpus Project, 2013).

its structure as a cycle of speeches between a noble sufferer who questions divine justice, and an orthodox friend who defends it, anticipates the structure of Job's dialogue (chs. 3–31). So perhaps the tradition of Job does not have a decisive beginning. Even the Hebrew version of the book is already a consequence of various traditions, which its authors and redactors drew from and brought into conversation.

Job the Soldier: A Christian Trajectory of Consequences

In line with its dynamic and dialogical origins, Jews, Christians, and Muslims have also continued to interpret the story of Job in vastly different ways, largely because they read different versions of it. For Christians in the first few centuries, the story was known not through the Hebrew book, but rather by way of the Old Greek and the Testament of Job, which differ considerably from the Hebrew version.

The Old Greek

The Old Greek (OG) version of the book of Job is not merely a witness to the putative original text, it is simultaneously a crucial part of the conversation provoked by the book, and a representative of the book itself. The very fact that the book of Job was translated and curated as a part of the cultural legacy of diasporic Jews in the Hellenistic period shows its enduring appeal several centuries after its literary production. As was the case for the other Greek translations of the Hebrew scriptures, the Old Greek version of Job is a product of Jews who spoke a different language and lived in a different cultural context from the book's first author(s). Yet they began the book of Job's transformation into a classic by their constructive participation in its ongoing re-production.

When the Christian scholar Origen collocated the different versions of the Old Testament in parallel columns around 235–245 CE, he noticed that the OG of Job was one-sixth shorter than the Hebrew, with 389 lines of the Hebrew not represented in the Old Greek.[27] He reported that the omissions occur sometimes in blocks of up to nineteen contiguous lines (*Ep. Afr.* 6.4; PG 11, 56.35).[28] Assuming that the longer version of the Hebrew, reflected as well in other Greek versions, is original,

---

27. The literature on the Greek book of Job is extensive, but see Markus Witte, "The Greek Book of Job," in *Das Buch Hiob und seine Interpretationen*, ed. Thomas Krüger et al., ATANT 88 (Zurich: TVZ, 2007), 33–54.

28. The largest block, 36:29–37:5a, has 20 lines rather than 19, though Origen had misconstrued the OG's translation of 37:1. See C. L. Seow, "Text Critical Notes on 4QJobª," *DSD* 22 (2015): 189–201, esp. 196–9.

he filled the lacunae with materials from Theodotion's more literal translation. Recent scholarship has corroborated the assumption that the OG has been attenuated from an originally longer version.[29] Yet the common characterization of the translation style of OG-Job as "free" or "paraphrastic" is pejorative, as if the translator were casual with the rendering of the text, when in fact the translation style of OG-Job may have been purposeful. Instead, OG-Job represents an expository translation that is reader-oriented, rather than the *interpres*-type of translation that is source-oriented.[30] In this case, orientation to the reader entails the accommodation of the translation to the culture of its readers in their Hellenistic context.[31] Indeed, more than a translation, OG-Job is a literary work in its own right.[32] OG-Job is the work of a translator who was also expositor, redactor, and even author.

Some scholars have suggested that the OG reflects a version deliberately altered to suit the theological scruples of the translator.[33] Yet, whatever the *Vorlage* of the OG might have been, whatever the translator might have intended, the result of the abridgements is significantly different from the face-value meaning of the Hebrew. An example will suffice to underscore this point.

The MT of Job 1:16 refers to a "fire of God" falling from the sky to destroy Job's sheep and shepherds. The OG, however, does not mention God, only that "fire fell from the sky," thus, whether intentional or not, avoiding the implication of divine ill-will against Job. According to the MT of Job 2:3, God admitted to having been incited by the Adversary

---

29. See Claude Cox, "Does a Shorter Hebrew Parent Text Underlie Old Greek Job?," in *In the Footsteps of Sherlock Holmes: Studies in the Biblical Text in Honour of Anneli Aejmelaeus*, ed. Kristin de Troyer, T. Michael Law, and Marketta Kiljeström, CBET 72 (Leuven: Peeters, 2014), 451–62.

30. For this distinction, see Sebastian P. Brock, "To Revise or Not to Revise: Attitudes to Jewish Biblical Translation," in *Septuagint, Scrolls and Cognate Writings*, ed. George J. Brooke and Barnabas Lindars, SCS 33l (Atlanta: Scholars Press, 1992), 301–38.

31. See Natalio Fernández Marcos, "The Septuagint Reading of the Book of Job," in *The Book of Job*, ed. Willem A. M. Beuken, BETL 114 (Leuven: Leuven University Press/Peeters, 1994), 251–66, esp. 256–61.

32. Fernández Marcos, "The Septuagint Reading of the Book of Job," 259–61.

33. So Gillis Gerleman, *Studies in the Septuagint, I: The Book of Job*, LUÅ 43/2 (Lund: Gleerup, 1946), 53–7; Henry S. Gehman, "The Theological Approach of the Greek Translator of Job 1–15," *JBL* 68 (1949): 231–40; Donald H. Gard, *The Exegetical Method of the Greek Translator of the Book of Job*, JBLMS 8 (Philadelphia: Society of Biblical Literature, 1952); Gard, "The Concept of Job's Character According to the Greek Translator of the Hebrew Text," *JBL* 72 (1953): 182–6.

to destroy Job gratuitously: "He is still holding fast to his integrity, although you have incited me against him to destroy him for naught." In the OG, however, God tells the Adversary, whom the translator calls *ho diabolos*, "You said to destroy his possessions for naught." The OG thus sidesteps the issue of divine susceptibility to the devil's instigation. Whereas the Hebrew has it that God had destroyed Job for naught, the Greek may be understood to mean that the devil was the one who brought destruction, a view more easily sustained in the OG on account of its rendering of Job 1:16. Furthermore, according to the OG, Job had not been destroyed, only his possessions were, which is in fact literally true, given that Job is still alive. However one accounts for the difference, the OG, as it stands, presents God in a manner consistent with theological orthodoxy.

Likewise, a different perspective on Job is signaled by the translation of the first verse. The Hebrew text has four descriptors for Job in 1:1 ("blameless and just, and a fearer of God, and one who turns away from evil"), but the Greek has five: "true, blameless, righteous, God-fearing, and one who eschews every evil thing." The four found in the Hebrew text are reiterated in 1:8 and 2:3. The term that stands out in the OG of 1:1, the one not repeated in the other two passages, is *dikaios*, "righteous." Most modern text critics evaluating this evidence would eliminate *dikaios* as an addition. Yet of all the descriptors in this verse, *dikaios* is the one that most defines Job. This term recurs in the OG in reference to Job (6:29; 9:15, 20; 12:4; 13:18; 32:1), culminating in 40:8. According to the Hebrew of 40:8, YHWH chastises Job for dismissing the deity's divine *mišpāṭ*: "Will you indeed dismiss my *mišpāṭ*? Will you condemn me that you may be right?" The OG renders the first line as an injunction instead of a question but is otherwise aligned with the Hebrew. The second line, however, is a rhetorical question in the Greek and it is substantially at variance with the Hebrew: "And do you think I have dealt with you in any other way than that you might appear to be *dikaios*?" (OG-Job 40:8b). Stated thus near the end of the book, the OG implies divine purposefulness in Job's suffering, namely, that Job might be found to be *dikaios*. This divine assertion vindicates Job, who ought to have known that his suffering was according to divine will. Indeed, Job himself had anticipated this vindication, according to the OG: "Behold, I am near [the end of] my trial; I know that I will be shown to be *dikaois*" (13:18).

In short, the term in 1:1 that scholars would typically eliminate on text-critical grounds turns out to be the most decisive one: Job was, above all, *dikaios* and his vindication as such by God was purposeful. Indeed, a MS of the Greek book of Job bears the title, "The Book of Righteous Job" (Paris, Bib. Nat., Coisl. 4; 13th–14th centuries), and another MS is named,

"The Life of Righteous Job" (Munich, Bayer. Staatsbibliothek, Gr. 148, 13th century). The Sahidic translation of the OG closes with a reference to "Job, the righteous," and the Syro-Hexapla has a colophon referring to "the book of Job the righteous." All these suggest that Job came to be read by Christians as hagiography.[34]

The Testament of Job

Translations are important in the life of classic texts, as they extend the ability of ancient voices to engage readers at a cultural, temporal, and spatial remove. Without translations, few texts, if any, could be considered world classics. Yet classics do not just engender translations, they also inevitably provoke rewritings and retellings. Moreover, many classics are themselves retellings of already popular stories. Shakespeare, for example, rewrote many of his plays from preexisting stories and dramas. One might point out that Shakespeare's *Macbeth* is itself a retelling of a story found in *Holinshed's Chronicles*, and *Othello* is a dramatized version of the story *Un Capitano Moro* by Cinthio.[35] In turn, Shakespeare's classic dramas have been put to many different uses over time. Mukherjee points out the global "mobility and circulation" of Shakespeare's classic plays opens them up to "audacious, sometimes irreverent, instances of Shakespeare love, authorship, and revisionism," as exemplified in various Indian rewritings and reimaginings of *Macbeth* and *Othello*.[36] These rewritings often re-contextualize and update particular elements of the story that have lost their resonance as language and culture change.

The book of Job has also been rewritten in order to reimagine its significance for new audiences. Perhaps the most influential of the early retellings of Job has been the *Testament of Job* (*T. Job*), a Hellenistic Jewish reimagination in Greek, largely based on the OG version of the story.[37] There are affinities between *T. Job* and other traditions of virtuous Jews, most notably Abraham in *Jubilees*, which itself is a consequence of the story of Job (see *Jub.* 12:1-8; 17:15–18:19). During the Roman era, the Christian community embraced *T. Job*; the continuities between the OG and *T. Job* are such that they were read as complementary accounts by the early church. The former touts Job as righteous, while the latter

---

34. See Berndt Schaller, "Das Testament Hiobs und die Septuaginta-Übersetzung des Buches Hiobs," *Bib* 61 (1980): 377–406.

35. See Kenneth Muir, *The Sources of Shakespeare's Plays* (London: Meuthuen, 1977), 182–95, 208–17.

36. Mukherjee, *What Is a Classic?*, 183.

37. Cf. Maria Haralambakis, *The Testament of Job: Text, Narrative and Reception History*, LSTS 80 (London: Bloomsbury T&T Clark, 2012).

emphasizes steadfast patience. While certain passages in the OG may hint at a less-than patient Job (so Job 6:11; 7:16; 17:13), Christian interpreters, beginning with the author of the Epistle of James, readily assumed that the righteous Job was, of course, patient. So the version of Job that was classic for many Christians was not just the OG, but rather the OG read in tandem with *T. Job*.

Apart from 1 Cor. 3:19, where Paul quotes OG-Job 5:13 as that which has been "written," the only other explicit reference to Job in the New Testament is in Jas 5:11: "You have heard of the *hypomonē* of Job." Yet the term *hypomonē*, "persistence/steadfastness/patience," does not occur in the OG of Job. It does appear in Theodotion's translation of Job 14:19c (14:18-19 are absent from the OG, but incorporated into the LXX by Origen), where Job's accuses God of destroying *hypomonē*: "And you destroyed human *hypomonē*." The related verb, *hypomenō*, occurs fourteen times in the Greek, but none pertain to Job's conduct as exemplary. In fact, in one case, Job insists that he cannot do it: "For what is my strength that I should persist" (*hypomenō*; Job 6:11). In another instance, Eliphaz urges him to do so: "Do not be stubborn, if you persist [*hypomeneis*], then your fruit will be good" (Job 22:21). By contrast, several terms for the exemplary conduct in Jas 5:7-11 are precisely those that recur in the *T. Job*: *hypomonē*, "persistence/steadfastness" (Jas 5:11; *T. Job* 1:5); *hypomenō*, "to persist/ be steadfast/be patient" (Jas 5:11; *T. Job* 4:6; 5:1; 26:4); *makrothymia*, "patience" (Jas 5:10; *T. Job* 27:7); *makrothymeō*, "to be patient" (Jas 5:7, 8; *T. Job* 11:10; 26:5; 27:7; 28:5; 35:4). These terms are used more or less synonymously to characterize Job's steadfast patience. This is not to say that one should simply equate the understanding of Job in Jas 5:7-11 with *T. Job* to the exclusion of other sources.[38] Rather, it appears that by the time the Epistle of James was composed, the story known through the Greek version had already merged with variations of the story, such as Aristeas the Historian's fragment preserved in Eusebius' *Praep. ev.* 9.25.1-4,[39] and some versions of *T. Job*.[40]

---

38. Patrick Gray, "Points and Lines: Thematic Parallelism in the Letter of James and the *Testament of Job*," *NTS* 50 (2004): 406–24.

39. It is quoted by Alexander Polyhistor, who flourished around the mid-first century BCE, which characterizes Job as *dikaios* and his suffering as a test of his steadfastness (*emmeinai*). Job was restored because of his *euphsychia*, "good courage." See Carl R. Holladay, *Fragments from Hellenistic Jewish Authors, Volume I: Historians, Texts and Translations 20* (Chico: Scholars Press, 1983), 261–75.

40. Compare also Jas 5:10, which seems to place Job among the prophets, with Sir. 49:9 in MS[B]; cf. Josephus, *C. Ap.* 1.40.

Job as a Type of Christ

It is not difficult to see why OG-Job would have been appealing to Christians. According to this version, Job was impeccably righteous (OG-Job 1:1), but he was allowed to suffer, according to divine will, in order that he may be shown to be righteous (OG-Job 40:8). Moreover, according to the Appendix to the OG: "it is written that he will rise again with those the Lord raises up" (Job 42:17). Hence, early Christian interpreters regard Job as a type of Christ.

To Origen, the book of Job, which is "even older than Moses himself,"[41] tells of how the devil had sought permission from God to put Job on trial (*Cels.* 6.43). Yet at issue is more than the trial of Job alone, for Job is a representative of all humanity. As Job himself says, life for humanity on earth is *peirastērion*, "a trial/temptation" (so OG-Job 7:1; Origen, *Or.* 29.1-2, 9; *Princ.* 3.2.7). Moreover, even though it was the devil who initiated it, the *peirastērion* which God granted (OG-Job 1:12) was in accord with divine purpose, as indeed Job is told at the end: "And do you think I have dealt with you in any other way than that you might appear to be righteous?" (OG-Job 40:8b; Origen, *Or.* 19.17). Job remained patient and did not sin, even though he had lost everything "on account of God" (Origen, *Hom. Gen.* 8.10; *Or.* 29.1-2; 30.2).[42] Drawing on the dual meaning of *peirastērion* as "trial" and "temptation," Origen portrayed the second test not in terms of Job's skin disease but as a temptation by his wife, who urged him to "say some word to the Lord and die!" (OG-Job 2:9e; *T. Job* 26:2). Yet Job, recognizing that it was the Tempter speaking through her,[43] rebuked her (OG-Job 2:10; *T. Job* 26:6). Thus, the devil was "conquered by the athlete of virtue" and proved a liar (Origen, *Or.* 30.2).

The reference to Job as an "athlete," as well as the battle imagery, are both derived from *T. Job*, where Job is called an "athlete" (*T. Job* 4:10; 27:3-5), his struggle to be faithful is characterized as a battle (*T. Job* 4:4; 18:2; 27:1), and his eventual success is called a conquest (*T. Job* 27:5).[44]

---

41. The emphasis on the book being "even older than Moses himself" is probably anti-Jewish. Elsewhere, Origen maintains with Justin Martyr that the fact that Job antedates Moses means that he lived before the Law, and yet he was righteous; e.g., *Comm. Rom.* 3.6.

42. The detail about Job suffering "on account of God" is not in the biblical versions but in *T. Job* 2:1–3:7.

43. This point is also not in the OG but is derived from *T. Job* 26:6, where Job tells her that the devil is standing behind her "so that he might deceive me too," for the devil will use "senseless women" to mislead their husbands.

44. Elsewhere, too, Origen says Job "did battle and nobly endured suffering" (*Hom. Luc.* 101.c). The metaphor of a "noble athlete" derives from the Hellenistic

Echoing *T. Job* 4:10-11; 27:3-5, Job is said to have "wrestled and conquered" twice. Yet Job did not enter the wrestling match again, says Origen, for the culminating third round of the contest was being "reserved for the Savior," as "it is written in the three Gospels," meaning the accounts of the temptation of Christ in Mt. 4:1-11; Mk 1:12-13; Lk. 4:1-13 (*Or.* 30.2). Accordingly, the "temptation" of Job by his wife prefigures the temptation of Christ, and Job's rebuke of his wife, which is his defeat of the devil, prefigures Christ's rebuke and defeat of the devil.

Origen's typological interpretation of Job, based on the OG and *T. Job*, shaped subsequent Christian understanding of Job. By the fourth century, Job 1–3 was among the liturgical readings in Lent and during Holy Week, for Job's suffering was viewed as a type of Christ's suffering. Thus Zeno of Verona preached a Lenten homily *On Job* some time near the end of the fourth century, where he presented Job as a type of Christ based on a series of perceived parallels between Job and Christ (*Tract.* I, 15.49-80; CCSL 22).[45] These parallels include the righteousness of both figures, the forsaking of treasures, conflict with the devil, and a blessed ending to their story.

In the same vein, a commentary by an anonymous Arian (Homoian) interpreter (CPG 1521; CSEL 96),[46] based on homilies preached during Holy Week, represents Job's sitting on a dunghill outside the city as a type of Christ, who suffered outside the city gate, according to Heb. 13:12 (CSEL 96, II, 32-33). Job, who persevered in his integrity, is a "type and figure" of the "immaculate lamb led to slaughter" (Jer. 11:19; CSEL 96, II, 10.23-25). The calf that Job offers for the possible sins of his children (Job 1:5) is a figure for Christ the lamb of God who takes away the sins of the world (CSEL 96, I, 31.3-10). Job's wife (2:9) was a temptress and thus a type of Eve (CSEL 96, II, 37.23-26).

Likewise Jerome, in a homily on Psalm 97 (Greek Psalm 96), follows Origen and others in seeing Job's wife as a type of Eve, through whom the devil tempted Job, a type of Adam, and affirms that Job foreshadows another Adam—Christ (CCSL 78, 444). The devil thought he could always deceive a woman, "as in the beginning," without considering that "just as one man has been destroyed through a woman, so now through a

---

athletic contest and is also found in *4 Macc.* 6:10, where the "noble athlete," despite all odds, persists till victory, and in 2 Tim. 2:5, a text frequently associated with Job in early Christian exegesis.

45. Bengt Löfstedt, ed., *Zenonis Veronensis Tractatus*, CCSL 22 (Turnhout: Brepols, 1971), 61–2.

46. Kenneth B. Steinhauser, with the assistance of H. Müller and D. Weber, eds., *Anonymi in Iob Commentarius*, CSEL 96 (Vienna: Verlag der Österreichischen Akademie der Wissenschaften, 2006).

woman the whole world is saved" (CCSL 78, 444-445). Thus, Eve is both a type of Job's wife and an antitype of Mary: "The former causes us to be cast out of Paradise, but the latter will lead us to heaven."

A similar exegesis is evident on the sarcophagus of the Roman Prefect, Junius Bassus,[47] who died in the year 359 CE. The Job scene, which reflects a number of themes in *T. Job*,[48] is juxtaposed with another scene depicting a Christian interpretation of Genesis 3. The broadly similar composition of these two scenes suggests how the story of Job and his wife was understood by the artist. Job is on the left side, as Adam is on the left; Job's wife is on the right, just as Eve is on the right. In between Adam and Eve is the snake representing the devil. So the figure at the center of the Job scene must be the devil, who, according to *T. Job*, comes to mortals disguised as a man.[49] The sculptor no doubt subscribes to the typological interpretation of Job as a Second Adam and his wife a Second Eve. The same composition—with Job, his wife with her hair shorn, and Satan in the middle—is attested as well in other sarcophagi in late antiquity,[50] all of them representing Job as a type of Christ.[51] In this view, Job's wife, like Eve, is a tool of the devil and her words in Job 2:9 are understood as a temptation to blaspheme.[52]

---

47. Now in Saint Peter's Sacristy, Vatican City; see Friedrich W. Deichmann, ed., *Repertorium der christlich-antiken Sarkophage, I. Rom und Ostia* (Wiesbaden: Franz Steiner, 1967), 279–83, pl. 104, no. 680.

48. So Dorothy H. Verkerk, "Job and Sitis: Curious Figures in Early Christian Funerary Art," *Mitteilungen zur christlichen Archäologie* 3 (1997): 20–9. For a detailed study of the iconography of the entire sarcophagus, see Elizabeth S. Malbon, *The Iconography of the Sarcophagus of Junius Bassus: Neofitus lit Ad Deum*, Princeton Legacy Library (Princeton: Princeton University Press, 1990).

49. A similar composition is found on another fourth-century sarcophagus; see Myla Perraymond, *La figura di Giobbe nella cultura paleocristiana tra esegesi patristica e manifestazioni iconografiche*, Studi di antichità cristiana 58 (Vatican City: Pontificio Istituto di Archeologia Cristiana, 2002), 94.

50. *Repertorium I*, 57–8, 129–30, pl. 19, no. 61; pl. 49, no. 215; Jutta Dresken-Weiland, ed., *Repertorium der christlich-antiken Sarkophage, II. Italien mit einem Nachtrag, Rom und Ostia, Dalmatien, Museen der Welt* (Mainz: Philipp von Zabern, 1998), 86, pl. 83, no. 248; Perraymond, *La figura di Giobbe*, 87–8, 89–100.

51. Hence, they have been classified with other "passion sarcophagi," that is, sarcophagi with scenes of the passion of Christ, on which, see, Sabine Schrenk, *Typos und Antitypos in der frühchristliche Kunst* (Münster: Aschendorffsche Verlagbuchhandlung, 1995), 35–51, 195–6.

52. This typological interpretation of Job and his wife persisted in Christian iconography at least until the fifteenth century. Thus, a woodcut by Anton Sorg in 1477 depicts Job tormented by his wife, while Satan confronts Jesus at the temptation. See

Exemplary Job

Alongside the notion of Job as a type of Christ is the even more pervasive view of him as an example of patience. This is not a trait of Job highlighted in the Hebrew book or the OG, but it is emphasized in *T. Job*, where it is illustrated by the metaphors of athletics and combat. All these are well attested in early Christian portrayals of Job, beginning with Origen (see above).

For example, Didymus the Blind frequently depicts Job as a courageous athlete who wrestled with the devil (*Comm. Job* 9.7–10.2; 40.16; 90.31).[53] Thus Job tearing his garments in mourning (1:21) is likened to an athletic "contestant" (*agōnistēs*) removing his clothing as he prepares to take on his opponent. Job's wrestled the devil in three bouts. The first was the assault on Job's property and his children, the second assault was on Job's own body, and the climactic third assault was by way of Job's wife's attempt to deceive him.

The athletic metaphor is a favorite for Chrysostom, who employs a great variety of sports idioms throughout his commentary on Job and elsewhere in his writings.[54] He imagined Job's struggle as a "spectacle" (*theatron*) that opens with Job the athlete entering the stadium (SC 346, 1.8.5; PTS 35, 11.8-9).[55] God's affirmation of Job's character in Job 1:8

Hie Vahet an das Register über die Bibeln des Alten Testaments (Augsburg: Gunther Zainer, 1477), fol. 225r. See also Albert Schramm, *Der Bilderschmuck der Frühdrucke*, 23 vols. (Leipzig: Hiersemann, 1920–43), vol. 4, pl. 40, fig. 306.

53. For the text, see Albert Henrichs, ed. and trans., *Didymos der Blinde, Kommentar zu Hiob (Tura-Papyrus), I–II*, 2 vols., Papyrologische Texte und Abhandlungen 1, 2 (Bonn: Habelt, 1968); Dieter Hagedorn, Ursula Hagedorn, and Ludwig Koenen, eds. and trans., *Kommentar zu Hiob, III (Tura-Papyrus)*, Papyrologische Texte und Abhandlungen 3 (Bonn: Habelt, 1968); *Kommentar zu Hiob, IV (Tura-Papyrus)*, Papyrologische Texte und Abhandlungen 33/1 (Bonn: Habelt, 1985).

54. Among the athletic terms in the commentary are *athlētēs* ("athlete"), *agōn* ("contest"), *agōnia* ("belonging to a contest"), *agōnizōmai* ("to contend"), *palē* ("wrestling"), *palaiō* ("to wrestle"), *palaismā* ("bout"), *pykteuō* ("sparring"), *apalthon* ("prize"). See, further, John A. Sawhill, *The Use of Athletic Metaphors in the Biblical Homilies of St. John Chrysostom* (Princeton: Princeton University Press, 1928).

55. There are two critical editions: Henri Sorlin with Louis Neyrand, eds. and trans., *Jean Chrysostome. Commentaire sur Job*, 2 vols., SC 346, 348 (Paris: Cerf, 1988), and Ursula Hagedorn and Dieter Hagedorn, eds. and trans., *Johannes Chrysostomos Kommentar zu Hiob*, PTS 35 (Berlin: de Gruyter, 1990). For an English translation, see Robert C. Hill, *St. John Chrysostom. Commentary on the Sage, I: Commentary on Job* (Brookline: Holy Cross Orthodox Press, 2006).

is like an athlete being "proclaimed," as in an athletic event. Job's declaration in 1:21, "naked I came," prompts the description of the naked athlete entering the contest.[56] The narrator's note in 1:20 that Job "fell to the ground," leads to the imagination of the devil scoring terrible blows against Job and throwing him down. Yet even as Job "fell to the ground" (1:20), he pulls the devil down as well. Just as athletes in such contests customarily bowed to the referees before they begin and then do so again upon winning, so too Job "fell to the ground and bowed down." The torn garments of Job are a testimony to the strength of his opponent. The devil is defeated in the first bout, but he challenges Job to a return match in the "Olympic contests" (SC 346, 2.3.22; PTS 35, 35.7).[57]

The trope of Job as an athlete pervades Christian writings in Greek, Latin, and Syriac through late antiquity and beyond.[58] The metaphor originally also entailed idioms of combat, meaning the spectacle of martial duels. Tertullian of Carthage wrote a treatise *On Patience*, where the devil's attacks on Job are expressed in idioms of warfare, though Job turned out to be a trophy that God established and a glorious banner that God raised over "the Enemy" (*Pat.* 14.4-6). Jerome too employed the military metaphor in a letter written in 406 to Julian, a Dalmatian patrician who had recently lost his wife and two daughters (*Epist.* 118; CSEL 55, 434-45).[59] Jerome avers that the "old enemy" who attacked Job is waging war again, attacking Julian, "a recruit of Christ" (*Epist.* 118.2; CSEL 55, 435-36). If Julian looks only to his present troubles, they will seem great, but if he looks to the "strong warrior," Job, his own troubles will seem like as child's play.[60]

---

56. In a similar scene, Job and his opponent are brought into the arena naked, which in Job's case meant that the spectators see him stripped of his wealth and other possessions. Yet they could see his fortitude, patience, and the "good condition of his soul." Job's opponent, who ranks among the highly skilled wrestlers, knew how to utilize his body strength and what tactics to use, and so forth (Chrysostom, *Stat.* 1.3; PG 49, 26.46–27.22).

57. So, too, Leontius of Constantinople imagines Job as an athlete and, in particular, as a boxer who trains in Olympia (*Hom.* V, 236–7). See Cornelis Datema and Pauline Allen, eds., *Leontii Presbyteri Constantinopolitan Homiliae*, CCSG 17 (Turnhout: Brepols; Leuven: Leuven University Press, 1987), 219.

58. Images of Job as an athlete are rare in iconography, though there is an illumination of a nude Job wrestling with Satan in a thirteenth-century MS of Gregory the Great's *Moralia* (Austria, Stiftsbibliothek Herzogenburg, MS 95, fol. 93r). The incipit reads: *QVOTIENS IN ARENE SPECTACULUM FORTIS ATHLETA DESCENDERIT.*

59. Isidorus Hilberg, ed., *Sancti Eusebii Hieronymi. Epistulae*, CSEL 54, 55 (Vienna: Tempsky / Leipzig: Freytag, 1910).

60. Similar imagery of Job as an athlete or warrior is also found in Cyprian of Carthage, *Pat.* 18; Basil of Caesarea, *Hom. quod mundanis adhaerendum* (PG 31,

All these views of Job are consequential for Gregory the Great in his *Moralia in Iob*,[61] where the imagery of warfare is paramount. The military analogy is set forth in the Preface, as Gregory speaks of Satan's relentless attacks on Job as a military assault (*Moral*. Praef. 4.9–5.12). Satan leads armies against Job, as if attacking a fortified city, and these troops are equipped with battering rams, siege engines, and other weaponry.[62] Job has to fend off the words of his enemies—his comforters—like armies on his flank, defending himself all around with "the shield of his steadfastness" and parrying their swords (*Moral*. 8.2.2). Throughout his commentary, Gregory refers to the pious as a soldier of God (*Moral*. 8.2.2; 31.34.73; 31.41.82; 31.43.84), a soldier of Christ (*Moral*. 31.34.73), or a heavenly soldier (*Moral*. 9.7.7; 31.40.80; 31.41.82). Through this warfare, God provides Christians with the lessons needed to lead one to spiritual maturity and salvation.[63] Therefore, by suffering adversities in this warfare, one will ironically be liberated.

Gregory is clear that the warfare he means is a spiritual one, a struggle against the temptation to surrender one's faith (*Moral*. 6.33.52; 30.25.75-77). Writing on Job 7:1, Gregory explains that life on earth is both *temptatio* (so the OL translation of the OG) and *militia* (so Jerome's translation from the Hebrew). While the two words sound different, Gregory maintains they actually amount to the same thing (*Moral*. 8.6.11; 23.24.47), a position that Jerome seems to have held, if not explicitly stated. Life on earth is full of distractions that will hinder one in the journey from the exterior to the interior. Such trials are inevitable as long as human beings are in their corruptible bodies (*Moral*. 6.33.51), but that warfare will come to an end with the resurrection of the body. Gregory makes this case in his comments on Job 14:14 (Vg.), where Job refers to the end of his days of warfare, when he expects his "change" to come (*Moral*. 12.13.17). That is, the "change" is understood here not as a changing of the guards or the end of a tour of mercenary duty, as Jerome had it, but as the changing of the human body. It is only then that the soldier is able to retire, as it were.

557-60); Cassiodorus, *Exp.Ps*. 37, 1.11-18 (CCSL 97, 342–3); Hilary of Poitiers, *Tract. in Iob* (CSEL 65, 230, frg. 1, lines 7–12).

61. Marci Adriaen, ed., *S. Gregorii Magni, Moralia in Iob*, CCSL 143, 143A, 143B (Turnhout: Brepols, 1979–85).

62. Such images are found in the book of Job, though with God as Job's enemy (Job 16:13-14; 19:11-12).

63. See Matthew Baasten, *Pride According to Gregory the Great: A Study of the Moralia*, Studies in the Bible and Early Christianity 7 (Lewiston: Mellen, 1986), 112–14.

Through the influence of Gregory's *Moralia*, the trope of Job as a soldier of Christ (in the spiritual sense) would later prompt Odo of Cluny in the tenth century to advocate harnessing the military power of those called to be soldiers in the material sense. Thus Odo maintained that the noble knight, Gerald of Aurillac, was a model of a soldier of Christ like Job.[64] Indeed, Gerald was "an athlete of the celestial hosts" (*athleta coelestis militiae*; *Vita* 2.1), like Job (29:17), who did not hesitate to deliver the weak from the wicked (*Vita* 1.8). It was not that he relished the use of military might. On the contrary, his aims were peaceful, and he only resorted to force when he had to (*Vita* 1.40). So Odo was not arguing for an aggressive Christian knighthood. His point was simply that lay people could be engaged in faithful *militia* as well as the clergy, who were hitherto the only ones called "soldiers of Christ." Nevertheless, by infusing literal warfare by Christians with religious and ethical meanings, Odo unwittingly laid the foundations for later justification for the crusades.[65] The First Crusade was launched with a passionate sermon at Clermont by Pope Urban II, who was once the abbot in Cluny.[66]

The nefarious consequences of the soldier metaphor extend far beyond the medieval period. It is manifest in the mystery play, *Das Spiel von Job dem Deutschen*, published by the Nazi propagandist Kurt Eggers in 1933. At one point in the play, "the Evil Enemy" urges military action for the sake of the Job-like, suffering Germany with words that hark back to Gregory's call for people to be soldiers of Christ, for "life on earth is a war":

> Ihr habt gut reden von dem Sieg,
> Denn ihr habt nichts zu leiden.
> Des Menschen Leben ist ein Krieg,
> Ein Hassen und ein Neiden.[67]

---

64. PL 133, 639–704, *Vita sancti Geraldi Auriliacensis comitis*. For comparisons of Gerald to Job, see *Vita* 1.18, 24, 28, 32, 41; 2.1; 3.2, 6.

65. Carl Erdmann, *The Origin of the Idea of Crusade*, trans. Marshall W. Baldwin and Walter Goffart (Princeton: Princeton University Press, 1977; German orig. 1935), 87–8. See, further, Giles Constable, "Cluny and the First Crusade," in *The Abbey of Cluny: A Collection of Essays to Mark the Eleventh-Hundredth Anniversary of Its Foundation*, Vita regularis 43 (Berlin: LIT, 2010), 197–211 (orig. published in 1997).

66. On all this, see C. L. Seow, "History of Consequences: The Case of Gregory's *Moralia in Iob*," *HBAI* 1 (2012): 368–87.

67. "You speak well of victory / Because you have nothing to suffer / The life of humans is a war / A hating and an envying." Kurt Eggers, *Das Spiel von Job dem Deutschen: Ein Mysterium* (Berlin: Volkschaft-Verlag, 1933), 11–12. See Carol A. Newsom, "Dramaturgy and the Book of Job," in *Das Buch Hiob und seine Interpretationen*, ed. T. Krüger et al., AThANT 88 (Zurich: TVZ, 2007), 375–93.

In Eggers' play, the Archangel Michael, "the Protector of the Germans," also echoes Gregory the Great's contention that the struggle of the soldiers of Christ leads to maturity.[68]

In all these cases, the "text" being interpreted is not the static written form in a pristine state, unencumbered by previous contributions. Rather, every text inevitably comes to the interpreter as shaped by its history, whether or not the reader is aware of that influence. The Job that functioned as a classic for Christians in the first few centuries was not the earlier Hebrew book, but instead various Greek forms of Job—initially the OG, but from the time of Origen onwards, supplemented by materials from Theodotion—which were inextricably tied to *T. Job*. What was received and used was not the static forms of the written texts, but also the narrative as formed and transformed through history. Job's status as a classic made it a useful interlocutor (and sometimes tool) for readers in the midst of contentious and even hostile disputes throughout history. Then, as now, these disputes often focus on questions of identity, belonging, and otherness. And yet, as a classic, Job does not provide simple answers—rather, it always remains open to new and different readings.

Different Texts, Different Trajectories: Jewish Consequences of Leviathan

In contrast to the Christian readings just surveyed, Jews had vastly different perspectives on Job, in part because they had access to different texts. The Tannaim in the first to the third centuries CE were conflicted about Job, with some regarding him favorably and others unfavorably.[69] The former views are continuous with the OG and *T. Job*, which were works produced by Jews after all. By the second and third centuries, however, these texts had been effectively Christianized, as Job came to be regarded as a type of Christ and as a role model for Christian conduct. Especially when Christians began to use these texts in anti-Jewish polemics, Jews responded by altering their own interpretations of Job. Beginning with the Amoraim in the third and fourth centuries, Job came to be uniformly interpreted not as the Prologue presents him, but rather

---

68. Eggers, *Das Spiel von Job*, 12.

69. See Jason Kalman, "Tannaim, Amoraim, and Targumim," in *The Many Faces of Job*, ed. C. L. Seow (Berlin: de Gruyter, forthcoming). In general, however, the book was relatively unimportant in the life of the synagogue. In contrast to the abundant and diverse output of Christian works that engaged Job in the first few centuries, there is relatively little Jewish exegetical engagement with Job in the same period.

according to his speeches in the poetic portions of the Hebrew book, as a rebel and blasphemer.[70] Yet it is not only the characterization of Job himself that differs between Jewish and Christian readings; the substantial differences between the Hebrew and Greek forms of the book influenced many other aspects of its reception as well. As a further illustration of the consequences of different texts of the book of Job, the remainder of this essay will compare the Jewish and Christian reception of Leviathan in 40:15–41:26 (ET 40:15–41:34).

The Greek Version and the Christian Trajectory

A brief analysis of OG Job 40–41 and its Christian consequences can provide contrast for Jewish interpretations. The OG renders Hebrew *bĕhēmôt* in Job 40:15 as *thēria*, a generic term for animalia, though it is clear that a singular beast is meant. As for *liwyātān* in 40:25, the OG has *drakōn*, "dragon," which it takes as a specific designation for the generic *thēria*. Moreover, in reference to the beast in 40:19b, the OG has "made to be mocked by my angels," which is similar to the OG's rendering of 41:25, where the dragon (Leviathan) is said to be "made to be mocked by my angels." These are translations borrowed from LXX Ps. 103:26b (MT Ps. 104:26b), "this dragon whom you formed to mock at him."[71] Moreover, the OG reads in Job 40:20b, "and he brought joy to the quadruped of Tartaros" and in 41:24a, "[he regards] Tartaros of the deep like a captive." These Greek renderings assume the beast to be a creature of the netherworld.

No one in the early church did more to shape Christian understanding of Leviathan than Origen. While the OG translates Hebrew *liwyātān* (Leviathan) in Job 40:25 as "a dragon," in 3:8 it has "the great sea monster" (*to mega kētos*): "Let him curse it who curses that day—the one who is about to overpower the great sea monster." The subject in 3:8 in the Hebrew is plural ("those who curse the day...to rouse Leviathan..."), but the OG has the singular ("let him...the one who is about to overpower..."), which Origen took to refer to Job as prefiguring Christ. The

---

70. See Jason Kalman, "Job Denied the Resurrection of Jesus? A Rabbinic Critique of the Church Fathers' Use of the Exegetical Traditions Found in the Septuagint and the Testament of Job," in *The Changing Face of Judaism, Christianity and Other Greco-Roman Religions in Antiquity*, ed Ian H. Henderson and George S. Oegema, with Sara Parks Ricker, Studien zu jüdischen Schriften aus hellenistisch-römischer Zeit 2 (Gütersloh: Gütersloher, 2006), 371–97.

71. For such "anaphoric translations" in OG-Job, see Homer Heater, Jr., *A Septuagint Translation Technique in the Book of Job*, CBQMS 11 (Washington, DC: The Catholic University of America, 1982), 126–7 et passim.

singular verb in the OG also allowed Origen to link this text with Jonah, who was swallowed by "the great sea monster" (*kētei megalō...tou kētous*; LXX Jon. 2:1-2; ET 1:17–2:1) and hence also with Mt. 12:40, where Jonah in the belly of the sea monster for three days and three nights is presented as a prefigure of Christ being in the netherworld for three days and three nights (Origen, *Or.* 13.4). So Origen asserts that Job 3:8 is a prophecy concerning Christ, who would subdue the "great sea monster," understood to mean the devil (*Comm. Jo.* 1.96; *Princ.* 4.1.5; *Hom. Lev.* 8.3.4). Moreover, given that Jonah in the belly is regarded as a type of Christ in the netherworld, Origen depicted the "great sea monster" as an allusion to Death (*Comm. Rom.* 5.10.10).[72] The association of Leviathan with the devil is suggested by Origen's mention of "the morning star" (*ho heōsphoros*) in Job 41:10 (OG) in reference to the eyes of Leviathan.[73] Origen paraphrases 40:25 as saying, "you will draw the apostate dragon with a hook," where "apostate dragon" is derived from 26:13, adding that "it is certain that the dragon is understood as the devil himself (*Princ.* 1.5.5).[74] Following Origen, Christian interpreters developed a robust theory of redemption based on Job 40:23-25, and the influence of this interpretation remains common in later Christian theology and is manifest in liturgies, literature, and the visual arts.[75]

The Hebrew Version and the Jewish Trajectory

Jewish views of Leviathan, on the other hand, derive from the Hebrew version, along with various rabbinic elaborations and legends. The MT identifies two creatures, Behemoth (Job 40:15-23) and Leviathan (40:24–41:26 [ET 40:24–41:34]). Unlike the Greek version, it does not associate Leviathan with the netherworld, nor does it suggest hostility between YHWH and Leviathan. In fact, in 41:1-5 (ET 41:9-13), God and Leviathan coalesce and terms used to describe Leviathan's appearance in 41:10-13 (ET 41:18-21) are those typically used of theophany.

---

72. For the background of all this in Origen's theology, see Henry Crouzel, *Origen*, trans. A. S. Worrall (San Francisco: Harper & Row, 1989; French orig. 1985), 21–2.

73. In a quotation attributed to Origen in the Job-Catena, see Ursula Hagedorn and Dieter Hagedorn, eds., *Die älteren griechischen Katenen zum Buch Hiob*, 3 vols., PTS 40, 48, 53 (Berlin: de Gruyter, 1994, 1997, 2000), 3:360.

74. Cf. Hagedorn and Hagedorn, eds., *Die älteren griechischen Katenen*, 3:344.

75. See Gregory of Nyssa, *Cat. Or.* 24.29-36; 26.4-10, 31-38; Athanasius, PG 28, 240.18-24; Pseudo-Chrysostom, PG 61, 753.70–754.10; PG 64, 23.20-32; Olympiodorus, *Comm. Job* 40.25-26; Gregory the Great, *Moral.* 33.7.14; Martin Luther, *LW* 22:24; cf. *LW* 26:27; WA 9:661; 40:640; 46:391; 57:129.

In the Greek version, the beast (Behemoth) is the dragon (Leviathan). Jewish traditions drawing primarily from the MT, however, regarded the two as different creatures, one of the land and the other the sea (*4 Ezra* 6:49-52; *2 Bar.* 29:4),[76] and they are often joined by a large mythological bird, Ziz (a term of uncertain meaning in Pss. 50:11; 80:14 [ET 80:13]), sometimes conflated with a fabulous bird known to the sages as *bar yôkānî* (*b. Bek.* 57b; *Yoma* 80a; *Suk.* 5b). These three represent the primordial beasts of the land, sea, and sky—creatures brought into existence on the fifth and sixth days of creation (Gen. 1:20-25).

Critical for understanding the history of Jewish interpretations are two points of translation. The MT of 40:30 (ET 41:6) reads: *yikrû ālâw ḥabbārîm // yeḥĕṣûhû bên kĕnaʿănîm*, which I would translate as, "Will partners haggle[77] over him? // Will they divide him up among merchants?" The Tg. derives *yikrû* from *krh*, "to give a feast" (cf. *kērâ*, "feast," 2 Kgs 6:23; so *b. B. Bat.* 74b),[78] and many interpreters assumed the same (Saadiah, Ibn Ezra, Ralbag, Meyuḥas). This translation underlies the legend that Leviathan will be served as food for the righteous at the messianic banquet (*2 Bar.* 29:4; *b. B. Bat.* 75a; *Lev. Rab.* 13:3), an interpretation based on Ps. 74:14, where a ravaged Leviathan is given as food to people. Yet, if Leviathan is to be eaten by the righteous, it must be kosher. To support the view that Leviathan is *dāg ṭāhôr*, a clean fish, the rabbis adduced Job 41:7a (ET 41:15), interpreted to mean "his scales are his pride," and 41:22a (ET 41:30), "sharpest potsherds are beneath him," interpreted to mean its fins. Such a fish, having scales and fins, is indeed fit to be eaten (*Sifra Shemini* 3:5, 49c/d; *b. Ḥul.* 67b; *Lev. Rab.* 22:10).[79] Furthermore, Job 40:31 (ET 41:7) reads in the MT: *hatmallēʾ bĕśukkôt ʿôrô // ûbĕṣilṣal dāgîm rōʾšô*, "Will you riddle his skin with harpoons,[80] // And his head with fishing

---

76. See K. William Whitney, *Two Strange Beasts: Leviathan and Behemoth in Second Temple and Early Rabbinic Judaism*, HSM 63 (Winona Lake: Eisenbrauns, 2006).

77. Hebrew *krh ʿl* is an idiom meaning "to buy on account of," hence, "to barter, make a transaction over," as evident in Job 6:27, but cf. also Deut. 2:6 and, possibly, Hos. 3:2.

78. Similarly, the OG and Symm.

79. For further discussion of how Leviathan was deemed kosher, see Michael Mulder, "Leviathan on the Menu of the Messianic Meal: The Use of Various Images of Leviathan in Early Jewish Tradition," in *Playing with Leviathan: Interpretation and Reception of Monsters from the Biblical World*, ed. Koert van Bekkum et al., Themes in Biblical Narrative 21 (Leiden: Brill, 2017), 115–30, esp. 122–6.

80. Ibn Ezra derives *śukkôt* from *śkk*, "to pierce," as also the noun *śikkîm*, "thorns" (Num. 33:55). Ramaq records this as a common view among interpreters. The root is

spears?" The Tg. presumes that *sukkôt* is a variant of *sukkot*, "booths,"[81] and many interpreters assume so (Saadiah, Additions to Rashi, Berechiah HaNaqdan). Moreover, the Tg. derives the term *ṣilṣal* from *ṣll*, "to be shelter," and this, too, finds support among medieval interpreters. These translations underlie the midrash that Leviathan's skin would be made into a booth for the righteous (*b. B. Bat.* 75a). Jews also understood Ps. 104:26 to mean that God created Leviathan for sport, with one legend suggesting that God plays with it three hours a day (*b. 'Abod. Zar.* 3b), and another that the righteous will hunt it for sport in the world to come (*Lev. Rab.* 13:3). The latter is related to the view in the *Tg.-Ps.* 104:26, which makes this sport an eschatological banquet: "…this Leviathan you created for the sport of the righteous at the meal of his dwelling place." Some authorities identified Leviathan as female and paired with Behemoth as its male counterpart (*b. B. Bat.* 74b), with Leviathan located in the lower cosmos (*Apoc. Ab.* 21:4; *1 En.* 60:7; *Pirq. R. El.* 9), but others posit two forms of Leviathan (*Apoc. Ab.* 10:10; *b. B. Bat.* 74b), an idea derived from Isa. 27:1, which refers to "Leviathan the fleeing serpent" (*liwyātān nāḥāš bārîaḥ*) and "Leviathan the writhing serpent" (*liwyātān nāḥāš 'ăqallātôn*), perhaps understood as "one below" and "one above" (cf. *m. Ḥag.* 2:1; *Apoc. Ab.* 10:9-10).[82] Related, too, is a tradition about a "cosmic Jordan," that flows into the mouth of Leviathan (cf. Job 40:23), though this view was rightly challenged, for the subject in Job 40:23 is Behemoth (*b. B. Bat.* 74b).[83] This is perhaps the origin of Leviathan as a cosmic *ouroboros*, a serpent that forms a circle by biting its own tail, thus encircling the cosmos. This view is evident in a *piyyûṭ* by Eleazar ben-Qallir on the battle between Behemoth and Leviathan.[84] The poem, which celebrates the revelation of the mystery of creation, includes the view that Leviathan has two

---

attested in Arabic *šakka*, "to pierce," including with spear or arrow, and *šikkat*, "arms, weapon" (Lane, 1582–3) and Akkadian *šikkatu/sikkatu*, "nail, peg" (*CAD*, S, 247–8). Perhaps the meaning is harpoon or an implement used to pull the creature out (cf. Aq: *anaphoreusin*, "lifting poles").

81. Many MSS in Kennicott and de Rossi indeed read *skwt*, though these are late and may be influenced by the Tg. and medieval exegesis.

82. Cf. Mulder, "Leviathan on the Menu of the Messianic Meal," 126–7; Andrei A. Orlov, "'What is Below?' Mysteries of Leviathan in Early Jewish Accounts and Mishnah Hagigah 2:1," in *Hekhalot Literature in Context: Between Byzantium and Babylonia*, ed. Ra'anan Boustan, Martha Himmelfarb, and Peter Schäfer, TSAJ 153 (Tübingen: Mohr Siebeck, 2003), 313–22.

83. See Whitney, *Two Strange Beasts*, 109–14.

84. Jefim Schirmann, "The Battle between Behemoth and Leviathan according to an Ancient Piyyûṭ," *PIASH* 4 (1971): 327–69.

forms—*liwyātān nāḥāš bārîaḥ* and *liwyātān nāḥāš 'ăqallātôn* (Isa. 27:1)— like a king over two armies, its mouth opened as it awaits the final banquet:

> His tail gripped tightly in his mouth,
> Encircling the Great Sea like ring.
> But when the great day comes,
> The Great King shall say,
> "Give him as food for a great nation!" (lines 76–80)

The poem goes on to describe the battle between Leviathan and Behemoth, as "the holy ones" witness God make sport of the beasts, and the messianic banquet that concludes the event. All these indicate that, for Jews, Leviathan was a symbol of eschatological hope in God's cosmic defeat of the forces of chaos.[85]

Certainly by the Gaonic period (589–1038 CE), Leviathan had begun to be identified as *Axis Mundi* and *Circuitus Mundi*, the former represented by *liwyātān nāḥāš bārîaḥ*, where *bryḥ* is interpreted as "bar, bolt" (properly, *bĕrîaḥ*),[86] and the latter by *liwyātān nāḥāš 'ăqallātôn*, where *'ăqallātôn* is understood to mean circular.[87]

These messianic themes are evident in Jewish art beginning in the medieval period. The *North French Hebrew Miscellany* (London, Brit. Lib. Add. MS 11639, fols. 517v, 518v, 519r) from the thirteenth century depicts the three primordial beasts, each on a page and identified by a caption. Behemoth is drawn as a wild ox poised to gore (fol. 519r); Leviathan is shown with sharp fins all around it (fol. 518b). These representations accord with a Jewish tradition concerning a deadly battle (*Lev. Rab.* 13:3). An illuminated Siddur from Austria, dated to around 1300, portrays Leviathan as a fish and Behemoth as a wild ox locked in combat (New York, Jewish Theological Seminary of America Library, MS 0017, fol. 2r). An illustrated Maḥzor from Leipzig, dated to around 1325, shows an enraged Behemoth confronting Leviathan, whose fins stick out of its body like blades, and on the left margin of the page stands a righteous Jew holding a *lulav* (palm branch) and *etrog* (a citrus fruit), symbols of the celebration of Sukkot (Leipzig, Karl-Marx-Universitätsbibliothek, MS Vollers 1102, II, fol. 181v). The association of Leviathan with Sukkot originated from an interpretation of the term *śukkôt* in Job 40:31 [ET 41:7]

---

85. Michael Fishbane, *The Exegetical Imagination: On Jewish Thought and Theology* (Cambridge: Harvard University Press, 1998), 41–55.

86. So *Pirqe R. El.* 9, "...*liwyātān nāḥāš bārîaḥ*, his dwelling in the lower waters and between its fins is the middle bar (*bĕrîaḥ*) of the earth."

87. See Whitney, *Two Strange Beasts*, 114–27.

and the legend that Leviathan's skin would be made into a booth for the righteous. The thirteenth-century Ambrosian Bible from Germany shows Behemoth, Leviathan, and Ziz in the top half of the page (Milan, Bib. Ambrosiana, MS B.30-32, fol. 136r). The bottom half presents the righteous with heads like those of birds,[88] crowned, and surrounding a table, presumably in anticipation of the messianic banquet where the beasts in the upper half of the page will be on the menu. With the exception of the Leipzig Mahzor, all Jewish manuscript illuminations interpret Leviathan as a serpentine fish, curled to form an open (incomplete) or a closed circle, that is, as *ouroboros*. Medieval exegetes imagined the circle formed by Leviathan as demarcating the heavens, even as it encircles the world.

The association of Leviathan with messianic hope through the provision of food and shelter for the righteous was turned, ironically, to belief in the beneficence of Leviathan itself. Indeed, Leviathan came to suggest divine providence, or even to represent divine presence on earth.[89] Beginning in the seventeenth century, therefore, Leviathan became a common feature in synagogues in Galicia. Leviathan as cosmic *ouroboros* frequently decorates the ceilings of synagogues.[90] On the dome of the *bimah* in the synagogue of Łańcut, Poland, the serpentine fish forms a circle within which one sees, as if through a roof-window, the heavens where birds fly (IJA, nos. 12567; 3705). The dome of the wooden synagogue in Myn'kivtsi, Ukraine, shows Leviathan encircling Jerusalem, which represents a microcosm of the cosmos (IJA, no. 134528). The ceiling of the wooden synagogue in Pakroujis, Lithuania, features Leviathan encircling a building, probably the synagogue itself (see IJA, no. 126110). Similarly, the ceiling of the Gwoździec Synagogue in Warsaw features Leviathan coiled around a city identified by the letter "W," the initial of the city (see IJA, no. 233134). Similar scenes are found on synagogue walls, both internal (as Kraśni and Dąbrowa Tarnowska, Poland) and external (in Pishchanka, Ukraine), and on Torah arks (in Sandomierz, Poland; Valkininkai/Olkieniki and Kėdainiai, Lithuania).

Leviathan is represented as well in various religious objects. A copper laver from Galicia displays two serpentine forms of Leviathan around it (IJA, nos. 465; 6684–6686). The upper serpent chases its own tail; the bottom serpent succeeds in biting it. On a tombstone in Banyliv,

---

88. Zofia Ameisenowa, "Animal-Headed Gods, Evangelists, Saints and Righteous Men," *Journal of the Warburg and Courtauld Institutes* 12 (1949): 21–45, esp. 28–34.

89. Marc M. Epstein, *Dreams of Subversion in Medieval Art and Literature* (University Park: Pennsylvania State University Press, 1997), 70–95.

90. See the examples in The Bezalel Narkiss Index of Jewish Art (IJA) at http://cja.huji.ac.il.

Ukraine, Leviathan is shown encircling a crown (IJA, no. 171805). The crown symbolizes the glorification of the righteous when they partake of the great messianic banquet (cf. the Ambrosian Bible where the Jews at the messianic banquet are crowned). Less common than the encircling Leviathan are examples of it in an elongated form, as on a synagogue lectern (IJA, no. 179559) and on the handle of a Kiddush cup (IJA, no. 18944).

Leviathan has continued to inspire artists as a symbol of hope in divine beneficence. Modern artistic renderings appear in many forms, including stained glass and mosaic compositions. Yet the traditional Jewish image of Leviathan forming a circle persists, as in Benny Ferdman's outdoor sculpture that forms a circle 13 feet in diameter. Entitled *Tsim-Tsum*; this piece was created for the Milken Community High School in Los Angeles in 2002.

No End

I have endeavored in this essay to tell a story about a classic that has no decisive beginning but is in fact pluriform. Yet it is necessarily an incomplete story, for there are many other trajectories and iterations that might be explored. One could consider, for instance, traditions of Job in Islam, which by and large were not derived from the Hebrew book of Job nor the Greek, nor even the Qur'ān, where Job ('Ayyûb) appears in only four passages (4:163; 6:84-85; 21:83-84; 38:41-44). These traditions are not strictly receptions of "the book of Job," though they have often been characterized as such. Indeed, many Muslim interpreters from the medieval period till the present have taken pains to isolate elements of the Islamic versions from "other people's texts"—describing them as *Isrā'iliyyāt*, that is, sources derived from the "Israelites" and, by extension, also Christians.

There are also other iterations of Leviathan that one might consider, such as Joseph Klein's 1998 musical composition, *Leviathan*, which is a reception of W. S. Merwin's poem of the same title in 1956, which is in turn a reception of Melville's *Moby-Dick* from 1851 and the *Exeter Book* from the tenth century, among other sources. Moreover, there are movies, heavy metal bands, board games, video games, and roller coasters—all named Leviathan. Most of these are in fact so genealogically distant from "the book of Job" that they cannot be regarded as receptions thereof, but rather as various iterations of the pluriform classic. So, just as there is no decisive beginning, there is certainly no end. Indeed, the object of one's study is less like a tree with a single root and stem, than like a rhizome, with a complex network of interconnected roots and nodes, as Gilles Deleuze and Félix Guattari have emphasized.[91] This undermines any firm disciplinary boundaries between the analysis of the book's development and reception, so scholars engaging with such literature must learn to become hermeneuts without borders—we are, after all, studying the "audacious, sometimes irreverent, instances of" Joban "authorship and revisionism."[92]

---

91. Gilles Deleuze and Félix Guattari, *A Thousand Plateaus: Capitalism and Schizophrenia,* trans. Brian Massumi (Minneapolis: University of Minnesota Press, 1987); cf. Brennan W. Breed, *Nomadic Text: A Theory of Biblical Reception History* (Indianapolis: University of Indiana Press, 2014).

92. Quote emended from Mukherjee, *What Is a Classic?*, 183.

Iconoclastic Readings:
Othering in Isaiah 44 and in Its Reception in Biblical Scholarship

Sonja Ammann

Introduction

Biblical scholars, as critical and historically informed readers, have a particular relationship to biblical texts. On the one hand, they are professional readers with a generally intimate relationship to their subject of study. As commentators, their task is to make sense of the biblical text, often for a confessional audience. On the other hand, through their education and academic context, they handle the text with methodological rigor and an awareness of its historically remote origins. In my contribution to this volume on "reading other peoples' texts," I would like to address how and to what extent the biblical text is "other peoples'" text or that of biblical scholars themselves. I will investigate this issue by comparing scholarly readings of one particular biblical text, Isa. 44:9-20. This approach allows for a narrowing down of the broader issue to the following more manageable question: *Do interpreters take on or refuse the role the text invites them to perform, or, put differently, do they identify with the implied reader?* Isaiah 44:9-20 is a polemical text on the fabrication of cult images. This text is particularly well-fitted for such a study for two reasons:

First, as a polemical text, Isaiah 44 emphasizes a particular construction of the Other, that is, those condemned in the text. This clear-cut distinction between Us and Them within the text itself will serve as a coordinate system for the self-positioning of the commentators: Do they locate themselves with the textual in-group or out-group, or do they take the position of an external observer?

The second reason for choosing Isaiah 44 as a case study is the interesting developments in the recent history of research on biblical texts aimed at iconic worship. While uncritical co-opting of the perspectives of the biblical authors once tended to be the rule in earlier commentaries, scholars in more recent times have increasingly refused to adopt the part that the polemical texts suggest the reader ought to play. In some cases, it seems that the iconoclastic impulse backfires on the biblical texts themselves: scholars treat the biblical authors (rather than the Babylonian practitioners of iconic cults) as ignoramuses and as worshippers of idols.[1]

Before I begin with the discussion of Isa. 44:9-20, I would like to briefly outline two concepts I use in this article to examine how scholars relate to the biblical texts on which they comment. First, I will make use of the term "implied reader" in the sense described by Jean-Louis Ska:

> The implied reader is…an intrinsic part of the structure of a narration. In the "drama of reading," the real reader, who accepts the contract proposed by the implied author, "becomes" the implied reader. In other words, the "implied reader" is less a person than a rôle that every concrete reader is invited to perform in the act of reading. Every narration contains an invitation to share a certain experience, to imagine and recreate a universe, to get in touch with certain values, feelings, decisions, and world-views. Such participation is another way to describe the "part" of the implied reader. It does not mean that every "real reader" will accept the values of the narration that he reads.[2]

---

1. Cf. Michael B. Dick, "Prophetic Parodies of Making the Cult Image," in *Born in Heaven, Made on Earth: The Making of the Cult Image in the Ancient Near East*, ed. Michael B. Dick (Winona Lake: Eisenbrauns, 1999), 1–53 (quoted below); George M. Soares-Prabhu, "Laughing at Idols: The Dark Side of Biblical Monotheism (an Indian Reading of Isaiah 44:9-20)," in *Reading from This Place: Vol. 2: Social Location and Biblical Interpretation in Global Perspective*, ed. Fernando F. Segovia and Mary A. Tolbert (Minneapolis: Fortress, 1995), 109–31, esp. 123–31 ("The religion of Second Isaiah, as seen from India, is in a sense as 'idolatrous' as that of the people he mocks," 125); cf. also Karel van der Toorn, "The Iconic Book: Analogies Between the Babylonian Cult of Images and the Veneration of the Torah," in *The Image and the Book: Iconic Cults, Aniconism, and the Rise of Book Religion in Israel and the Ancient Near East*, ed. Karel van der Toorn, CBET 21 (Leuven: Peeters, 1997), 229–48, on functional analogies between cult images and the Torah. For an early representative of such a critical reading cf. Bernhard Duhm, *Das Buch Jesaja*, 5th ed. (Göttingen: Vandenhoeck & Ruprecht, 1968), 336.

2. Jean-Louis Ska, *'Our Fathers Have Told Us': Introduction to the Analysis of Hebrew Narratives*, SubBi 13 (Rome: Pontificio Istituto Biblico, 1990), 42–3. The "implied reader" is adapted from W. C. Booth's concept of the "implied author," cf. Wayne C. Booth, *The Rhetoric of Fiction*, 2nd ed. (Chicago: University of Chicago Press, 1983), 138 ("The author creates, in short, an image of himself [= the 'implied author,' S.A.] and another image of his reader; he makes his reader, as he makes his

To this definition, one should add that both the implied author and the implied reader are a construction by the real readers of a text.[3] Real readers whose readings correspond to the implied reader they construe are readers who "accept the contract." By contrast, readers who refuse to perform the role of the implied reader—by rejecting, for instance, statements, values, and points of view expressed in the text—deliberately read the text against the grain. For our investigation, the degree of overlap between the implied reader and the reading performed by the scholar in question will be used as an indicator of the extent to which they are reading the text as "their own" or "other peoples'."

Second, I will use the terms "textual in-group" and "textual out-group" to discuss how scholars identify with characters and groups described and addressed in the text. The concept of "in-group" and "out-group" was developed in social psychology and in social identity theory especially.[4] This concept is at stake when we talk about Us versus Them. In biblical scholarship, social identity theory has been fruitfully applied to investigate how biblical texts relate to and interact with their socio-historical contexts.[5] This terminology might also be helpful to think about how readers construe texts as "their own" or "other peoples'." To distinguish this use of the "in-group/out-group" concept from a reconstruction of the socio-historical groups targeted by the polemics in their ancient contexts, I will use the terms "textual in-group/out-group." Like biblical texts opposing "Israelites" to "Canaanites," texts like Isaiah 44 imply a polemical distinction between Us and Them. Even where a first person plural is not explicit in the text, readers are invited to join the implied author in distinguishing themselves from a group of Others construed in the text. Performing the implied reader's role is thus not the act of an

second self, and the most successful reading is one in which the created selves, author and reader, can find complete agreement"). The concept of the "implied reader" was developed by Wolfgang Iser, *Der implizite Leser: Kommunikationsformen des Romans von Bunyan bis Beckett* (Munich: Fink, 1972); ET: Iser, *The Implied Reader: Patterns of Communication in Prose Fiction from Bunyan to Beckett* (Baltimore: Johns Hopkins University Press, 2011); Iser, *Der Akt des Lesens: Theorie ästhetischer Wirkung*, 4th ed., UTB (1976; repr., Munich: Fink, 1994), 50–67.

3. Cf. Wolf Schmid, *Narratology: An Introduction*, trans. Alexander Starritt, De Gruyter Textbook (Berlin: de Gruyter, 2010), 51–2.

4. Cf. Henri Tajfel, "Social Identity and Intergroup Behaviour," *Social Science Information* 13, no. 2 (1974): 65–93.

5. Cf., e.g., the seminal study by Philip F. Esler, *Conflict and Identity in Romans: The Social Setting of Paul's Letter* (Minneapolis: Fortress, 2003).

isolated individual, it involves taking sides and identifying with one group as opposed to an Other. I propose to use the term "textual in-group" for this implicit "us" construed in the text, comprising the implied author(s) and the implied reader(s). A real reader accepting the role of the implied reader will identify with this textual in-group and, I would say, read the text as "his / her own." In contrast, the textual out-group comprises those who are presented as the "others" in the text. The implied readers are supposed to distinguish themselves from this out-group.

Othering in Isaiah 44:9-20[6]

[9] Makers of cult images are all nothing, and their darlings are of no use. Their witnesses are they: they do not see and do not know, so that they will be put to shame.

[10] Who would fashion a god and cast a cult image, without any use?

[11] Look, all its companions will be put to shame, and the craftsmen, they are [merely] human. They all assemble, they stand up, they tremble and are put to shame altogether.

[12] An iron smith makes[7] an axe with coal fire, he shapes it with hammers and makes it with his strong arm, yet he is hungry and has no strength, he did not drink water and is tired.

[13] A carpenter lays out a cord, he traces it out with a pencil, he makes it with carving knives and traces it out with a compass. He made it in human form, with human splendor, to live in a house.

[14] He cut down[8] for himself firs and took a holm tree or an oak and let [it] grow strong among the trees of the forest. He planted laurel and rain made [it] grow.

[15] And it served for humans as fuel. He took from it and warms himself; further, he lights [it] and bakes bread; further, he makes a god out of it and prostrates himself. He made a cult image and bowed down before it!

---

6. I discuss this text (and its translation) in more detail in Sonja Ammann, *Götter für die Toren: Die Verbindung von Götterpolemik und Weisheit im Alten Testament*, BZAW 466 (Berlin: de Gruyter, 2015), 82–103.

7. Reading יפעל in place of ופעל, cf. Silvia Schroer, *In Israel gab es Bilder: Nachrichten von darstellender Kunst im Alten Testament*, OBO 74 (Fribourg: Universitätsverlag; Göttingen: Vandenhoeck & Ruprecht, 1987), 219.

8. The verse begins with an infinitive construct (לכרת). Most commentators emend to a finite form or insert a finite verb, e.g., David Winton Thomas, "Isaiah XLIV.9-20: A Translation and Commentary," in *Hommages à André Dupont-Sommer* (Paris: Adrien-Maisonneuve, 1971), 319–30, esp. 326; Claus Westermann, *Das Buch Jesaja, Kap. 40–66*, 4th ed., ATD 19 (Göttingen: Vandenhoeck & Ruprecht, 1981), 118 n. 4.

¹⁶ Half of it, he burned in the fire, on half of it, he roasts⁹ meat, he eats roasted [meat] and is sated. Further, he warms himself and says: "Ah, I have warmed myself and seen the fire!"

¹⁷ The rest of it he makes into a god, his cult image. He bows down to it and prostrates himself and prays to it and says: "Save me, for you are my God!"

¹⁸ They do not know and they do not understand, for plastered are their eyes, so that they do not see, and their hearts, so that they do not comprehend.

¹⁹ He does not consider in his heart, and he does not have knowledge nor understanding to say: "Half of it I have burnt in the fire, and also I have baked bread on its coals, I roast meat and eat [it], and of its rest I make an abomination, I bow before a log of wood."

²⁰ He who gets involved with ashes, the deluded heart guides him away, and he does not save his live, and does not say: "Is there not deceit in my right hand?"

This text casts the makers of cult images in a negative light and disparages them with invectives from the very beginning ("they are all nothing!," Isa. 44:9), Othering them. Readers are thus invited to join in the condemnation of the makers of images. "They" lack understanding, make an abomination, and will be put to shame. Beyond that, the precise contours of the underlying in-group/out-group differentiation are not made explicit, opening a range of possible interpretations. First, the text uses the third person throughout, containing no explicit references to its speaker or its audience. A specific textual in-group—namely, the Us in contrast to Them—that readers are supposed to identify with is not explicitly present at the surface of the text. While some interpreters understand Isa. 44:9-20 as part of a discourse in which Yʜᴡʜ addresses his people (see 44:6-8, 21-22), others reckon with a text that bears no close relation to its context and needs to be treated on its own.¹⁰ The identity of the makers and worshippers of images is not specified in this text, and scholars differ in their assessment of whether they belong to Yʜᴡʜ's people addressed in vv. 6-8, or to a group or nation that does not worship Yʜᴡʜ. Based on the Deutero-Isaianic context and setting, scholars who locate the makers

---

9. Following K. Elliger's suggestion to invert יבאל and יצלה (cf. v. 19 and LXX), cf. Karl Elliger, *Deuterojesaja. Teilbd. 1. Jesaja 40,1–45,7*, BK (Neukirchen-Vluyn: Neukirchener, 1978).

10. In particular, many scholars consider Isa. 44:9-20 a secondary addition that interrupts the speech addressing Yʜᴡʜ's people in the 2nd person, cf. Duhm, *Buch Jesaja*, 333; Westermann, *Buch Jesaja*, 119; Elliger, *Deuterojesaja*, 416–17; Rosario P. Merendino, *Der Erste und der Letzte. Eine Untersuchung von Jes 40–48*, VTSup 31 (Leiden: Brill, 1981), 385; Joseph Blenkinsopp, *Isaiah 40–55: A New Translation with Introduction and Commentary*, AB 19A (New York: Doubleday, 2002), 240.

and worshippers of images in Isaiah 44 among the nations often assume that the polemics are aimed at Babylonians.[11] Although the text mentions technical details of their fabrication (vv. 12-13) and the anthropomorphic appearance of the images (v. 13), the description of the images and the context of their fabrication and use remains ambiguous. The text leaves open whether the craftsmen are fabricating images of YHWH, or of other deities, and for what cultic or ritual context.[12] Moreover, it is not clear what exactly the text takes issue with—the fabrication of particular images or of divine images in general, the cultic use of images, or a particular cult that competes with the people's trust in YHWH? Depending on the assumed (religio-)historical background and identity of the makers and worshippers of images, the purpose and function of Isa. 44:9-20 can be cast in various ways.

Thus, while it seems clear that the implied reader's role is to judge negatively the textual out-group of the makers and worshippers of images, the text contains gaps and ambiguities that commentators need to fill in order to determine the boundaries between the in-group and the out-group.

Scholarly Readings of Isaiah 44

The polemical text in Isa. 44:9-20 presents a construction of an out-group, namely, the makers and worshippers of cult images, and invites the reader to identify with the textual in-group. In the following, I will examine how commentators construe the textual in-group and out-group, and how they comply with the role of the implied reader. Of course, the four ways of reading Isaiah 44 that I will present are by no means exhaustive. I have chosen as examples four commentators with a Christian background whose readings nonetheless differ considerably. These readings are exemplary in

---

11. Most scholars locate the redaction of Second Isaiah in Babylonia; but this is by no means certain, cf. e.g., Blenkinsopp, *Isaiah*, 103; Hans M. Barstad, *The Babylonian Captivity of the Book of Isaiah: "Exilic" Judah and the Provenance of Isaiah 40–55* (Oslo: Novus, 1997).

12. While Isa. 44:15-17 refer to a domestic context, this seems less likely for the collaborative work by professionals described in vv. 12-13, where the "house" (בית, v. 13) could be taken as a reference to a temple. Some scholars consider Isa. 44:9-20 to be a composite text (e.g., Elliger, *Deuterojesaja*, 417–22; and cf. my discussion of this issue in Ammann, *Götter*, 82–90). In any case, both the vague descriptions in vv. 9-11, 18 and the juxtaposition of competing descriptions of the subjects and settings in vv. 14-17 and 19-20 on the one hand, and vv. 12-13 on the other, add to the ambiguity of the text.

the sense that each of them represents a type of reading that can be found with little variation in the works of other commentators.

Claus Westermann (Reading as an Enlightened Protestant)

Claus Westermann (1909–2000) was a German Protestant scholar. A member of the *Bekennende Kirche*, he served as a pastor in Berlin and later taught Old Testament at the University of Heidelberg.[13] His commentary on Isaiah 40–66 was first published in 1966 (4th revised edition, 1981). Westermann considers Isa. 44:9-20 to be a secondary addition in its present context, but praises its literary qualities.[14] He states that the text denigrates "idol makers" ("Götzenbildner") and "worshippers of images" ("Bilderanbeter").[15] According to Westermann, Isa. 44:9-20 does not address Israelites.[16] Thus, in this reading, the polemics clearly target an out-group that stands in contrast to the ancient author and his audience as well as to Westermann's own viewpoint. Westermann does not question the condemnation of iconic worship (which he understands in a rather general sense). Rather, he marvels at the "spirit of enlightenment" ("Geist der Aufklärung") he senses in this text.[17] At this point, Westermann—quoting Greek and Latin authors—brings his own classical education in, which conforms in his reading to the biblical author's perspective.[18] Almost with regret, he admits that the text's depiction of iconic worship

---

13. An account of his life by Westermann himself can be found in Manfred Oeming, ed., *Claus Westermann: Leben – Werk – Wirkung*, Beiträge zum Verstehen der Bibel 2 (Münster: LIT, 2003). For a short presentation of Westermann and his work in English, cf. Walter Brueggemann, "Westermann, Claus," in *Dictionary of Biblical Interpretation*, ed. John H. Hayes, 2 vols. (Nashville: Abingdon, 1999), 633–4.

14. He calls it "ein Musterbeispiel satirischer Dichtung," Westermann, *Buch Jesaja*, 121. In earlier commentaries, scholars who ascribe the passage to a later redactor often consider its literary and theological quality inferior to "original" Second Isaiah texts, cf., e.g., Duhm, *Buch Jesaja*, 333; R. Norman Whybray, *Isaiah: 2. Isaiah 40–66*, NCB (London: Oliphants, 1975), 100 ("rather poor writing by an author who was trying to imitate Deutero-Isaiah").

15. Westermann, *Buch Jesaja*, 121.

16. As opposed to Hos. 13:2, cf. Westermann, *Buch Jesaja*, 123.

17. See his commentary on v. 14: "Die letzte Bemerkung 'ein Haus zu bewohnen' zeigt besonders deutlich den aufklärerischen Geist, in dem die Satire verfasst ist," and on vv. 15-17: "Hier, an seinem Ziel, in diesen Versen 15-17 zeigt der Dichter des Spottliedes am deutlichsten den Geist, aus dem er spricht: es ist der Geist der Aufklärung"; Westermann, *Buch Jesaja*, 122.

18. "Es ist daher gar nicht erstaunlich, dass wir hierzu eine Parallele aus der lateinischen Klassik kennen, die den gleichen ironischen Kontrast vorbringt: bei Horaz in den Satiren I; 8,1ff."; Westermann, *Buch Jesaja*, 122.

does not match actual practice and explains this "oversimplification" ("Vergröberung") as part of the polemical strategy of the text.[19]

Westermann therefore comfortably positions himself as part of the text's in-group. He shares the Enlightened criticism of iconic worship that he perceives in the text. His attitude towards the text and its author's skills are generally positive, and no distancing language is used in his discussion of the passage. This way of reading—an uncritical agreement (theological and rational) with a general condemnation of iconic worship (which is perceived as the message of the text)—is common in Protestant commentaries from the twentieth century.[20]

I would like to contrast this reading with a religio-historical reading that places more emphasis on the Mesopotamian perspective.

Angelika Berlejung (Reading as an Assyriologist)

Angelika Berlejung (born 1961) is also a German Protestant scholar. She is Professor of Hebrew Bible/Old Testament at the University of Leipzig and has a strong background in Assyriology. Her book, *Die Theologie der Bilder: Herstellung und Einweihung von Kultbildern in Mesopotamien und die alttestamentliche Bilderpolemik* (*The Theology of Images: Manufacturing and Induction of Cult Images in Mesopotamia and Biblical Polemics against Images*) is a religio-historical rather than a biblical study. Thus, Berlejung discusses the existence of cult images in ancient Israel starting with the archaeological evidence. The first part of the book deals with the manufacturing and theology of cult images in Mesopotamia. In the second part, Berlejung discusses biblical texts against cult images, including Isaiah 44. She explains the

---

19. "Alle Ausleger weisen darauf hin, dass das Spottgedicht die Wirklichkeit des Bilderdienstes nicht trifft…. Man kann dem nicht ausweichen, dass hier mindestens eine Vergröberung vorliegt. Das ist im Wesen des Spottliedes begründet; ihm liegt keinerlei Absicht, zu verstehen, zugrunde; es will 'heruntermachen.'" Westermann, *Buch Jesaja*, 123.

20. Cf., e.g., Elliger, *Deuterojesaja*, 440–1; Klaus Baltzer, *Deutero-Jesaja*, KAT 10/2 (Gütersloh: Gütersloher Verl.-Haus, 1999), 251–67; John D. W. Watts, *Isaiah 34–66*, WBC 25 (Waco: Word, 1987), 146, "The ridiculous futility and self-deception of idol worship is portrayed in the comic satire it deserves." In the revised edition ([Nashville: Thomas Nelson, 2005], 688), this line has been softened by omitting "ridiculous" and "it deserves," probably reflecting the developments in the history of research pointed out in the introduction of the present essay. I would like to thank Ken Brown for bringing this change in Watts' commentary to my attention. Also Whybray, *Isaiah*, 100, despite his critical comments about the literary qualities of the text (see above, n. 14), attributes to its author "a sound theological instinct."

polemics as a comprehensive and precise rebuttal of ancient Near Eastern conceptions of cult images.[21] In contrast to Westermann, Berlejung uses (text-)descriptive and analytical language and clearly distinguishes the author's voice from her own.[22] While Westermann designates the speaking voice simply as "the poet (of the taunt-song)," Berlejung labels the textual in-group as the "opponents of images" ("Perspektive der Bilderfeinde"),[23] as opposed to the textual out-group of the "craftsmen" ("Handwerker") or more generally the "worshippers of images" ("Bildverehrer").[24] In this way, Berlejung highlights that both the speaker and those who are the objects of his attack represent a particular position on iconic worship.

Thus, Berlejung does not identify with a textual in-group, but describes both positions—for and against images—from an outsider's perspective. The fact that she interprets the biblical polemics against the backdrop of ancient Near Eastern image theology implies that the use and theology of cult images is considered the normal state of affairs, to which the biblical polemics relate. The textual out-group of Isaiah 44—that is, the Babylonian practitioners of iconic worship—are allowed to speak up through their own texts.

Some scholars with a religio-historical approach similar to Berlejung's go further. In their readings, they not only allow the Babylonian practitioners of iconic cults to speak up; they even privilege the (reconstructed) Babylonian point of view over against the biblical writer's. Thus, Michael B. Dick concludes regarding the prophetic texts against iconic worship: "As clever as these prophetic parodies were, they were both unoriginal and methodologically flawed.... Deutero-Isaiah's method is also flawed, for he has contrasted a phenomenological description of the Mesopotamian practice with a theological portrayal of Yahwism. His argument does not reflect the culpable ignorance of the Israelite religion about other religions...but a conscious distortion forged in polemic."[25] Dick clearly

---

21. Cf. Angelika Berlejung, *Die Theologie der Bilder: Herstellung und Einweihung von Kultbildern in Mesopotamien und die alttestamentliche Bilderpolemik*, OBO 162 (Fribourg: Universitätsverlag; Göttingen: Vandenhoeck & Ruprecht, 1998), 386–7.

22. For instance, she writes that Isa. 44:18-20 "shows that the writer of these verses was of the opinion that..." ("zeigt..., daß der Verfasser der Verse der Ansicht war..."; Berlejung, *Die Theologie der Bilder*, 384); cf. also 381, for a careful reflection on the presuppositions underlying the writer's line of argumentation.

23. Berlejung, *Die Theologie der Bilder*, 382; cf. also "Perspektive der Bildergegner" and "[d]er Verfasser der bilderpolemischen Verse," ibid., 387.

24. Berlejung, *Die Theologie der Bilder*, 387.

25. Dick, "Prophetic," 45.

refuses the role of the implied reader and assigns the interpretational prerogative to the textual out-group.

The more moderate religio-historical reading of the text by Berlejung has also had an impact on theological commentaries on Isaiah 44 and is quoted extensively in Ulrich Berges' commentary on Second Isaiah,[26] to which I will refer below.

We have seen so far two ways of reading Isaiah 44 that are quite different in terms of identification with the implied reader and with the textual in-group: a particular Protestant reading by Claus Westermann and a religio-historical reading by Angelika Berlejung. In searching for further scholarly readings with a different profile, I will turn now to a couple of Catholic commentaries on Isaiah 44.

José Severino Croatto (An Argentinian Liberationist Reading)

Thinking of the great contributions of the Fribourg School to the study of iconography in ancient Israel and Judah,[27] one could assume that scholars from a Catholic tradition might approach the topic of images with a particular sensitivity. For instance, Ulrich Berges comments on the story of the person who makes himself an idol in verses 15-17: "Present makers of religious art would protest, too, and rightly so, if they were alleged to use waste wood to produce crucifixes and statues of Mary."[28] This quote provides a rare example of a Catholic scholar hinting at possible parallels between the image worshipped in Isa. 44:14-17 and Catholic iconic practices. Yet none of the Catholic commentaries I examined explicitly raises a concern that texts like Isaiah 44 might imply a criticism against any current Catholic practice.[29] Some Catholic commentators point out

---

26. Ulrich Berges, *Jesaja 40–48*, HThKAT (Freiburg i.B.: Herder, 2008).

27. Schroer, *In Israel gab es Bilder*; Silvia Schroer and Othmar Keel, *Die Ikonographie Palästinas-Israels und der Alte Orient: Eine Religionsgeschichte in Bildern*, 4 vols. (Fribourg: Academic Press, 2005–18); Othmar Keel and Christoph Uehlinger, *Göttinnen, Götter und Gottessymbole. Neue Erkenntnisse zur Religionsgeschichte Kanaans und Israels aufgrund bislang unerschlossener ikonographischer Quellen*, 5th ed. (Freiburg i.B.: Herder, 2001), to name but a few classics.

28. "Auch die heutigen Hersteller religiöser Kunst würden zu Recht protestieren, unterstellte man ihnen, sie verwendeten Abfallholz zur Produktion von Kruzifixen und Marienstatuen!" (Berges, *Jesaja 40–48*, 347).

29. However, the text provokes reactions that might indicate some commentators perceive it as offensive. See, for instance, Blenkinsopp, *Isaiah*, 241: "It should be said at once that this reads like a willful misunderstanding of the function of the image in cults throughout the ancient and, for that matter, the modern world. The dictionary definition of idolatry as 'the worship of a physical object as a god' very clearly implies

that the criticism voiced in Isaiah 44 is not directed against images in general, but only against certain kinds and uses of images.³⁰ Some consider the theological message of the text not to be about iconic worship at all but rather about worship of other gods besides Yhwh, or the lack of trust in Yhwh.³¹ There is, however, and unsurprisingly so, not one single reader's role performed by each and every Catholic commentator. Out of the broad variety of Catholic readings of the text, I would like to present two readings that take very different perspectives from Westermann's and Berlejung's, starting with a reading by José Severino Croatto.

Croatto (1930–2004) was a Professor of Philosophy and History of Religions at the University of Buenos Aires before becoming Professor of Hebrew Bible at the Instituto Superior Evangélico de Estudios Teológicos (ISEDET; Buenos Aires). A specialist in philology and trained in historical-critical exegesis in Rome and Jerusalem, he made important contributions to liberation hermeneutics. In his commentary on Isaiah,³² he treats Isa.

---

that the term is prejudicial and that it entails a subjective and, more often than not, false judgment on certain religious expressions. An image can focus the energy and concentrate the attention of a group engaged in common worship. It can give concrete expression to the sense of the real presence of the divinity. That the sense of divine presence fills a powerful and understandable human need can be seen in the incident of the Golden Calf (Exod 32–34). Like any other expression of religious sentiment or conviction, an image is subject to abuse and can degenerate into superstition, but a religion that claims to dispense with such assurances of divine presence expressed by physical symbols can also end up being heartless, cruel, and monomaniacally fanatical. Throughout Christian history, at any rate, the prohibition of images—as in eighth- and ninth-century Byzantium—has had very limited success. Taken individually and out of context, such acts (familiar in the Neo-Babylonian homeland) as making an image, clothing and feeding it, and giving it life by the ceremony of 'washing the mouth,' seem pointless and futile. To those involved, however, they make sense in a ritual context that gives expression to and draws the worshiper into a world of symbolic meanings."

30. Thus, while in Westermann's understanding Isa. 44 disparages "worshippers of images" ("Bilderanbeter"), Catholic commentators tend to use different terms. Bonnard, for instance, thinks that the criticism targets worshippers of "false gods" ("faux-dieux"). Cf. also Berges, *Jesaja*, 59 ("Bilder werden nicht generell abgelehnt, wohl aber Kultgegenstände, die nicht auf den Willen und die Inspiration JHWHs zurückgehen [Ex 32, 1–4.23 f.; 1 Kön 12, 28–33; vgl. Jes 48, 5; Hab 2, 18 f.]").

31. Cf. Merendino, *Erste*, 390; Pierre-Émile Bonnard, *Le second Isaïe, son disciple et leurs éditeurs* (Paris: Gabalda, 1972), 161.

32. J. Severino Croatto, *Isaías: La palabra profética y su relectura hermenéutica. Vol. II: 40–55: La liberación es posible*, Colección Comentario bíblico (Buenos Aires: Editorial Lumen, 1994).

44:9-20 as a central unit within Isaiah 40–49. His attitude towards the text is generally appreciative insofar as he does not voice any criticism of its style nor its theology. The positive assessment of the text's message is based on Croatto's socio-political reading of it. Croatto assumes that the text constitutes an admonition towards Israelites. It thus addresses the textual in-group and is not a criticism or mockery of other religions.[33]

Croatto places this admonition in the historical context of the Babylonian exile and reads Isaiah 44 as "a text of countercultural resistance" ("textos de resistencia contracultural"), a term used here with positive connotations.[34] Croatto explicitly states that the theological issue in Isaiah 44 is not about iconic worship: "Therefore, the issue dealt with in verses 9-20 is not the images but rather *which God* is effective in history."[35] The central theological issue, according to Croatto, is touched upon in verse 17: the maker of the cult image—an Israelite—addresses a prayer for liberation to a god other than YHWH. Given the centrality of the theme of liberation in Croatto's theological approach, it is noteworthy that he translates the prayer "Liberate [or: Free] me, for you are my God" ("libérame, porque mi Dios eres tú").[36] The aim of the text, according to Croatto, is to "*convince* with excellent rhetoric that *Yahweh* and no other God *is willing* and *able* to save, and that *only he* can do it."[37]

Although Croatto detects irony and mockery in the text, he does not relish in the mockery, and does not add to it with degrading language for the maker of cult images. Rather, he reads behind the irony the broken relationship between the maker of images and YHWH as "something tragic" ("algo trágico").[38]

Clearly, Croatto does not read the text observing and evaluating it from an outside perspective. There is no discussion of historical accuracy, et cetera, as in religio-historical readings like Berlejung's (and Berges'). Rather, Croatto intends to comply with the role of the implied reader, paying attention to the clues provided by the text itself (e.g., repetitions

---

33. Croatto, *Isaías*, 2:104.
34. Cf. Croatto, *Isaías*, 2:104.
35. "El problema, por lo tanto, de los vv. 9-20 no es el de las imágenes sino el de *qué Dios* es eficaz en la historia"; Croatto, *Isaías*, 2:104. According to Croatto, the images mentioned in Isaiah 44 (as in the Decalogue) are always representations of gods other than YHWH (ibid., 2:107–8).
36. Croatto, *Isaías*, 2:107. The Hebrew term הצילני (Hiphil of נצל) could also be rendered "save me."
37. "*convencer* con una excelente retórica que *Yavé* y no otro Dios *quiere y puede* salvar, y que *él solo* puede hacerlo"; Croatto, *Isaías*, 2:107.
38. Croatto, *Isaías*, 2:107, speaking of v. 17.

of words, structure, and allusions to other passages). The theological message of the text, analyzed against its socio-historical context, remains a valid message for present readers, and Croatto talks about it in highly positive terms (e.g., "a powerful text," "texto poderoso"[39]).

For the theme of the present volume, it is particularly interesting to note that Croatto performs and advocates a strict in-group reading. The text does not address "other people" and is not meant to be read by them. The reader's contract with the text, so to say, presupposes a contract with a particular theological (social, and/or religious) commitment: the message of the text only makes sense within a community bound to YHWH. As Croatto emphasizes, the text cannot be applied to worshippers of other gods outside the YHWH-community. Within the YHWH-community, however, criticism of certain forms of religious practice is legitimate.

Dominic Sundararaj Irudayaraj (Reading as an Indian Catholic)

Dominic S. Irudayaraj is a Jesuit scholar. Originally from Andhra Province in India, he did his postgraduate studies at the Jesuit School of Theology in Berkeley, California. He currently teaches Old Testament at Hekima University College in Kenya. In his published dissertation on Isaiah 63, he uses a social identity approach, examining constructions of identity and of otherness.[40] In his reading of Isa. 44:9-20, he first notices a debasement of iconic worship and perceives it as offensive.[41] It is noteworthy that such empathy is rarely found in European theological readings of Isaiah 44, but seems to be more common in Indian readings of anti-iconic texts.[42]

---

39. Croatto, *Isaías*, 2:107, cf. also the use of terms like "importance" ("importancia," ibid., 2:104) and "greatness" ("magnitud," ibid., 2:107).

40. Dominic S. Irudayaraj, *Violence, Otherness and Identity in Isaiah 63:1-6: The Trampling One Coming from Edom*, LHBOTS 633 (London: Bloomsbury T&T Clark, 2017). Although this book focusses on a different biblical text, the theoretical framework of social identity theory set up on pp. 39–50 also provides background for Irudayaraj's discussion of Isaiah 44.

41. "The idol-taunt in Isaiah 44:9-20 sounds problematic from an image-rich Indian Christian perspective," Dominic S. Irudayaraj, "Idol-taunt and Exilic Identity: A Dalit Reading of Isaiah 44:9-20," in *Myths of Exile: History and Metaphor in the Hebrew Bible*, ed. Anne K. de Hemmer Gudme and Ingrid Hjelm (London: Routledge, 2015), 125–36, and cf. p. 126 on images in Indian Christian churches.

42. Cf. Soares-Prabhu, "Laughing at Idols," 109–31, and the contributions by Anthony John Baptist in Marie-Theres Wacker, *Baruch and the Letter of Jeremiah*, Wisdom Commentary 31 (Collegeville: Liturgical, 2016). Among European commentators, Blenkinsopp (*Isaiah*, 241), for instance, takes a critical stance on the condemnation of "idolatry."

However, Irudayaraj does not reject the role proposed to the reader in Isaiah 44 altogether. Rather, he opts for a sympathetic reading,[43] and finds a way to work around the issue of images. Like Croatto, he reads Isaiah 44 against the socio-political background of the Babylonian exile.[44] He parallels the exilic experience with the experience of Dalits (i.e., the population considered "untouchable" in the caste system) in contemporary India.[45] Moreover, he points out shared features between Isa. 44:9-20 and Dalit literature, both kinds of texts using ridicule and reversal to resist a hegemonic discourse. Irudayaraj suggests that the function of Isaiah 44 is similar to Dalit "counter-cultural literature":[46] "the prophet resists the pervasive presence and persuasive appeal of the empire. Therefore, much like the Dalit literature, the icon parody in Isaiah is an apt instance of 'Resistance Literature'."[47]

Thus, reading the images in Isaiah 44 as symbols of the empire rather than as cult statues in general allows Irudayaraj to identify positively with the textual in-group. As he puts it, "The chosen focus on the identity construction helps to tone down the anti-iconic sentiments within the idol-taunt, especially for someone who reads it from the image-rich Indian perspective."[48] The makers of images in Isaiah 44 are the textual out-group in this reading, but they are Othered as representatives of the empire rather than as worshippers of images.

Conclusion

The four exemplary interpretations of Isa. 44:9-20 have shown that biblical scholars read this text as "their own" in different ways. The picture that emerges from comparing their readings seems to indicate that this is not a specific effect triggered by particular features of Isa. 44:9-20. Some of the conclusions I will draw in the following are therefore likely to hold for the interpretation of other biblical texts, too.

As we have seen in the readings I presented, all but Berlejung's religio-historical reading comply with the role of the implied reader and identify

---

43. As he states explicitly, cf. Irudayaraj, "Idol," 133.

44. Irudayaraj draws here on the socio-political reading suggested by Nathaniel B. Levtow, *Images of Others: Iconic Politics in Ancient Israel*, BJSUCSD 11 (Winona Lake: Eisenbrauns, 2008).

45. "Much like the exilic experience, Dalit history is marked by experiences of trauma." Irudayaraj, "Idol-taunt," 127.

46. Irudayaraj, "Idol-taunt," 127.

47. Irudayaraj, "Idol-taunt," 131–2.

48. Irudayaraj, "Idol-taunt," 133–4.

with the textual in-group. However, their understandings of the text's message as well as their characterizations of the textual in-group and out-group differ considerably. In Croatto's reading, for instance, there is no out-group, since he considers the makers and worshippers of images to be Israelites, too. The following chart provides a summary of the variety of interpretations:

	Textual in-group	Textual out-group	Self-positioning
Westermann	Israelites	worshippers of images	in-group
Berlejung	opponents of images	worshippers of images	outsider's perspective
Croatto	Israelites in exile	(no Othering)	in-group
Irudayaraj	Israelites in exile	the empire and its representatives	in-group

In short, the variety of interpretations highlights that the commitment to the text as "one's own" is prior to, and to a certain extent apparently independent of, the actual content of the text. The tension this can create is most obvious in Irudayaraj's reading: He first perceives the text as an insult and empathizes with the textual out-group.[49] However, he then decides to perform a "sympathetic reading"[50] and—redefining the images as symbols of the empire—finds a way to identify with the textual in-group. Thus, the willingness to comply with the implied reader's role and to identify (or at least: to sympathize) with the textual in-group can have a creative effect in a positive sense: the committed scholar will not just dismiss a disturbing text, but dig deeper to produce a satisfying reading of the text.[51]

On the other hand, Croatto's and Irudayaraj's readings draw attention to the potentially prejudicial effects of such an identification with the textual in-group: readers identifying themselves with the textual in-group easily join the choir of othering the textual out-group. We have seen such an attitude, for example, in Westermann's reading. Moreover, contemporary readers identifying with the textual in-group generally seek for contemporary relevance of the text, which means that the textual out-group, too, can be related to people in the present. Croatto and Irudayaraj propose two different solutions to the ethical issue inherent in reading Isaiah 44 as "their own." Their readings have in common that they propose to read the

---

49. Cf. Irudayaraj, "Idol-taunt," 125–6.
50. Irudayaraj, "Idol-taunt," 134.
51. By "committed," I do not mean religious commitment in particular. Scholars in other fields outside biblical studies are often as devoted to their respective subject as certain biblical scholars are to canonical literature.

text from below. Identifying the textual in-group with the powerless and oppressed prevents from othering the vulnerable in present applications of the text. The theological and ethical guidelines for reading the text in both cases are prior and external to the text itself, as is the decision to identify with the textual in-group.

Biblical Scholars' Ethos of Respect: Original Meanings, Original Texts, and Reception History of Ecclesiastes

Brennan Breed

Introduction: The Constitutive Problem of Reading

No matter where you mark the point of origin of biblical scholarship—whether with the work of Richard Simon, or Baruch Spinoza, or Lorenzo Valla, or Rashi, or Jerome, or Origen, or Ezra—biblical scholars have from the beginning understood their shared task in similar terms: namely, as reading other people's texts.[1] And as biblical scholars often note, none

---

1. On Simon, see John Barton, *The Nature of Biblical Criticism* (Louisville: Westminster John Knox, 2007), 125, and Jean Steinmann, *Biblical Criticism* (London: Burns & Oates, 1959), 46–8; on Spinoza, see John Sandys-Wunsch, "Spinoza—The First Biblical Theologian," *ZAW* 93 (1981): 327–41, esp. 331, and Ronald [S.] Hendel, "Mind the Gap: Modern and Postmodern in Biblical Studies," *JBL* 133 (2014): 422–43, esp. 438; on Valla, see Marjorie O'Rourke Boyle, "Evangelism and Erasmus," in *The Cambridge History of Literary Criticism: Vol. 3, The Renaissance*, ed. Glyn P. Norton (Cambridge: Cambridge University Press, 1999), 44–52, esp. 44; on Rashi, see Eran Viezel, "The Formation of Some Biblical Books, According to Rashi," *JTS* 61 (2010): 16–42; Jerome is where Richard Simon himself starts his story of biblical criticism (published in 1685), see Richard Simon, *Critical History of the Text of the New Testament: Wherein is Established the Truth of the Acts on which the Christian Religion is Based*, trans. Andrew W. R. Hunwick, NTTSD 43 (Leiden: Brill, 2013), xv; on Origen, see Barton, *Nature of Biblical Criticism*, 9; and Gilles Dorival, "Origen," in *The New Cambridge History of the Bible, Vol. 1: From the Beginnings to 600*, ed. James Carleton Paget and Joachim Schaper (Cambridge: Cambridge University Press, 2013), 605–28. For an overview of the history of philology, which overlaps almost entirely with the question of the origins of biblical scholarship, see James Turner, *Philology: The Forgotten Origins of the Modern Humanities* (Princeton: Princeton University Press, 2014), 18–61.

of these readers were merely reading. One can always quibble about the definition of the concept of "reading," and whether it includes acts such as preservation, editing, organization, and selection, but nevertheless such curating acts, at a minimum, must precede any act of reading—or one would not have a text at hand that one might read.[2]

In the prologue to the Greek translation of Ben Sira, for example, the grandson casts himself and Ben Sira as both readers and producers of texts that were intended for others, but over time and with geographical relocation and cultural transformation, became incomprehensible.[3] Reading and writing find no sharp delineation in this prologue. Moreover, even in the second century BCE, these not-yet biblical texts have already slipped from their supposedly original audiences into the hands of those who still feel the need to read them even though they are so "Other" that they cannot understand them. Thus, the emergence of the biblical text came well after the disappearance of the original audience to whom the text made complete sense—if either original audience or a complete sense proper to the biblical text existed at all. We might say that the biblical text is always already someone else's text. And, in many ways, this is not unique to biblical texts. Indeed, I would argue that this is a constitutive problem of texts in general.

While there are many ways that biblical scholars have construed their own identities, the identities of biblical texts, and the identities of the communities that produced and transmitted the texts over time, the basic constellation of elements remains fairly stable, and it is indistinguishable from the general task of reading texts. K. M. Newton describes the basic coordinates of textual study: "The central concern of…the study of literature is the problem created by the fact that texts written in the past continue to exist and to be read while their authors and the historical context which produced them have passed away in time."[4]

---

2. Origen created the Hexapla and the Masoretes organized textual traditions, selected them, and added vowels. On the difficult borders between composition, editing, and reception in the history of the biblical text, see Brennan W. Breed, *Nomadic Text: A Theory of Biblical Reception History* (Bloomington: Indiana University Press, 2014), 1–74. For a particular example, see Nathan Mastnjak, "Jeremiah as Collection: Scrolls, Sheets, and the Problem of Textual Arrangement," *CBQ* 80 (2018): 25–44.

3. On the complex issue of Ben Sira as a literary and historical persona, see Eva Mroczek, *The Literary Imagination in Jewish Antiquity* (Oxford: Oxford University Press, 2016), 90–103.

4. K. M. Newton, *Interpreting the Text: A Critical Introduction to the Theory and Practice of Literary Interpretation* (New York: Harvester/Wheatsheaf, 1990), 40–1.

In other words, whenever I read, I am always in some sense reading other people's texts. Even when I revisit something I wrote myself, I encounter something that requires interpretation, however slightly, if I am to read it.[5] Likewise, whenever I read texts that my community (whether religious, ethnic, institutional, regional, national, etc.) claims are central to its identity, I always encounter many layers of linguistic and cultural differences.[6] And whenever I dig through the historical record concerning my tradition and the texts that it holds sacred, I always find a multiplicity of authors, contexts, communities, and traditions that coexist in ways that are irreducibly complex. The Bible, because of its long history of production and re-production, editing and formatting, is always Other to anyone who would pick it up—even to the presumed original authors of the texts that comprise it, since they would find themselves bewildered not only by the codex form of the book, but also by the very concept of binding their work together with dozens of other texts with similarly long histories of production and transmission.[7]

Would any ancient Israelite or Judahite prophet recognize the biblical book that bears their name as their own, a seamless identity with themselves? It seems few, if any, biblical scholars would argue as much today. As Martti Nissinen explains, "In their present contexts, even the passages that might refer to prophetic words once pronounced on the mouths of Isaiah, Jeremiah, Amos, or Hosea, are completely recontextualized. They are edited from the point of view of communities that have read and reread them according to their own needs and preferences, creating their own constructs of prophets and prophecy."[8] If somehow he was given access to the scrolls at Qumran, Isaiah of Jerusalem would doubtless detect within the texts that bear his name many different layers

---

5. See Jacques Derrida, *Limited Inc.*, trans. Samuel Weber and Jeffrey Mehlman, ed. Gerald Graff (Evanston: Northwestern University Press, 1988), 47–51. See also Geoffrey Bennington, "Derrida's 'Eighteenth Century,'" *Eighteenth-Century Studies* 40 (2007): 381–93, esp. 392.

6. One can notice an otherness even within biblical texts that function as touche stones for the identities of various groups—see, for example, the tension between Israelite and ancestral forms of religion in Genesis; R. W. Moberly, *The Old Testament of the Old Testament: Patriarchal Narratives and Mosaic Yahwism* (Eugene: Wipf & Stock, 2001).

7. Even the modern concept of authorship would likely surprise them: see Karel van der Toorn, *Scribal Culture and the Making of the Hebrew Bible* (Cambridge: Harvard University Press, 2007), 40–8.

8. Martti Nissinen, *Ancient Prophecy: Near Eastern, Biblical, and Greek Perspectives* (Oxford: Oxford University Press, 2017), 149. See also Brad Kelle, "The Phenomenon of Israelite Prophecy in Contemporary Scholarship," *CurBR* 12 (2014): 275–320, and van der Toorn, *Scribal Culture*, 173–204.

of hands and voices and interests that contributed to the production of something that ended up at least minimally Other to everyone involved in the process. And yet, the text of Isaiah's scroll has played a crucial role in the production of a wide variety of identities and communities. Likewise, the ancient Israelite kings described in the book of Kings would likely be baffled by its monotheistic Yahwism, the supposition of Judahite dominance, the cultic centrality at Jerusalem, and the covenantal antimonarchism—all of which are inseparable from its putatively "original" form.[9] The texts that comprise the Hebrew Bible are, at least in this sense, Other to everyone, at home in no specific historical context and the product of no individual mind or even specific community.[10] And yet, even a cursory glance at the history of biblical production, transmission, and reception reveals the powerful, extensive, and often horrific effects of identification and othering that constitute and emanate from encounter with this textual tradition.[11]

While the biblical text is at least minimally Other to any potential reader, it is in another sense a book that so many individuals and communities consider their own—for some, even *constitutive* of their own identity—that it is rarely treated as purely Other. And yet, the various communities who identify with these texts tend to construe the texts and their own identity in divergent ways. Thus, the identity of the biblical text is not universal from the diverse vantage points of the various groups whose identities depend upon it: rather, the biblical texts of these groups are incommensurable, incongruent, and irreducibly different. For example, the Samaritan Pentateuch is not merely a smaller version of the Jewish *Tanakh*, and neither of these are merely smaller versions of the Eastern Orthodox Bible. All three communities claim these textual artifacts to be the same thing—namely, the sacred scripture of the God YHWH—and yet they are irreducibly different even at the points of textual overlap.[12]

---

9. See, for instance, the essays in Francesca Stavrakopoulou and John Barton, eds., *Religious Diversity in Ancient Israel and Judah* (London: T&T Clark, 2010); see also Carol Meyers, "From Household to House of Yahweh: Women's Religious Culture in Ancient Israel," in *Congress Volume: Basel, 2001*, ed. André Lemaire, VTSup 92 (Leiden: Brill, 2002), 283–301.

10. On this point, see Breed, *Nomadic Text*, 75–114.

11. See, for example, the introductory essay to this volume, Ken Brown and Brennan Breed, "Social Identity and Scriptural Interpretation: An Introduction." Also see David Whitford, *The Curse of Ham in the Early Modern Era: The Bible and the Justifications for Slavery*, St. Andrews Studies in Reformation History (London: Routledge, 2009).

12. See Emanuel Tov, *Textual Criticism of the Hebrew Bible*, 3rd rev. exp. ed. (Minneapolis: Fortress, 2012), 23–154.

Some solve this problem by referring to Bibles, but the plural creates as many (if not more) problems as it solves—many of these different communities claim that their scriptures are the *real* scriptures, to the exclusion of the others.[13] But even with an individual who believes he or she truly and seamlessly identifies with the Bible, the tension between the modern reader and the biblical text emerges in ways that cannot be ignored. This can be detected, for example, in the many jokes in conservative Christian communities about the common experience of Leviticus derailing most plans to read the Bible in canonical order. As one Evangelical devotional book puts it, "Leviticus becomes the graveyard where read-through-the-Bible-in-a-year plans go to die."[14] Does pluralizing the noun solve the problem of Otherness that troubles any act of identification?

It is this dialectic of Otherness-within-identity, of the recognition of a constitutive gap in textuality that nevertheless demands to be bridged in countless different interpretive ways, that this essay will endeavor to examine. I will focus first on the ways that biblical scholars tend to conceptualize and attempt to cross this gap, which requires asking about their (our) identities, about the identity of the text, and about the identity of the individual or community that is understood to stand behind the text. I will then turn to the book of Qohelet/Ecclesiastes to think of different ways that we might construe this identification and otherness of the biblical text, with attention to the concept of reception history.

Biblical Theology and the Ethos of Respect

Within the variegated and fuzzily bordered field of biblical scholarship, one can find a wide variety of metaphors and images that conceptualize the constitutive gap of biblical interpretation. One interesting and oft-used trope is "respect": One must respect the text, one must respect the original context, one must respect the authors who wrote this material by attending to their intended meanings.[15] The word "respect," in this context, connotes

---

13. On the problems of textual nominalism, see Breed, *Nomadic Text*, 61–4.

14. Michael J. Akers, *Morning and Evening Meditations from the Word of God: Education, Challenge, Inspiration, and Encouragement* (Bloomington: WestBow, 2014), 162.

15. Respecting the text, the context, and the author are, in many ways, very different propositions, and reflect the theoretical orientation of the biblical scholar. E. D. Hirsch, Jr. championed the idea of respecting the author and the author's intentions in interpretive practices, and many biblical scholars have followed his lead (see E. D. Hirsch, Jr., "Objective Interpretation," *Publications of the Modern Language Association of America* 75 [1960]: 463–79, esp. 470–5; and, for example, Michael V.

politeness, deference, empathy, and courtesy; it implies that the reader of a biblical text is listening to the voice of someone else speaking, and that the reader should care about the speaker by listening carefully and thoughtfully.[16] It implies difference between speaker and listener, but also an attempt to identify with the one speaking.

Many confessional biblical scholars use this discourse of "respect" in a specific manner. Christopher Seitz, for example, argues that readers of the biblical text should cultivate

> a proper respect—reverence is not too strong a term—for what an honor it is to read this literature at all.... The basic challenge of the Old Testament is not historical distance, overcome by historical-critical tools, or existential disorientation, overcome by a hermeneutics of assent or suspicion. The Old Testament tells a particular story about a particular people and their particular God, who in Christ we confess as our God.... We have been read into a will, a first will and testament, by Christ. If we do not approach the literature with this basic stance—of estrangement overcome, of an infusion properly called "adoption"—historical-critical methods or a hermeneutics of assent will stand outside and fail to grasp that God is reading us.[17]

Seitz thinks of himself, and of the model reader of the biblical text, as participating in a particular tradition—including privileged intertexts and

---

Fox, "Job 38 and God's Rhetoric," *Semeia* 19 [1981]: 53–61, esp. 53). Umberto Eco's maxim "respect the text, not the author," with his own caveats of certain contexts in which the author or speaker's intention is "absolutely important," is doubtless influential here (see Eco, *Interpretation and Overinterpretation*, ed. S. Collini [Cambridge: Cambridge University Press, 1992], 66). Yet in biblical studies in particular, Eco's plea to respect the text over author in interpretation has not won out; in fact, the object of respect in the discourse of biblical studies is often the presumed author, following Hirsch. For an example of the discourse of respect of context in biblical studies, see John J. Collins, *A Short Introduction to the Hebrew Bible* (Augsburg: Fortress, 2007), 13–14: "I view the text in its historical context, relating it where possible to the history of the time and respecting the ancient literary traditions."

16. See examples of this trope in J. P. Fokkelman, *Narrative Art and Poetry in the Books of Samuel: Vol. 3, Throne and City (II Sam. 2–8 & 21–24)*, SSN 27 (Assen/Maastricht: Van Gorcum, 1990), 333; Amy Plantinga Pauw, *Proverbs and Ecclesiastes*, Belief: A Theological Commentary on the Bible (Louisville: Westminster John Knox, 2015), 61; Ingeborg Mongstad-Kvammen, *Toward a Postcolonial Reading of the Epistle of James: James 2:1-13 in its Roman Imperial Context*, BibInt 119 (Leiden: Brill, 2013), xiii; Antony F. Campbell, *1 Samuel*, FOTL 7 (Grand Rapids: Eerdmans, 2003), 1.

17. Christopher Seitz, *Word Without End: The Old Testament as Abiding Theological Witness* (Grand Rapids: Eerdmans, 1998), 11.

practices—that requires existential identification for proper engagement. In short, if you become part of the community, with the appropriate posture of reverence and appropriate understanding of the existential and relational distances that lie between the reader and the meaning of the text, then it becomes possible to read the text. Seitz presses the point with his multiple metaphors concerning relationships: the ideal reader begins in a place of "estrangement" that must be "overcome" by an "adoption," or perhaps by being "read into a will"—elsewhere in the same essay, Seitz refers to this as "reading someone else's mail."[18] Yet these metaphors of adoption and post-mortem inheritance emphasize that the relationship between ideal reader and text is not natural, seamless, or automatic: In the beginning there was a chasm, which must be crossed. To Seitz, the historical-critical project does not help one to cross it; true identification cannot happen without faith.[19] The text (and the one who is its ultimate author, God) is cast as the *paterfamilias*, the one due respect and reverence, and the one with powers to adopt outsiders and include readers and grant them the inheritance of comprehension.

Biblical Criticism and the Ethos of Respect

In response, many scholars since the Enlightenment have sought to interpret the biblical text with, in the words of Sherwood and Moore, "'objectivity,' 'neutrality,' 'disinterestedness,' and all the other related

---

18. Seitz, *Word Without End*, 4. On the metaphor of reading someone else's mail, see Paul van Buren, "On Reading Someone Else's Mail: The Church and Israel's Scriptures," in *Die Hebräische Bibel und ihre zweifache Nachgeschichte: Festschrift für Rolf Rendtorff zum 65. Geburtstag*, ed. Erhard Blum, Christian Macholz, and Ekkehard Stegemann (Neukirchen-Vlyun: Neukirchner Verlag, 1990), 595–606.

19. See also Seitz, *Word Without End*, 12: "Historical criticism offered for generations of readers of the Old Testament something to do: entire careers have been built fine-tuning the documentary hypothesis or wrestling with whether the early Israelites were donkey or camel nomads. Yet the question may not have been asked whether a universal point of view, based upon an authorial intent or a refined historical reconstruction, is the point of access the Old Testament itself assumes to be ours." To be very clear: this logic is problematic to me, even within my confessional identity as a Christian, because it seems to suggest that Christians have displaced Jews as the rightful yet adopted heirs of Yhwh, and have had their theological inheritance handed over in their place. There is also the abundant evidence that scholars of faiths other than Christianity, and scholars of no faith at all, have proven time and again to be astute readers who have closed the hermeneutical distance to produce important readings of biblical texts. There is no faith requirement to be an excellent biblical scholar.

and foundational values of biblical studies as an academic discipline."[20] The new "historical-critical method" allowed scholars to "historicize and defamiliarize the Bible, making it a new book, written by ancient authors and rooted in the culture of ancient Israel."[21]

Among these critical scholars, one also finds the trope of respect as a common model for biblical interpretation, but they employ it in a different manner than Seitz. The critical version of the trope differs in terms of both the identity of the reader and the identity of the text. Instead of attempting to adopt oneself into the identity of the text and ancient community that produced it, the critical scholar first attempts to bracket his or her own theological and cultural assumptions.[22] Then, the scholar notes the precise coordinates of historical, cultural, and linguistic difference that lies between the critic and the text's presumed authors.[23] This gap cannot be mystically collapsed by existential commitment; it can only be bridged by the hard work of philology, textual criticism, and literary study.

Lorenzo Valla and his discovery of the context of origin for the *Donation of Constantine* plays an important role in the production of this model of the biblical critic: As John Barton claims, this is "regarded by many as the first example of historical criticism."[24] Valla disrespected tradition, ecclesial authority, and common scholarly practice, relying instead on logic and careful philological analysis to determine what, exactly, he was reading.[25] Only then could Valla understand the *Donation* for what

---

20. Stephen D. Moore and Yvonne Sherwood, *The Invention of the Biblical Scholar: A Critical Manifesto* (Minneapolis: Fortress, 2011), 40.

21. Hendel, "Mind the Gap," 439. See Jonathan Sheehan, *The Enlightenment Bible: Translation, Scholarship, Culture* (Princeton: Princeton University Press, 2005); Moore and Sherwood, *Invention of the Biblical Scholar*, 47–9.

22. See Barton, *Nature of Biblical Criticism*, 58, 171–5; Philip R. Davies, *Whose Bible Is It Anyway?*, JSOTSup 204 (Sheffield: Sheffield Academic, 1995); Ronald A. Simkins, "Biblical Studies as a Secular Discipline: The Role of Faith and Theology," *Journal of Religion and Society* 12 (2011): 1–17.

23. See F. W. Dobbs-Allsopp, "Rethinking Historical Criticism," *BibInt* 7 (1999): 235–71; John J. Collins, "Is a Critical Biblical Theology Possible?," in *The Hebrew Bible and Its Interpreters*, ed. Douglas A. Knight and Gene M. Tucker (Atlanta: Scholars Press, 1990), 1–17; John Barton, "Historical-Critical Approaches," in *The Cambridge Companion to Biblical Interpretation*, ed. John Barton (Cambridge: Cambridge University Press, 1998), 9–20.

24. Barton, *Nature of Biblical Criticism*, 128. See also Jerry Bentley, "Biblical Philology and Christian Humanism: Lorenzo Valla and Erasmus as Scholars of the Gospels," *The Sixteenth Century Journal* 8, no. 2 (1977): 8–28.

25. For the text of Valla's study see Lorenzo Valla, *On the Donation of Constantine*, trans. G. Bowersock (Cambridge: Harvard University Press, 2008).

it really was: not an ancient contract between an emperor and a bishop of Rome, but rather a medieval forgery.[26] The truth emerged because Valla respected the text's precise language and its historical context. As it turns out, that text did not deserve all the respect it had acquired—but perhaps the same can be said of biblical texts. They were not written by Moses or Mark, they did not originate from when they were thought to have been written, and they did not record history as a matter of fact. But nevertheless, one could discover the *truth*: namely, the identity of the authors of these texts, when and where they wrote, and what they were actually trying to say. Scholars had to disrespect religious tradition and its constraints in order to respect the otherness of the actual textual artifacts and their producers and thus discover their true meaning. Ronald Hendel claims that biblical criticism has the potential to "disrupt networks of authority," and if practiced properly, it "disrupts the unquestioned habits of Christian faith."[27] Instead of *paterfamilias*, the text has been wrongly imprisoned by the *doxa* of religious authorities and tradition.

In the view of critical scholars, the reader of the Bible begins as an Other, but through methodological rigor, the reader can identify the hidden secrets of a text and discover its meaning. Respecting the text, and respecting the ancient author, means challenging the tradition that has obscured its true identity. And the reader does not need to be a member of a certain group—the reader's identity is not constrained in any way. As Gerd Theissen argues:

> Historical criticism is addressed to anyone capable of understanding it, and not just to a privileged group handing on a particular tradition. By its very nature, historical criticism is concerned to make particular traditions generally accessible.... It is concerned with understanding, and therefore with breaking down the barriers between people with different cultural backgrounds, different religions or different views of the world.... Only an attitude of this kind can command unconditional respect from members of any tradition....[28]

Biblical criticism, then, makes a bridge that anyone can cross by discovering the precise contours of the text's otherness, and thus making a democratic dialogue possible for any who wish to encounter the text.

---

26. See Turner, *Philology*, 35–9.

27. Ronald [S.] Hendel, *Steps to a New Edition of the Hebrew Bible*, TCSt 10 (Atlanta: SBL, 2016), 298, 300.

28. Gerd Theissen, *On Having a Critical Faith* (London: SCM, 1979), 203. Quoted in Barton, *Nature of Biblical Criticism*, 176.

Through the effacement of the interpreter's identity and the assertion of a common logic, criticism produces the universal space of the philologists. As Barton claims, "the neutral, bracketing-out approach proper to biblical criticism not only is essential, but actually expresses more respect for the text than does a so-called theological hermeneutic."[29] Since Barton envisions that there is a single correct answer to a text—namely, what he calls its plain meaning—he argues that critical readings that yield the plain meaning show respect for the text, while theological readings that yield other sorts of meaning show less respect—perhaps even disrespect.[30] For Barton, neutrality is essential to critical reading, because identification with a theology (or ideology) would skew the outcome of the reading process.[31]

Barton, in an introduction to biblical criticism, writes:

> Rather than believing that we can know the truth of a text by approaching it with the correct predispositions and presuppositions, biblical critics think that the meaning emerges from reading the text cold, without a prior commitment to its truth or a ready-made framework (such as the church's faith) within which it is read. Critics think of this as showing the text more *respect* than a committed reading, because it does not limit what the text might mean on the basis of an already existing theory about what this meaning is bound to be.[32]

For Barton, the subtraction from ecclesial expectations and community convictions creates space to "encounter the text cold," in a neutral state—which is the precondition for showing respect for the text. But Barton has his prescribed predispositions and presuppositions, too—he just happens to think they are right. For example, Barton calls his position a "literary perspective," and names his presuppositions as attentiveness to form criticism and attention to what he calls the "original historical context."[33]

---

29. Barton, *Nature of Biblical Criticism*, 27.
30. Barton, *Nature of Biblical Criticism*, 69–117.
31. Some biblical critics might differ with Barton's search for the singular plain meaning of the text in theory, but agree with it in practice. Concepts like the "ideal reader," or phrases such as "the most likely meaning" of the text cover over the concept of "original meaning" without displacing its structuring logic.
32. John Barton, "Strategies for Reading Scripture," in *The HarperCollins Study Bible*, ed. Harold W. Attridge and Wayne A. Meeks, rev. ed. (San Francisco: HarperCollins, 2006), xxxix–xliii, here xlii.
33. Barton, "Strategies for Reading Scripture," xli.

Like Theissen, Barton envisions a universally generic reader using universally generic critical tools, thus rhetorically depersonalizing the reader. In other words, if a reader is to approach the text with proper respect, then that reader must take up a subject position that literally any other reader in the world could occupy, and they are to discern the exact same plain meaning that anyone else would discern. As Alisdair MacIntyre writes about Enlightenment thinkers, Barton and other critical scholars believe that "all rational persons conceptualize data in one and the same way and that therefore any attentive and honest observer, unblinded and undistracted by the prejudices of prior commitment to belief would report the same data, the same facts."[34] There is a striking loss, or perhaps forgetting, of self implied in these schematic representations of the act of biblical criticism. Yet neutral space in theory is rarely neutral space in practice. Time and again, readers who do not fit the expected identity of such supposedly neutral reading spaces— namely, white, male, Christian, and from an elite institution—have found themselves excluded precisely because of their particularity.[35] The supposedly universal position of criticism is deeply inflected by assumptions about identity and belonging.[36] When unexpected Others occupy the position of critical interpretation, they often produce "other" sorts of meanings that end up fitting only in the books and conference sessions that focus on identity. One critical biblical scholar described a call to "hear the voices" of scholars who have particular lived knowledge of "racist, sexist, homophobic, colonizing, and other dehumanizing" uses of scripture as the "agonistics of local narratives (or, more colloquially,

---

34. Alisdair MacIntyre, *Three Rival Versions of Moral Enquiry: Encyclopaedia, Genealogy, and Tradition* (Notre Dame: Notre Dame University Press, 1990), 16.

35. See Barbara A. Holdrege, "Beyond the Guild: Liberating Biblical Studies," in *African Americans and the Bible: Sacred Texts and Social Textures*, ed. Vincent L. Wimbush with Rosamond C. Rodman (New York: Continuum, 2000), 138–60; Francisco Lozada Jr., "Toward Latino/a Biblical Studies: Foregrounding Identities and Transforming Communities," *Latino/a Biblical Hermeneutics: Problematics, Objectives, Strategies*, ed. Francisco Lozada Jr. and Fernando F. Segovia (Atlanta: SBL Press, 2014), 187–202; Elisabeth Schüssler Fiorenza, *Democratizing Biblical Studies: Toward an Emancipatory Educational Space* (Louisville: Westminster John Knox, 2009), 68–70.

36. See, for example, the explanation of why Jews have felt unwelcome in the supposedly ecumenical conversation about biblical theology in Jon D. Levenson, *The Hebrew Bible, the Old Testament, and Historical Criticism: Jews and Christians in Biblical Study* (Louisville: Westminster John Knox, 1993), 33–61.

'the airing of grievances')."³⁷ The assumption of a univocal universality always runs afoul of empirical plurality. So many people have read biblical texts—even with the exact same critical tools—and come out with different answers. Are they all wrong but one?

Self-described critical biblical scholars often describe those who do not read the Bible with critical neutrality as pathological failures. As Hendel argues in his work on the book of Genesis, the "plain senses of Genesis are never lost as long as people pay attention to the verbal details and resonances of the text," but "modern biblical scholarship also argues that much of the history of the interpretation of Genesis is a history of error."³⁸ Why did Hendel write an entire book on the history of how people read the book of Genesis, then? Because, as he puts it, even though "much of its afterlife in Western civilization has been false, or based on faulty premises," nevertheless "people and cultures need illusions," and "the afterlife of Genesis...mostly consists of such creative illusions."³⁹ Hendel's particular approach to reception history emanates directly from his conception of critical scholarship. He assumes that there is a natural and objective dichotomy between "the book's original meanings—those that are properties of the 'plain' or grammatical sense of the ancient Hebrew words, sentences, and narratives—and its later interpretations," which take "liberties with the plain sense."⁴⁰ Thus, according to Hendel, there is one true, plain meaning of the text, which is a substantial and singular thing, and then there are innumerable interpretive errors, which are all illusions.

Perhaps, though, the actual illusion is the faith in a singular true plain sense meaning to each biblical text that is, or should be, identical for every reader throughout history. According to adherents of this faith, readers should arrive at the precise meaning that (certain) biblical critics have determined to be correct. Yet Hendel's own text-critical project is constructed on the premise that there is *not* one true shape to every biblical text—as we now know, there were multiple, irreducibly different versions of biblical texts in circulation before there was any concept of

---

37. Hendel, "Mind the Gap," 443, quoting from Moore and Sherwood, *Invention of the Biblical Scholar*, 133. See also Hendel's dismissal of issues of identity in his "Farewell to SBL: Faith and Reason in Biblical Studies," *BAR* 36, no. 4 (2010): 28, 74.

38. Ronald [S.] Hendel, *The Book of Genesis: A Biography*, Lives of Great Religious Books (Princeton: Princeton University Press, 2012), 6.

39. Hendel, *The Book of Genesis*, 7.

40. Hendel, *The Book of Genesis*, 4.

canonicity or textual stability.[41] Likewise, it seems illusory to suggest that there is one plain sense of any given biblical text: every biblical book shows signs of scribal composition that extend beyond a single pen, and in many instances the process of composition seems to have spanned many generations, multiple geographical and cultural locations, and numerous socio-cultural and linguistic shifts within particular cultures.[42] For example, what is the singular plain sense meaning of Jacob's dream at Bethel in Genesis 28? Which presumed scribal author gets to say what the true meaning is: the pre-extant forms of the Jacob story attested by Hosea 12, the non-Priestly sources in Genesis 25, the Priestly scribes who rewrote the story in Genesis 35, or the redactors who sewed these different stories together into a Jacob cycle and added material to Genesis 28—or is it the scribes who situated this story within the larger frame of Genesis, or who edited the Torah into a broad, albeit uneven, narrative?[43] Presumably, these scribes were all Other to each other, and did not have completely identical ideas about what this story means—hence their redacting and rewriting. Who, then, gets to occupy the place of true meaning, and who among these ancient scribes is relegated to the status of illusory error? How can we respect the differences, and the different identities, that we find layered behind every text that we encounter in the Bible?

An Alternate Approach: The Ethos of "In This Respect"

It seems to me that Barton is correct that confessional, theologically motivated readings often suspiciously end up saying exactly what the

---

41. See Hendel, *Steps to a New Edition*, 25–8, 37–9. See also Breed, *Nomadic Text*, 15–74.

42. On the anachronism of "book," see John Barton, "What is a Book? Modern Exegesis and the Literary Conventions of Ancient Israel," in *Intertextuality in Ugarit and Israel: Papers Read at the Tenth Joint Meeting of the Society for Old Testament Study and Het Oudtestamentisch Werkgezelschap in Nederland en België, Held at Oxford, 1997*, ed. Johannes C. de Moor, OtSt 40 (Leiden: Brill, 1998), 1–14.

43. See, for example, Erhard Blum, "Noch einmal: Jakobs Traum in Bethel – Genesis 28,10-22," in *Rethinking the Foundations: Historiography in the Ancient World and in the Bible, Essays in Honour of John Van Seters*, ed. S. McKenzie and T. Römer, BZAW 294 (Berlin: de Gruyter, 2000), 33–54; Albert de Pury, "The Jacob Story and the Beginning of the Formation of the Pentateuch," in *A Farewell to the Yahwist? The Composition of the Pentateuch in Recent European Scholarship*, ed. Thomas B. Dozeman and Konrad Schmid, SymS 34 (Atlanta: SBL, 2006), 51–72, esp. 64–5; David Carr, *Reading the Fractures of Genesis: Historical and Literary Approaches* (Louisville: Westminster John Knox, 1996), 85–9.

interpreter wanted them to say all along.[44] Critical thought *can* open up distance between the interpreter and text in a way that is productive, not simply reductive. Yet perhaps there is a way to use critical tools to open up a space of difference between the reader and the text, while rejecting the foundational assumptions of many biblical critics that the goal of such work is to find a singular, true meaning to a text that fits perfectly into an original context. In order to retain critical distance without collapsing the differences within the text, and within the history of reception, including readers today, I argue that we must reconceive the relationship of identity and otherness.

The trope of respect typically assumes a setting of one-on-one interpersonal dialogue that requires us all to hear an identical, universal message from a text. But there is another use of the word "respect" that I find scattered throughout the discourse of biblical criticism that may be much more helpful for critical thought: namely, the phrase "in this respect." This phrase construes "respect" in a manner similar to the word "aspect." It is, at root, an admission that the object under analysis is not exhausted by the observation that is to follow. If I say, "In this respect, the book of Ecclesiastes is a skeptical book," then I am saying that there are other aspects or angles of vision on Ecclesiastes that one could defensibly take. "In this respect" cautions that a particular, contingent, limited point is about to follow, and that there are admittedly other respects to the object under discussion. This is, to my mind, a more properly analytical trope.[45] It concedes both the multiplicity of the object of analysis and the multiple perspectives an observer might take that would cast the object in different light, reveal some occluded aspects, and hide others that were prominent.[46]

Perhaps the work of analysis is not the practice of demystifying illusions and revealing the singular truth of each text. Instead, one can analyze a biblical text as a multifaceted, pluriform, open-ended system. And ironically, as Eva Mroczek has recently shown, the notion of an

---

44. "To me it seems that proponents of confessing readings of the Bible risk requiring the interpreter to live inside a religious community that has closed boundaries and in which it is taken for granted that the believer has privileged access to the meaning of biblical texts." Barton, *Nature of Biblical Criticism*, 176.

45. If analysis is the careful examination of the elements or structure of an object, then accounting for the irreducible differences in contexts of production, authorial and redactional voices, and potential meanings and uses is a constitutive aspect of analysis, and reductive concepts like "the plain sense" and "the original context" are not properly analytical. See Breed, *Nomadic Text*, 75–115.

46. For a more detailed argument, see Breed, *Nomadic Text*, 116–32.

open-ended, pluriform, and polyvalent sacred text is actually much closer to the conception of sacred literature in Second Temple Judaism than the critical biblical ideal of a stable, published text with a singular plain meaning.[47] According to Mroczek's detailed analysis of the literary imaginations and expectations of texts, authors, and meaning in ancient Judah, sacred texts were often understood to be incomplete fragments of an unrepresentable, hidden body of teaching connected to a famous figure. Solomon's three thousand proverbs and one thousand and five songs (1 Kgs 5:12 [ET 4:32]) and David's three thousand, six hundred psalms mentioned in 11QPsalms[a] testify to this expectation that there was much more sacred literature besides what was available, but it was always beyond the grasp of any individual person.[48] Moreover, in Ben Sira and *Jubilees*, Mroczek finds descriptions of sacred textuality that presuppose an intergenerational, geographically mobile process incorporating various genres, which themselves are only partial glimpses of "the multiple and multiform ways God has communicated with Israel."[49] All of this leads Mrozcek to argue that the literary imagination of ancient Judaism conceived of texts as "open books": Any physical instantiation of a text was an interim statement that could be re-edited while it was in circulation.[50] This should transform our expectations about identity in relation to reading biblical books: Reading is not a dialogue with a single partner who has a singular message to share with anyone and everyone, and neither is it an adoptive process reserved for those who already belong to the chosen community. Rather, reading is an engagement with a shifting, many-layered process.[51] It can yield different "plain senses" even when conducted by the self-same reader, depending on which of the many voices one engages, which questions the reader brings to the process, and which criteria the reader chooses to judge the production of meaning.[52]

Elsewhere, I have argued that biblical scholars would benefit from thinking of their objects of study as a process with manifold potential

---

47. Mroczek, *Literary Imagination*.
48. Mroczek, *Literary Imagination*, 63, 178–89.
49. Mroczek, *Literary Imagination*, 154.
50. Mroczek, *Literary Imagination*, 184–9.
51. See James E. Bowley and John C. Reeves, "Rethinking the Concept of 'Bible': Some Theses and Proposals," *Henoch* 25 (2003): 3–18. For a discussion of the structure of processes and the importance of divergence, see Manuel DeLanda, *Intensive Science and Virtual Philosophy* (New York: Continuum, 2002), 9–39, esp. 21.
52. See Breed, *Nomadic Text*, 204–6.

outcomes.⁵³ Instead of trying to respect a singular context, text, author, and/or meaning by deeming the rest illusory, I suggest that we think of our readings and the readings of others as different potential outcomes of the process of reading; thus, any particular reading is necessarily a *limitation* of the potential meaning that a text can produce. Readings that work with the raw materials for meaning provided by a text are all real, actual construals of a given text. There are many other potential readings that one could have ended up with, and they are *also* real. The philosopher Gilles Deleuze argues against the typical distinction between the "real"—whatever is the current state of affairs—and the "possible"—whatever might be extant but is not, and thus is not real. Instead, Deleuze encourages us to think of anything that could potentially happen as *real*, but not yet *actualized*. Whatever currently exists, he calls the *actual*, and what exists only in potential form—much like potential energy, which is very much real and present—the *virtual*.⁵⁴ Both the actual and the virtual are real, according to Deleuze. If we think this way, we can distinguish between *actual* readings (that is, the reading that someone has activated at a particular moment) and *virtual* readings of a text (that is, potential readings that are not actualized at the moment). Reception history, then, would not necessarily reveal a genealogy of illusions and failures, save the few lucky readers who happened to get the singular right answer. Rather, reception history traces the history of a text's actualizations, and by collecting and analyzing these actualizations, we can sense something of the text's virtual dimension—that is, its structure of potentiality.

Critical biblical scholarship is, for the most part, comprised of impressively productive tools, and it has opened many otherwise unimaginable avenues of inquiry. Nevertheless, the dominant ideology of critical biblical scholarship has, for the past several centuries, required singular interpretations of texts to compete in agonistic struggle with one another. Yet a particular reading of a biblical text is *a particular reading* of a biblical text—in one, and only one, respect. Critical biblical scholars can observe a text from a wide variety of different perspectives, thinking

---

53. Brennan W. Breed, "Nomadology of the Bible: A Processual Approach to Biblical Reception History," *BibRec* 1 (2012): 299–322; Breed, "What Can a Text Do? Reception History as an Ethology of the Biblical Text," in *Reception History and Biblical Studies: Theory and Practice*, ed. Emma England and William John Lyons, LHBOTS 615/Scriptural Traces 6 (London: Bloomsbury T&T Clark, 2015), 95–106.

54. See Gilles Deleuze, *Difference and Repetition*, trans. Paul Patton (New York: Columbia University Press, 1995), 163–87, 211–14. For an introduction to this concept, see Todd May, *Gilles Deleuze: An Introduction* (Cambridge: Cambridge University Press, 2005), 48–9.

about its function in different historical contexts, thinking about the role of different layers of scribal hands that contributed to the work, and perhaps they can understand their conclusions as a single actualization of a textual potentiality that could produce many different actualizations. What would allow one to judge between these readings, organizing them into a hierarchy of better or worse readings (or versions of texts)? Only *local*, not universal, criteria—that is, one might be looking for the form and function of a particular text in the Iron Age, or perhaps one is asking about the same text in the Hellenistic era, or perhaps in the rabbinic community in Late Antiquity, or among Italian visual artists of the trecento. None of these are naturally more important than any other, and while the text is translated and read through a variety of contexts, of course its potentiality will shift, and new types of readings will emerge. The rules and criteria for critical biblical scholars who are focused on recovering—and respecting—particular groups of readers from the Iron Age through the Hellenistic era are not necessarily the rules and criteria for all readers everywhere, and there is no universal, objective hierarchy of such rules. Can we respect those who read in other respects?

Readings produced according to different sets of rules may be defensible or indefensible—it seems clear to me that there are readings that simply do not actualize virtual potentialities of a text. In other words, yes, there are wrong readings.[55] If one wants to judge readings of a text as readings—there are, of course, other ways to judge—then even Jacques Derrida agrees that one must stay "within the text" that one reads, and that reading cannot "transgress the text" by saying whatever one wants.[56] But at the same time, one must be able to, in reading, produce a supplement of substitutive significations that requires, at a minimum, putting things "in other words." A commentary that reproduced the text exactly as it is found would show the utmost respect for the source text, but it would not reveal a reading of that text. In order to produce a reading and offer a particular construal of what the text means, the reader must substitute some words, rearrange others, omit still more, in their synthetic retelling of the text. As Geoffrey Bennington observes, "There could be no reading absolutely respectful of a text, for a total respect would forbid one from even touching the text."[57] Reading requires changing, rearranging, emphasizing, minimizing, and the particular substitutions are not regulated by any singularly

---

55. See Breed, *Nomadic Text*, 127–31.

56. Jacques Derrida, *Of Grammatology*, trans. Gayatri C. Spivak, corrected ed. (Baltimore: Johns Hopkins University Press, 1998), 158.

57. Geoffrey Bennington and Jacques Derrida, *Jacques Derrida*, trans. Geoffrey Bennington (Chicago: University of Chicago Press, 1993), 165.

applicable transcendental rule. We are always reading other people's texts, and thus we are always rearranging other people's texts.

In short, attention to reception history can help scholars chart the actual effects of biblical texts and offer hypotheses concerning their virtual structure—and both of these are anything but illusory. Discerning the contours of a text's otherness over time, its excess and lack of precise fit within any given historical context, is an attempt to understand its identity. This identity, though, is not constant, nor is it a shadow of some static ideal: instead, it is a differential identity. It is an identity based on difference, much like the identity of a river shifts and changes over time based on differential forces between water and soil, differential pressures in the earth's crust producing earthquakes that shift the landscape, differences in topology that direct the potential energy of water to actualize itself in particular patterns, and differential climactic forces that lead to floods and droughts.[58] The river is an actual thing, of course, but its stable appearance, or what we might think is a reliable identity, is actually a product of manifold differential forces that together constitute a field of potentialities. A semantic network such as a sacred text has a similar differential identity.

The Reception of Qohelet:
A Dialectic of Identity and Otherness

But how does this work in practice? For a brief example of how I think identity and difference function in biblical texts, I turn to the book of Ecclesiastes and its main character (or perhaps author, or authorial character, depending on how the reader conceives of the structure of the work), who goes by the odd title "Qohelet."[59] As many biblical scholars

---

58. On differential identities, see Breed, *Nomadic Text*, 65–74; Ferdinand de Saussure, *Course in General Linguistics*, ed. Charles Bally and Albert Schehaye, trans. Roy Harris (Chicago: Open Court, 1983), 65–70; Bennington and Derrida, *Jacques Derrida*, 23–41; Geoffrey Bennington, "Saussure and Derrida," in *The Cambridge Companion to Saussure*, ed. Carol Sanders (Cambridge: Cambridge University Press, 2005), 186–204.

59. See Carolyn Sharp, "Ironic Representation, Authorial Voice, and Meaning in Qohelet," *BibInt* 12 (2004): 37–68; Kyle Greenwood, "Debating Wisdom: The Role of Voice in Ecclesiastes," *CBQ* 74 (2012): 476–91. See also a reading in the context of royal inscriptions, Y. V. Koh, *Royal Autobiography in the Book of Qoheleth*, BZAW 369 (Berlin/New York: de Gruyter, 2006), and in the context of Israelite literature, Jennie [Grillo] Barbour, *The Story of Israel in the Book of Qohelet: Ecclesiastes as Cultural Memory* (Oxford: Oxford University Press, 2012).

have noted, and as Jennifer Koosed has explored with subtlety, "Qohelet" is a feminine participle meaning "assembler," and yet it is almost exclusively the subject of masculine verbs.[60] It appears that there are at least a few scribes who have contributed to the production of this text, since the superscription (Eccl. 1:1-2), epilogue (12:8-11), and one seeming editorial insertion (7:27) refer to Qohelet in the third person, and many scholars have argued that there is evidence of at least two distinct scribal voices in the epilogue.[61] Which one is the real Qohelet? Which ones are the others?

Some interpreters, such as Tremper Longman, have argued that the framing texts are the true voice of the author, and that the pessimistic words of Qohelet are staged to show the danger of speculative thought.[62] Others, such as Michael Fox, see the presentation of Qohelet as the product of a scribe who wants to use this character to help the reader think about life's contradictions.[63] Still others, such as James Loader, see the framing work as a failed, desperate editorial attempt to obscure the radical message found in the book.[64] And others, such as Choon-Leong Seow, argue that the epilogue and the ensuing postscript serve as an authorization for the book that precedes them, in accordance with ancient Near Eastern traditions concerning didactic texts, and that they are not in essential conflict with the rest of the book.[65] I certainly have my own opinions about how I read the framing materials, but it is more important for the purposes of this essay to note that there are many different ways that careful, trained, creative scholars have grappled with the virtual potentials offered by this text, and they have actualized them in a variety of ways. Many (perhaps not all) of these constructions are defensible readings given the raw materials offered by the book of Qohelet.

But even if the entirety of the book of Ecclesiastes comes from one hand, problems of identity remain: First, the text is rife with apparent

---

60. See Jennifer Koosed, *(Per)mutations of Qohelet: Reading the Body in the Book*, LHBOTS 429 (London: Bloomsbury T&T Clark, 2006), 74–85.

61. See Thomas Bolin, *Ecclesiastes and the Riddle of Authorship* (New York: Routledge, 2017), 58–75.

62. Tremper Longman III, *The Book of Ecclesiastes*, NICOT (Grand Rapids: Eerdmans, 1998), 38.

63. Michael V. Fox, "Frame-Narrative and Composition in the Book of Qohelet," *HUCA* 48 (1977): 83–106.

64. See James A. Loader, *Polar Structures in the Book of Qohelet*, BZAW 152 (Berlin: de Gruyter, 1979).

65. Choon-Leong Seow, *Ecclesiastes: A New Translation, with Introduction and Commentary*, AB 18C (New York: Doubleday, 1997), 131–2.

contradictions.⁶⁶ In one example, Qohelet claims that the words of a poor yet wise person are despised in favor of the mighty, but then immediately says that the words of a calm, wise person are heeded more than a shouting king (Eccl. 9:16-17).⁶⁷ If the reader is supposed to gain access to a single, coherent meaning with the help of philology, Qohelet seems to present a difficult obstacle. At least some of these contradictions can be overcome by hermeneutical maneuvering: Perhaps Qohelet is quoting a text only to refute it, or perhaps Qohelet changes opinions throughout the course of the book, or perhaps some seeming contradictions are the work of editors who either sloppily or consciously altered the message of the book—or perhaps Qohelet's point is communicated primarily through contradiction itself.⁶⁸ Not all solutions to the problem of Qohelet's inconsistency are equally convincing—but there are nevertheless a variety of ingenious and defensible responses to the problem of the identity of Qohelet's message that are irreducibly different, and not all of them can be ruled out of hand.

Another problem with Qohelet's identity concerns the vague relationship with royalty and utter lack of proper names other than "David." While the superscription introduces him as "son of David, king in Jerusalem" (Eccl. 1:1), he introduces himself later as "king over Israel in Jerusalem" (1:12), conjugating the verb in such a manner that it would translate as a past tense verb ("I *was* king"), which suggests a potential abdication of the throne. No king named Qohelet is known, and while "son of David" could connote a later Davidic king, it would most likely signal Solomon, David's son who ruled over Israel in Jerusalem.⁶⁹ Moreover, the epilogue treats Qohelet as purely a teacher, not a king at all (Eccl. 12:9).⁷⁰ And

66. See, for example, Michael V. Fox, *Qohelet and His Contradictions*, JSOTSup 71 (Sheffield: Almond, 1989), and James L. Crenshaw, "Qoheleth in Current Research," *HAR* 7 (1984): 41–56, where Crenshaw writes: "Unless I am mistaken the essential issue for more than fifty years has been the search for an adequate means of explaining inconsistencies within the book" (43).

67. For other examples: Eccl. 4:2-3 vs. Eccl. 9:4-6; Eccl. 1:17 vs. Eccl. 2:13-16; 7:11-12.

68. See George A. Barton, *A Critical and Exegetical Commentary on the Book of Ecclesiastes*, ICC (Edinburgh: T. & T. Clark, 1908), 43–6; Theodore A. Perry, *Dialogues with Kohelet: The Book of Ecclesiastes* (College Park: Penn State University Press, 1993), 33–48; Norbert Lohfink, *Qoheleth*, trans. Sean McEvenue, CC (Minneapolis: Fortress, 2003), 139–44; R. Norman Whybray, "The Identification and Use of Quotations in Ecclesiastes," in *Congress Volume Vienna 1980*, ed. John A. Emerton, VTSup 32 (Leiden: Brill, 1981), 435–51. Note the exceptionally helpful overview in Bolin, *Riddle of Authorship*, 58–75.

69. See Seow, *Ecclesiastes*, 95–9.

70. See Seow, *Ecclesiastes*, 390–414.

while the royal section in Eccl. 1:12–2:26 casts Qohelet in a somewhat Solomonic guise, it pointedly refrains from claiming the name Solomon. After chapter 2, the Solomonic guise drops, and for the duration of the book Qohelet appears to see the king as someone to be feared (cf. Eccl. 10:20). So, perhaps Qohelet merely pretends to be king in order to lead the reader on a thought experiment, as Choon-Leong Seow suggests: the "intent of the author [is] to evoke memory of Solomon, the wise king par excellence and the best example of one who has it all."[71] Thus, Qohelet, speaking in Eccl. 1:12, wants the reader, at least for a time, to think of Solomon when hearing Qohelet. And perhaps the frame narrator, speaking in 1:1, wants the reader to think of the whole book as coming from the lips of Solomon. How does one find a singular plain sense in all this, and how would one show respect to it?

It is all confusing at best. As a result, the identity of Qohelet has proven ripe for creative interpretations that struggle with the coordinates of this problem. Many interpreters throughout history, such as *Targum Qohelet*, understood Ecclesiastes as the product of an elderly Solomon who had been expelled from his throne for misconduct (Eccl. 1:12).[72] Some of these readers see Ecclesiastes as the pious product of his repentance, and others see it as the detritus of his apostasy before he reconverted.[73] And I must admit, I myself can understand a reading of Qohelet as more or less pious—after all, much of the book can be compared to other examples from the generally pious corpus of Israelite wisdom literature, including the rejection of an afterlife. I can also understand a reading of Qohelet that casts it as an impious mess, because it does at times counsel the reader to limit religious observance to a bare minimum (cf. Eccl. 4:17–5:6 [ET 5:1–7]), and it never once uses the Tetragrammaton.[74] Both of these

---

71. Seow, *Ecclesiastes*, 37.

72. *The Targum of Qohelet*, trans. Peter S. Knobel, ArBib 15 (Edinburgh: T. & T. Clark, 1991), 22. See also Gregory of Nyssa, *Homilies on Ecclesiastes*, trans. Stuart George Hall (Berlin: de Gruyter, 1993), 48–59, quoted in Jennie Grillo, "Qohelet and the Marks of Modernity: Reading Ecclesiastes with Matthew Arnold and Charles Taylor," *Religions* 7 (2016): 1–9.

73. For an overview of Jewish interpretation, see Louis Ginzberg, *Legends of the Jews, vol. 4*, trans. Henrietta Szold and Paul Radin (Philadelphia: Jewish Publication Society, 1913), 123–76. See Bolin, *Riddle of Authorship*, 80–102.

74. Tremper Longman, *Ecclesiastes*, 151, takes 4:17–5:6 "not as an assertion of divine power, but of divine distance, perhaps even of indifference." See also Michael Payne, "The Voices of Ecclesiastes," *College Literature* 15 (1988): 262–8, who sees the book as a collage of voices that include piety and impiety, quoted in Bolin, *Riddle of Authorship*, 72, 79.

construals of Ecclesiastes respect the text—they merely use the raw textual materials provided by Ecclesiastes in different ways.

But is this all a big mistake? There was, doubtless, an actual historical set of circumstances (or perhaps several) that fostered the production of the book of Ecclesiastes. Are there not wrong answers to the question, "Who wrote this book?" I would agree that there is a correct historical reconstruction, and that the epistemological uncertainty of any historical reconstruction is no reason to forgo the task. But perhaps there are other questions just as worthy of answers, and perhaps these may illuminate the text in other ways. If one only wants to consider the book in light of its actual process of composition, one might miss what Qohelet's persona might have meant in that same historical context. As Eva Mroczek points out, the literary persona of Ben Sira functions like that of Moses and David: his sprawling text may be a compilation of many sources, and some of it may not be from his hand at all, but Ben Sira is an ideal sage who ties together a sacred text and gestures to more revelation that lies outside it.[75] In a similar manner, Qohelet is said to have arranged many proverbs—reminiscent of Solomon's activity in 1 Kgs 5:12 [ET 4:32]—which may not refer to the book of Ecclesiastes itself.[76]

In other words, the text contains the raw materials needed to interpret Ecclesiastes as deploying the dominant trope of ancient Jewish sacred textuality: namely, Ecclesiastes the text is but a fragmentary presentation of an ungraspable, incalculably large body of divine revelation that is hidden in an idealized past and presented in the name of Qohelet. Yet it would be possible, as well, to see this identification as ironic, or a criticism of the dominant ancient Jewish literary imagination because of the ways that Qohelet and Ecclesiastes push back against this morphology of text and understanding of revelation.[77] Instead of the untold depths of sacred wisdom offered by the limitless libraries created by sages like Solomon and David, and instead of the wondrous heavenly mysteries mediated by Enoch and Daniel, Qohelet's wisdom might simply be the fragmented, graspable material that one can see in the textual artifact. As Qohelet says again and again: there is nothing beyond this world that can be known. Qohelet tried to find the חשבון—the sum of everything, the explanation, the meaning of life—and found instead that a חשבון such as this does not

---

75. See Mroczek, *Literary Imagination*, 90–103.

76. See Seow, *Ecclesiastes*, 385.

77. According to the interpretive logic of James L. Crenshaw, *Qoheleth: The Ironic Wink*, Studies on Personalities of the Old Testament (Columbia: University of South Carolina Press, 2013).

exist (7:23-29).[78] For those who want to ascend to the heavenly realm, Qohelet reminds us that we are not able to transcend this world (Eccl. 5:1 [ET 5:2]).[79] Thus, the epilogist's statement that Qohelet had many משלים could appear to signal the dominant trope of ancient Jewish scripturality, but then collapse that transcendent infinitude into the limited, immanent "words" that he "wrote" (12:9-10).[80] The epilogist pivots to a warning to beware anything that is not in the collected words of the sages—perhaps a reference to the written text mentioned in the previous verse (12:10-11). The ensuing warning about scrolls and endings might then caution the reader not to seek after the endless, ungraspable teachings of the sages that beckon one towards transcendent heights (12:12). In short, the epilogue to Ecclesiastes could well be a cautionary tale about sacred textuality itself: its actual existing otherness, however limited and fragmentary in meaning, is all that can be found in this world—or beyond. This is, of course, one potential actualization of the epilogue to Ecclesiastes, in one respect. Doubtless, it can be read otherwise, in other respects.[81]

Thomas Bolin has recently analyzed the history of Qohelet's reception—not the book as a whole, Ecclesiastes, but rather the literary character of Qohelet.[82] Bolin sorts the wide variety of interpretations of Qohelet's identity, his personality, and his teaching, into five semantic nodes: (1) Qohelet as Solomon; (2) Qohelet as an unidentified royal; (3) Qohelet as a teacher of contradictions; (4) Qohelet as either a saint or a sinner or both; (5) Qohelet as a philosopher. These categories do not exhaust potential construals of Qohelet, but they provide an excellent starting point for considering the overall impact of Qohelet's persona, and Bolin offers an example of what Gilles Deleuze would describe as "counteractualization."[83] In Deleuze's description of reality as comprising

---

78. See Seow, *Ecclesiastes*, 260–1, 271.

79. See Anton Schoors, *The Preacher Sought to Find Pleasing Words: A Study of the Language of Qoheleth. Part II: Vocabulary*, OLA 143 (Leuven: Peeters, 2004), 104.

80. On משלים, see Jacqueline Vayntrub, *Beyond Orality: Biblical Poetry on Its Own Terms*, The Ancient Word (New York: Routledge, 2019), 36–60.

81. See, for example, the very different, but careful, reading of T. A. Perry, *The Book of Ecclesiastes (Qohelet) and the Path to Joyous Living* (New York: Cambridge University Press, 2015).

82. Bolin, *Riddle of Authorship*.

83. See James Williams, *The Transversal Thought of Gilles Deleuze: Encounters and Influences* (Manchester: Clinamen, 2005), 49; Gilles Deleuze, *The Logic of Sense*, ed. Constantin Boundas, trans. Mark Lester and Charles Stivale (New York: Columbia University Press, 1990), 150; Deleuze, *Difference and Repetition*, 252.

both the virtual and the actual, he argues that humans can only directly perceive the actual. When we observe change, we see transitions between actual states, from which we can intuit some of the contours of the virtual dimension of an object. For example, when an artist makes a new shape out of a particular medium, they are often using their knowledge of the potential capacities of that medium to imagine something new that they have not seen before. In other words, the artist is using collected observations to counteractualize the medium, discerning some potentials that they had not yet observed and perhaps had not yet known were possible.

In a similar manner, Bolin amasses hundreds of particular actualizations of Qohelet's identity and organizes them not into categories of Jewish and Christian interpretation, or artistic versus exegetical engagement. Rather, he organizes them into categories based on what potential capacities of the text a particular engagement actualizes. Bolin does not approve of all these interpretations as readings, it should be said: he explicitly denies that some of these are engagements with the text that account for its textual features in any sufficient way. One might say that these misreadings fail to respect the text of Ecclesiastes, at least as a reading. They may be beautiful, or ethically compelling, or theologically fascinating, but they do not work as *readings* per se.[84]

So, if I am to *respect* Qohelet, it seems to me that I should do one of two things: either offer a reading of Ecclesiastes that seeks to construe the language of the text in one particular manner, which limits its potentials while at the same time actualizing some of them, or analyze the many readings of Ecclesiastes that already exist and see if I can find patterns that reveal some of the contours of the virtual structuration of the text's potentials. In neither case am I finding the singular truth of the text; nevertheless, both procedures use the logic and tools of critical studies, including philology.

In reviewing the history of Qohelet's reception, one dimension of Qohelet's virtual structure involves the dialectic between identity and otherness.[85] Readers from the ancient world to the modern are forced to grapple with a voice that seems both strongly personal and fragmentary, a set of seemingly contradictory teachings that are equally at home as a pious exemplar of ancient Near Eastern thought and a radical Hellenistic revolt against the tired maxims of Yahwistic orthodoxy, a voice that is comfortable with the tradition while standing outside of it, a literary sage who pretends to be a king and might be a successful entrepreneur.

---

84. See also Breed, *Nomadic Text*, 127–41.
85. See Bolin, *Riddle of Authorship*, and Eric S. Christianson, *Ecclesiastes through the Centuries*, BBC (Malden: Wiley-Blackwell, 2007).

Many readers take Qohelet to be one of them, though for some that is a stable member of a particular community, and for others it validates their exclusion from a community. Many readers are wary of Qohelet and wonder if he is even a true part of their tradition; these readers tend to be conservative, hewing close to what they see as the traditions of their communities, but others consider themselves true rebels and see in Qohelet a would-be iconoclast who ends up unwittingly reinforcing the theological status quo.[86]

What happens when Others read Ecclesiastes? Perhaps this is the only way one can engage it; everyone feels Other when reading the book. It is difficult to imagine anyone, even the putative original author, identifying entirely with it and respecting it without remainder. But perhaps this is a feature, not a bug, of its construction. That is, perhaps the never-ending dialectic of identity and difference is an irreducible dimension of Ecclesiastes itself. The book constantly poses questions about identity and introduces obstacles to easy identification—and it pushes you, the reader, take a position on the questions of Qohelet's identity, on Qohelet's relationship to the communities of ancient Israel and Second Temple Judaism and various contemporary communities, and on your own relationship to these groups, as you read it. And since there is not a single correct answer to those questions, perhaps we can learn to respect the variety of actualizations that we will doubtless encounter in any attempt to read Ecclesiastes' readings.

---

86. See Mark R. Sneed, *The Politics of Pessimism in Ecclesiastes: A Social-Science Perspective*, AIL 12 (Atlanta: SBL, 2012).

Bibliography

Aageson, James W. "Written Also for Our Sake: Paul's Use of Scripture in the Four Major Epistles, with a Study of 1 Corinthians 10." In *Hearing the Old Testament in the New Testament*, edited by Stanley E. Porter, 152–81. Grand Rapids: Eerdmans, 2006.
Achenbach, Reinhard. *Die Vollendung der Tora: Studien zur Redaktionsgeschichte des Numeribuches im Kontext von Hexateuch und Pentateuch*. BZABR 3. Wiesbaden: Harrassowitz, 2003.
Acheraïou, Amar. *Questioning Hybridity, Postcolonialism and Globalization*. London: Palgrave Macmillan, 2011.
Adriaen, Marci, ed. *S. Gregorii Magni, Moralia in Iob*. CCSL 143, 143A, 143B. Turnhout: Brepols, 1979–85.
Agha, Asif. *Language and Social Relations*. Studies in the Social and Cultural Foundations of Language 24. Cambridge: Cambridge University Press, 2007.
Akers, Michael J. *Morning and Evening Meditations from the Word of God: Education, Challenge, Inspiration, and Encouragement*. Bloomington: WestBow Press, 2014.
Albertz, Rainer. "Das Buch Numeri jenseits der Quellentheorie: Eine Redaktionsgeschichte von Num 20–24 (Teil 1)." *ZAW* 123 (2011): 171–83.
Albertz, Rainer, and Jakob Wöhrle, eds. *Between Cooperation and Hostility: Multiple Identities in Ancient Judaism and the Interaction with Foreign Powers*. Journal of Ancient Judaism Supplements 11. Göttingen: Vandenhoeck & Ruprecht, 2013.
Alexander, T. Desmond. "Further Observations on the Term 'Seed' in Genesis." *TynBul* 48 (1997): 363–7.
Alston, Richard. "Philo's 'In Flaccum': Ethnicity and Social Space in Roman Alexandria." *Greece and Rome* 44 (1997): 165–75.
Althusser, Louis. "Ideology and Ideological State Apparatuses (Notes towards an Investigation)." In *Lenin and Philosophy and Other Essays*, 127–86. Translated by Ben Brewster. New York: Monthly Review Press 1971.
Ameisenowa, Zofia. "Animal-Headed Gods, Evangelists, Saints and Righteous Men." *Journal of the Warburg and Courtauld Institutes* 12 (1949): 21–45.
Amit, Yairah. "The Dual Causality Principle and Its Effects on Biblical Literature." *VT* 37 (1987): 385–400.
Ammann, Sonja. *Götter für die Toren: Die Verbindung von Götterpolemik und Weisheit im Alten Testament*. BZAW 466. Berlin: de Gruyter, 2015.
Anderson, Andrew Runni. "Heracles and His Successors: A Study of a Heroic Ideal and the Recurrence of a Heroic Type." *HSCP* 39 (1928): 7–58.
Anderson, Benedict. *Imagined Communities: Reflections on the Origin and Spread of Nationalism*. Rev. ed. London: Verso, 1991.
Anderson, Graham. *The Second Sophistic: A Cultural Phenomenon in the Roman Empire*. London: Routledge, 1993.

Anderson, John R. *Cognitive Psychology and its Implications*. 8th ed. New York: Worth, 2015.
Anderson, Robert T., and Terry Giles. *The Samaritan Pentateuch: An Introduction to Its Origin, History, and Significance for Biblical Studies*. RBS 72. Atlanta: Society of Biblical Literature, 2012.
Annus, Amar, and Alan Lenzi. *Ludlul bēl Nemeqi: The Standard Babylonian Poem of the Righteous Sufferer*. SAACT 7. Helsinki: Neo-Assyrian Text Corpus Project, 2010.
Anthony, John Baptist. Various Sidebars in Marie-Theres Wacker, *Baruch and the Letter of Jeremiah*. Wisdom Commentary 31. Collegeville: Liturgical Press, 2016.
Anzaldúa, Gloria. *Borderlands/La Frontera: The New Mestiza*. San Francisco: Aunte Lute, 1999.
Appelbaum, Robert, and John Wood Sweet, eds. *Envisioning an English Empire: Jamestown and the Making of the North Atlantic World*. Philadelphia: University of Pennsylvania Press, 2005.
Armstrong, Catherine. *Writing North America in the Seventeenth Century: English Representations in Print and Manuscript*. Hampshire, UK: Ashgate, 2007.
Asamoah-Gyadu, J. Kwabena. "From Prophetism to Pentecostalism: Religious Innovation in Africa and African Religious Scholarship." In *African Traditions in the Study of Religion in Africa: Emerging Trends, Indigenous Spirituality and the Interface with Other World Religions, Essays in Honour of Jacob Kehinde Olupona*, edited by Afe Adogame, Ezra Chitando, and Bolaji Bateye, 161–75. Surrey: Ashgate, 2012.
Ashcroft, Bill, Gareth Griffiths and Helen Tiffin, eds. *The Empire Writes Back: Theory and Practice in Postcolonial Literatures*. New York: Routledge, 1989.
Ashley, Timothy R. *The Book of Numbers*. NICOT 4. Grand Rapids: Eerdmans, 1993.
Awabdy, Mark A. *Immigrants and Innovative Law: Deuteronomy's Theological and Social Vision for the גר*. FAT 2/67. Tübingen: Mohr Siebeck, 2014.
Baasten, Matthew. *Pride According to Gregory the Great: A Study of the Moralia*. Studies in the Bible and Early Christianity 7. Lewiston: Mellen, 1986.
Baden, Joel S. *J, E and the Redaction of the Pentateuch*. FAT 68. Tübingen: Mohr Siebeck, 2009.
Bailey, Randall C. "Academic Biblical Interpretations among African Americans in the United States." In *African Americans and the Bible: Sacred Texts and Social Textures*, edited by Vincent L. Wimbush with Rosamond C. Rodman, 696–711. New York: Continuum, 2000.
Bakhtin, Mikhail M. *The Dialogic Imagination: Four Essays*. Edited by Michael Holquist. Translated by Caryl Emerson and Michael Holquist. Austin: University of Texas Press, 1981.
Bakhtin, Mikhail M. *Problems of Dostoevsky's Poetics*. Translated by Caryl Emerson. Introduction by Wayne Booth. Theory and History of Literature 8. Minneapolis: University of Minnesota Press, 1984.
Banana, Canaan. "The Case for a New Bible." In *"Rewriting the Bible": The Real Issues*, edited by Isabel Mukonyora, James L. Cox and Frans J. Verstraelen, 17–32. Gweru: Mambo, 1993.
Bandstra, Andrew J. "Interpretation in 1 Corinthians 10:1–11." *CTJ* 6 (1971): 5–21.
Barclay, John M. G. *Jews in the Mediterranean Diaspora: From Alexander to Trajan (323 BCE–117 CE)*. Edinburgh: T. & T. Clark, 1996.
Barclay, John M. G. *Paul and the Gift*. Grand Rapids: Eerdmans, 2015.
Barish, Jonas. *The Antitheatrical Prejudice*. Berkeley: University of California Press, 1981.

Barr, James. *History and Ideology in the Old Testament: Biblical Studies at the End of the Millennium. The Hensley Henson Lectures for 1997 Delivered to the University of Oxford*. Oxford: Oxford University Press, 2000.

Barrett, Rob. *Disloyalty and Destruction: Religion and Politics in Deuteronomy and the Modern World*. LHBOTS 511. London: T&T Clark, 2009.

Barstad, Hans M. *The Babylonian Captivity of the Book of Isaiah: "Exilic" Judah and the Provenance of Isaiah 40–55*. Oslo: Novus, 1997.

Barstad, Hans M. *The Myth of the Empty Land: A Study in the History and Archaeology of Judah during the 'Exilic' Period*. SO 28. Oslo: Scandinavian University Press, 1996.

Barth, Fredrik, ed. *Ethnic Groups and Boundaries: The Social Organization of Culture Difference*. Oslo: Scandinavian University Press, 1969. Repr., Long Grove: Waveland, 1998.

Barthes, Roland. *S/Z: An Essay*. Translated by Richard Miller. New York: Hill & Wang, 1974.

Barton, George A. *A Critical and Exegetical Commentary on the Book of Ecclesiastes*. ICC. Edinburgh: T. & T. Clark, 1908.

Barton, John. "Historical-Critical Approaches." In *The Cambridge Companion to Biblical Interpretation*, edited by John Barton, 9–20. Cambridge: Cambridge University Press, 1998.

Barton, John. *The Nature of Biblical Criticism*. Louisville: Westminster John Knox, 2007.

Barton, John. "Strategies for Reading Scripture." In *The HarperCollins Study Bible*, edited by Harold W. Attridge and Wayne A. Meeks, xxxix–xliii. Rev. ed. San Francisco: HarperCollins, 2006.

Barton, John. "What Is a Book? Modern Exegesis and the Literary Conventions of Ancient Israel." In *Intertextuality in Ugarit and Israel: Papers Read at the Tenth Joint Meeting of the Society for Old Testament Study and Het Oudtestamentisch Werkgezelschap in Nederland en België, Held at Oxford, 1997*, edited by Johannes C. de Moor, 1–14. OtSt 40. Leiden: Brill, 1998.

Batovici, Dan, and Kristin De Troyer, eds. *Authoritative Texts and Reception History: Aspects and Approaches*. BibInt 151. Leiden: Brill, 2017.

Baumgarten, A. I. "The Pharisaic Paradosis." *HTR* 80 (1987): 63–77.

Beauvoir, Simone de. *The Second Sex*. Translated by Constance Borde and Sheila Malovany-Chevallier. 1949. Repr. New York: Random House, 2009.

Bechtel, Lyn M. "What If Dinah Is Not Raped? (Genesis 34)." *JSOT* 62 (1994): 19–36.

Becking, Bob. "'We All Returned as One!' Critical Notes on the Myth of the Mass Return." In *Judah and the Judeans in the Persian Period*, edited by Oded Lipschits and Manfred Oeming, 3–18. Winona Lake: Eisenbrauns, 2006.

Ben Zvi, Ehud and Diana V. Edelman, eds. *Imagining the Other and Constructing Israelite Identity in the Early Second Temple Period*. LHBOTS 456. London: Bloomsbury, 2014.

Bennington, Geoffrey. "Derrida's 'Eighteenth Century.'" *Eighteenth-Century Studies* 40 (2007): 381–93.

Bennington, Geoffrey. "Saussure and Derrida." In *The Cambridge Companion to Saussure*, edited by Carol Sanders, 186–204. Cambridge: Cambridge University Press, 2005.

Bennington, Geoffrey, and Jacques Derrida. *Jacques Derrida*. Translated by Geoffrey Bennington. Chicago: University of Chicago Press, 1993.

Bentley, Jerry. "Biblical Philology and Christian Humanism: Lorenzo Valla and Erasmus as Scholars of the Gospels." *The Sixteenth Century Journal* 8, no. 2 (1977): 8–28.

Berges, Ulrich. *Jesaja 40–48*. HThKAT. Freiburg i.B.: Herder, 2008.

Berlejung, Angelika. *Die Theologie der Bilder: Herstellung und Einweihung von Kultbildern in Mesopotamien und die alttestamentliche Bilderpolemik*. OBO 162. Fribourg: Universitätserlag; Göttingen: Vandenhoeck & Ruprecht, 1998.

Berner, Christoph. "Das Wasserwunder von Rephidim (Ex 17,1–7) als Schlüsseltext eines nachpriesterschriftlichen Mosebildes." *VT* 63 (2013): 193–209.

Bernstein, Moshe. "'Rewritten Bible': A Generic Category Which Has Outlived Its Usefulness?" *Textus* 22 (2005): 169–96.

Berthelot, Katell. "The Paradoxical Similarities between the Jews and the Roman Other." In *Perceiving the Other in Ancient Judaism and Early Christianity*, edited by Michal Bar-Asher Siegal, Wolfgang Grünstäudl and Matthew Thiessen, 95–109. WUNT 394. Tübingen: Mohr Siebeck, 2017.

Berthelot, Katell. "Philon d'Alexandrie, lecteur d'Homère: quelques éléments de réflexion." In *Prolongements et renouvellements de la tradition classique*, edited by Anne Balansard, Gilles Dorival, and Mireille Loubet, 145–57. Aix-en-Provence: Publications de l'Université Provence, 2011.

Betz, Hans Dieter. *Galatians: A Commentary on Paul's Letter to the Churches in Galatia*. Hermeneia. Philadelphia: Fortress, 1979.

Bhabha, Homi K. *The Location of Culture*. 2md ed. London: Routledge, 2004.

Blank, David. "Reading Between the Lies: Plutarch and Chrysippus on the Uses of Poetry." *Oxford Studies in Ancient Philosophy* 40 (2011): 237–64.

Blenkinsopp, Joseph. *Isaiah 40–55. A New Translation with Introduction and Commentary*. AB 19A. New York: Doubleday, 2002.

Bloom, Harold. *The Anxiety of Influence*. New York: Oxford University Press, 1973.

Bloom, Harold. *The Breaking of the Vessels*. Chicago: University of Chicago Press, 1982.

Blot, Richard K., ed. *Language and Social Identity*. Westport: Praeger, 2003.

Blum, Erhard. "Noch einmal: Jakobs Traum in Bethel – Genesis 28,10-22." In *Rethinking the Foundations: Historiography in the Ancient World and in the Bible, Essays in Honour of John Van Seters*, edited by. S. McKenzie and T. Römer, 33–54. BZAW 294. Berlin: de Gruyter, 2000.

Boccaccini, Gabrielle, and Carlos A. Segovia, eds. *Paul the Jew: Rereading the Apostle as a Figure of Second Temple Judaism*. Minneapolis: Fortress, 2016.

Boda, Mark J., and Paul L. Redditt, eds. *Unity and Disunity in Ezra–Nehemiah: Redaction, Rhetoric, and Reader*. HBM 17. Sheffield: Sheffield Phoenix, 2008.

Boer, Roland. "Louis Althusser: The Difficult Birth of Israel in Genesis." In *Marxist Criticism of the Hebrew Bible*, 23–46. London: Bloomsbury T&T Clark, 2015.

Boer, Roland. *Marxist Criticism of the Hebrew Bible*. London: Bloomsbury T&T Clark, 2015.

Boer, Roland. *The Sacred Economy of Ancient Israel*. Library of Ancient Israel. Louisville: Westminster John Knox, 2015.

Boer, Roland, and Jorunn Økland, eds. *Marxist Feminist Criticism of the Bible*. The Bible in the Modern World 14. Sheffield: Sheffield Phoenix, 2008.

Bohlinger, Tavis A. "The Akedah in Pseudo-Philo: A Paradigm of Divine–Human Reciprocity." *JSP* 25 (2016): 189–227.

Bolin, Thomas. *Ecclesiastes and the Riddle of Authorship*. New York: Routledge, 2017.

Bond, Edward L. "England's Soteriology of Empire and the Roots of Colonial Identity in Early Virginia." *Anglican and Episcopal History* 66 (1997): 471–99.

Bonnard, Pierre-Émile. *Le second Isaïe, son disciple et leurs éditeurs*. Paris: Gabalda, 1972.

Booth, Wayne [C.] "Introduction." In *Problems of Dostoevsky's Poetics*, by Mikhail M. Bakhtin, xiii–xxvii. Translated by Caryl Emerson. Theory and History of Literature 8. Minneapolis: University of Minnesota Press, 1984.

Booth, Wayne C. *The Rhetoric of Fiction*. 2nd ed. Chicago: University of Chicago Press, 1983.

Bornkamm, Heinrich. *Luther and the Old Testament*. Translated by Eric W. and Ruth C. Gritsch. Mifflintown, PA: Sigler, 1997.

Bourgel, Jonathan. "The Destruction of the Samaritan Temple by John Hyrcanus: A Reconsideration." *JBL* 135 (2016): 505–23.

Bowersock, Glen W. *Greek Sophists in the Roman Empire*. Oxford: Clarendon, 1969.

Bowley, James E., and John C. Reeves. "Rethinking the Concept of 'Bible': Some Theses and Proposals." *Henoch* 25 (2003): 3–18.

Boyarin, Daniel. *Intertextuality and the Reading of Midrash*. Indiana Studies in Biblical Literature. Bloomington: Indiana University Press, 1990.

Boyarin, Daniel. *A Radical Jew: Paul and the Politics of Identity*. Contraversions 1. Berkeley: University of California Press, 1994.

Brah, Avtar. "Diaspora, Border and Transnational Identities." In *Feminist Postcolonial Theory: A Reader*, edited by Reina Lewis and Sara Mills, 613–34. New York: Routledge, 2003.

Brawley, Robert [L.] "Evocative Allusions in Matthew: Matthew 5:5 as a Test Case." In *Literary Encounters with the Reign of God*, edited by Sharon Ringe and H. C. Paul Kim, 127–48. New York: T&T Clark, 2004.

Brawley, Robert L. *Text to Text Pours Forth Speech: Voices of Scripture in Luke–Acts*. Indiana Studies in Biblical Literature. Bloomington: Indiana University Press, 1995.

Breed, Brennan W. *Nomadic Text: A Theory of Biblical Reception History*. Bloomington: Indiana University Press, 2014.

Breed, Brennan W. "Nomadology of the Bible: A Processual Approach to Biblical Reception History." *Biblical Reception* 1 (2012): 299–322.

Breed, Brennan [W.] "What Can a Text Do? Reception History as an Ethology of the Biblical Text." In *Reception History and Biblical Studies: Theory and Practice*, edited by Emma England and William John Lyons, 95–106. LHBOTS 615 / Scriptural Traces 6. London: Bloomsbury T&T Clark, 2015.

Brett, Mark G., ed. *Ethnicity and the Bible*. BibInt 19. Leiden: Brill, 1996.

Brock, Sebastian P. "To Revise or Not to Revise: Attitudes to Jewish Biblical Translation." In *Septuagint, Scrolls and Cognate Writings*, edited by George J. Brooke and Barnabas Lindars, 301–38. SCS 33l. Atlanta: Scholars Press, 1992.

Brown, Ken. *The Dynamic Development of the Bible: Revision and Reception*. Forthcoming.

Brown, Ken. "Temple Christology in the Gospel of John: Replacement Theology and Jesus as the Self-Revelation of God." MA Thesis, Trinity Western University, 2010. https://www.academia.edu/8870006/.

Brueggemann, Walter. "Westermann, Claus." In *Dictionary of Biblical Interpretation*, edited by John H. Hayes, 633–4. 2 vols. Nashville: Abingdon, 1999.

Budd, Philip J. *Numbers*. WBC 5. Waco: Word, 1984.

Buren, Paul van. "On Reading Someone Else's Mail: The Church and Israel's Scriptures." In *Die Hebräische Bibel und ihre zweifache Nachgeschichte: Festschrift für Rolf Rendtorff zum 65. Geburtstag*, edited by Erhard Blum, Christian Macholz, and Ekkehard Stegemann, 595–606. Neukirchen-Vluyn: Neukirchener, 1990.

Burnside, Jonathan P. "Why Was Moses Banned from the Promised Land? A Radical Retelling of the Rebellions of Moses (Num 20:2-13 and Exod 2:11-15)." *ZABR* 22 (2016): 111–59.

Byrskog, Samuel, Raimo Hakola, and Jutta Maria Jokiranta, eds. *Social Memory and Social Identity in the Study of Early Judaism and Early Christianity*. NTOA/SUNT 116. Göttingen: Vandenhoeck & Ruprecht, 2016.

Calvino, Italo. *The Literature Machine: Essays*. Translated by Patrick Creagh. Repr., London: Vintage, 1997.

Campbell, Antony F. *1 Samuel*. FOTL 7. Grand Rapids: Eerdmans, 2003.

Canny, Nicholas, and Anthony Pagden, eds. *Colonial Identity in the Atlantic World, 1500–1800*. Princeton: Princeton University Press, 1989.

Carasik, Michael, ed. *The Commentators' Bible: The JPS Miqra'ot Gedolot, Numbers* במדבר. Philadelphia: Jewish Publication Society, 2011.

Carr, David. *Reading the Fractures of Genesis: Historical and Literary Approaches*. Louisville: Westminster John Knox, 1996.

Carson, D. A., Peter T. O'Brian and Mark A. Seifrid, eds. *Justification and Variegated Nomism*. 2 vols. WUNT 140, 181. Tübingen: Mohr Siebeck, 2001, 2004.

Cave, Alfred A. "Canaanites in a Promised Land: The American Indian and the Providential Theory of Empire." *American Indian Quarterly* 12 (1988): 277–97.

Chazon, Esther G. "'Gather the Dispersed of Judah': Seeking a Return to the Land as a Factor in Jewish Identity of Late Antiquity." In *Heavenly Tablets: Interpretation, Identity and Tradition in Ancient Judaism*, edited by Lynn LiDonnici and Andrea Lieber, 159–73. JSJSup 119. Leiden: Brill, 2007.

Cheon, Samuel. *The Exodus Story in the Wisdom of Solomon: A Study in Biblical Interpretation*. JSPSup 23. Sheffield: Sheffield Academic, 1997.

Christianson, Eric S. *Ecclesiastes through the Centuries*. BBC. Malden: Wiley-Blackwell, 2007.

Coetzee, John. "What Is a Classic? A Lecture." In *Stranger Shores: Essays, 1986–1999*, 1–19. London: Vintage, 1992.

Cohen, Anthony P. *The Symbolic Construction of Community*. London: Routledge, 1985.

Cohen, Gerson D. "Esau as Symbol in Early Medieval Thought." In *Studies in the Variety of Rabbinic Cultures*, 243–69. Philadelphia: The Jewish Publication Society, 1991.

Collins, C. John [Jack]. "Galatians 3:16: What Kind of Exegete Was Paul?" *TynBul* 54 (2003): 75–86.

Collins, C. John (Jack). "A Syntactical Note (Genesis 3:15): Is the Woman's Seed Singular or Plural." *TynBul* 48 (1997): 139–48.

Collins, John J. "Is a Critical Biblical Theology Possible?" In *The Hebrew Bible and Its Interpreters*, edited by Douglas A. Knight and Gene M. Tucker, 1–17. Atlanta: Scholars Press, 1990.

Collins, John J. *A Short Introduction to the Hebrew Bible*. Augsburg: Fortress, 2007.

Connolly, Joy. "Like the Labors of Heracles: Andreia and Paideia in Greek Culture Under Rome." In *Andreia: Studies in Manliness and Courage in Classical Antiquity*, edited by Ralph M. Rosen and Ineke Sluiter, 287–318. Mnemosyne: Bibliotheca Classica Batava. Leiden: Brill, 2003.

Constable, Giles. "Cluny and the First Crusade." In *The Abbey of Cluny: A Collection of Essays to Mark the Eleventh-Hundredth Anniversary of Its Foundation*, 197–211. Vita regularis 43. Berlin: LIT Verlag, 2010. Orig, published in 1997.

Cox, Claude. "Does a Shorter Hebrew Parent Text Underlie Old Greek Job?" In *In the Footsteps of Sherlock Holmes: Studies in the Biblical Text in Honour of Anneli Aejmelaeus*, edited by Kristin de Troyer, T. Michael Law, and Marketta Kiljeström, 451–62. CBET 72. Leuven: Peeters, 2014.

Cranfield, C. E. B. *A Critical and Exegetical Commentary on the Epistle to the Romans*. Edinburgh: T. & T. Clark, 1975.

Crashaw, William. *A Sermon Preached in London before the Right Honourable the Lord Lawarre, Lord Governour and Captaine Generall of Virginea, and Others of His Maiesties Counsell for that Kingdom, and the Rest of the Adventurers in that Plantation*. London: W. Welby, 1610.

Crenshaw, James L. "Qoheleth in Current Research." *HAR* 7 (1984): 41–56.

Crenshaw, James L. *Qoheleth: The Ironic Wink*. Studies on Personalities of the Old Testament. Columbia: University of South Carolina Press, 2013.

Croatto, J. Severino. *Isaías: La palabra profética y su relectura hermenéutica, Volume 2: 40–55: La liberación es posible*. Colección Comentario bíblico. Buenos Aires: Editorial Lumen, 1994.

Crouzel, Henry. *Origen*. Translated by A. S. Worrall. San Francisco: Harper & Row, 1989. French orig. 1985.

Culler, Jonathan. *Structuralist Poetics: Structuralism, Linguistics and the Study of Literature*. Ithaca: Cornell University Press, 1975.

Cyrino, Monica Silveira. "Heroes in D(u)ress: Transvestism and Power in the Myths of Herakles and Achilles." *Arethusa* 31 (1998): 207–41.

Damrosch, David. *What Is World Literature?* Princeton: Princeton University Press, 2003.

Datema, Cornelis, and Pauline Allen, eds. *Leontii Presbyteri Constantinopolitan Homiliae*. CCSG 17. Turnhout: Brepols; Leuven: Leuven University Press, 1987.

Davies, Philip R. *Whose Bible Is It Anyway?* JSOTSup 204. Sheffield: Sheffield Academic, 1995.

Day, John, ed. *Temple and Worship in Biblical Israel*. LHBOTS 422. London: T&T Clark, 2005.

De Lacy, Phillip. "Stoic Views of Poetry." *AJP* 69 (1948): 241–71.

Deichmann, Friedrich W., ed. *Repertorium der christlich-antiken Sarkophage, I. Rom und Ostia*. Wiesbaden: Franz Steiner, 1967.

DeLanda, Manuel. *Intensive Science and Virtual Philosophy*. New York: Continuum, 2002.

Deleuze, Gilles. *Difference and Repetition*. Translated by Paul Patton. New York: Columbia University Press, 1995.

Deleuze, Gilles. *The Logic of Sense*. Edited by Constantin Boundas. Translated by Mark Lester and Charles Stivale. New York: Columbia University Press, 1990.

Deleuze, Gilles, and Félix Guattari. *A Thousand Plateaus: Capitalism and Schizophrenia*. Translated by Brian Massumi. Minneapolis: University of Minnesota Press, 1987.

Dell, Katharine, and Will Kynes, eds. *Reading Job Intertextually*. LHBOTS 574. New York: Bloomsbury, 2013.

Derrida, Jacques. *Limited Inc*. Edited by Gerald Graff. Translated by Samuel Weber and Jeffrey Mehlman. Evanston: Northwestern University Press, 1988.

Derrida, Jacques. *Of Grammatology*. Translated by Gayatri C. Spivak. Corrected ed. Baltimore: Johns Hopkins University Press, 1998.

Di Mattei, Steven. "Paul's Allegory of the Two Covenants (Gal 4.21–31) in Light of First-Century Hellenistic Rhetoric and Jewish Hermeneutics." *NTS* 52 (2006): 102–22.

Dick, Michael B. "Prophetic Parodies of Making the Cult Image." In *Born in Heaven, Made on Earth: The Making of the Cult Image in the Ancient Near East*, edited by Michael B. Dick, 1–53. Winona Lake: Eisenbrauns, 1999.

Dillmann, August. *Die Genesis*. Leipzig: S. Hirzel, 1882.

Dillmann, August. *Genesis: Critically and Exegetically Expounded*. Translated by William B. Stevenson. 2 vols. Edinburgh: T. & T. Clark, 1897.

Dobbs-Allsopp, F. W. "Rethinking Historical Criticism." *BibInt* 7 (1999): 235–71.

Donaldson, Laura E. *Decolonising Feminisms: Race, Gender, and Empire Building*. Chapel Hill: University of North Carolina Press, 1992.

Donaldson, Terence L. *Paul and the Gentiles: Remapping the Apostle's Convictional World*. Minneapolis: Fortress, 1997.

Dorival, Gilles. "Origen." In *The New Cambridge History of the Bible, Volume 1: From the Beginnings to 600*, edited by James Carleton Paget and Joachim Schaper, 605–28. Cambridge: Cambridge University Press, 2013.

Dozeman, Thomas B., and Konrad Schmid, eds. *Farewell to the Yahwist? The Composition of the Pentateuch in Recent European Interpretation*. SymS 34. Atlanta: Society of Biblical Literature, 2006.

Dresken-Weiland, Jutta, ed. *Repertorium der christlich-antiken Sarkophage, II. Italien mit einem Nachtrag, Rom und Ostia, Dalmatien, Museen der Welt*. Mainz: Philipp von Zabern, 1998.

Dube, Musa W. "The Bible in the Bush: The First 'Literate' Batswana Bible Readers." *Translation* 2 (2013): 79–103.

Dube, Musa W. "Boundaries and Bridges: Journeys of a Postcolonial Feminist Biblical Scholar." *Journal of the European Society of Women in Theological Research* 22 (2014): 139–56.

Dube, Musa W. "Consuming a Colonial Cultural Bomb: Translating *Badimo* into 'Demons' in Setswana Bible." *JSNT* 73 (1999): 33–59.

Dube, Musa W. "Curriculum Transformation: Dreaming of Decolonization in Theological Education." In *Border Crossings: Cross-Cultural Hermeneutics*, edited by P. N. Premnath, 121–38. Maryknoll, NY: Orbis, 2007.

Dube, Musa W. "Decolonizing the Darkness." In *Soundings in Cultural Criticism: Perspectives and Methods in Culture, Power and Identity in New Testament*, edited by Francisco Lozada Jr. and Greg Carey, 31–44. Minneapolis: Fortress, 2013.

Dube, Musa W. "An Introduction: How We Come to 'Read With'." *Semeia* 73 (1996): 7–17.

Dube, Musa W. *Postcolonial Feminist Interpretation of the Bible*. St. Louis: Chalice, 2000.

Dube, Musa W. "Readings of *Semoya*: Batswana Women Interpretations of Matt 15:21-28." *Semeia* 73 (1996): 111–29.

Dube, Musa W. "The Scramble for Africa as the Biblical Scramble for Africa: Postcolonial Perspectives." In *Postcolonial Perspectives in African Biblical Interpretations*, edited by Musa W. Dube, Andrew Mbuvi, and Dora Mbuwayesango, 1–29. Global Perspectives on Biblical Scholarship 13. Atlanta: SBL, 2012.

Dube, Musa W. "Towards a Postcolonial Feminist Interpretation of the Bible." *Semeia* 78 (1997): 11–26.

Dube, Musa W., Andrew M. Mbuvi, and Dora R. Mbuwayesango, eds. *Postcolonial Perspectives in African Biblical Interpretations*. GPBS 13. Atlanta: Society of Biblical Literature, 2012.

Duhm, Bernhard. *Das Buch Jesaja*. 5th ed. Göttingen: Vandenhoeck & Ruprecht, 1968.

Dunn, James D. G. *The New Perspective on Paul*. 2nd ed. Grand Rapids: Eerdmans, 2008.

Dunn, James D. G. *Romans 1–8*. WBC 38A. Dallas: Word, 1988.
Eco, Umberto. *Interpretation and Overinterpretation*. Edited by S. Collini. Cambridge: Cambridge University Press, 1992.
Edwards, Catharine. *The Politics of Immorality in Ancient Rome*. Cambridge: Cambridge University Press, 1993.
Eggers, Kurt. *Das Spiel von Job dem Deutschen: Ein Mysterium*. Berlin: Volskschaft-Verlag, 1933.
Eliot, T. S. *What Is a Classic? An Address Delivered Before the Virgil Society on the 16th of October 1944*. London: Faber & Faber, 1945.
Elliger, Karl. *Deuterojesaja. Teilbd. 1. Jesaja 40,1–45,7*. BK. Neukirchen-Vluyn: Neukirchener Verlag, 1978.
Ellis, E. Earle. *Paul's Use of the Old Testament*. Grand Rapids: Eerdmans, 1957.
England, Emma, and William John Lyons, eds. *Reception History and Biblical Studies: Theory and Practice*. LHBOTS 615 / Scriptural Traces 6. London: Bloomsbury T&T Clark, 2015.
Enns, Peter E. "The 'Moveable Well' in 1 Cor 10:4: An Extrabiblical Tradition in an Apostolic Text." *BBR* 6 (1996): 23–38.
Epstein, Marc M. *Dreams of Subversion in Medieval Art and Literature*. University Park, PA: Pennsylvania State University Press, 1997.
Erdmann, Carl. *The Origin of the Idea of Crusade*. Translated by Marshall W. Baldwin and Walter Goffart. Princeton: Princeton University Press, 1977. German orig. 1935.
Esler, Philip F. *Conflict and Identity in Romans: The Social Setting of Paul's Letter*. Minneapolis: Fortress, 2003.
Fabian, Johannes. *Time and the Other: How Anthropology Makes Its Object*. New York: Columbia University Press, 1983. Repr. 2014.
Fanon, Frantz. *The Wretched of the Earth*. Translated by Constance Farrington. London: Paladin, 1963.
Fausz, J. Frederick. "An 'Abundance of Blood Shed on Both Sides': England's First Indian War, 1609–1614." *Virginia Magazine of History and Biography* 98 (1990): 3–56.
Feder, Yitzhaq. "The Defilement of Dina: Uncontrolled Passions, Textual Violence, and the Search for Moral Foundations." *BibInt* 24 (2016): 281–309.
Fee, Gordon D. *The First Epistle to the Corinthians*. NICNT. Grand Rapids: Eerdmans, 1987.
Fee, Gordon D. "Who are Abraham's True Children? The Role of Abraham in Pauline Argumentation." In *Perspectives on Our Father Abraham: Essays in Honor of Marvin R. Wilson*, edited by Steven A. Hunt, 126–37. Grand Rapids: Eerdmans, 2010.
Feldman, Louis H. "Philo, Pseudo-Philo, Josephus, and Theodotus on the Rape of Dinah." *JQR* 94 (2004): 253–77.
Fishbane, Michael. *Biblical Interpretation in Ancient Israel*. New York: Oxford University Press, 1985.
Fishbane, Michael. *The Exegetical Imagination: On Jewish Thought and Theology*. Cambridge, MA: Harvard University Press, 1998.
Fisk, Bruce N. *Do You Not Remember? Scripture, Story and Exegesis in the Rewritten Bible of Pseudo-Philo*. JSPSup 37. Sheffield: Sheffield Academic, 2001.
Fitzmyer, Joseph A. *First Corinthians: A New Translation with Introduction and Commentary*. AB 32. New Haven: Yale University Press, 2008.
Fitzmyer, Joseph A. *Romans: A New Translation with Introduction and Commentary*. AB 33. New York: Doubleday, 1993.

Fokkelman, J. P. *Narrative Art and Poetry in the Books of Samuel, Volume 3: Throne and City (II Sam. 2–8 & 21–24)*. SSN 27. Assen/Maastricht: Van Gorcum, 1990.

Foster, Robert B. *Renaming Abraham's Children: Election, Ethnicity, and the Interpretation of Scripture in Romans 9*. WUNT 2/421. Tübingen: Mohr Siebeck, 2016.

Fox, Michael V. "Frame-Narrative and Composition in the Book of Qohelet." *HUCA* 48 (1977): 83–106.

Fox, Michael V. "Job 38 and God's Rhetoric." *Semeia* 19 (1981): 53–61.

Fox, Michael V. *Qohelet and His Contradictions*. JSOTSup 71. Sheffield: Almond, 1989.

Freedman, David Noel, and David Miano. "People of the New Covenant." In *The Concept of the Covenant in the Second Temple Period*, edited by Stanley E. Porter and Jacqueline C. R. De Roo, 7–26. JSJSup 71. Leiden: Brill, 2003.

Frey, Jörg, Ursula Schattner-Rieser, and Konrad Schmid, eds. *Die Samaritaner und die Bibel: Historische und literarische Wechselwirkungen zwischen biblischen und samaritanischen Traditionen / The Samaritans and the Bible: Historical and Literary Interactions between Biblical and Samaritan Traditions*. SJ 70 / StSam 7. Berlin: de Gruyter, 2012.

Fried, Lisbeth S. *Ezra: A Commentary*. A Critical Commentary. Sheffield: Sheffield Phoenix, 2015.

Friedheim, Emmanuel. "Quelques notes sur la signification historique du silence philonien à propos de la Bibliothèque d'Alexandrie." In *The Library of Alexandria: A Cultural Crossroads of the Ancient World*, edited by Christophe Rico and Anca Dan, 245–55. Proceedings of the Second Polis Institute Interdisciplinary Conference. Jerusalem: Polis Institute, 2017.

Friesen, Courtney J. P. "Dying Like a Woman: Euripides' Polyxena as Exemplum between Philo and Clement of Alexandria." *GRBS* 56 (2016): 623–45.

Friesen, Courtney J. P. "Gluttony and Drunkenness as Jewish and Christian Virtues: From the Comic Heracles to Christ in the Gospels." In *Envisioning God in the Humanities: Essays on Christianity, Judaism, and Ancient Religion in Honor of Melissa Harl Sellew*, edited by Courtney J. P. Friesen, 243–61. Westar Seminar on God and the Human Future. Eugene: Wipf & Stock, 2018.

Frymer-Kensky, Tikva. *In the Wake of the Goddesses: Women, Culture, and the Biblical Transformation of Pagan Myth*. New York: Ballantine, 1992.

Gadamer, Hans-Georg. *Truth and Method*. 2nd ed. Translated by Joel Weinsheimer and Donald G. Marshall. New York: Crossroad, 1990.

Galbraith, Deane. "Interpellation, Not Interpolation: Reconsidering Textual Disunity in Numbers 13–14 as Variant Articulations of a Single Ideology." *The Bible & Critical Theory* 10 (2014): 29–48.

Galinsky, G. Karl. *The Herakles Theme: The Adaptations of the Hero in Literature from Homer to the Twentieth Century*. Oxford: Blackwell, 1972.

Gambetti, Sandra. *The Alexandrian Riots of 38 CE and the Persecution of the Jews: A Historical Reconstruction*. JSJSup 135. Leiden: Brill, 2009.

García Martínez, Florentino. "The Heavenly Tablets in the *Book of Jubilees*." In *Between Philology and Theology: Contributions to the Study of Ancient Jewish Interpretation*, by Florentino García Martínez, edited by Hindy Najman and Eibert Tigchelaar, 51–69. Leiden: Brill, 2013.

García Martínez, Florentino, and Eibert J. C. Tigchelaar, eds. *The Dead Sea Scrolls Study Edition*. Leiden: Brill, 1999.

Gard, Donald H. "The Concept of Job's Character According to the Greek Translator of the Hebrew Text." *JBL* 72 (1953): 182–6.

Gard, Donald H. *The Exegetical Method of the Greek Translator of the Book of Job*. JBLMS 8. Philadelphia: Society of Biblical Literature, 1952.

Garland, Robert. *Surviving Greek Tragedy*. London: Bloomsbury, 2004.

Garnsey, Peter, and Richard Saller. *The Roman Empire: Economy, Society and Culture*. Berkeley: University of California Press, 1987.

Garton, Roy E. *Mirages in the Desert: The Tradition-Historical Developments of the Story of Massah-Meribah*. BZAW 492. Berlin: de Gruyter, 2017.

Gaston, Lloyd. *Paul and the Torah*. Vancouver: University of British Columbia Press, 1987.

Geertz, Clifford. *The Interpretation of Cultures*. New York: Basic, 1973.

Gehman, Henry S. "The Theological Approach of the Greek Translator of Job 1–15." *JBL* 68 (1949): 231–40.

Gerleman, Gillis. *Studies in the Septuagint, I: The Book of Job*. LUÅ 43/2. Lund: Gleerup, 1946.

Ginzberg, Louis. *The Legends of the Jews*. Translated by Henrietta Szold, Paul Radin, and Boaz Cohen. Philadelphia: Jewish Publication Society of America, 1909–1938.

Glicksman, Andrew T. *Wisdom of Solomon 10: A Jewish-Hellenistic Reinterpretation of Early Israelite History through Sapiential Lenses*. DCLS 9. Berlin: de Gruyter, 2011.

Goff, Barbara, ed. *Classics and Colonialism*. London: Duckworth, 2005.

Gohrisch, Jana, and Ellen Grünkemeier, eds. *Postcolonial Studies Across the Disciplines*. Cross/Cultures 170. Amsterdam: Rodopi, 2013.

Grabbe, Lester L. *Ezra–Nehemiah*. OTR. London: Routledge, 1998.

Grabbe, Lester L. *A History of the Jews and Judaism in the Second Temple Period*. 2 vols. LSTS 47, 68. London: T&T Clark, 2004, 2008.

Grabbe, Lester L. *An Introduction to Second Temple Judaism: History and Religion of the Jews in the Time of Nehemiah, the Maccabees, Hillel and Jesus*. London: T&T Clark, 2010.

Grabbe, Lester L., ed. *Leading Captivity Captive: "The Exile" as History and Ideology*. JSOTSup 278. Sheffield: Sheffield Academic, 1998.

Graf, Fritz. "Comedies and Comic Actors in the Greek East: An Epigraphical Perspective." In *Athenian Comedy in the Roman Empire*, edited by C. W. Marshall and Tom Hawkins, 117–29. London: Bloomsbury, 2015.

Gray, Alison. "Reception of the Old Testament." In *The Hebrew Bible: A Critical Companion*, edited by John Barton, 405–30. Princeton: Princeton University Press, 2016.

Gray, Patrick. "Points and Lines: Thematic Parallelism in the Letter of James and the *Testament of Job*." *NTS* 50 (2004): 406–24.

Gray, Robert. *A Good Speed to Virginia*. London: W. Welbie, 1609.

Green, Arthur. "Shekhinah, the Virgin Mary, and the Song of Songs: Reflections on a Kabbalistic Symbol in Its Historical Context." *AJSR* 26 (2002): 1–52.

Greenwood, Kyle. "Debating Wisdom: The Role of Voice in Ecclesiastes." *CBQ* 74 (2012): 476–91.

Gregory of Nyssa. *Homilies on Ecclesiastes*. Translated by Stuart George Hall. Berlin: de Gruyter, 1993.

Grillo, Jennie. "Qohelet and the Marks of Modernity: Reading Ecclesiastes with Matthew Arnold and Charles Taylor." *Religions* 7 (2016): 1–9.

[Grillo] Barbour, Jennie. *The Story of Israel in the Book of Qohelet: Ecclesiastes as Cultural Memory*. Oxford: Oxford University Press, 2012.

Grondin, Jean. "The Hermeneutical Circle." In *The Blackwell Companion to Hermeneutics*, edited by Niall Keane and Chris Lawn, 299–305. Malden: John Wiley & Sons, 2015.

Gruen, Erich S. "Jewish Literature and the Second Sophistic." In *The Oxford Handbook to the Second Sophistic*, edited by Daniel S. Richter and William A. Johnson, 639–54. Oxford: Oxford University Press, 2017.

Guardiola-Sáenz, Leticia A. "Border-Crossing and Its Redemptive Power in John 7:53–8:11: A Cultural Reading of Jesus and the Accused." In *John and Postcolonialism: Travel Space and Power*, edited by Musa W. Dube and John Staley, 129–52. Sheffield: Sheffield Academic, 2002.

Guardiola-Sáenz, Leticia A. "Borderless Women and Borderless Texts: A Cultural Reading of Matthew 15:21-28." *Semeia 78* (1997): 69–81.

Gumperz, John J., ed. *Language and Social Identity*. Studies in Interactional Sociolinguistics 2. Cambridge: Cambridge University Press, 1982.

Gunkel, Hermann. *Genesis*. Translated by Mark E. Biddle. Macon: Mercer University Press, 1997.

Hagedorn, Dieter, Ursula Hagedorn, and Ludwig Koenen, eds. and trans. *Kommentar zu Hiob, III (Tura-Papyrus)*. Papyrologische Texte und Abhandlungen 3. Bonn: Habelt, 1968.

Hagedorn, Dieter, Ursula Hagedorn, and Ludwig Koenen, eds. and trans. *Kommentar zu Hiob, IV (Tura-Papyrus)*. Papyrologische Texte und Abhandlungen 33/1. Bonn: Habelt, 1985.

Hagedorn, Ursula, and Dieter Hagedorn, eds. *Die älteren griechischen Katenen zum Buch Hiob*. 3 vols. PTS 40, 48, 53. Berlin: de Gruyter, 1994, 1997, 2000.

Hagedorn, Ursula, and Dieter Hagedorn, eds. and trans. *Johannes Chrysostomos Kommentar zu Hiob*. PTS 35. Berlin: de Gruyter, 1990.

Hall, Stuart. "Cultural Identity and Diaspora." In *Identity: Community, Culture, Difference*, edited by Jonathan Rutherford, 222–37. London: Lawrence & Wishart, 1990.

Halliwell, Stephen. "Plato's Repudiation of the Tragic." In *Tragedy and the Tragic: Greek Theatre and Beyond*, edited by M. S. Silk, 332–49. Oxford: Clarendon, 1996.

Halpern-Amaru, Betsy. *Rewriting the Bible: Land and Covenant in Post-Biblical Jewish Literature*. Valley Forge: Trinity Press International, 1994.

Hanke, Lewis. *The Spanish Struggle for Justice in the Conquest of America*. Philadelphia: University of Pennsylvania Press, 1949.

Hanson, K. C., and Douglas E. Oakman. *Palestine in the Time of Jesus: Social Structures and Social Conflicts*. 2nd ed. Minneapolis: Fortress, 2008.

Haralambakis, Maria. *The Testament of Job: Text, Narrative and Reception History*. LSTS 80. London: Bloomsbury T&T Clark, 2012.

Hardwick, Lorna, and Carol Gillespie, eds. *Classics in Post-Colonial Worlds*. Oxford: Oxford University Press, 2007.

Harlow, Daniel C. et al., eds. *The "Other" in Second Temple Judaism: Essays in Honor of John J. Collins*. Grand Rapids: Eerdmans, 2011.

Harrill, James Albert. *Paul the Apostle: His Life and Legacy in Their Roman Context*. Cambridge: Cambridge University Press, 2011.

Harrington, D. J. "Pseudo-Philo (First Century A.D.): A New Translation and Introduction." In *The Old Testament Pseudepigrapha*, edited by James H. Charlesworth, 2:297–377. 2 vols. ABRL. New York: Doubleday, 1983–1985.

Harrison, George W. M. "Positioning of Satyr Drama and Characterization in the *Cyclops*." In *Satyr Drama: Tragedy at Play*, edited by George W. M. Harrison, 237–58. Swansea: Classical Press of Wales, 2005.

Hartenstein, Friedhelm, and Konrad Schmid, eds. *Abschied von der Priesterschrift? Zum Stand der Pentateuchdebatte*. Leipzig: Evangelische Verlagsanstalt, 2013.

Hayes, Christine E. *Gentile Impurities and Jewish Identities: Intermarriage and Conversion from the Bible to the Talmud*. Oxford: Oxford University Press, 2002.

Hayes, John H. "The Usage of the Oracles against Foreign Nations in Ancient Israel." *JBL* 87 (1968): 81–92.

Hays, Richard B. *The Conversion of the Imagination: Paul as Interpreter of Israel's Scripture*. Grand Rapids: Eerdmans, 2005.

Hays, Richard B. *Echoes of Scripture in the Letters of Paul*. New Haven: Yale University Press, 1989.

Hays, Richard B. *The Faith of Jesus Christ: An Investigation of the Narrative Substructure of Galatians 3:1–4:11*. Grand Rapids: Eerdmans, 2002.

Hays, Richard B. *Reading Backwards: Figural Christology and the Fourfold Gospel Witness*. Waco: Baylor University Press, 2014.

Hearn, Maxwell K. *How to Read Chinese Paintings*. New Haven: Yale University Press, 2008.

Heater, Homer, Jr. *A Septuagint Translation Technique in the Book of Job*. CBQMS 11. Washington, DC: The Catholic University of America, 1982.

Heidegger, Martin. *Identity and Difference*. Translated by Joan Stambaugh. New York: Harper & Row, 1969.

Heidegger, Martin. *Sein und Zeit*. 7th ed. Tübingen: Max Niemeyer, 1953.

Heidegger, Martin. *Unterwegs zur Sprache*. Pfullingen: Neske, 1960.

Heim, Erin M. *Adoption in Galatians and Romans: Contemporary Metaphor Theories and the Pauline* huiothesia *Metaphors*. BibInt 153. Leiden: Brill, 2017.

Hekster, Olivier. "Propagating Power: Hercules as an Example for Second-Century Emperors." In *Herakles and Hercules: Exploring a Graeco-Roman Divinity*, edited by Louis Rawlings and Hugh Bowden, 205–21. Swansea: Classical Press of Wales, 2005.

Hendel, Ronald [S.] *The Book of Genesis: A Biography*. Lives of Great Religious Books. Princeton: Princeton University Press, 2012.

Hendel, Ronald S. "Farewell to SBL: Faith and Reason in Biblical Studies." *BAR* 36, no. 4 (2010): 28, 74.

Hendel, Ronald [S.] "Mind the Gap: Modern and Postmodern in Biblical Studies." *JBL* 133 (2014): 422–43.

Hendel, Ronald [S.] *Steps to a New Edition of the Hebrew Bible*. TCSt 10. Atlanta: SBL, 2016.

Hengel, Martin. "The Pre-Christian Paul." In *The Jews among Pagans and Christians*, edited by Judith Lieu, John North, and Tessa Rajak, 29–52. London: Routledge, 1992.

Hening, William Waller. *The Statutes at Large: Being a Collection of All the Laws of Virginia from the First Session of the Legislature, in the Year 1619*. Richmond: S. Pleasants, 1809.

Henrichs, Albert, ed. and trans. *Didymos der Blinde, Kommentar zu Hiob (Tura-Papyrus), I–II*. 2 vols. Papyrologische Texte und Abhandlungen 1, 2. Bonn: Habelt, 1968.

Hensel, Benedikt. *Juda und Samaria: Zum Verhältnis zweier nach-exilischer Jahwismen*. FAT 110. Tübingen: Mohr Siebeck, 2016.

Hilberg, Isidorus, ed. *Sancti Eusebii Hieronymi. Epistulae*. CSEL 54, 55. Vienna: Tempsky / Leipzig: Freytag, 1910.

Hill, Robert C. *St. John Chrysostom. Commentary on the Sage, I: Commentary on Job*. Brookline: Holy Cross Orthodox, 2006.

Hirsch, E. D., Jr. "Objective Interpretation." *Publications of the Modern Language Association of America* 75 (1960): 463–79.

Hodge, Caroline Johnson. *If Sons, then Heirs: A Study of Kinship and Ethnicity in the Letters of Paul*. New York: Oxford University Press, 2007.

Hofreiter, Christian. *Making Sense of Old Testament Genocide: Christian Interpretations of* Herem *Passages*. Oxford: Oxford University Press, 2018.

Holdrege, Barbara A. "Beyond the Guild: Liberating Biblical Studies." In *African Americans and the Bible: Sacred Texts and Social Textures*, edited by Vincent L. Wimbush with Rosamond C. Rodman, 138–60. New York: Continuum, 2000.

Holladay, Carl R. *Fragments from Hellenistic Jewish Authors, Volume I: Historians, Texts and Translations 20*. Chico: Scholars Press, 1983.

Hollander, John. *The Figure of Echo: A Mode of Allusion in Milton and After*. Berkeley: University of California Press, 1981.

hooks, bell. "The Oppositional Gaze: Black Female Spectators." In *Black Looks: Race and Representation*, 115–31. Boston: South End, 1992.

Horn, James. "The Conquest of Eden: Possession and Dominion in Early Virginia." In *Envisioning an English Empire: Jamestown and the Making of the North Atlantic World*, edited by Robert Appelbaum and John Wood Sweet, 25–48. Philadelphia: University of Pennsylvania Press, 2005.

Horowitz, Elliott. *Reckless Rites: Purim and the Legacy of Jewish Violence*. Jews, Christians, and Muslims from the Ancient to the Modern World. Princeton: Princeton University Press, 2006.

Hošek, Radislave. "Herakles auf der Bühne der alte attischen Komödie." In *GERAS: Studies Presented to George Thomson on the Occasion of his 60th Birthday*, edited by Ladislav Varcl and Ronald F. Willetts, 119–27. AUC Philosophica et historica 1, Graecolatina Prasgensia 2. Prague: Charles University Press, 1963.

Hübner, Hans. *Die Weisheit Salomons: Liber Sapientiae Salomonis*. ATD Apokryphen 4. Göttingen: Vandenhoeck & Ruprecht, 1999.

Hunn, Debbie. "Galatians 3:6-9: Abraham's Fatherhood and Paul's Conclusions." *CBQ* 78 (2016): 500–514.

Irudayaraj, Dominic S. "Idol-taunt and Exilic Identity: A Dalit Reading of Isaiah 44:9-20." In *Myths of Exile: History and Metaphor in the Hebrew Bible*, edited by Anne K. de Hemmer Gudme and Ingrid Hjelm, 125–36. London: Routledge, 2015.

Irudayaraj, Dominic S. *Violence, Otherness and Identity in Isaiah 63:1-6: The Trampling One Coming from Edom*. LHBOTS 633. London: Bloomsbury T&T Clark, 2017.

Iser, Wolfgang. *The Act of Reading: A Theory of Aesthetic Response*. Baltimore: Johns Hopkins University Press, 1978.

Iser, Wolfgang. *Der Akt des Lesens: Theorie ästhetischer Wirkung*. 4th ed., UTB. 1976. Repr., Munich: Fink, 1994.

Iser, Wolfgang. *The Implied Reader: Patterns of Communication in Prose Fiction from Bunyan to Beckett*. Baltimore: Johns Hopkins University Press, 2011.

Iser, Wolfgang. *Der implizite Leser: Kommunikationsformen des Romans von Bunyan bis Beckett*. Munich: Fink, 1972.

Jacobson, Howard. *A Commentary on Pseudo-Philo's Liber Antiquitatum Biblicarum, with Latin Text and English Translation*. AGJU 31. Leiden: Brill, 1996.

Jenkins, Richard. *Social Identity*. 4th ed. London: Routledge, 2014.

Jennings, Willie James. *The Christian Imagination: Theology and the Origins of Race*. New Haven: Yale University Press, 2010.

Johnson, Robert. *The New Life of Virginia*. London: F. Kyngston, 1612. Repr. in volume 8 of *Collections of the Massachusetts Historical Society*, 199–227. 2nd ed. Boston: N. Hale, 1826.

Joseph, Alison L. *Portrait of the Kings: The Davidic Prototype in Deuteronomistic Poetics*. Minneapolis: Fortress, 2015.

Joseph, Alison L. "Understanding Genesis 34:2: *'Innâ*." *VT* 66 (2016): 663–8.

Joseph, Alison L. "Who Is the Victim in the Dinah Story?" *TheTorah.com*. 30 November 2017, http://thetorah.com/who-is-the-victim-in-the-dinah-story/.

Joyce, Paul M. "'Even if Noah, Daniel, and Job were in it…' (Ezekiel 14:14): The Case of Job and Ezekiel." In *Reading Job Intertextually*, edited by Katharine Dell and Will Kynes, 118–28. LHBOTS 574. New York: Bloomsbury, 2013.

Kahneman, Daniel. *Thinking, Fast and Slow*. New York: Farrar, Straus & Giroux, 2013.

Kahneman, Daniel, and Amos Tversky. "On the Psychology of Prediction." *Psychological Review* 80 (1973): 237–51.

Kalimi, Isaac. "The Hiding of the Temple Vessels in Jewish and Samaritan Literature." In *Fighting over the Bible: Jewish Interpretation, Sectarianism and Polemic from Temple to Talmud and Beyond*, 208–16. BRLJ 54. Leiden: Brill, 2017.

Kalimi, Isaac. "Martin Luther, the Jews, and Esther: Biblical Interpretation in the Shadow of Judeophobia." *JR* 100 (2020): 42–74.

Kalimi, Isaac, ed. *New Perspectives on Ezra–Nehemiah: History and Historiography, Text, Literature, and Interpretation*. Winona Lake: Eisenbrauns, 2012.

Kalman, Jason. "Job Denied the Resurrection of Jesus? A Rabbinic Critique of the Church Fathers' Use of the Exegetical Traditions Found in the Septuagint and the Testament of Job." In *The Changing Face of Judaism, Christianity and Other Greco-Roman Religions in Antiquity*, edited by Ian H. Henderson and George S. Oegema, with Sara Parks Ricker, 371–97. Studien zu jüdischen Schriften aus hellenistisch-römischer Zeit 2. Gütersloh: Gütersloher Verlag, 2006.

Kalman, Jason. "Tannaim, Amoraim, and Targumim." In *The Many Faces of Job*, edited by C. L. Seow. Berlin: de Gruyter, forthcoming.

Kasprzyk, Dimitri, and Christophe Vendries. *Spectacles et désordre à Alexandrie: Dion de Pruse, Discours aux Alexandrins*. Histoire ancienne. Rennes: Presses Universitaires de Rennes, 2012.

Kaufmann, Thomas. *Luthers Juden*. 2nd ed. Stuttgart: Reclam, 2015.

Keel, Othmar, and Christoph Uehlinger. *Göttinnen, Götter und Gottessymbole. Neue Erkenntnisse zur Religionsgeschichte Kanaans und Israels aufgrund bislang unerschlossener ikonographischer Quellen*. 5th ed. Freiburg i.B.: Herder, 2001.

Kelle, Brad. "The Phenomenon of Israelite Prophecy in Contemporary Scholarship." *CurBR* 12 (2014): 275–320.

Kelley, Shawn. *Racializing Jesus: Race, Ideology and the Formation of Modern Biblical Scholarship*. New York: Routledge, 2002.

Kessler, John. "Persian's Loyal Yahwists: Power Identity and Ethnicity in Achaemenid Yehud." In *Judah and the Judeans in the Persian Period*, edited by Oded Lipschits and Manfred Oeming, 91–121. Winona Lake: Eisenbrauns, 2006.

Kisiel, Theodore. "The Language of the Event: The Event of Language." In volume 3 of *Martin Heidegger: Critical Assessments*, edited by Christopher Macann, 151–67. London: Routledge, 1992.

Klauck, Hans-Josef et al., eds. *Encyclopedia of the Bible and Its Reception*. Berlin: de Gruyter, 2009–.

Klawans, Jonathan. "The Essene Hypothesis: Insights from Religion 101." *DSD* 23 (2016): 51–78.

Klawans, Jonathan. "Idolatry, Incest, and Impurity: Moral Defilement in Ancient Judaism." *JSJ* 29 (1998): 391–415.

Klein, Jacob. "*Man and His God*: A Wisdom Poem or a Cultic Lament?" In *Approaches to Sumerian Literature: Studies in Honor of H. L. Vanstiphout*, edited by Piotr Michalowski and Niek Veldhuis, 123–43. CM 35. Leiden: Brill, 2006.

Klein, Jacob. "'Personal God' and Individual Prayer in Sumerian Religion." In *Vorträge gehalten auf der 28. Rencontre assyriologique Internationale in Wien 6.–10. Juli 1981*, edited by Hermann Hunger and Hans Hirsch, 295–306. AfOB 19. Austria: Ferdinand Berger & Sons, 1982.

Knobel, Peter S., trans. *The Targum of Qohelet*. ArBib 15. Edinburgh: T. & T. Clark, 1991.

Knoppers, Gary N. *Jews and Samaritans: The Origins and History of Their Early Relations*. Oxford: Oxford University Press, 2013.

Knoppers, Gary N., and Kenneth A. Ristau, eds. *Community Identity in Judean Historiography: Biblical and Comparative Perspectives*. Winona Lake: Eisenbrauns, 2009.

Koh, Y. V. *Royal Autobiography in the Book of Qoheleth*. BZAW 369. Berlin/New York: de Gruyter, 2006.

Koosed, Jennifer. *(Per)mutations of Qohelet: Reading the Body in the Book*. LHBOTS 429. London: Bloomsbury T&T Clark, 2006.

Kramer, Samuel Noah. "Man and His God: A Sumerian Variation on the 'Job' Motif." In *Wisdom in Israel and the Ancient Near East Presented to Harold Henry Rowley by the Editorial Board of Vetus Testamentum in Celebration of his 65th Birthday, 24 March 1955*, edited by Martin Noth and D. Winton Thomas, 170–82. VTSup 3. Leiden: Brill, 1960.

Kramer, Samuel Noah. "The Oldest Literary Catalogue: A Sumerian List of Literary Compositions Compiled about 2000 B.C." *BASOR* 88 (1942): 10–19.

Kratz, Reinhard G. "The Idea of Cultic Centralization and Its Supposed Ancient Near Eastern Analogies." In *One God–One Cult–One Nation: Archaeological and Biblical Perspectives*, edited by Reinhard G. Kratz and Hermann Spieckermann, 121–44. BZAW 405. Berlin: de Gruyter, 2010.

Kratz, Reinhard G. "'The Place which He Has Chosen': The Identification of the Cult Place of Deut. 12 and Lev. 17 in 4QMMT." *Meghillot* 5–6 (2007): *57–*80.

Kratz, Reinhard G., and Hermann Spieckermann, eds., *One God–One Cult–One Nation: Archaeological and Biblical Perspectives*. BZAW 405. Berlin: de Gruyter, 2010.

Krishna, Sankaran. *Globalisation and Postcolonialism: Hegemony and Resistance in the Twenty-First Century*. New York: Rowman & Littlefield, 2009.

Kristeva, Julia. *Desire in Language: A Semiotic Approach to Literature and Art*. Edited by Leon S. Roudiez. Translated by Thomas Gora, Alice Jardine, and L. Roudiez. New York: Columbia University Press, 1980.

Kristeva, Julia. "Psychoanalysis and the Polis." *Critical Inquiry* 9 (1982): 77–92.

Kuenen, Abraham. "Beitraege zur Hexateuchkritik: VI. Dina und Sichem (Gen. 34)." In *Gesammelte Abhandlungen zur biblischen Wissenschaft*, 255–76. Freiburg i.B: Mohr, 1894.

Kugel, James L. "The Contradictions in the *Book of Jubilees*." In *A Walk Through* Jubilees: *Studies in the* Book of Jubilees *and the World of Its Creation*, 227–96. JSJSup 156. Leiden: Brill, 2012.

Kugel, James L. "The Story of Dinah in the *Testament of Levi*." *HTR* 85 (1992): 1–34.

Kugel, James L. *Traditions of the Bible: A Guide to the Bible as It Was at the Start of the Common Era*. Cambridge: Harvard University Press, 1998.
Kupperman, Karen Ordahl. *The Jamestown Project*. Cambridge: Belknap, 2007.
LaCoste, Nathalie. *Waters of the Exodus: Jewish Experiences with Water in Ptolemaic and Roman Egypt*. JSJSup 190. Leiden: Brill, 2018.
Laird, Donna. *Negotiating Power in Ezra–Nehemiah*. AIL 26. Atlanta: Society of Biblical Literature, 2016.
Lambert, Wilfred G. "The Babylonian Theodicy." In *Babylonian Wisdom Literature*, 63–91. Oxford: Oxford University Press, 1960.
Lamos, Colleen. *Deviant Modernism: Sexual and Textual Errancy in T. S. Eliot, James Joyce, and Marcel Proust*. Cambridge: Cambridge University Press, 1998.
de Las Casas, Bartolomé. *A Short Account of the Destruction of the Indies*. Edited and translated by Nigel Griffen. 1552. Repr., London: Penguin, 1992.
de Las Casas, Bartolomé. *The Spanish Colonie*. Translated by M. M. S. London: T. Dawson, 1583.
Lazarus, Neil, ed. *The Cambridge Companion to Postcolonial Literary Studies*. Cambridge: Cambridge University Press, 2004.
Lazarus, Neil. "Introducing Postcolonial Studies." In *The Cambridge Companion to Postcolonial Literary Studies*, edited by Neil Lazarus, 1–18. Cambridge: Cambridge University Press, 2004.
Levenson, Jon D. *The Hebrew Bible, the Old Testament, and Historical Criticism: Jews and Christians in Biblical Study*. Louisville: Westminster John Knox, 1993.
Levine, Baruch A. *Numbers 1–20: A New Translation with Introduction and Commentary*. AB 4. New York: Doubleday, 1993.
Levinson, Bernard M. *Deuteronomy and the Hermeneutics of Legal Innovation*. New York: Oxford University Press, 1997.
Levinson, Bernard M. "The First Constitution: Rethinking the Origins of Rule of Law and Separation of Powers in Light of Deuteronomy." *Cardozo Law Review* 27, no. 4 (2006): 1853–88.
Levinson, Bernard M. *A More Perfect Torah: At the Intersection of Philology and Hermeneutics in Deuteronomy and the Temple Scroll*. Critical Studies in the Hebrew Bible. Winona Lake: Eisenbrauns, 2013.
Levison, John R. "Torah and Covenant in Pseudo Philo's *Liber Antiquitatum Biblicarum*." In *Bund und Tora: Zur theologischen Begriffsgeschichte in alttestamentlicher, frühjüdischer und urchristlicher Tradition*, edited by Friedrich Avemarie and Hermann Lichtenberger, 111–27. WUNT 92. Tübingen: Mohr, 1996.
Levtow, Nathaniel B. *Images of Others: Iconic Politics in Ancient Israel*. BJSUCSD 11. Winona Lake: Eisenbrauns, 2008.
LiDonnici, Lynn, and Andrea Lieber, eds. *Heavenly Tablets: Interpretation, Identity and Tradition in Ancient Judaism*. JSJSup 119. Leiden: Brill, 2007.
Lieb, Michael, Emma Mason and Jonathan Roberts, eds. *The Oxford Handbook of the Reception History of the Bible*. Oxford: Oxford University Press, 2011.
Lieu, Judith M. *Marcion: The Making of a Heretic*. Cambridge: Cambridge University Press, 2015.
Lincicum, David. "Philo's Library." *SPhiloA* 26 (2014): 99–114.
Lincicum, David. "A Preliminary Index to Philo's Non-Biblical Citations and Allusions." *SPhil* 25 (2013): 139–67.
Lipka, Hilary. *Sexual Transgression in the Hebrew Bible*. Sheffield: Sheffield Phoenix, 2006.

Loader, James A. *Polar Structures in the Book of Qohelet*. BZAW 152. Berlin: de Gruyter, 1979.
Löfstedt, Bengt, ed. *Zenonis Veronensis Tractatus*. CCSL 22. Turnhout: Brepols, 1971.
Lohfink, Norbert. *Qoheleth*. Translated by Sean McEvenue. CC. Minneapolis: Fortress, 2003.
Lohr, Joel N. *Chosen and Unchosen: Conceptions of Election in the Pentateuch and Jewish-Christian Interpretation*. Siphrut 2. Winona Lake: Eisenbrauns, 2009.
Longman, Tremper, III. *The Book of Ecclesiastes*. NICOT. Grand Rapids: Eerdmans, 1998.
Lozada, Francisco, Jr. "Toward Latino/a Biblical Studies: Foregrounding Identities and Transforming Communities." In *Latino/a Biblical Hermeneutics: Problematics, Objectives, Strategies*, edited by Francisco Lozada Jr. and Fernando F. Segovia, 187–202. Atlanta: SBL, 2014.
Luther, Martin. "Preface to the Old Testament." In Volume 35 of *Luther's Works*, edited by E. Theodore Bachmann, 235–36. Philadelphia: Muhlenberg, 1960.
Luther, Martin. *Sämtliche Schriften*, Volume 8. Edited by Johann G. Walch. Groß Oesingen: Harms, 1987.
MacDonald, Nathan. "Anticipations of Horeb: Exodus 17 as Inner-Biblical Commentary." In *Studies on the Text and Versions of the Hebrew Bible in Honour of Robert Gordon*, edited by Geoffrey Khan and Diana Lipton, 7–19. Leiden: Brill, 2012.
MacDonald, Nathan. *Deuteronomy and the Meaning of "Monotheism."* 2nd ed. FAT II/1. Tübingen: Mohr Siebeck, 2012.
MacIntyre, Alisdair. *Three Rival Versions of Moral Enquiry: Encyclopaedia, Genealogy, and Tradition*. Notre Dame: Notre Dame University Press, 1990.
Magen, Yitzhak. "The Dating of the First Phase of the Samaritan Temple on Mount Gerizim in Light of the Archaeological Evidence." In *Judah and the Judeans in the Fourth Century B.C.E*, edited by Oded Lipschits, Gary N. Knoppers and Rainer Albertz, 157–212. Winona Lake: Eisenbrauns, 2007.
Malbon, Elizabeth S. *The Iconography of the Sarcophagus of Junius Bassus: Neofitus lit Ad Deum*. Princeton Legacy Library. Princeton: Princeton University Press, 1990.
Malherbe, Abraham J. "Heracles." In *Light from the Gentiles: Hellenistic Philosophy and Early Christianity*, edited by Carl R. Holladay et al., 2:651–74. 2 vols. NovTSup 150. Leiden: Brill, 2014.
Manahan, Karen B. "Robert Gray's *A Good Speed to Virginia*." In *The Literature of Justification*, edited by Edward J. Gallagher. Lehigh University Digital Library, 2006. http://digital.lib.lehigh.edu/trial/justification/jamestown/essay/4/.
Mantzavinos, C. "Hermeneutics." In *The Stanford Encyclopedia of Philosophy*. June 22, 2016, https://plato.stanford.edu/entries/hermeneutics/.
Marcos, Natalio Fernández. "The Septuagint Reading of the Book of Job." In *The Book of Job*, edited by Willem A. M. Beuken, 251–66. BETL 114. Leuven: Leuven University Press/Peeters, 1994.
Marcovich, Miroslav. *Pseudo-Iustinus: Cohortatio ad Graecos, De monarchia, Oratio ad Graecos*. PTS 32. Berlin: de Gruyter, 1990.
Martyn, J. Louis. *Galatians: A New Translation with Introduction and Commentary*. AB 33A. New York: Doubleday, 1997.
Mastnjak, Nathan. "Jeremiah as Collection: Scrolls, Sheets, and the Problem of Textual Arrangement." *CBQ* 80 (2018): 25–44.
Matlock, R. Barry. "Detheologizing the ΠΙΣΤΙΣ ΧΡΙΣΤΟΥ Debate: Cautionary Remarks from a Lexical Semantic Perspective." *NovT* 2 (2000): 1–23.

Matter, E. Ann. *The Voice of My Beloved: The Song of Songs in Western Medieval Christianity*. Philadelphia: University of Pennsylvania Press, 1990.
May, Natalie Naomi. "'I Read the Inscriptions from before the Flood…' Neo-Sumerian Influences in Ashurbanipal's Royal Self-Image." In *Time and History in the Ancient Near East: Proceedings of the 56th Rencontre Assyriologique Internationale at Barcelona, 26–30 July 2010*, edited by L. Feliu et al., 199–210. Winona Lake, IN: Eisenbrauns, 2013.
May, Todd. *Gilles Deleuze: An Introduction*. Cambridge: Cambridge University, 2005.
Maza, Sarah. *Thinking About History*. Chicago: University of Chicago Press, 2017.
Mbuwayesango, Dora. "How Local Divine Powers Were Suppressed: A Case of Mwari of the Shona." In *Other Ways of Reading: African Women and the Bible*, edited by Musa W. Dube, 63–77. Atlanta: SBL, 2000.
Meeks, Wayne. "'And Rose Up to Play': Midrash and Paraenesis in 1 Corinthians 10:1-22." *JSNT* 16 (1982): 64–78.
Mercer, Kobena. "Diaspora Culture and the Dialogic Imagination: The Aesthetics of Black Independent Film in Britain." In *Welcome to the Jungle: New Positions in Black Cultural Studies*, 53–66. New York: Routledge, 1994.
Merendino, Rosario P. *Der Erste und der Letzte. Eine Untersuchung von Jes 40–48*. VTSup 31. Leiden: Brill, 1981.
Meyers, Carol. "From Household to House of Yahweh: Women's Religious Culture in Ancient Israel." In *Congress Volume: Basel, 2001*, edited by André Lemaire, 283–301. VTSup 92. Leiden: Brill, 2002.
Michal Bar-Asher Siegal, Wolfgang Grünstäudl and Matthew Thiessen, eds. *Perceiving the Other in Ancient Judaism and Early Christianity*. WUNT 394. Tübingen: Mohr Siebeck, 2017.
Middlemas, Jill. *The Templeless Age: An Introduction to the History, Literature and Theology of the 'Exile'*. Louisville: Westminster John Knox, 2007.
Milgrom, Jacob. *The JPS Torah Commentary: Numbers* במדבר. Philadelphia: Jewish Publication Society, 1990.
Moberly, R. W. *The Old Testament of the Old Testament: Patriarchal Narratives and Mosaic Yahwism*. Eugene: Wipf & Stock, 2001.
Mojola, Aloo. "How the Bible is Received in Communities: A Brief Overview with Particular Reference to East Africa." In *Scripture Community and Mission: Essays in Honor of Preman Niles*, edited by Philip L. Wickeri, 1–17. Hong Kong: Christian Council of Asia, 2002.
Mongstad-Kvammen, Ingeborg. *Toward a Postcolonial Reading of the Epistle of James: James 2:1-13 in its Roman Imperial Context*. BibInt 119. Leiden: Brill, 2013.
Moore, Stephen D., and Yvonne Sherwood. *The Invention of the Biblical Scholar: A Critical Manifesto*. Minneapolis: Fortress, 2011.
Mor, Menachem, and Friedrich V. Reiterer, with Waltraud Winkler, eds. *Samaritans: Past and Present, Current Studies*. SJ 53 / StSam 5. Berlin: de Gruyter, 2010.
Moran, William L. "Rib-Hadda: Job at Byblos?" In *Biblical and Related Studies Presented to Samuel Iwry*, edited by Ann Kort and Scott Morschauser, 173–81. Winona Lake: Eisenbrauns, 1985.
Mroczek, Eva. *The Literary Imagination in Jewish Antiquity*. Oxford: Oxford University Press, 2016.
Mudimbe, V. Y. *The Invention of Africa: Gnosis, Philosophy, and the Order of Knowledge*. Bloomington: Indiana University Press, 1988.
Muir, Kenneth. *The Sources of Shakespeare's Plays*. London: Methuen, 1977.

Mukherjee, Ankhi. "'What Is a Classic?': International Literary Criticism and the Classic Question." *PMLA* 124 (2010): 1026–42.

Mukherjee, Ankhi. *What Is a Classic? Postcolonial Rewriting and Invention of the Canon.* Stanford: Stanford University Press, 2014.

Mulder, Michael, "Leviathan on the Menu of the Messianic Meal: The Use of Various Images of Leviathan in Early Jewish Tradition." In *Playing with Leviathan: Interpretation and Reception of Monsters from the Biblical World*, edited by Koert van Bekkum et al., 115–30. Themes in Biblical Narrative 21. Leiden: Brill, 2017.

Mullen, Theodore E. *Ethnic Myths and Pentateuchal Foundations: A New Approach to the Formation of the Pentateuch.* SemeiaSt 35. Atlanta: Scholars Press, 1997.

Muraoka, T. *A Greek–English Lexicon of the Septuagint.* Leuven: Peeters, 2009.

Murphy, Frederick J. "Divine Plan, Human Plan: A Structuring Theme in Pseudo-Philo." *JQR* 77 (1986): 5–14.

Murphy, Frederick J. "The Eternal Covenant in Pseudo-Philo." *JSP* 3 (1988): 43–57.

Murphy, Frederick J. "God in Pseudo-Philo." *JSJ* 19 (1988): 1–18.

Murphy, Frederick J. *Pseudo-Philo: Rewriting the Bible.* New York: Oxford University Press, 1993.

Myers, Jacob M. *Ezra, Nehemiah: Introduction, Translation, and Notes.* AB 14. Garden City: Doubleday, 1965.

Najman, Hindy. "Reconsidering *Jubilees*: Prophecy and Exemplarity." In *Enoch and the Mosaic Torah: The Evidence of Jubilees*, edited by Gabriele Boccaccini and Giovanni Ibba, 229–43. Grand Rapids: Eerdmans, 2009.

Najman, Hindy. *Seconding Sinai: The Development of Mosaic Discourse in Second Temple Judaism.* JSJSup 77. Leiden: Brill, 2003.

Najman, Hindy. "The Vitality of Scripture Within and Beyond the 'Canon'." *JSJ* 43 (2012): 497–518.

Nederveen Pieterse, Jan. *Globalization and Culture: Global Mélange.* 3rd ed. Lanham: Rowman & Littlefield, 2015.

Needham, R. "Polythetic Classification: Convergence and Consequences." *Man* NS 10 (1975): 349–69.

Neusner, Jacob. *The Tosefta: Translated from the Hebrew with a New Introduction.* 2 vols. Peabody: Hendrickson, 2002.

Newsom, Carol A. "Dramaturgy and the Book of Job." In *Das Buch Hiob und seine Interpretationen*, edited by T. Krüger et al., 375–93. AThANT 88. Zurich: TVZ, 2007.

Newsom, Carol A. "Spying Out the Land: A Report from Genology." In *Bakhtin and Genre Theory in Biblical Studies*, edited by Roland Boer, 19–30. SemeiaSt 63. Atlanta: Society of Biblical Literature, 2007.

Newsom, Carol A. "Woman and the Discourse of Patriarchal Wisdom: A Study of Proverbs 1–9." In *Gender and Difference in Ancient Israel*, edited by Peggy L. Day, 142–60. Minneapolis: Fortress, 1989.

Newton, K. M. *Interpreting the Text: A Critical Introduction to the Theory and Practice of Literary Interpretation.* New York: Harvester/Wheatsheaf, 1990.

Nickelsburg, George W. E. "Good and Bad Leaders in Pseudo-Philo's *Liber Antiquitatum Biblicarum*." In *Ideal Figures in Ancient Judaism: Profiles and Paradigms*, edited by John J. Collins, and George W. E. Nickelsburg, 49–65. Chico: Scholars Press, 1980.

Nickerson, Raymond S. "Confirmation Bias: A Ubiquitous Phenomenon in Many Guises." *Review of General Psychology* 2 (1998): 175–220.

Niehoff, Maren R. "Philo and Plutarch on Homer." In *Homer and the Bible in the Eyes of Ancient Interpreters*, edited by Maren R. Niehoff, 127–53. Jerusalem Studies in Religion and Culture 16. Leiden: Brill, 2012.

Niehoff, Maren R. *Philo of Alexandria: An Intellectual Biography*. Anchor Yale Bible Reference Library. New Haven: Yale University Press, 2018.

Nissinen, Martti. *Ancient Prophecy: Near Eastern, Biblical, and Greek Perspectives*. Oxford: Oxford University Press, 2017.

Novak, David. *The Election of Israel: The Idea of the Chosen People*. Cambridge: Cambridge University Press, 1995.

Novenson, Matthew V. *Christ among the Messiahs: Christ Language in Paul and Messiah Language in Ancient Judaism*. Oxford: Oxford University Press, 2012.

Ntloedibe Kuswani, Gomang Seratwa. "Translating the Divine: The Case of Modimo in the Setswana Bible." In *Other Ways of Reading: African Women and the Bible*, edited by Musa W. Dube, 78–100. Atlanta: SBL Press, 2000.

Nussbaum, Martha C. "Poetry and the Passions: Two Stoic Views." In *Passions and Perceptions: Studies in Hellenistic Philosophy of Mind. Proceedings of the Fifth Symposium Hellenisticum*, edited by Jacques Brunschwig and Martha C. Nussbaum, 97–149. Cambridge: Cambridge University Press, 1993.

Nussbaum, Martha C. "Tragedy and Self-Sufficiency: Plato and Aristotle on Fear and Pity." *Oxford Studies in Ancient Philosophy* 10 (1992): 107–59.

O'Rourke Boyle, Marjorie. "Evangelism and Erasmus." In *The Cambridge History of Literary Criticism, Volume 3: The Renaissance*, edited by Glyn P. Norton, 44–52. Cambridge: Cambridge University Press, 1999.

Oeming, Manfred, ed. *Claus Westermann: Leben–Werk–Wirkung*. Beiträge zum Verstehen der Bibel 2. Münster: LIT, 2003.

Olupona, Jacob K., and Terry Rey, eds. *Òrìṣà Devotion as World Religion: The Globalization of Yorùbá Religious Culture*. Madison: University of Wisconsin Press, 2008.

Orlov, Andrei A. "'What is Below?' Mysteries of Leviathan in Early Jewish Accounts and Mishnah Hagigah 2:1." In *Hekhalot Literature in Context: Between Byzantium and Babylonia*, edited by Ra'anan Boustan, Martha Himmelfarb, and Peter Schäfer, 313–22. TSAJ 153. Tübingen: Mohr Siebeck, 2003.

Oshima, Takayoshi. *The Babylonian Theodicy*. SAACT 9. Helsinki: The Neo-Assyrian Text Corpus Project, 2013.

Otto, Eckart. "Treueid und Gesetz: Die Ursprünge des Deuteronomiums im Horizont neuassyrischen Vertragsrechts." *ZABR* 2 (1996): 1–52.

Parker, John. "Religion and the Virginia Colony, 1609–1610." In *The Westward Enterprise: English Activities in Ireland, the Atlantic, and America 1480–1650*, edited by K. R. Andrews, N. P. Canny, and P. E. H. Hair, 245–70. Liverpool: Liverpool University Press, 1978.

Parpola, Simo. "Assyrian Library Records." *JNES* 42 (1983): 1–29.

Payne, Michael. "The Voices of Ecclesiastes." *College Literature* 15 (1988): 262–8.

Peckham, George. "A True Report of the Late Discoveries, and Possession Taken in the Right of the Crowne of England of the Newfound Lands." In volume 8 of *The Principal Navigations Voyages Traffiques & Discoveries of the English Nation*, edited by Richard Hakluyt, 89–131. 1589. Repr., Glasgow: James MacLehose & Sons, 1904.

Perraymond, Myla. *La figura di Giobbe nella cultura paleocristiana tra esegesi patristica e manifestazioni iconografiche*. Studi di antichità cristiana 58. Vatican City: Pontificio Istituto di Archeologia Cristiana, 2002.

Perrot, C., and P.-M. Bogaert. *Pseudo-Philon: Les Antiquités Bibliques*. SC 229, 230. Paris: Gabalda, 1976.

Perry, T. A. *The Book of Ecclesiastes (Qohelet) and the Path to Joyous Living*. New York: Cambridge University Press, 2015.

Perry, T. A. *Dialogues with Kohelet: The Book of Ecclesiastes*. College Park: Penn State University Press, 1993.

Petit, Madeleine. *Quod omnis probus liber sit: introduction, texte, traduction et notes*. Les oeuvres de Philon d'Alexandrie 28. Paris: Cerf, 1974.

Phillips, Anthony. "Nebalah: A Term for Serious Disorderly and Unruly Conduct." *VT* 25 (1975): 237–42.

Pitt-Rivers, Julian. *The Fate of Shechem or the Politics of Sex*. Cambridge: Cambridge University Press, 1977.

Plantinga Pauw, Amy. *Proverbs and Ecclesiastes*. Belief: A Theological Commentary on the Bible. Louisville: Westminster John Knox, 2015.

Propp, William H. C. *Exodus 1–18: A New Translation with Introduction and Commentary*. AB 2. New York: Doubleday, 1998.

Pui-lan, Kwok. *Discovering the Bible in the Non-Biblical World*. Maryknoll: Orbis, 1995.

Pui-lan, Kwok. *Postcolonial Imagination and Feminist Theology*. London: SCM, 2004.

Pury, Albert de. "The Jacob Story and the Beginning of the Formation of the Pentateuch." In *A Farewell to the Yahwist? The Composition of the Pentateuch in Recent European Scholarship*, edited by Thomas B. Dozeman and Konrad Schmid, 51–72. SymS 34. Atlanta: SBL, 2006.

Rad, Gerhard von. "Typological Interpretation of the Old Testament." In *Essays on Old Testament Interpretation*, edited by Claus Westermann, 17–39. London: SCM, 1963.

Reardon, B. P. *Courants littéraires grecs des IIe et IIIe siècles après J.-C.*, Annales littéraires de l'Université de Nantes 3. Paris: Les belles lettres, 1971.

Redford, Donald. "Some Observations on the Traditions Surrounding 'Israel in Egypt'." In *Judah and the Judeans in the Achaemenid Period: Negotiating Identity in an International Context*, edited by Oded Lipschits, Gary N. Knoppers, and Manfred Oeming, 279–364. Winona Lake: Eisenbrauns, 2011.

Reese, James M. *Hellenistic Influence on the Book of Wisdom and Its Consequences*. AnBib 41. Rome: Pontifical Institute, 1970.

Reinmuth, Eckart. "Beobachtungen zum Verständnis des Gesetzes im *Liber Antiquitatum Biblicarum* (Pseudo-Philo)." *JSJ* 20 (1989): 151–70.

Reinmuth, Eckart. "'Nicht vergeblich' bei Paulus und Pseudo-Philo, *Liber Antiquitatum Biblicarum*." *NovT* 33 (1991): 97–123.

Reuter, Eleonore. *Kultzentralisation: Entstehung und Theologie von Dtn 12*. BBB 87. Frankfurt: Hain, 1993.

Riffaterre, Michael. *Semiotics of Poetry*. Advances in Semiotics. Bloomington: Indiana University Press, 1978.

Roberts Gaventa, Beverly. "On the Calling-Into-Being of Israel: Romans 9:6-29." In *Between Gospel and Election: Explorations in the Interpretation of Romans 9–11*, edited by Florian Wilk, J. Ross Wagner, and Frank Schleritt, 255–69. WUNT 257. Tübingen: Mohr Siebeck, 2010.

Rochberg-Halton, Francesca. "Canonicity in Cuneiform Texts." *JCS* 36 (1984): 127–44.

Rofé, Alexander. "Defilement of Virgins in Biblical Law and the Case of Dinah (Genesis 34)." *Biblica* 86 (2005): 369–75.

Rokem, Freddie. "The Bible on the Hebrew/Israeli Stage: Hanoch Levin's *The Torments of Job* as a Modern Tragedy." In *The Book of Job: Aesthetics, Ethics, Hermeneutics*, edited by Leora Batinsky and Ilana Pardes, 185–212. Perspectives on Jewish Texts and Contexts 1. Berlin: de Gruyter, 2015.
Rom-Shiloni, Dalit. "Facing Destruction and Exile: Inner-Biblical Exegesis in Jeremiah and Ezekiel." *ZAW* 117 (2005): 189–205.
Roskies, David G. *Against the Apocalypse: Responses to Catastrophe in Modern Jewish Culture*. Cambridge: Harvard University Press, 1984.
Rowley, H. H. "The Interpretation of the Song of Songs." *JTS* 38 (1937): 337–63.
Said, Edward W. *Culture and Imperialism*. New York: Vintage, 1994.
Said, Edward W. *Orientalism*. New York: Random House, 1978. Repr., 2014.
Sanders, E. P. *Paul and Palestinian Judaism: A Comparison of Patterns of Religion*. Philadelphia: Fortress, 1977.
Sanders, E. P. "Paul's Jewishness." In *Paul's Jewish Matrix*, edited by Thomas G. Casey and Justin Taylor, 51–73. Mahwah: Paulist, 2011.
Sanders, E. P. *Paul, the Law, and the Jewish People*. Minneapolis: Fortress, 1983.
Sanders, E. P. et al., eds. *Jewish and Christian Self-Definition*. 3 vols. Philadelphia: Fortress, 1980–82.
Sanders, Seth L. *The Invention of Hebrew*. Urbana: University of Illinois Press, 2009.
Sanders, Seth L. "What Was the Alphabet For? The Rise of Written Vernacular and the Making of Israelite National Literature." *Maarav* 11 (2004): 25–56.
Sandys-Wunsch, John. "Spinoza: The First Biblical Theologian." *ZAW* 93 (1981): 327–41.
Satlow, Michael L. *How the Bible Became Holy*. New Haven: Yale University Press, 2014.
Satlow, Michael L. "Narratives or Sources? Active Learning and the Teaching of Ancient Jewish History and Texts." *Teaching Theology and Religion* 15 (2012): 48–60.
Satlow, Michael L. "Paul's Scriptures." In *Strength to Strength: Essays in Honor of Shaye J. D. Cohen*, edited by Michael L. Satlow, 257–73. Providence: Brown Judaic Studies, 2018.
Saussure, Ferdinand de. *Course in General Linguistics*. Edited by Charles Bally and Albert Schehaye. Translated by Roy Harris. Chicago: Open Court, 1983.
Sawhill, John A. *The Use of Athletic Metaphors in the Biblical Homilies of St. John Chrysostom*. Princeton: Princeton University Press, 1928.
Schaller, Berndt. "Das Testament Hiobs und die Septuaginta-Übersetzung des Buches Hiobs." *Bib* 61 (1980): 377–406.
Schirmann, Jefim. "The Battle between Behemoth and Leviathan according to an Ancient Piyyût." *PIASH* 4 (1971): 327–69.
Schmid, Konrad. "Post-Priestly Additions in the Pentateuch: A Survey of Scholarship." In *The Formation of the Pentateuch: Bridging the Academic Cultures of Europe, Israel, and North America*, edited by Jan C. Gertz et al., 589–606. FAT 111. Tübingen: Mohr Siebeck, 2016.
Schmid, Wolf. *Narratology: An Introduction*. Translated by Alexander Starritt. De Gruyter Textbook. Berlin: de Gruyter, 2010.
Schmidt, Ethan A. *The Divided Dominion: Social Conflict and Indian Hatred in Early Virginia*. Boulder: University of Colorado Press, 2015.
Schmidt, Ludwig. "Der Stab des Mose in der vor- und nach-priesterlichen Redaktion des Pentateuch." In *Post-Priestly Pentateuch: New Perspectives on Its Redactional Development and Theological Profiles*, edited by Federico Giuntoli and Konrad Schmid, 253–76. FAT 101. Tübingen: Mohr Siebeck, 2015.

Schmitz, Thomas. *Bildung und Macht: Zur sozialen und politischen Funktion der zweiten Sophistik in der griechischen Welt der Kaiserzeit*. Zetemata 97. Munich: Beck, 1997.

Schnabel, Eckhard J. *Der erste Brief des Paulus an die Korinther*. HTANT. Wuppertal: Brockhaus, 2006.

Schoeps, Hans-Joachim. *Paul: The Theology of the Apostle in the Light of Jewish Religious History*. Translated by Harold Knight. Philadelphia: Westminster, 1961.

Schoors, Anton. *The Preacher Sought to Find Pleasing Words: A Study of the Language of Qoheleth. Part II: Vocabulary*. OLA 143. Leuven: Peeters, 2004.

Schorch, Stefan. "The Samaritan Version of Deuteronomy and the Origin of Deuteronomy." In *Samaria, Samarians, Samaritans: Studies on Bible, History and Linguistics*, edited by József Zsengellér, 23–37. SJ 66 / StSam 6. Berlin: de Gruyter, 2011.

Schottroff, Luise. "'Give to Caesar What Belongs to Caesar and to God What Belongs to God': A Theological Response of the Early Christian Church to Its Social and Political Environment." In *The Love of Enemy and Nonretalitation in the New Testament*, edited by Willard Swartley, 223–57. Louisville: Westminster John Knox, 1992.

Schramm, Albert. *Der Bilderschmuck der Frühdrucke*. 23 vols. Leipzig: Hiersemann, 1920–1943.

Schrenk, Sabine. *Typos und Antitypos in der frühchristliche Kunst*. Münster: Aschendorffsche Verlagbuchhandlung, 1995.

Schroer, Silvia. *In Israel gab es Bilder. Nachrichten von darstellender Kunst im Alten Testament*. OBO 74. Fribourg: Universitätsverlag / Göttingen: Vandenhoeck & Ruprecht, 1987.

Schroer, Silvia, and Othmar Keel. *Die Ikonographie Palästinas-Israels und der Alte Orient: Eine Religionsgeschichte in Bildern*. 4 vols. Fribourg: Academic Press, 2005–2018.

Schüssler Fiorenza, Elisabeth. *Democratizing Biblical Studies: Toward an Emancipatory Educational Space*. Louisville: Westminster John Knox, 2009.

Schwartz, Seth. *Josephus and Judaean Politics*. Leiden: Brill, 1990.

Sechrest, Love L. *A Former Jew: Paul and the Dialectics of Race*. LNTS 410. New York: T&T Clark, 2009.

Segal, Michael. *The Book of Jubilees: Rewritten Bible, Redaction, Ideology, and Theology*. JSJSup 117. Leiden: Brill, 2007.

Segal, Michael. "Rewriting the Story of Dinah and Shechem: The Literary Development of Jubilees 30." In *The Hebrew Bible in Light of the Dead Sea Scrolls*, edited by Norá Dávid et al., 337–56. FRLANT 239. Göttingen: Vandenhoeck & Ruprecht, 2011.

Segovia, Fernando F. *Decolonizing Biblical Studies*. Maryknoll: Orbis, 2000.

Segovia, Fernando F. "Towards a Hermeneutics of the Diaspora: A Hermeneutics of Otherness and Engagement." In *Reading from the Place, Volume 1: Social Location and Biblical Interpretation in the United States*, edited by Fernando F. Segovia and Mary A. Tolbert, 57–78. Minneapolis: Fortress, 1995.

Segovia, Fernando F., and Mary Ann Tolbert, eds. *Teaching the Bible: The Discourses and Politics of Biblical Pedagogy*. Maryknoll: Orbis, 1998.

Seitz, Christopher. *Word Without End: The Old Testament as Abiding Theological Witness*. Grand Rapids: Eerdmans, 1998.

Seow, Choon-Leong (C. L.). *Ecclesiastes: A New Translation, with Introduction and Commentary*. AB 18C. New York: Doubleday, 1997.

Seow, C. L. "History of Consequences: The Case of Gregory's *Moralia in Iob*." *HBAI* 1 (2012): 368–87.

Seow, C. L. *Job 1–21: Interpretation and Commentary*. Illuminations. Grand Rapids: Eerdmans, 2013.

Seow, C. L. "Text Critical Notes on 4QJob[a]." *DSD* 22 (2015): 189–201.

Sharp, Carolyn. "Ironic Representation, Authorial Voice, and Meaning in Qohelet." *BibInt* 12 (2004): 37–68.

Shaw, Carl A. *Satyric Play: The Evolution of Greek Comedy and Satyr Drama*. Oxford: Oxford University Press, 2014.

Sheehan, Jonathan. *The Enlightenment Bible: Translation, Scholarship, Culture*. Princeton: Princeton University Press, 2005.

Sherwood, Yvonne. *A Biblical Text and Its Afterlives: The Survival of Jonah in Western Culture*. Cambridge: Cambridge University Press, 2000.

Sherwood, Yvonne. "Comparing the 'Telegraph Bible' of the Late British Empire to the Chaotic Bible of the Sixteenth Century Spanish Empire: Beyond the Canaan Mandate into Anxious Parables of the Land." In *In the Name of God: The Bible in the Colonial Discourse of Empire*, edited by C. L. Crouch and Jonathan Stökl, with Cat Quine, 4–62. BibInt 126. Leiden: Brill, 2014.

Sherwood, Yvonne. "Francisco de Vitoria's More Excellent Way: How the Bible of Empire Discovered the Tricks of [the Argument from] Trade." *BibInt* 21 (2013): 215–75.

Shohat, Ella, and Robert Stam. *Unthinking Eurocentrism: Multiculturalism and the Media*. New York: Routledge, 1994.

Simkins, Ronald A. "Biblical Studies as a Secular Discipline: The Role of Faith and Theology." *Journal of Religion and Society* 12 (2011): 1–17.

Simon, Richard. *Critical History of the Text of the New Testament: Wherein is Established the Truth of the Acts on which the Christian Religion is Based*. Translated by Andrew W. R. Hunwick. NTTSD 43. Leiden: Brill, 2013.

Ska, Jean-Louis. *'Our Fathers Have Told Us': Introduction to the Analysis of Hebrew Narratives*. SubBi 13. Rome: Pontificio Istituto Biblico, 1990.

Skinner, John. *A Critical and Exegetical Commentary on Genesis*. ICC. Edinburgh: T. & T. Clark, 1969.

Smallwood, E. Mary. *The Jews Under Roman Rule: From Pompey to Diocletian: A Study in Political Relations*. SJLA 20. Leiden: Brill, 1976.

Smith, John. *Advertisements for the Unexperienced Planters of New-England, or Any-Where*. London: J. Haviland, 1631. Repr. in volume 3 of *The Complete Works of John Smith (1580–1631) in Three Volumes*, edited by Philip L. Barbour, 259–307. The Institute of Early American History and Culture. Williamsburg: University of North Carolina Press, 1986.

Sneed, Mark R. *The Politics of Pessimism in Ecclesiastes: A Social-Science Perspective*. AIL 12. Atlanta: SBL, 2012.

Snell, Bruno, et al. *Tragicorum graecorum fragmenta*. 5 vols. Göttingen: Vandenhoeck & Ruprecht, 1971–2004.

Soares-Prabhu, George M. "Laughing at Idols: The Dark Side of Biblical Monotheism (an Indian Reading of Isaiah 44:9–20)." In *Reading from This Place, Volume 2: Social Location and Biblical Interpretation in Global Perspective*, edited by Fernando F. Segovia and Mary A. Tolbert, 109–31. Minneapolis: Fortress Press, 1995.

Sommer, Benjamin D. "Dating Pentateuchal Texts and the Danger of Pseudo-Historicism." In *The Pentateuch: International Perspectives on Current Research*, edited by Thomas B. Dozeman, Konrad Schmid, and Baruch J. Schwartz, 85–108. FAT 78. Tübingen: Mohr Siebeck, 2011.

Sommer, Benjamin D. *A Prophet Reads Scripture: Allusion in Isaiah 40–66*. Stanford: Stanford University Press, 1998.
Sorg, Anton. *Hie Vahet an das Register über die Bibeln des Alten Testaments*. Augsburg: Gunther Zainer, 1477.
Sorlin, Henri, with Louis Neyrand, eds. and trans. *Jean Chrysostome. Commentaire sur Job*. 2 vols. SC 346, 348. Paris: Cerf, 1988.
Spaulding, Mary B. *Commemorative Identities: Jewish Social Memory and the Johannine Feast of Booths*. LNTS 396. London: T&T Clark, 2009.
Specht, Herbert. "Die Verfehlung Moses und Aarons in Num 20,1-13* P." In *Torah and the Book of Numbers*, edited by Christian Frevel, Thomas Pola and Aaron Schart, 273–313. FAT 2/62. Tübingen: Mohr Siebeck, 2013.
Spiegel, Shalom. "Noah, Danel and Job: Touching on Canaanite Relics in the Legends of the Jews." In *Louis Ginzberg Jubilee Volume on the Occasion of His Seventieth Birthday*, 305–55. New York: The American Academy of Jewish Research, 1945.
Spivak, Gayatri C. *In Other Worlds: Essays in Cultural Politics*. New York: Routledge, 1988.
Spivak, Gayatri C. "The Rani of Sirmur: An Essay in Reading the Archives." *History and Theory* 24 (1985): 247–72.
Spivak, Gayatri C. "Three Women's Texts and a Critique of Imperialism." *Critical Inquiry* 12 (1985): 243–61.
Sprinkle, Preston M. "The Hermeneutic of Grace: The Soteriology of Pseudo-Philo's *Biblical Antiquities*." In *This World and the World to Come: Soteriology in Early Judaism*, edited by Daniel M. Gurtner, 50–67. LSTS 74. London: T&T Clark, 2011.
Stavrakopoulou, Francesca, and John Barton, eds. *Religious Diversity in Ancient Israel and Judah*. London: T&T Clark, 2010.
Steck, Odil Hannes. *Israel und das gewaltsame Geschick der Propheten: Untersuchungen zur Überlieferung des deuteronomistischen Geschichtsbildes im Alten Testament, Spätjudentum und Urchristentum*. Neukirchen-Vluyn: Neukirchener Verlag, 1967.
Stegemann, Ekkehard, and Wolfgang Stegemann. *The Jesus Movement: A Social History of Its First Century*. Translated by O. C. Dean, Jr. Minneapolis: Fortress, 1999.
Steinhauser, Kenneth B., with the assistance of H. Müller and D. Weber, eds. *Anonymi in Iob Commentarius*. CSEL 96. Vienna: Verlag der Österreichischen Akademie der Wissenschaften, 2006.
Steinmann, Jean. *Biblical Criticism*. London: Burns & Oates, 1959.
Stern, Philip D. *The Biblical Ḥerem: A Window on Israel's Religious Experience*. BJS 211. Atlanta: Scholars Press, 1991.
Stone, Lawrence. *The Causes of the English Revolution, 1529–1642*. New York: Harper & Row, 1972.
Storey, Ian C. "But Comedy Has Satyrs Too." In *Satyr Drama: Tragedy at Play*, edited by George W. M. Harrison, 201–18. Swansea: Classical Press of Wales, 2005.
Sugirtharajah, Rasiah S. *Exploring Postcolonial Biblical Criticism: History, Method, Practice*. Chichester: Wiley-Blackwell, 2011.
Sugirtharajah, Rasiah S., ed. *The Postcolonial Biblical Reader*. New York: Blackwell, 2006.
Sugirtharajah, Rasiah S. *Postcolonial Criticism and Biblical Interpretation*. Oxford: Oxford University Press, 2009.
Suleiman, Susan Rubin. "Pornography, Transgression, and the Avant-Garde: Bataille's *Story of the Eye*." In *The Poetics of Gender*, edited by Nancy Miller, 117–36. Gender and Culture. New York: Columbia University Press, 1986.

Sutton, Dana F. *The Greek Satyr Play*. Beiträge zur klassischen Philologie 90. Meisenheim: Anton Hain, 1980.
Swain, Simon. *Hellenism and Empire: Language, Classicism, and Power in the Greek World AD 50–250*. Oxford: Clarendon, 1996.
Tajfel, Henri. "Social Identity and Intergroup Behaviour." *Social Science Information* 13. no. 2 (1974): 65–93.
Taleb, Nassim Nicholas. *The Black Swan: The Impact of the Highly Improbable*. New York: Random House, 2007.
Taylor, Charles. *Sources of the Self: The Making of the Modern Identity*. Cambridge: Harvard University Press, 1989.
Theissen, Gerd. *On Having a Critical Faith*. London: SCM, 1979.
Thiessen, Matthew. *Contesting Conversion: Genealogy, Circumcision, and Identity in Ancient Judaism and Christianity*. New York: Oxford University Press, 2011.
Thiessen, Matthew. *Paul and the Gentile Problem*. Oxford: Oxford University Press, 2016.
Thiessen, Matthew. "'The Rock Was Christ': The Fluidity of Christ's Body in 1 Corinthians 10.4." *JSNT* 36 (2013): 103–26.
wa Thiong'o, Ngugi. *Decolonising the Mind: The Politics of Language in African Literature*. London: James Currey, 1986.
Thiselton, Anthony C. *The First Epistle to the Corinthians: A Commentary on the Greek Text*. NIGTC. Grand Rapids: Eerdmans, 2000.
Thomas, David Winton. "Isaiah XLIV.9-20: A Translation and Commentary." In *Hommages à André Dupont-Sommer*, 319–30. Paris: Adrien-Maisonneuve, 1971.
Tobin, Thomas H. "What Shall We Say that Abraham Found? The Controversy behind Romans 4." *HTR* 88 (1995): 437–52
Toorn, Karel van der. *Family Religion in Babylonia, Syria and Israel: Continuity and Change in the Forms of Religion*. SHANE 7. Leiden: Brill, 1996.
Toorn, Karel van der. "The Iconic Book: Analogies Between the Babylonian Cult of Images and the Veneration of the Torah." In *The Image and the Book. Iconic Cults, Aniconism, and the Rise of Book Religion in Israel and the Ancient Near East*, edited by Karel van der Toorn, 229–48. CBET 21. Leuven: Peeters, 1997.
Toorn, Karel van der. *Scribal Culture and the Making of the Hebrew Bible*. Cambridge: Harvard University Press, 2007.
Toorn, Karel van der. "Theodicy in Akkadian Literature." In *Theodicy in the World of the Bible: The Goodness of God and the Problem of Evil*, edited by Antti Laato and Johannes C. de Moor, 57–89. Leiden: Brill, 2003.
Tov, Emanuel. *Textual Criticism of the Hebrew Bible*. 3rd ed. Minneapolis: Fortress, 2012.
Trible, Phyllis. *Texts of Terror: Literary-Feminist Readings of Biblical Narratives*. OBT. Minneapolis: Fortress, 1984.
Tsedaka, Benyamim, with Sharon Sullivan, eds. *The Israelite Samaritan Version of the Torah*. Grand Rapids: Eerdmans, 2013.
Tucker, J. Brian, and Coleman A. Baker, eds. *T&T Clark Handbook to Social Identity in the New Testament*. London: Bloomsbury T&T Clark, 2014.
Turner, James. *Philology: The Forgotten Origins of the Modern Humanities*. Princeton: Princeton University Press, 2014.
Turpie, D. M. *New Testament View of the Old: A Contribution to Biblical Introduction and Exegesis*. London: Hodder and Stoughton, 1872.
Tuval, Michael. *From Jerusalem Priest to Roman Jew*. WUNT 357. Tübingen: Mohr Siebeck, 2013.

Tversky, Amos, and Daniel Kahneman. "Availability: A Heuristic for Judging Frequency and Probability." *Cognitive Psychology* 5 (1973): 207–32.

Unnik, W. C. van. "Once Again: Tarsus or Jerusalem." In *Sparsa Collecta: The Collected Essays of W. C. van Unnik*, 321–7. SNN 29. Leiden: Brill, 1973.

Unnik, W. C. van. *Tarsus or Jerusalem: The City of Paul's Youth*. London: Epworth, 1962.

Uzanne, Octave. "Conversations and Opinions of Victor Hugo." *Scribner's Magazine* 12 (1892): 558–76.

Valla, Lorenzo. *On the Donation of Constantine*. Translated by G. Bowersock. Cambridge: Harvard University Press, 2008.

VanderKam, James C. *The Book of Jubilees*. Sheffield: Sheffield Academic, 2001.

VanderKam, James [C.] "Jubilees as the Composition of One Author?" *RevQ* 26 (2014): 501–16.

VanderKam, James C. "The Putative Author of the Book of Jubilees." In *From Revelation to Canon: Studies in the Hebrew Bible and Second Temple Literature*, 439–47. Leiden: Brill, 2000.

VanLandingham, Chris. *Judgment & Justification in Early Judaism and the Apostle Paul*. Peabody: Hendrickson, 2006.

Vayntrub, Jacqueline. *Beyond Orality: Biblical Poetry on Its Own Terms*. The Ancient Word. New York: Routledge, 2019.

Verkerk, Dorothy H. "Job and Sitis: Curious Figures in Early Christian Funerary Art." *Mitteilungen zur christlichen Archäologie* 3 (1997): 20–9.

Viezel, Eran. "The Formation of Some Biblical Books, According to Rashi." *JTS* 61 (2010): 16–42.

Walls, Andrew. "British Missions." In *Missionary Ideologies in the Imperialist Era: 1880–1920*, edited by Torben Christensen and William Hutchinson, 8–24. Aarhus: Aros, 1982.

Watson, Francis. *Paul and The Hermeneutics of Faith*. Edinburgh: T. & T. Clark, 2004.

Watson, Francis. *Paul, Judaism, and the Gentiles: Beyond the New Perspective*. Rev. ed. Grand Rapids: Eerdmans, 2007.

Watts, John D. W. *Isaiah 34–66*. WBC 25. Waco: Word, 1987.

Watts, John D. W. *Isaiah 34–66*. 2nd ed. WBC 25. Nashville: T. Nelson, 2005.

Weinfeld, Moshe. "Job and Its Mesopotamian Parallels: A Typological Analysis." In *Text and Context: Old Testament and Semitic Studies for F.C. Fensham*, edited by W. T. Claassen, 217–26. JSOTSup 48. Sheffield: JSOT, 1988.

Welborn, Larry L. "Towards Structural Marxism as a Hermeneutic of Early Christian Literature, Illustrated with Reference to Paul's Spectacle Metaphor in 1 Corinthians 15:30–32." *The Bible & Critical Theory* 8 (2012): 27–35.

Westermann, Claus. *Das Buch Jesaja, Kap. 40–66*. 4th ed. ATD 19. Göttingen: Vandenhoeck & Ruprecht, 1981.

Whitford, David. *The Curse of Ham in the Early Modern Era: The Bible and the Justifications for Slavery*. St. Andrews Studies in Reformation History. London: Routledge, 2009.

Whitney, K. William. *Two Strange Beasts: Leviathan and Behemoth in Second Temple and Early Rabbinic Judaism*. HSM 63. Winona Lake: Eisenbrauns, 2006.

Whitmarsh, Tim. *Beyond the Second Sophistic: Adventures in Greek Postclassicism*. Berkeley: University of California Press, 2013.

Whitmarsh, Tim. *Greek Literature and the Roman Empire: The Politics of Imitation*. Oxford: Oxford University Press, 2001.

Whitmarsh, Tim. *The Second Sophistic*. Greece and Rome: New Surveys in the Classics 35. Oxford: Oxford University Press, 2005.
Witte, Markus. "The Greek Book of Job." In *Das Buch Hiob und seine Interpretationen*, edited by Thomas Krüger et al., 33–54. ATANT 88. Zurich: TVZ, 2007.
Whybray, R. Norman. "The Identification and Use of Quotations in Ecclesiastes." In *Congress Volume Vienna 1980*, edited by John A. Emerton, 435–51. VTSup 32. Leiden: Brill, 1981.
Whybray, R. Norman. *Isaiah: 2. Isaiah 40–66*. NCB. London: Oliphants, 1975.
Williams, James. *The Transversal Thought of Gilles Deleuze: Encounters and Influences*. Manchester: Clinamen, 2005.
Williamson, Hugh G. M. *Ezra, Nehemiah*. WBC 16. Waco: Word, 1985.
Wimbush, Vincent L., ed. *African Americans and the Bible: Sacred Texts and Social Textures*. With Rosamond C. Rodman. New York: Continuum, 2000.
Wineburg, Sam. *Historical Thinking and Other Unnatural Acts: Charting the Future of Teaching the Past*. Philadelphia: Temple University Press, 2001.
Winston, David. *The Wisdom of Solomon: A New Translation with Introduction and Commentary*. AB 43. Garden City: Doubleday, 1979.
Witherington, Ben, III. *Conflict and Community in Corinth: A Socio-Rhetorical Commentary on 1 and 2 Corinthians*. Grand Rapids: Eerdmans, 1995.
Wright, N. T. *The Climax of the Covenant: Christ and the Law in Pauline Theology*. Edinburgh: T. & T. Clark, 1991.
Wright, N. T. "Messiahship in Galatians?" In *Galatians and Christian Theology: Justification, the Gospel, and Ethics in Paul's Letter*, edited by Mark W. Elliott, Scott J. Hafemann, N. T. Wright, and John Frederick, 3–23. Grand Rapids: Baker Academic, 2014.
Wright, N. T. "Paul and the Patriarch: The Role(s) of Abraham in Galatians and Romans." In *Pauline Perspectives: Essays on Paul, 1978-2013*, 558–63. Minneapolis: Fortress, 2013.
Wyles, Rosie. "Heracles' Costume from Euripides' *Heracles* to Pantomime Performance." In *Performance in Greek and Roman Theatre*, edited by George W. M. Harrison and Vayos Liapis, 181–98. Mnemosyne Supplements 353. Leiden: Brill, 2013.
Zahn, Molly M. "Genre and Rewritten Scripture: A Reassessment." *JBL* 131 (2012): 271–88.
Zahn, Molly M. "Innerbiblical Exegesis: The View from Beyond the Bible." In *The Formation of the Pentateuch: Bridging the Academic Cultures of Europe, Israel, and North America*, edited by Jan C. Gertz et al., 107–20. FAT 111. Tübingen: Mohr Siebeck, 2016.
Zahn, Molly M. *Rethinking Rewritten Scripture: Composition and Exegesis in the 4QReworked Pentateuch Manuscripts*. STDJ 95. Leiden: Brill, 2011.
Zimmermann, Ruben. *Puzzling the Parables of Jesus: Methods and Interpretation*. Minneapolis: Fortress, 2015.
Zsengellér, József, ed. *Samaria, Samarians, Samaritans: Studies on Bible, History and Linguistics*. SJ 66 / StSam 6. Berlin: de Gruyter, 2011.
Zuckerman, Bruce E. *Job the Silent: A Study in Historical Counterpoint*. New York/ Oxford: Oxford University Press, 1991.
Zwickel, Wolfgang. *Der Tempelkult in Kanaan und Israel: Studien zur Kulturgeschichte Palästinas von der Mittelbronzezeit bis zum Untergang Juda*. FAT 10. Tübingen: Mohr Siebeck, 1994.

Index of References

Ancient Near Eastern Sources		15:1 LXX	137	23:2	4

Ancient Near Eastern Sources
Man and His God (Babylonian) 173

Man and His God (Sumerian) 172–74

The Babylonian Theodicy 174–75

Hymn to Marduk (Ugarit) 173

Ludlul Bēl Nēqemi
I.33-34   174
II.33-38   174

Middle Assyrian Laws
55–56   86

Hebrew Bible/Old Testament
Genesis
1:20-25   190
2:24   86
3   182
3:18   144
4:8-10   82
6:19-20   99
6:22   106
7:2-3   99
7:12   99
7:24   99
12:1-3   127
12:7-8   17
12:7   128, 131
13:15 LXX 144
15   136, 137, 143
15:1 LXX 137
15:2-3   137
15:4   137, 149
15:5-6   147
15:5   132, 137, 143
15:6   136, 137
15:6 LXX 138, 148
15:7 LXX 76
15:13   129
15:18   128
15:18 LXX 76
16   141
16:6   87
16:9   87
17   96, 126–8, 136, 141–3, 149
17:1-2   128
17:1   126, 128
17:2   126
17:4   126
17:4 LXX 127
17:5   136, 143
17:6-8   127
17:7   126
17:8   128
17:8 LXX 144
17:11   143
17:14   127
17:16   128
17:19 LXX 144
20:9   88
22:17   132, 139, 146
22:17 LXX 144
22:17-18 145, 146
22:18   145
22:18 LXX 144, 145
23   4
23:2   4
23:6   93
24:7 LXX 144
25:1-7   17
26:34   99
27   98
27:41-45 98
27:46–28:5 99
27:46   98
28   224
28:6-9   99
28:16   23
29:26   88
34   28, 83–5, 89, 97–101
34:1-26   86
34:2   87, 89, 92, 94
34:3   91, 92
34:5   94–6
34:7   88–90, 92, 94
34:8   95
34:9   96
34:12   95
34:13   92, 94, 96
34:14   89, 93
34:15-16 96
34:15   93
34:19   89, 91, 92
34:22   93
34:25   97
34:26   91
34:27   94, 96
34:30   95
35   224
35:23-25 93
36:2-5   93
36:12-15 93
36:17   93

Index of References

41:45	91	34:6-7	75	20:8	104, 108, 112, 118
46:10	101	40:16	106		
47:27	93			20:9-12	104, 105
49	97	*Leviticus*		20:10	106, 108, 112, 117, 118
49:5-7	97	4:22	93		
		17–27	86	20:11-12	106
Exodus		18	95	20:11	104, 108, 112, 118
6:6	118	18:20	96		
7:14-26	107	18:24	11, 95	20:12	106
7:14-24	108	18:27-28	95	20:13	104, 108, 118, 120
7:15	108	20	95		
7:17	108	26:3-4	131	20:24	106, 117, 120
7:18	108	26:9-10	131	21:4-9	108
7:19	108			21:5-9	114
7:20	108	*Numbers*		25	93
7:21	108	5:11-31	95	27:12-23	120
7:24	108	7	93	27:14	120
17	103, 105, 106, 108, 117, 118, 121	8:3	106	32:30	93
		11–25	112	33:55	190
		13–14	105, 106, 117, 120	34	93
17:1-7	103, 104				
17:1-7 LXX	107	13:18	105	*Deuteronomy*	
17:1	103, 105, 108, 112, 118	13:19	105	1:31-36	120
		13:23	106	2:6	190
17:2-6	118	13:26	105	4:34	118
17:2-4	104	13:28	105	5:3	24
17:2	104, 108, 112, 114, 118	13:29	105	5:14-15	24
		13:32	105	5:18	20
17:3	104, 105, 108, 118	14:11	120	7:1-6	19
		14:14	105	7:2-3	92, 96
17:5-6	104	14:21-23	106	8:5	108
17:5	104, 108	14:25	105	8:15	108, 113, 118
17:6	104, 106, 108, 112, 113, 118	14:27-30	106	8:15 LXX	108
		14:45	105	12	18, 19, 23
		17:11 ET	106	12:1-7	18
17:7	104, 108, 114	17:26	106	12:1	24
17:9	14	20	29, 103, 105, 108, 116–19, 121	12:2-4	18
20–23	19			12:5	19
20:5	77			12:8-12	18
20:14	20	20:1-13	103, 104	12:11	19
20:17 ET	20	20:1-2	103	12:13-23	18
20:22-26	18	20:1	105, 119	12:13-14	17, 23
20:24	18	20:2-6	104	12:14	19
22	97	20:2	105, 108, 118	12:18	19
22:15-16	86, 89, 90	20:3	104	12:21	19
32–34	206	20:5	104–6, 108, 112, 117, 118	12:26	19
32:1-4	206			12:29-31	18
32:9-10	131	20:6-8	104	12:31	11
32:10	131	20:6	105	13:16	96
32:23-24	206	20:8-12	105	18:10-12	11

Deuteronomy (cont.)
20:16-18	19
21	87
21:11-14	87
22	87, 97
22:23-24	87
22:25-27	87
22:28-29	86, 87, 90, 92
26:5	24
26:11 2	4
27:4	20
32	113
32:4	113
32:10-14	108
32:10	108
32:13	113
32:15	113
32:17	114
32:18	113
32:21	114
32:30	113
32:31	113
32:37	113

Joshua
1–4	120
2	43
17	3, 17
17:14-18	2
17:14	3
22:9	93
22:19	93
24:2	134

Judges
6:20	106

1 Samuel
1:3	17
2:2	114
7:17	17
18:25-27	89

2 Samuel
7	147
7:12-14	147
7:12	78, 147
7:14	147
13	91
13:12	88

13:15	91
22:3	114
22:32	114
22:47	114

1 Kings
4:32 ET	226, 233
5:12	226, 233
8:16	20
11	99
12	99
12:28-33	206
18:20-46	17
20:25	106

2 Kings
6:23	190
12:9	93
23:27	20

Isaiah
5	78
5:2	78
11:15–12:3	118
13–23	109
17:10	114
20:2	106
26:4	114
27:1	191, 192
30:29	114
35:1-7	118
40–55	118
40–49	207
41:18-20	118
41:18	118
43:20	118
44	196, 201, 203, 205–10
44:6-8	200
44:8	114
44:9-20	30, 196, 197, 199–202, 207–9
44:9-11	201
44:9	200
44:12-13	201
44:13	201
44:14-17	201, 205
44:15-17	201, 202, 205
44:17	207

44:18-20	204
44:18	201
44:19-20	201
44:19 LXX	200
44:21-22	200
48:5	206
48:20-21	118
48:20	118
48:21	118
51:3	118
58:11-14	118

Jeremiah
2:1-3	108
11:19	181
21:5-6	118
25–31 LXX	109
31:29-30	77
31:30	77
42–44	110
46–51	109

Ezekiel
9:4-6	118
11:9	118
14:14	172
14:20	172
18:2	77
18:6	95
20:34-38	118
22:11	95
25–32	109
37:16-22	4
40–48	118

Hosea
2:14-15 ET	108
2:16-17	108
3:2	190
11:1	108
12	224
13:4-5	108

Joel
4:3	93

Amos
1	109

Jonah
1:17–2:1 ET	189
2:1-2 LXX	189
4:2	75

Habakkuk
1:12	114
2:18-19	206

Zechariah
8:5	93

Psalms
2	147
2:7	147
17:3 LXX	114
17:32 LXX	114
17:47 LXX	114
18:2 ET	114
18:3	114
18:31 ET	114
18:32	114
18:46 ET	114
18:47	114
22	70
31:1-2 LXX	138
32:1-2	138
36 LXX	76
36:9 LXX	76
36:11 LXX	76
36:22 LXX	76
36:29 LXX	76
36:34 LXX	76
37:11	76
49:14 LXX	23
50:11	190
50:14	23
71:11 LXX	146
71:17 LXX	146
72	146
72:1-2	147
72:1	146
72:5	146
72:7-8	146
72:9	146
72:11	146
72:17	146
74:14	190
77:35 LXX	114
78:35	114
78:68	20
80:8 LXX	108
80:13 ET	190
80:14	190
81:7	108
81:8	108
88:27 LXX	114
89:26 ET	114
89:27	114
97	181
103:26 LXX	188
104:26	191
105:30-31 LXX	142
106:5-6 LXX	108
106:31-32	142
107:5-6	108
113:8 LXX	108
114:8	108
135:16 LXX	108
136:16	108
137:1-6	33

Job
1–3	181
1:1	177, 180
1:1 OG	177, 180
1:5	181
1:8	177, 183
1:8 OG	177
1:12 OG	180
1:16	176
1:16 OG	176
1:20	184
1:21	183–84
2:3	176–77
2:3 OG	177
2:9	181, 182
2:9 OG	180–2
2:10 OG	180
3–31	175
3:8	188
3:8 OG	188, 189
4:17-19	174
5:8-16	174
5:13	179
5:17-18	174
5:19-26	174
6:11 OG	179
6:27	190
6:29 OG	177
7:1 OG	180, 185
7:1 OL	185
7:16 OG	179
9:15 OG	177
9:20 OG	177
12:4 OG	177
13:18 OG	177
14:14 Vg.	185
14:18-19 LXX	179
14:19 LXX	179
16:13-14	185
17:13 OG	179
19:11-12	185
22:21 OG	179
26:13	189
29:17	186
32:1 OG	177
36:29–27:5	175
37:1 OG	175
40–41 OG	188
40:8 OG	177, 180
40:15–41:34 ET	188
40:15–41:26 ET	188
40:15-23	189
40:15 OG	188
40:19 OG	188
40:20 OG	188
40:23-25	189
40:23	191
40:24–41:34 ET	189
40:24–41:26	189
40:25	188, 189
40:25 OG	188
40:30	190
40:31	190, 192
41:1-5	189
41:6 ET	190
41:7	190
41:7 ET	190, 192
41:9-13 ET	189
41:10-13	189
41:10 OG	189
41:15 ET	190
41:18-21 ET	189
41:22	190
41:24 OG	188
41:25 OG	188
41:30 ET	190
42:17 OG	180
42:17 Sahidic	178

Ecclesiastes/Qohelet		15:21-28	43, 45	4:5	136
1:1-2	230	28:18-20	43	4:6-8	138
1:1	231, 232			4:9-17	138
1:12–2:26	232	*Mark*		4:9-10	142
1:12	231, 232	1:12-13	181	4:9	136, 139
1:17	231	11:27	78	4:11-12	148
2	232	12:1-9	77	4:11	136, 139, 142, 143
2:13-16	231	12:1	78		
4:2-3	231	12:12	78	4:12	136, 142
4:17–5:6	232	15:34	70	4:13	136, 139, 143, 147
5:1-7 ET	232				
5:1	234	*Luke*		4:14-15	144
5:2 ET	234	1:33	78	4:14	136
7:11-12	231	4:1-13	181	4:16	136-39, 142, 144, 148
7:23-29	234	6:30	80		
7:27	230	6:35	80	4:17-18	136, 147
9:4-6	231	24:46-47	79	4:17	136, 139, 143
9:16-17	231			4:18-22	142
10:20	232	*John*		4:18	136, 143
12:8-11	230	4:1-42	43	4:19	136
12:9-10	234	4:20	22	4:20	136
12:9	231	4:21	22	4:22-23	136
12:10-11	234	4:23	22, 23	4:23-24	140
12:12	234	6:25-40	114	4:24-25	142
		6:41-58	114	4:24	136
Esther		7:37-39	113	5:6	138
2:4	106	19:34	113	5:8	138
				5:10	138
Ezra		*Acts*		5:12-21	149
4:1-2	21	2:29-36	78	5:15	138
4:2	21	4:34-35	80	5:21	138
4:3	21	21:20	74	6:3	116
4:6-16	22	22:2-5	64	9–11	138
4:10	21	22:23	64	9	140
9–10	92			9:1–11:36	125
		Romans		9:3-6	115
Nehemiah		1:2-4	125, 146	9:5	142
1:8-2	20	1:3	147	9:6-18	138
4–6	22	2:28-29	115	9:6	115
13	92	3:1-9	125	9:7-9	139
		3:27	138	9:7	139
2 Chronicles		4	136, 143	9:8	148
6:5-6	20	4:1-8	137	9:10-13	139, 141
7:12	20	4:1	142, 148	9:11	139
		4:2-4	142	9:12	139
NEW TESTAMENT		4:2-3	138, 143	9:15-18	139
Matthew		4:2	142	9:24-26	139
4:1-11	181	4:3	136	10:17	140
5:5	76, 139	4:4-5	137	11:1	125
12:40	189	4:4	138, 140, 148	11:2	138

11:5	138	3:7-9	140, 148	2:5	139
11:17-24	115	3:7	140	11:4	82
11:32	138	3:8	144, 145	13:12	181
12:6	138	3:9	149		
15:7-12	146	3:14	139, 140	*James*	
15:8-9	147	3:15-16	144	5:7-11	179
15:8	144	3:16-18	148	5:7	179
		3:16	144–6	5:8	179
1 Corinthians		3:17	143	5:10	179
3:10	138	3:19-26	149	5:11	179
5:9	112	3:22	149		
8–10	114	3:23-24	143	*1 Peter*	
8:7	114	3:26-29	140	1:23	140
10	29, 103, 112,	3:27	116		
	113, 117, 122	3:29	115, 147	APOCRYPHA	
10:1-22	112	4	140	*Wisdom of Solomon*	
10:1-6	112	4:1-5	149	1:1	109
10:1-4	116	4:1-3	143	5:16-23	111
10:2	116	4:4	125	6:1	109
10:4	113	4:7	143	6:9	109
10:6-11	116	4:18	143	6:21	109
10:9	114	4:21-31	140, 148	10:15	110
10:14-22	116	4:23	140	11–19	107, 109
10:16	114	4:25	113	11	29, 103, 107,
10:18	115, 116	4:28	141		108, 117, 122
10:20	114	4:29	140, 141	11:1-14	109
10:22	114	4:30–5:2	141	11:1	110
12:2	115	4:31	141	11:3	110
15:9-10	138	6:16	115	11:4-10	107
				11:4	108
2 Corinthians		*Ephesians*		11:5	108, 110
3:17	113	4:7	138	11:6-7	109
4:6	149			11:6	108, 109
4:15	138	*Philippians*		11:7-9	109
4:17	138	3:2-3	148	11:7	108
4:18-22	138	3:3	115	11:8-10	108
8:9	138	3:5	64, 125	11:8	108, 110
9:15	138			11:9	108, 114
		1 Thessalonians		11:14	108
Galatians		1:4-5	140	11:15–15:19	109
2:14	138	2:13	140	12:6	110
2:15	125			12:18-22	109
3–4	139, 143	*2 Thessalonians*		12:22	110
3	136, 139, 145	1:12	138	15:2	109
3:2-5	138			15:4	109
3:2	140	*2 Timothy*		16–19	109
3:5-6	140	2:5	181	16:1-4	109
3:5	140			16:2	109
3:6-9	115, 149	*Hebrews*		16:5-14	108, 109
3:6	136	1:5	147	16:6	109

Wisdom of Solomon (cont.)
16:8	110
16:11	109
16:15-29	109
16:20	109
17	109
17:1–18:4	109
17:7-8	109
18:2-3	109
18:3	109
18:5-25	109
18:5	109
18:6	110
18:8	109, 110
18:10	110
18:20	109
18:22	110
19:1-17	109
19:1-8	109
19:7	109
19:9-22	109
19:10	109
19:13-14	111
19:18-22	109

Ecclesiasticus/Ben Sira
Prologue	213
44:19-21	126, 139
44:9 MS^B	179

1 Maccabees
2:52	126

PSEUDEPIGRAPHA
2 Baruch
29:4	190

1 Enoch
60:7	191

4 Ezra
6:49-52	190

4 Maccabees
6:10	181

Apocalypse of Abraham
10:9-10	191
10:10	191
21:4	191

Jubilees
6:32	57
6:36-37	57
12:1-8	178
17:3	139
17:15–18:19	178
19:21	139
22:14	139
23:10	126
30	100
32:18	139

Liber Antiquitatum Biblicarum
4:11	126–28, 130
4:16	126
4:17	134
6:3-4	133
6:9	133, 134
6:10	133
6:11	133, 134
6:17-18	134
7:4	127, 133, 134
8:3	127–28
9	128
9:3	129, 135
9:4	129, 130
9:5	150
9:7-8	130
9:7	130, 134
9:8	130
9:13	128
9:15	128
10:2	130
10:7	113
11:5	130, 131
11:15	113
12:4	129, 131
12:9	129
13:10	130–32
14:2	129
15:5	129
16:5	135
18:1-6	134
18:3	129
18:5	132, 134
18:10	150
18:11	129
18:13-14	150
19:2	132
19:6	135
21:9-10	130
21:9	129, 131
23:1-14	130
23:5	134
23:11	129, 131
23:13	129
25–28	129
26:1	129
27:13	129
28:4	135
30:7	130
31:5	135
32:1-4	134
32:1	134, 135
32:4	134
32:14	130
33:2	129
33:5	129, 135
35:2	131
35:3	130
39:7	135
40:2	134
43:5	150
43:7	150
46:1	129
47:2	129
47:12	129
49:6	131
51:6	129
53:12	129
56:1	129
61:3	129
62:2	129
62:4	129

Psalms of Solomon
17:4	147
17:23	147

Testament of Job
1:5	179
2:1–3:7	180
4:4	180
4:6	179
4:10-11	181
4:10	180
5:1	179
11:10	179
18:2	180

26:2	180	*Ḥullin*		2.84	108
26:4	179	67b	190	2.86	113
26:5	179			3.202	162
26:6	180	*Sukkah*			
27:1	180	5b	190	*Quod omnis probus*	
27:3-5	180, 181			*liber sit*	
27:5	180	*Yoma*		1–61	156
27:7	179	80a	190	17–18	156
28:5	179	Midrash		22	159–60
35:4	179	*Genesis Rabbah*		25	162
		80:11	101	62-160	156
Dead Sea Scrolls				75–91	156
4QFlor				92–96	163
1:10-13	147	*Leviticus Rabbah*		98	156
1:18-19	147	13:3	190–2	99	157, 162
		22:10	190	101	157
4QMMT				102	157
B 51–66	20	*Mekilta Exodus*		103	157
		14:31	139	116	160
CD				118-20	163
3:2	126	*Pirqe Rabbi Eliezer*		141	160
		9	191, 192	143	160
Targums				145	159
Targum Psalms		*Sifra Shemini*			
104:26	191	3:5, 49c/d	190	*De vita Mosis*	
				1.155	139
Targum Job		Philo of Alexandria		1.210	108
40:30	190, 191	*De aeternitate mundi*			
		5	159	Josephus	
Targum Qohelet	232	30	159	*Antiquitates judaicae*	
		144	159	4.1	166
Mishnah				4.2	166
Ḥagigah		*De decalogo*		12.8	110
2:1	191	1.16	108	13.10.6	62
				13.10.56	62
Tosefta		*Quod deterius potiori*		13.254-56	22
Sukkah		*insidiari soleat*		19.281	110
3:11-13	113, 122	1.115	113	20.251	77, 80
Babylonian Talmud		*De Josepho*		*Contra Apionem*	
'Abodah Zarah		78	162	1.40	179
3b	191			2.35	110
		Legatio ad Gaium		2.42	110
Baba Batra		79	165		
74b	191	90–91	165	*Bellum judaicum*	
75a	190, 191	90	165	1.62-65	22
		151	163	2.487	110
Bekorot					
57b	190	*Legum allegoriae*			
		1.7	159		

Index of References

CLASSICAL GREEK AND
ROMAN LITERATURE
Aelian
Varia historia
2.13   159

Apollodorus
2.6.3   156

Appian
Bella civilia
3.2.16   166

Aristophanes
Aves
1604   158

Ecclesiazusae
879   154

Lysistrata
44   154

Pax
741-42   158

Ranae
     165
45–47   155
46   154
463   155
495-97   155
503-48   158
522-28   155
579-88   155
1491-99   159

Thesmophoriazusae
138   154

Vespae
60   158

Aristotle
De poetica   162
1457   74
1457b   74

Artemidorus Daldianus
Onirocritica
4.59   162

Athenaeus
Deipnosophistae
4.148c   166
4.158e   159
10.411e-412b   157
12.537f   164

Cassius Dio
Historia Romana
56.36.3   164
56.36.4   164
56.36.5   164
59.26.7   165

Cicero
Epistulae ad Atticum
9.2a.2   160

Paradoxa Stoicorum
5   156

Orationes philippicae
2.104   166

Dio Chrysostom
Ad Alexandrinos
32.94   154, 158

De dicendi exercitatione
18.7   160

De regno i
1.59-63   164
84   165

Diodorus Siculus
4.31.5-8   156

Diogenes Laertius
2.18   159
2.22   159

Epictetus
Diatribai
1.24.15-16   161
4.1   156

Epicharmus
frag. 18 K.-A.   158

Euripides
Alcestis
747-72   158

Chrysippus (frag.)
TrGF (Snell et al.)
5.839.12-14   159

Hecuba
548-51   160

Hercules furens
465   157

Syleus (frag.)
TrGF (Snell et al.)
5.687   156–57, 162
5.688   157
5.691   157
5.692-94   162

Heraclitus
Allegoriae
22.11   159

Homer
Iliad   171

Horace
Satirae
I, 8.1ff   202

Hyginus
Fabulae
32   156

Ion
Omphale (frag.)
TrGF (Snell et al.)
1.22   154
1.24-25   154

Isocrates
Philippus
5.105-14   164

Lucretius
2.991-1006   159

Macrobius
Saturnalia
2.7.16-17   164

Marcus Aurelius
7.50   159

Ovid
Heroides
9.26   166
9.47   166
9.63   166
9.65   166
9.101-2   167
9.111-12   166
9.117   166

Philostratus
Vitae sophistarum
    152

Plato
Respublica
10.603c-606b   160

Pliny the Elder
Naturalis historia
5.73   163
14.28.148   166

Plutarch
Antonius
4.1   166
4.2 [4.3]   166
4.2 [4.4]   166

Quomodo adolescens poetas audire debeat
    161
34b   160

Consolatio ad Apollonium
10.106d   160

Sextus Empiricus
Adversus Mathematicos
6.17   159

Sophocles
Trachiniae
248-53   156

Stobaeus
4.8.3   160

Suetonius
Nero
21.1   164

Theocritus
Idylls
17.26-27   164

TrGF (Snell et al.)
5 T A.1.IA.3 159
5.275.3-4   160
5.893.1   159

Virgil
Aeneid   44, 171

Vitruvius
8 praef. 1   159

ANCIENT, MEDIEVAL AND PRE-MODERN CHRISTIAN LITERATURE
Anonymous (Arian)
CSEL 96
I. 31.3-10   181
II. 10.23-25   181
II. 32-33   181
II. 37.23-26   181

Athanasius
PG 28
240.18-24   189

Basil of Caesarea
De Spiritu Sancto
XXVI 62   23

Hom. quod mundanis adhaerendum
PG 31
557-60   184

Cassiodorus
Expositio Psalmorum
37, 1.11-18   185

John Chrysostom
Homiliae de statuis ad populum Antiochenum
1.3   184

SC
346, 1.8.5   183
346, 2.3.22   184

Pseudo-Chrysostom
PG 61
753.70–754.10   189
PG 64
23.20-32   189

Cinthio
Un Capitano Moro 178

Clement of Alexandria
Stromata
4.7.49.4   160
5.11.70.2   159
6.2.23   159

Cyprian
De bono patientiae
18   184

Didymus the Blind
Commentarii in Job
9.7–10.2   183
40.16   183
90.31   183

Eusebius
Praeparatio evangelica
6.6.2   162
9.25.1-4   179

Gregory of Nyssa
Catechetical Oration
24.29-36   189
26.4-10   189
26.31-38   189

Gregory the Great
Expositio in Librum Job, sive Moralium libri xxv 185–7
Praef. 4.6–5.12   185
6.33.51   185
6.33.52   185
8.2.2   185
8.6.11   185
9.7.7   185
12.13.17   185
23.24.47   185
30.25.75-77   185
31.34.73   185
31.40.80   185
31.41.82   185
31.43.84   185
33.7.14   189

Hilary of Poitiers
Tractate in Job
Frag. 1
ll. 7-12   185

Jerome
Epistulae
118   184
118.2   184

Homiliae in Psalmos
97   181–82

Justin Martyr (spur.)
De monarchia   161

Lactantius
Divinarum institutionum libri VII
1.9   154

Leontius
Homiliae
V, 236-7   184

Luther
Sämtliche Schriften
8:78–79   122

Works
22:24   189
26:27   189

WA
9:661   189
18:76
  ll. 4-8   26
24:12
  ll. 3-7   26
40:640   189
46:391   189
57:129   189

Odo of Cluny
Vita
1.8   186
1.18   186
1.24   186
1.28   186
1.32   186
1.40   186
1.41   186
2.1   186
3.2   186
3.6   186

Olympiodorus
Commentarius in Job
40.25-26   189

Origen
De principiis
1.5.5   189
3.2.7   180
4.1.5   189

Contra Celsum
3.22   154
3.23   154
4.77   159
6.43   180

Commentarius in Job
1.96   189

Commentarii in Romanos
3.6   180
5.10.10   189

Epistula ad Africanum
6.4   175

Homiliae in Genesim
8.10   180

Homiliae in Leviticum
8.3.4   189

Homiliae in Lucam
101c   180

De oratione
13.4   189
19.17   180
29.1-2   180
29.9   180
30.2   180, 181

Michael Psellus
Poemata
21.275-76   162

Shakespeare
Macbeth   178
Act V, Scene
V ll. 23-28   71

Othello   178

Tertullian   166–67
De pallio
4.3   154

De patientia
14.4-6   184

Zeno of Verona
Tract I,
15.49-80   181

QUR'ĀN
4.163   194
21.83-84   194
38.41-44   194
684-85   194

MEDIEVAL JEWISH
LITERATURE
Abraham ibn Ezra
Commentary on Job
40:30   190

Berechiah HaNeqdan
Commentary on Job
40:31   191

Eleazar ben-Qallir
Piyyût
ll. 76-80   191–92

Levi ben Gershon (Ralbag)
Commentary on Job
40:30   190

Saadiah Gaon
Commentary on Job
40:30   190
40:31   191

MANUSCRIPTS AND ART
Ambrosian Bible
(13th cent.; Biblioteca
Ambrosiana, Milan;
MS B.30-32)
fol. 136r   193

The Book of Righteous Job
(13th–14th cent.;
Bibliotheque Nationale,
Paris; Coisl. 4)   177

Han Gan
Night Shining White
             171

IJA
465   193
3705   193
6684-6686   193
18944   194
12567   193
126110   193
134528   193
171805   194
179559   194
233134   193

Illuminated Maḥzor
(ca. 1325; Karl-Marx-
Universitätsbibliothek,
Leipzig;
MS Vollers 1102, II)
fol. 181v   192

Illuminated Moralia,
Gregory the Great
(Stiftsbibliothek
Herzogenburg, Austria;
MS 95)
fol. 93r   184

Illuminated Siddur (ca.
1300; Jewish Theological
Seminary of America,
New York; MS 0017)
fol. 2r   192

*Northern French Hebrew
Miscellany* (British
Library, London; Add. MS
11639)
fol. 517v   192
fol. 518b   192
fol. 518v   192
fol. 519r   192

Index of Authors

Aageson, J. W. 112, 113
Achenbach, R. 105, 117
Adriaen, M. 185
Agha, A. 8
Akers, M. J. 216
Albertz, R. 103, 105, 117
Alexander, D. T. 146
Allen, P. 184
Alston, R. 111
Althusser, L. 15
Ameisenowa, Z. 193
Amit, Y. 99
Ammann, S. 107, 199, 201
Anderson, A. R. 164, 166
Anderson, B. 24
Anderson, G. 152
Anderson, J. R. 55
Anderson, R. T. 20
André, G. 94
Annus, A. 173
Anzaldúa, G. 35
Appelbaum, R. 2
Armstrong, C. 13
Asamoah-Gyadu, J. K. 48, 49
Ashcroft, B. 35
Ashley, T. R. 104
Awabdy, M. A. 24

Baasten, M. 185
Baden, J. S. 104
Bailey, R. C. 40
Baker, C. A. 7
Bakhtin, M. M. 14, 72, 81
Baltzer, K. 203
Banana, C. 48
Bandstra, A. J. 112
Barbour, J. 229
Barclay, J. M. G. 110, 129, 138, 139, 150
Barish, J. 161
Barr, J. 50

Barrett, R. 25
Barstad, H. M. 119, 201
Barth, F. 8
Barthes, R. 69, 70
Barton, G. A. 231
Barton, J. 212, 215, 219–22, 224, 225
Batovici, D. 7
Baumgarten, A. I. 62
Beauvoir, S. de 9
Bechtel, L. M. 85
Becking, B. 119
Ben Zvi, E. 7
Bennington, G. 214, 228
Bentley, J. 219
Berges, U. 205, 206
Berlejung, A. 203–5, 209, 210
Berner, C. 104, 105, 121
Bernstein, M. 58
Berthelot, K. 14, 158
Betz, H. D. 144
Bhabha, H. K. 9, 10, 36, 80
Blank, D. 161
Blenkinsopp, J. 200, 201, 205, 208
Bloom, H. 73, 74, 81, 82
Blot, R. K. 8
Blum, E. 224
Boccaccini, G. 64
Boda, M. J. 22
Boer, R. 15, 16, 80
Bogaert, P.-M. 126
Bohlinger, T. A. 134, 135
Bolin, T. 230, 232, 234, 235
Bond, E. L. 2
Bonnard, P.-E. 206
Booth, W. 80, 197
Bornkamm, H. 26
Bourgel, J. 22
Bowersock, G. W. 152
Bowley, J. E. 226
Boyarin, D. 70, 71, 115

Index of Authors

Brah, A. 35, 36, 49
Brawley, R. L. 73, 74, 76
Breed, B. W. 7, 14, 83, 100, 102, 195, 213, 215, 216, 224–9, 235
Brett, M. G. 7
Brock, S. P. 176
Brown, K. 23, 102, 114
Brueggemann, W. 202
Budd, P. J. 105
Buren, P. van 218
Burnside, J. P. 106
Byrskog, S. 7

Calvino, I. 169
Campbell, A. F. 217
Canny, N. 5
Carasik, M. 122
Carr, D. M. 224
Carson, D. A. 115
Cave, A. A. 2, 3, 11
Chazon, E. G. 119
Cheon, S. 107–9, 111
Christianson, E. S. 235
Coetzee, J. 170
Cohen, A. P. 8
Cohen, G. D. 14
Collins, C. J. 144, 145
Collins, J. J. 217, 219
Connolly, J. 165
Conrad, J. 44
Constable, G. 186
Cox, C. 176
Cranfield, C. E. B. 142
Crashaw, W. 4, 5, 12
Crenshaw, J. L. 231, 233
Croatto, J. S. 205–8, 210, 211
Crouzel, H. 189
Culler, J. 70
Cyrino, M. S. 154, 156, 167

Damrosch, D. 169
Datema, C. 184
Davies, P. R. 219
De Lacy, P. 161
De Troyer, K. 7
DeLanda, M. 226
Deichmann, F. W. 182
Deleuze, G. 195, 227, 234
Dell, K. 172
Derrida, J. 14, 214, 228, 229

Di Mattei, S. 141
Dick, M. B. 197, 204, 205
Dillmann, A. 85
Dobbs-Allsopp, F. W. 219
Donaldson, L. E. 44
Donaldson, T. L. 115
Dorival, G. 212
Dozeman, T. B. 85
Dresken-Weiland, J. 182
Dube, M. W. 10, 11, 27, 37–9, 41–8
Duhm, B. 197, 200, 202
Dunn, J. D. G. 64, 115, 142

Eco, U. 217
Edelman, D. V. 7
Edwards, C. 161
Eggers, K. 186, 187
Eliot, T. S. 170, 171
Elliger, K. 200, 201, 203
Ellis, E. E. 63, 145
England, E. 7
Enns, P. E. 113
Epstein, M. M. 193
Erdmann, C. 186
Esler, P. F. 198

Fabian, J. 9
Fanon, F. 10
Faulkner, W. 71, 72
Fausz, J. F. 3
Feder, Y. 89, 91, 95, 96
Fee, G. D. 112–15, 139
Feldman, L. H. 100
Fernández Marcos, N. 176
Fishbane, M. 75, 192
Fisk, B. N. 125, 131
Fitzmyer, J. A. 112–15, 142
Fokkelman, J. P. 217
Foster, R. B. 115
Fox, M. V. 217, 230, 231
Freedman, D. N. 132
Frey, J. 20
Fried, L. S. 21
Friedheim, E. 163
Friesen, C. J. P. 158, 160
Frymer-Kensky, T. 89

Gadamer, H.-G. 51, 53, 54, 57
Galbraith, D. 16
Galinsky, G. K. 153, 158, 164

Gambetti, S. 111
Gamsey, P. 80
Gard, D. H. 176
Garland, R. 158
Garton, R. E. 105
Gaston, L. 136
Gaventa, B. R. 139
Geertz, C. 56
Gehman, H. S. 176
Gerleman, G. 176
Gerstenberger, E. 87
Gillespie, C. 170
Ginzberg, L. 113, 232
Glicksman, A. T. 109–11
Goff, B. 170
Gohrisch, J. 9
Grabbe, L. L. 22, 119
Graf, F. 162
Gray, A. 83
Gray, P. 179
Gray, R. 2–5, 10, 11, 17
Green, A. 16
Greenwood, K. 229
Griffiths, G. 35
Grillo, J. 232
Grondin, J. 53
Gruen, E. S. 153
Grünkemeier, E. 9
Grünsta:udl, W. 7
Guardiola-Sáenz, L. A. 36, 37, 40
Guattari, F. 195
Gumperz, J. J. 8
Gunkel, H. 84, 94

Hagedorn, D. 183, 189
Hagedorn, U. 183, 189
Hakola, R. 7
Hall, S. 8
Halliwell, S. 160
Halpern-Amaru, B. 119, 129, 132
Hanke, L. 3
Hanson, K. C. 77
Haralambakis, M. 178
Hardwick, L. 170
Harrill, J. A. 64
Harrington, D. J. 113, 126
Harrison, G. W. M. 162
Hartenstein, F. 85
Hayes, C. E. 103
Hayes, J. H. 110

Hays, R. B. 25, 64, 115, 116, 136, 142, 146
Hearn, M. K. 171
Heater, H., Jr. 188
Heidegger, M. 53, 54, 69, 79
Heim, E. M. 149
Hekster, O. 164
Hendel, R. S. 212, 219, 220, 223, 224
Hengel, M. 65
Hening, W. W. 1, 3
Henrichs, A. 183
Hensel, B. 20, 21
Hilberg, I. 184
Hill, R. C. 183
Hirsch, E. D., Jr. 216
Hofreiter, C. 19
Holdrege, B. A. 222
Holladay, C. R. 179
Hollander, J. 73
hooks, b. 16
Horn, J. 2
Horowitz, E. 1, 14
Hošek, R. 158
Hübner, H. 110, 112
Hugo, V. 169
Hunn, D. 149

Irudayaraj, D. S. 208–10
Iser, W. 70, 198

Jacobson, H. 127, 128, 132
Jenkins, R. 8, 13, 152
Jennings, W. 10
Johnson Hodge, C. 136, 140, 147
Johnson, R. 12
Jokiranta, J. M. 7
Joseph, A. L. 87, 99, 101
Joyce, P. M. 172

Kahneman, D. 54
Kalimi, I. 22, 26
Kalman, J. 187, 188
Kasprzyk, D. 154
Kaufmann, T. 26
Keel, O. 205
Kelle, B. 214
Kelley, S. 40, 42
Kessler, J. 119
Kinnyatti, M. wa 44
Kipling, R. 44

Kisiel, T. 69
Klauck, H.-J. 7
Klawans, J. 62, 86, 92, 94
Klein, J. 173
Knoppers, G. N. 19–22, 103
Koenen, L. 183
Koh, Y. V. 229
Koosed, J. 230
Kramer, S. N. 173, 174
Kratz, R. G. 18–20, 24
Krishna, S. 34
Kristeva, J. 69, 70, 72, 79
Kuenen, A. 85, 86
Kugel, J. L. 60, 61, 100, 113
Kupperman, K. O. 2, 12, 13
Kuswani, G. S. N. 46
Kynes, W. 172

LaCoste, N. 110
Laird, D. 21
Lambert, W. G. 174
Lamos, C. 170
Las Casas, B. de 5
Lazarus, N. 10
Lenzi, A. 173
Levenson, J. D. 222
Levine, B. A. 104
Levinson, B. M. 18, 19, 24, 25, 60, 82, 98
Levison, J. R. 126–8, 130–2
Levtow, N. B. 209
LiDonnici, L. 103
Lieb, M. 7
Lieber, A. 103
Lieu, J. M. 66
Lincicum, D. 158, 162
Lipka, H. 87–9, 94–6
Loader, J. A. 230
Löfstedt, B. 181
Lohfink, N. 231
Lohr, J. N. 19
Longman, T., III 230, 232
Lozada, F., Jr. 222
Luther, M. 25, 122
Lyons, W. J. 7

MacDonald, N. 19, 121
MacIntyre, A. 222
Magen, Y. 21
Malbon, E. S. 182
Malherbe, A. J. 153, 154

Manahan, K. B. 2
Mantzavinos, C. 53
Marcovich, M. 161
Martínez, F. G. 20, 58
Martyn, J. L. 139, 145
Mason, E. 7
Mastnjak, N. 213
Matlock, R. B. 136
Matter, E. A. 16
May, N. N. 173, 174
May, T. 227
Maza, S. 55
Mbuvi, A. M. 11
Mbuwayesango, D. R. 11, 46
Meeks, W. 112, 114
Melville, H. 194
Mercer, K. 8
Merendino, R. P. 200, 206
Merwin, W. S. 194
Meyers, C. 215
Miano, D. 132
Middlemas, J. 119
Milgrom, J. 106
Moberly, R. W. 214
Moffat, T. 40, 41
Mojola, A. 46
Mongstad-Kvammen, I. 217
Moore, S. D. 219
Mor, M. 20
Moran, W. L. 174
Mositi, T. 44
Mroczek, E. 102, 213, 226, 233
Mudimbe, V. Y. 10
Muir, K. 178
Mukherjee, A. 170, 178, 195
Mulder, M. 190, 191
Mullen, T. E. 117
Müller, H. 181
Muraoka, T. 127
Murphy, F. J. 125, 127, 129, 132, 134, 135, 150
Myers, J. M. 21

Najman, H. 59, 97, 98, 100, 102
Needham, R. 8
Neusner, J. 122
Newsom, C. A. 8, 16, 186
Newton, K. M. 213
Neyrand, L. 183
Nickelsburg, G. W. E. 125, 129

Nickerson, R. S. 54
Niehoff, M. R. 156, 159, 163
Nissinen, M. 214
Novak, D. 124
Novenson, M. V. 146
Nussbaum, M. C. 160, 161

O'Brien, P. T. 115
O'Rourke Boyle, M. 212
Oakman, D. E. 77
Oeming, M. 202
Olupona, J. K. 48
Orlov, A. A. 191
Oshima, T. 174
Otto, E. 24

Pagden, A. 5
Parker, J. 2
Parpola, S. 173
Pauw, A. P. 217
Payne, M. 232
Peckham, G. 3
Perraymond, M. 182
Perrot, C. 126
Perry, T. A. 231, 234
Petit, M. 156
Phillips, A. 88
Pieterse, J. N. 10
Pitt-Rivers, J. 73
Propp, W. H. C. 104, 121
Pui-lan, K. 10, 40
Pury, E. de 224

Rad, G. von 76
Reardon, B. P. 152
Redditt, P. L. 22
Redford, D. 110
Reese, J. M. 109–11
Reeves, J. C. 226
Reinmuth, E. 129, 131, 149
Reiterer, F. V. 20
Reuter, E. 17, 18
Rey, T. 48, 49
Riffaterre, M. 73
Ristau, K. A. 103
Roberts, J. 7
Rochberg-Halton, F. 173
Rofé, A. 85, 93, 94, 97
Rokem, F. 169
Rom-Shiloni, D. 118

Roskies, D. G. 1
Rowley, H. H. 16

Said, E. W. 9, 34, 35, 38, 42
Saller, R. 80
Sanders, E. P. 7, 64, 115
Sanders, S. L. 24
Sandys-Wunsch, J. 212
Satlow, M. L. 22, 52, 61, 63, 65
Saussure, F. de 229
Sawhill, J. A. 183
Schaller, B. 178
Schattner-Rieser, U. 20
Schirmann, J. 191
Schmid, K. 20, 85
Schmid, W. 198
Schmidt, E. A. 3
Schmidt, L. 105
Schmitz, T. 152
Schnabel, E. J. 115
Schoeps, H.-J. 145
Schoors, A. 234
Schorch, S. 20
Schottroff, L. 80
Schramm, A. 183
Schrenk, S. 182
Schroer, S. 199, 205
Schüssler Fiorenza, E. 222
Schwartz, S. 65
Sechrest, L. L. 142
Segal, M. 60, 61
Segovia, C. A. 64
Segovia, F. F. 34, 40, 41
Seifrid, M. A. 115
Seitz, C. 217, 218
Seow, C. L. 169, 173, 175, 186, 230–4
Sharp, C. 229
Shaw, C. A. 161
Sheehan, J. 219
Sherwood, Y. 3, 5–7, 219
Shohat, E. 40, 47
Siegal, M. B. 7
Simkins, R. A. 219
Simon, R. 212
Ska, J.-L. 197
Skinner, J. 84
Smallwood, E. M. 110, 111
Smith, J. 12
Sneed, M. R. 236
Snell, B. 155

Soares-Prabhu, G. M. 197, 208
Sommer, B. D. 51, 118
Sorg, A. 182, 183
Sorlin, H. 183
Spaulding, M. B. 113
Specht, H. 104, 105
Spiegel, S. 172
Spiekermann, H. 18
Spivak, G. C. 9
Sprinkle, P. M. 129, 132, 134, 135, 150
Stam, R. 40, 47
Stavrakopoulou, F. 215
Steck, O. H. 129
Stegemann, E. 76
Stegemann, W. 76
Steinhauser, K. B. 181
Steinmann, J. 212
Stern, P. D. 19
Stone, L. 56
Storey, I. C. 162
Sugirtharajah, R. S. 10, 40
Suleiman, S. R. 79
Sullivan, S. 20
Sutton, D. F. 161, 162
Swain, S. 152
Sweet, J. W. 2

Tajfel, H. 198
Taleb, N. N. 55
Taylor, C. 68, 79
Theissen, G. 220
Thiessen, M. 7, 113, 114, 127, 140, 141, 144, 147
Thiong'o, N. 37
Thiselton, A. C. 114, 115
Thomas, D. W. 199
Tiffin, H. 35
Tigchelaar, E. J. C. 20
Tobin, T. H. 142
Tolbert, M. A. 41
Toorn, K. van der 17, 18, 174, 197, 214
Tov, E. 215
Trible, P. 41
Tsedaka, B. 20
Tucker, J. B. 7
Turner, J. 212, 220
Turpie, D. M. 63
Tuval, M. 65
Tversky, A. 54

Uehlinger, C. 205
Unnik, W. C. van 64, 65
Uzanne, O. 169

Valla, L. 219
VanLandingham, C. 133
VanderKam, J. C. 60, 61
Vayntrub, J. 234
Vendries, C. 154
Verkerk, D. H. 182
Viezel, E. 212

Wacker, M.-T. 208
Walls, A. 42
Watson, F. 136, 137, 140, 143
Watts, J. D. W. 203
Weber, D. 181
Weinfeld, M. 174
Welborn, L. L. 16
Westermann, C. 199, 200, 202, 203, 210
Whitmarsh, T. 152, 153
Whitney, K. W. 190–2
Whybray, R. N. 202, 203
Williams, J. 234
Williamson, H. G. M. 21
Wimbush, V. L. 40
Wineburg, S. 52
Winkler, W. 20
Winston, D. 107–12
Witherington, B., III 114
Witte, M. 175
Wöhrle, J. 103
Wright, N. T. 137, 142, 143, 145
Wyles, R. 156, 157, 164

Zahn, M. M. 58, 59, 102
Zimmermann, R. 78
Zuckerman, B. E. 172
Zwickel, W. 17

Index of Subjects

Abraham (biblical figure)
   analogies with later peoples 139–41
   comparison of Paul's and *LAB*'s depictions 125–7, 133–50
   depiction in *LAB* 125–7, 133–5
   passivity/trust in God 134, 135, 138, 139
   prefiguring of Christ-narrative 144–8
African Independent Churches (Botswana) 44, 45
African biblical interpretation 47–9
Alexandria (Egypt)
   Jewish community 110, 111
   library/scholastic community 151
Anaxagoras 159
apophrades (figure of speech) 74, 75, 77, 78
Aristeas the Historian 179
Ashurbanipal, King 173
askesis (figure of speech) 74, 78
Augustus, Emperor 164
Aurillac, Gerald of 186
author(s), mode of address *see under* reader(s)

Badimo (ancestors), transposed into figures of evil 45, 46
Bassus, Junius, sarcophagus of 182
Ben Sira, Shimon ben Yeshua ben Eliezer 213, 226, 233
Berlejung, Angelika 203–5, 209, 210
Berlin Conference (1884) 37, 38
Bible
   multiplicity of texts 17–26, 102, 169–78, 187–95, 223, 224
   pre-canonical texts 83–101, 121, 171–5, 223, 224
   translation 40–1, 45–7, 65, 111–12, 114, 151, 175–9, 188, 190–1, 207, 213, 228

Biblical Studies
   critical approach 196, 197, 218–24, 227, 228
   impact of colonialism 1–17, 37, 38, 41, 42, 43, 44
   impact of social identity 1–26, 28, 30, 31, 36–8, 44–9, 68, 78–84, 101, 120–5, 198–216, 229–36
   methodology of 1–17, 27, 28, 50–2, 55–7, 61, 62, 66–82, 196–9, 209–36
Botswana
   Bible studies 44, 45, 46–9
   church communities 44, 45
   missionaries in 40, 41
   situation of immigrants in 33, 34
   traditional cultural/religious beliefs 40, 41
"By the Rivers of Babylon" (song) 33, 34

Caligula, Emperor 111
Canaanites, colonized peoples/opposing forces identified with 2, 4, 11, 12
Catholic commentaries, on image-worship 205–9, 206, 210, 211
   (lack of) analogy with modern Catholic practice 205, 206
   range of perspectives 206
Chinese art 170, 171
circumcision, social/cultural significance
   explored by Paul 141–3
   in story of Abraham 127, 128, 141–3
   in story of Dinah 84, 86, 89, 91, 96
clinamen (figure of speech) 74, 75
colonialism 1–6, 10–13, 27, 34, 35
   biblical justifications 2–5, 11, 17, 23, 37, 38
   impact on biblical studies 37, 38, 41–4
   demonization of natives 4, 5, 9–14, 18, 19, 40, 41, 45, 46

Conrad, Joseph, *Heart of Darkness* 44
conversion (religious) 13
covenant (of God and Abraham) 127–50
    and character of Abraham 133–5
    fleshly symbolism 128, 141–3
    manner of fulfillment 137–9, 140, 141
    perpetuity 127, 128
    relationship with other covenants 130–2
    survival of Israelite disobedience 129–30
    unbreakability 128–30
Crashaw, William, Rev. 4, 5, 12, 13
Croatto, José Severino 205–8, 210, 211
crusades 186

daemonization (figure of speech) 74, 75
Dalits ("untouchables"), in Indian society 209
David (biblical character), referenced in Ecclesiastes 231
Dead Sea Scrolls 60, 65
Deleuze, Gilles 227, 234, 235
Deuteronomy, Book of 11, 17–26, 82
    construction of identity 11, 17–25
    form of address to readers 23, 24, 26
    Jewish/Samaritan differences over interpretation 20–3, 26
    on locations for sacrifice/worship 17–20
    rejection by Luther 25, 26
    on sexual relations/intermarriage 87, 92, 96, 97
diaspora
    Israelite, 8th–6th cent. BCE 33, 34, 102, 103, 110, 112
    modern, social conditions of 33, 34
Donation of Constantine 219, 220
Dostoevsky, Fyodor 71, 81
dual causality 99

Ecclesiastes, Book of 31, 216, 225, 229–36
    authorship 230, 231, 232, 233
    range of interpretations 230, 233, 234
    self-contradictions 230, 231–3
    vocabulary 233, 234
    see also Qohelet
Eggers, Kurt, *Das Spiel von Job dem Deutschen* 186, 187

Egypt *see* Alexandria
Essenes 61, 62
Exodus, Book of
    Christian symbolism 112–16, 122
    citation/rewriting in later books 29, 75, 103–23
    contradicted by Deuteronomy 17–18, 82

Faulkner, William, *The Sound and the Fury* 71, 72
Ferdman, Benny 194
Fernández de Enciso, Martín 3
figures of speech, classification of 74, 75
Flaccus, A. Avilius 111
France, colonial policy in New World 5
Fribourg School 205

Gaius, Emperor 165
Genesis, Book of
    analyzed/adapted by Paul 136, 137, 138, 141–3, 145–6, 149
    compositional history 124, 125
    later retellings 125, 126 (*see also* Liber Antiquitatum Biblicarum)
    rewritings/variant versions 224
    scholars' readings of 223, 224
    see also Genesis 34
Genesis 34, "Dinah" story 28, 29, 83–101
    characterization of Dinah's brothers 84, 88, 90, 91, 97
    characterization of Jacob 90, 92, 95, 97
    compositional history 84, 85, 92, 93, 98, 99
    generic characteristics 85
genocide, calls for 92, 96
globalization 34
    economy of 35
    impact on religious studies 48, 49
Gray, Robert, Rev. 2–5, 10–11, 17
Greco-Roman studies 38–41
    (alleged) Eurocentrism 39, 40
Greek, Bible translations into 107–11, 175–89, 213

Han Gan 171
Heracles (legendary figure) 151–68
    comic portrayals 29, 30, 151, 152, 154–5, 157, 158, 162, 163, 166, 167

cross-dressing episodes 154, 155, 166, 167
    early Christian attitudes to 153, 154
    as model for rulers 164–6
    serious/heroic depictions 163–7
    traditional appearance/garb 155, 156
hermeneutical circle 53, 54
historiography 55–7, 61, 62
Homer 158, 160, 161, 171

iconoclasm 196–211
identity
    of author with readership 15, 16
    collective 23–6
    complexity of 7, 8
    impact of conquest/resettlement 20, 21
    impact of migration 10, 20, 21, 27, 33, 34
    impact on biblical studies 30, 31, 224, 225
    and interpretation 14–17, 31, 32
    and legitimation 78–81
    and marriage 28, 29
    and otherness 7–14, 25, 26, 33–6, 120–3, 235, 236
    role of location 17–20
    as social/cultural construct 7–9, 25, 30, 31
    social theory of 7–14, 198, 199, 208
images, making of 199–211
    biblical text 199, 200
in-groups/out-groups
    defined 198, 199
    readers' neutral positioning 204, 205
    readers' self-positioning as "in" 202, 203, 207, 208
India, social conditions 209
indigenous languages, Bible translations into 45–7
intermarriage 28, 29, 83–101
    biblical strictures against 92, 96, 97, 99, 100
    biblical tolerance of 85, 86, 91, 99
    mass retribution for 84, 92, 95, 96
    viewed as shameful 88–90
intertextuality 68–82, 100, 101
    biblical instances 70, 75–81, 172, 173
    diachronic/synchronic 73, 74
    dialogical character 72

figuration of 72–5
inevitability of 68–72
as misinterpretation 73, 74, 81
power moves in 81, 82
shifts of function 74, 75
Irudayaraj, Dominic S. 208, 209, 210, 211
Isaiah, Book of
    compositional history 214–15 (*see also* Isaiah 44)
    rewriting of Exodus 118
Isaiah 44 (on making of images) 196, 197, 199–211
    (alleged) oversimplification 202, 203
    ambiguities 200, 201
    Catholic commentaries 205–9, 210, 211
    construction of Other 196, 200
    critical readings 205, 206, 208
    "in-group" readings 202, 203, 207, 208
    neutral readings 204, 205
    range of readings 201–11
    text 199, 200
    use of irony/mockery 203, 207

James VI of Scotland/I of England 4
Jamestown, VA, British colony 1–6, 10–14, 17
    Royal Charter 1, 3
Jesus, (alleged) prefiguring in Old Testament
    in Exodus (in Pauline analysis) 112–16, 122
    in Genesis (in Pauline analysis) 138, 144–8
    in Job 180–2, 188, 189
Job, Book of 169–95
    characterization of Job 178, 179, 183, 184, 187, 188
    characterization of Job's wife 181–3
    Greek vs. Hebrew versions 30, 175–8, 188–94
    illustrations 182, 183
    cultural antecedents 172–5
    Job as Christ-figure 180–2, 188, 189
    Job as exemplar of patience 183–7
    later retellings 178, 179, 186, 187
    metaphor of athletics 180, 181, 183, 184

military imagery/applications 185–7
   range of interpretations 169–70, 187, 188
   Transjordanian elements 172
John Hyrcanus I, King 22, 62
Joshua, Book of, cited as justification for conquest 2–5, 11, 17
Jubilees, Book of 28, 51, 52, 57–63, 66, 100, 226
   authorship/dating 62, 63
   compositional history 58, 60–3
   generic characteristics 58–60
   purpose 60, 62, 63

kenosis (figure of speech) 81, 82
   biblical examples 77, 78
   defined 74, 77
Kipling, Rudyard, "The White Man's Burden" 44
Klein, Joseph, *Leviathan* (song) 194

language, acquisition of 69
Leviathan, figure of 30, 171, 188–94
   artistic representations 192–4
   early Christian interpretations 188, 189
   identified with/distinguished from Behemoth 190, 191, 192
   Jewish interpretations 189–94
   in modern (popular) culture 194
   poetic depictions (post-biblical) 191, 192
   translation issues 190, 191
Leviticus, Christian reception of 216
Liber Antiquitatum Biblicarum 113, 125–35
   characterization of Abraham 125–7, 133–5
   relationship with source material 127, 128, 141
   similarities/contrasts with Paul 139, 141, 142, 144, 148–50
   treatment of covenant 127–35
Lincoln, Abraham 52
Luke, Gospel of, relationship with Israelite scripture 79–81
Luther, Martin
   attitudes to Jews 25, 26, 122
   rejection of Mosaic Law 25, 26
   translation of Pentateuch 25

Mackenzie, John 41
Marcion of Sinope 66, 81
Mark Antony (M. Antonius) 165, 166
Matthew, Gospel of
   mistranslations 45, 46
Melville, Herman, *Moby-Dick* 194
Merwin, W. S., "Leviathan" (poem) 194
Mesopotamia, image-worship in 203
migration
   global scale 34, 35
   impact on identity 10, 33, 34
missionaries
   attitudes to native people 40, 41, 43
   letters/papers 40, 41
   role in colonizing process 37, 38
Moffat, Robert 40, 41
Moses (biblical character)
   death 119, 120
   literary persona 233
   negative portrayal/punishment 104, 106, 116–17, 119, 122
Mositi, Torontle, *The Victims* 44

Native Americans *see* Powhatan
Nazi regime, appropriation of biblical imagery 186, 187
Nero, Emperor 151
Numbers, Book of
   compositional history 117
   differences in detail 105
   positive aspects 120
   retelling of Exodus 103–7, 116–20
   reversal of authorial attitude/characterization 103, 104, 106, 107, 116, 117, 118, 119, 121, 122
   verbal/structural parallels 104–6

Odo of Cluny 186
Other/otherness 9–14
   Bibles viewed as 215, 216
   biblical constructions of 96, 97, 101, 121, 196, 200
   colonized peoples viewed as 2–7, 45–8
   commonality of identity with 13
   reader as 221–3, 235, 236
   role in construction of identity 9, 10
ourobouros, Leviathan depicted as 191, 193, 194

Paul 28, 29, 51, 52, 63–6
  biography 63, 64, 65, 112
  citing of scriptural authorities 64
  commentary on/departures from
    Genesis 136, 137, 138, 141–3, 145, 146, 149
  Old vs. New Perspectives on 137, 138
  target readership 65, 66
  treatment of Abrahamic narrative 124, 125, 136–50
Pentateuch, source-critical/redaction-critical scholarship 117
  see also individual books
Pharisees 61, 62
Philip of Macedon 164
Philo of Alexandria 29, 30, 62, 110, 158, 159
  admiration/citation of Euripides 158–62, 167, 168
  commentary on figure of Heracles 151, 152, 156–8, 167, 168
  modern commentaries 153
  On the Eternity of the World 159
  That Every Good Person Is Free 153, 156–8, 159, 160, 163, 167, 168
piyyûṭ (Jewish poetry) 191, 192
Pocahontas 12
postcolonialism 9, 10, 34
  Bible readings 47–9
  continuance of Christian faith 42, 43
postmodernism 53, 54
Powhatan people 14
  conflict with colonists 1, 3
  viewed as savages/heathens 4, 11–13
preconception, role in literary/ethical judgments 52–5
Psalms
  on exile/diaspora 33, 34
  referencing in later books 76, 77
Pseudo-Philo 29
  see also Liber Antiquitatum Biblicarum

Qohelet (character/narratorial voice) 229–36
  enigmatic nature 233, 234
  etymology 229, 230
  inconsistency 230, 231
  literary reception of character 234–6
  problem of identity 231, 232
  range of interpretations 230, 234–6
  vocabulary 233, 234

Rahab's Reading Prism 41
rape
  distinguished from other illicit sexual activity 87
  penalties for 87
reader(s)
  assumed class/background 15, 16, 23, 24, 28, 222
  depersonalization 222
  "implied" 197–9, 201
  mode of address to 15–17, 23, 24, 201
  as Other 221–3, 235, 236
reading, as constructive activity 28
reception criticism 6, 7, 14–26, 31–2, 41–9, 51–5, 68–82, 97–103, 120–3, 151–3, 169–71, 194–9, 209–29
redaction 83–5
  as reception 97–101
"respect," in Biblical Studies
  alternative significance 225, 226
  for biblical text 216–18; text vs. author 216, 217
  in critical approach 218–24
Roman Empire 110, 111
  administrative system 76, 77, 79, 80

sacrifice, proper location for 17–23
Sadducees 61, 62
Samaritans
  interpretation of Deuteronomy 20–3, 26
  places of worship 20–3
  scriptural texts 215
satyr play, generic characteristics 161, 162
Second Sophistic movement 152, 153
Second Temple period 29, 52, 102, 107, 122, 123, 124, 226
Setswana (language), Bible translations into 45–7
  offence to native beliefs 45, 46
  patriarchalizing 46
sexual relations (before/outside marriage)
  mass retribution for 84, 92, 95, 96
  penalties/precedents 85, 86, 95
  shame attached to 88–90, 94, 95
  vocabulary of 87, 94–6

Shakespeare, William 170
   Macbeth 71, 178
   Othello 178
Smith, John, Capt. 12
Socrates 159
Solomon (biblical character), possible
  identification of Qohelet with 231, 232
Sorg, Anton, woodcut of Job 182, 183
The Sound and the Fury 71, 72
Spain, colonial policy in New World 3
Sumerian literature 172, 173
supersessionism 82

Ten Commandments, in Deuteronomy 24
tessera (figure of speech) 74, 76, 77
Testament of Job
   relationship with source material 178, 179
   influence on Christian reception of Job 179–81, 187
"texts of terror" 41, 45, 46
Tiberius, Emperor 164
Trajan, Emperor 164
translation
   role in circulation of classics 178
   significance for interpretation of Job 190, 191
   see also Bible; Greek; indigenous languages

Vineyard, Parable of 77, 78
Virgil, *Aeneid* 44, 171
Virginia Company 1–6
   Royal Charter 1–3
   tracts/broadsides 13

Westermann, Claus 202, 203, 210
Whitaker, Alexander, Rev. 12
Wisdom of Solomon, Book of 103, 107–12
   compositional history 110, 111
   contrasted with 1 Corinthians/Numbers 108, 120–2
   identification of readership 116, 117
   parallels with Exodus 107, 108
   selective use of material 109
   target audience 109–12
   use of antithesis 108, 109
   vocabulary 108, 109
women, lack of autonomy 88, 90
Wookey Bible (1903) 45, 46

www.ingramcontent.com/pod-product-compliance
Lightning Source LLC
Chambersburg PA
CBHW072125290426
44111CB00012B/1777